PETER TIBORIS

A MUSICAL ODYSSEY

ALEXANDER KITROEFF

Publisher: Arkadia Publications
608 Terrace Place
Baldwin, NY 11510
jhoward@midamerica_music.com
Year of Publication: December 2023
Copyright: Alexander Kitroeff
ISNB 979-8-218-31767-6
Library of Congress Control Number: 2023921501:
Book cover photo of Carnegie Hall appears with permission from the
Carnegie Hall Corporation

TABLE OF CONTENTS

FOREWORD

BY JOHN RUTTER, CBE

If I was running a bookstore I would have trouble deciding where to shelve 'Peter Tiboris: a Musical Odyssey'. Does it belong with biography, social history, music, business studies, travel, or is it a self-help book? It encompasses all of these categories and more, with the utterly absorbing story of an American musician from a small town in Wisconsin, the grandson of Greek immigrants, who dreams of great things in his chosen world of music and makes them come true. His odyssey leads him to New York as the founder and head of a company that brings thousands of musicians from all over America to perform in Carnegie Hall and takes thousands more to perform in the great music-making cities of Europe and beyond. We learn of his Greek heritage, of the poverty which led his grandparents to seek a new life in America, of the Orthodox Christian faith and tradition which his family steadfastly maintained in a new land and which has sustained him to this day. We see the family ties which so strongly underpin Greek-American life, and the moral and work ethic gently instilled into him by his kindly father.

I am a Brit; for centuries my ancestors plied their artisan trades somewhere or other in our damp islands until the wider educational opportunities of the twentieth century elevated us into the professional classes – hardly the stuff of an enthralling narrative. I find it awe-inspiring to reflect that behind almost every American lies a dramatic family history, often of poverty or persecution . . . the pain of leaving a beloved homeland, the hopes and fears experienced by the immigrants as they started their lives again in a new land, the assimilation into a new culture, the success stories enjoyed by some, the quest for ancestral roots that may come with a later generation. In Peter Tiboris' case we have all of this; as an aside he recalls that he would not be living in America if it had not been for a fungal blight afflicting the French grape harvest in the 1880s. (You can find out why in Chapter One.)

Alexander Kitroeff chronicles this part of the extraordinary history of America, reflected through the story of a young man finding his way in the world of music – surely a case of the old saying that you don't choose music as a way of life, it chooses you. We meet Peter's mentors and learn of the early influences upon him, but then events take an unpredictable turn as he becomes drawn into the parallel universe of business entrepreneurship – not from any desire for riches or acclaim but in pursuit of a vision to elevate amateur and student musicians into the world of high-level professional performance by offering them . . . Carnegie Hall.

This is where I enter the story. Starting in 1988, at Peter's invitation I have guest-conducted over 130 concerts, most of them in Carnegie Hall, and I have been as uplifted by the experience as I hope the performers have been. To see 200 teenage (or indeed adult) singers turn in forty-eight hours from 'show me' skepticism to pure joy as they prepare, say, the Mozart or Brahms requiems is the experience every music teacher wants to have, and I do believe that this is what drives Peter also. One of the best and most rewarding things we can do in life is to pass on what we know and love to a younger generation or to our peers. It becomes obvious as we read this chronicle of Peter's life that he can be labelled as 'musician', 'conductor' and 'entrepreneur', but I think he also has 'teacher' engraved in his soul.

I cannot, of course, be impartial, but I try to be objective about the performances I am involved in, and I would say that the framework Peter and his MidAmerica colleagues have created for the performances we give is just about as ideal as it can be, with meticulously planned schedules, intense and thorough rehearsals, and a sense of mounting excitement as we prepare to take the stage. Do we always pull it off when we get there? My assessment is overwhelmingly positive: of the 130+ performances I have conducted, perhaps half a dozen were miraculous (when something inexplicable and amazing happens), most of the rest were plus or minus of 'very presentable indeed' – and inevitably there were a few where I was awfully glad we didn't have the New York Times critic in the front row.

Peter is a multi-faceted musician, and conducting has been an important thread running through his entire life. As you read this book you will get a sense of what drives a conductor to risk everything standing in front of perhaps hundreds of performers – with an audience as the wild animal at his or her back. I confess I'm still not sure I know the answer to this myself, but I have enjoyed getting closer to the secret by reading his thoughts on this most visible yet intangible form of musical activity.

It is fitting that Alexander Kitroeff's account of Peter's odyssey ends by taking him back to his ancestral homeland of Greece. If you have never visited the idyllic island of Syros, where his Festival of the Aegean is held annually, you should. The festival is now in the capable hands of Peter's amazing opera-singer wife Eilana, and if you visit at festival time, she and her team will guarantee you an experience to cherish for years to come.

Could anyone have accomplished what Peter has accomplished? Well, if it's true that anyone can be President of the United States, then yes; if we are more realistic, then no. Peter's combination of musical insight, vision, energy, commitment, and determination to make the most of whatever opportunities life offers is to say the least, uncommon. He is modest enough to claim "it's all about the music," and of course it is, but I believe you will come away from reading this book thinking "yes, but there's a lot more to it than that." I for one have been inspired by reading about it all, in this engaging chronicle of a remarkable life.

Music is a moral law.

It gives soul to the universe,

Wings to the mind,

Flight to the imagination,

A charm to sadness,

Gaiety and life to everything.

It is the essence of order

And

Lends to all that is

Good, just and beautiful.

— Plato

CHAPTER ONE

CHURCH ORGANIST IN SHEBOYGAN, WISCONSIN

The end of all good music is to affect the soul — Claudio Monteverdi

To sing is to pray twice — St Augustine

For thousands of Americans, many of them members of amateur and semi-professional bands, choirs, wind ensembles and orchestras the answer to the question "How do you get to Carnegie Hall" is Peter Tiboris, the music professor who became an orchestra conductor and entrepreneur and did something revolutionary. The company that he created in the mid-1980s began a program which enabled music organizations from all over the country and beyond to come and perform at the illustrious Carnegie Hall, the ultimate concert stage in what was for almost all of them a once-in-a-lifetime opportunity. They sponsored their own way in order to perform, but MidAmerica guaranteed a smoothly-run operation which guaranteed they would perform at the most prestigious music venue in the world, an experience that left them overwhelmed with pride, emotions and memories. What was revolutionary about Tiboris' vision and the way he implemented it was not only that it was such an innovative idea but also because it represented a democratization of New York's classical music world by making the Carnegie Hall experience available to all.

By combining the production of concerts with the core of its purpose – to bring music organizations to New York – MidAmerica became one of the major production companies associated with Carnegie Hall. It is the most prolific presenter of choral concerts in the history of Carnegie Hall dating back to May 5, 1891, the day of the opening of the hall when Tchaikovsky himself conducted the first concert. The table below presents the exact figures:

TABLE I: NUMBER OF CONCERTS PRESENTED BY
MIDAMERICA PRODUCTIONS AT CARNEGIE HALL

*The very first concert MidAmerica presented at Carnegie Hall
was on April 30, 1986, in the Main Hall (Stern Auditorium/Perelman Stage).*

Number of concerts in Stern Auditorium/Perelman
Stage from April 30, 1986-September 20, 2023: 686

Number of concerts in Weill Recital Hall at
Carnegie Hall from April 30, 1986-September 20, 2023: 379

Number of concerts in Zankel Hall at
Carnegie Hall from April 30, 1986-September 20, 2023: 1

Total number of concerts from April 30, 1986-September 20, 2023: 1,066

*It is challenging to rank outside presenters; however, MidAmerica Productions would
be in the top 5 among all outside presenters at Carnegie Hall since May 5, 1891.*

SOURCE: THE ROSE ARCHIVES AND MUSEUM AT CARNEGIE HALL
PROVIDED BY KATHLEEN SABOGAL, CARNEGIE HALL ARCHIVIST.

Moreover, MidAmerica Productions achieved its success with a small staff and meager resources, but it succeeded because Tiboris proved to be a relentless leader. As one of his closest associates put it, Peter Tiboris was, and is, an unstoppable force as well as an immovable object, a combination that ensured the success of his vision. And MidAmerica's success was recognized maybe grudgingly by a few highbrow music critics but more importantly by leading musicians who performed

or conducted or were otherwise associated with its programs.[1] And on the wings of that artistic and business venture Tiboris was able to build an equally successful career as an internationally recognized symphonic orchestra conductor. The creation of an acclaimed summer festival on the Aegean island of Syros was the capstone of his career.

Many of Tiboris' associates over the years recognize his multiple talents and his stature as a conductor, but credit him primarily with his success in enabling thousands of choirs and thousands of music artists to perform at Carnegie Hall. Tim Sharp, the longtime Executive Director of the American Choral Directors Association who worked for MidAmerica considers that Tiboris' singular, huge contribution is to have elevated choral music and taken it to the world's premier concert stage. And he did it on his own in the sense that he was the first to think of it, to try it out, and he eventually succeeded by making a fine art of what he did, time and time again, for forty years. Moreover he overcame a series of obstacles because of his clear understanding of what he was doing and through his dogged perseverance. Sharp suggests that Tiboris promoted choral music with a singular vision and success in the way Brian Epstein promoted the Beatles and made them a success. [2]

Peter Tiboris' background and life in his hometown where he grew up provides a few indications that he was going to become a classical music conductor and producer of music concerts. One of them was that at the age of nine he began playing the organ at his Greek Orthodox church, St. Spyridon. The grandson of Greek immigrants, he grew up as an American. That would suggest, at least in theory, that he could have chosen any profession he wanted. But even Americans are shaped by their family histories and their cultural heritage. Indeed, there was a unique set of choices Peter made in addition to the influences of his family background. Peter is a third generation Greek-American, in other words it was his grandparents who emigrated from Greece and settled in the United States. As was the case with so many other European ethnic groups who arrived in America in the early twentieth century, the pattern the family followed was that the first generation most commonly engaged in some type of manual work or opened a small business, and thanks to their hard work their children, boys especially, were able to go on and study and pursue a career as white-collar professionals. And that was even more the case with their children, such as Peter and his younger brother Gus. Their father was able to study and became a dentist; and Gus did the same. In contrast, Peter followed a different path, he studied music, he became a music professor, and went on to become an internationally recognized music conductor and concert producer.

GREEKS AND CLASSICAL MUSIC AND OPERA IN AMERICA

In the case of Greek-American families especially, this was a notably unique career path. Unlike other European origin ethnic groups, such as Jews or Italians, the Greek-Americans did not have a rich tradition of classical music composers and performers in the Old World or the New. There were very few Greek names in the world of American classical music when Peter was born in 1947, albeit big ones. Dimitri Mitropoulos was the principal conductor of the Minneapolis Symphony Orchestra, a position in which he had served since 1937. He later reached the pinnacle of classical music in America as music director and conductor of the New York Philharmonic, whose home was Carnegie Hall. Yet Mitropoulos was always considered a European who had entered America's classical music world. The even greater name, Maria Callas, was barely known when Peter was born. A year earlier she had made her debut abroad, in Italy in 1946, and her Metropolitan Opera debut would come in 1956. And although she was the daughter of Greek immigrants and born in New York City, Callas was a worldly opera diva whose Greek American identity was very quickly surpassed by her stature as a globally recognized figure. This meant there would be virtually no role models for Peter in terms of his ethnic background. Less well known to the general public was Nicola Moscona, an operatic bass who was born in Greece and made his New York debut at the Metropolitan Opera in 1937 and sang there until 1971; an impressive total of 719 performances. After his retirement, Moscona taught at the Academy of Vocal Arts in Philadelphia, the city in which he died in 1975 just before his sixty-eighth birthday. In 1940 Moscona had performed in New York to raise funds to aid Greece in its World War II effort and the pianist was an American-born Greek Constantine Callinicos. Born in New York City in 1913, Callinicos would be the exception to the rule that saw most children of Greek immigrants pursue a career in business or become doctors or lawyers. Callinicos was not only a pianist but also a conductor – his debut as a New York City Opera conductor was in 1958 – and became known as the long-time accompanist to the famous Italian-American baritone Mario Lanza. There were a few other Greek Americans in the classical music world of the United States who were Tiboris' contemporaries, and we will encounter most them later on in this book.

Yet there was a type of music Greek immigrants were familiar with and which they brought with them to America at the turn of the twentieth century. It was the Byzantine era liturgical music of their religion, Greek Orthodoxy, which had survived through the centuries, although it had gone through changes. Greek Orthodoxy is

the version of Christianity that prevailed in the Eastern Mediterranean and Eastern Europe, and whose title 'Orthodoxy' means 'the true doctrine' – it does not denote a conservative version of Christianity the way Orthodox Judaism does for that faith. A popular version of that Byzantine music had been developed in Greece by Ioannis Sakellarides (1853–1938), a Greek musician and psaltis (chanter) who proffered a simplified version of the received repertory of Byzantine chant that he claimed to have purified of oriental influences.

The ascent of Western musical styles in the churches of Athens coincided with the rise of Greek immigration to the United States. The immigrants brought to the New World both traditional Byzantine chant and the new Athenian liturgical music but found that their new cultural environment was more hospitable to the latter. Russian-style works were not unheard in America, but it was the music of Sakellarides that soon came to be accepted as 'traditional' in its Greek Orthodox churches. This was evidently due in part to its simplicity, the ready availability of its frequently reprinted staff-notation editions, and the close melodic resemblance of much of it to more traditional forms of chant. Also important was its active cultivation by prominent musicians and clergy. Several disciples of Sakellarides immigrated to the United States and assumed key musical posts: George Anastasiou (Washington, DC and later Tarpon Springs, Florida), Angelos Desfis (Los Angeles), and Christos Vryonides (1894-1961), the first professor of Byzantine chant at the Holy Cross Greek Orthodox School of Theology, the archdiocesan seminary now located in Brookline, Massachusetts. Continuity in musical development along Western lines was assured by the support of Archbishops Athenagoras (1931-49), Michael (1949-59), and Iakovos (1959-96), all of whom promoted mixed choirs with organs.[3] Peter's father Ernest was one of many children of Greek immigrants who embraced this religious music, and he expressed his love for it by becoming the psaltis and later on choir director at the church the family attended regularly, St. Spyridon, in Sheboygan Wisconsin. As we will see, his father's involvement in church music would have a profound influence on Peter and can be said to have been his entry point into the wider world of music.

FROM PELOPONNESOS TO SHEBOYGAN, WISCONSIN

Peter Tiboris' grandparents were among the thousands of Greeks who immigrated to the United States in the early twentieth century. The family name was Tsibouris at that time and his grandfather Panayotis Anastasios was one of thousands of Greeks who sought a better future in the United States at the turn of the century. The village where Panayotis was born in 1871 and which he left behind was Dedebey. It was nestled in the southwestern part of Arcadia, the central region of Peloponnesus. Dedebey was too small to merit a mention in the numerous historical or travelers' accounts of Peloponnesus during the nineteenth century. Among the very few is one that has Theodoros Kolokotronis, the military chieftain who led the Greek revolution against the Ottomans in 1821, arriving there that year and pausing to consider his next move in one of the early battles of the campaign. Dedebey also appears in a book by the British antiquarian topographer William Martin Leake titled Peloponnesiaca published in 1848. In 1927 a Greek government commission tasked with renaming Turkish-sounding names of villages into Greek ones renamed Dedebey 'Tripotamo' which means three rivers. It was a decision based on the village's location near the Alpheios river and two of its tributaries. The river Alpheios that flowed near the village was, in mythology, one of the rivers rerouted by Hercules in his fifth labor in order to cleanse the filth of the Augean Stables.

As was the custom at the time, Panayotis Anastasios Tsibouris married a woman from his village. Calliope Fotopoulos was born in Dedebey in 1880, and they married in 1897 when he was 26 and she was 16. Calliope was one of ten children, nine girls and one boy. The large number of her siblings was not rare, rural families tended to have many children because mortality rates were high, although on the way down in Peloponnesus in the last two decades of the nineteenth century. Children also helped rural families with the work in the fields. Calliope gave birth to a son, Constantinos in 1898 and a daughter, Assimo a few years later.

Dedebey and the rest of Peloponnesos had enjoyed a brief spell of prosperity in the 1880s when its grapes replaced the French grapes in international markets because the vineyards in France were struck by a blight. Farmers in Peloponnesos and the neighboring Ionian islands switched to the cultivation of grapes. Most of them possessed small plots of land, generally no more than four acres, but this did not prevent them from responding to the rising price of the currants. The currants were seedless grapes that were dried and exported as currants which were high in demand in Europe and especially Britain. The currants were used in the various English puddings, which were a staple of that country's cuisine. Greece even managed to export its currants to the United States, despite the opposition of growers of a similar fruit, the raisin, in California. When in 1896 the raisin growers succeeded in persuading the government to impose a tariff on the incoming currants, the New York Times commented the measure had not "helped the consumer much. Later on, the demand for the Greek currants will be created by the vast difference in flavor and its seedless character and its quality."[4] Alas for Greece, however, France overcame the blight and demand for Greek currents took a sudden dive and never recovered. The small farmer who had become a small entrepreneur now had to become an immigrant in order to pay the family's debts and help it sustain one of its main duties in rural Greece, to provide a respectable dowry for its daughters to get married.

That is when transatlantic immigration began. Most of the Greek immigrants from Arcadia made their way to the Midwestern states in response to the job opportunities open at the time. Although the vast majority of Greeks were from rural areas and had been engaged in agriculture, they chose to take any type of job an unskilled laborer could undertake or one that required relatively quick on-the-job training. The idea was that they would earn a lot of good money and return to Greece after a few years. Ultimately, fewer than one in four of them managed to do that: the rest settled permanently in the United States, as did Panayotis Tsibouris. The first immigrants from the Peloponnesian regions of Arcadia, Laconia and Messenia settled in Chicago, so many of them in fact that the Greeks called it 'Chicagoupolis'. Others headed to St. Louis, which was the gateway to the west and jobs in mines and on the railroad. Others, including Tsibouris, ventured north into Wisconsin, and he was among those who settled in Sheboygan. The decision to settle there in a climate that was so brutally colder than that of Greece was a testament to their determination to find work and make the most of their decision to come to America.

When I visited Tripotamo with Tiboris in March of 2023 the village was deserted. Most small rural villages in Greece are empty but there was an additional reason for Tripotamo. Using the right of eminent domain, the Greek electricity company was about to extend its nearby mining for lignite and swallow up the village. The village is in the process of being moved to another location close by, and in the summer of 2022, a final service was held in the local church, in which one of the chandeliers was donated by the Tsibouris family. The church is also being relocated but the priest, Fr. Vasilios Darras, had the keys to the half-empty church and showed us the engraving of the name Tsibouris on the chandelier which is about to be dismantled and brought to the new church. As we were walking around the village we ran into a local resident, who had come that day to remove some plants from the garden of his house before they would be swept away by the electricity company's bulldozers. He knew the names of several Tripotamo residents who had gone to America. Peter

Tiboris had not heard of them, and they had not settled anywhere near Sheboygan in Wisconsin where they could have maintained ties with his grandfather. It was only when very large numbers of immigrants from the same place immigrated to America that they were able to form some sort of society, usually known as a 'brotherhood'. Tripotamo did not have the numbers for such a luxury.

Panayotis Tsibouris arrived in Boston in March of 1903 aboard a vessel belonging to the Dominion Line company after a voyage that lasted almost four weeks. Calliope stayed behind, but Panayotis brought Constantino and Assimo, their two children, with him so they could start their education, and as a sign that he expected to stay in the United States for the long term. This was not the case with most Greek immigrants who hoped they would make enough money and return after a few years. That year saw a record number of arrivals from Greece – over 14,000. The numbers peaked to about 45,000 departures annually by 1907. By the time the United States drastically limited emigration from Southeastern Europe in the early 1920s, there were about 350,000 Greeks in the country. The rising xenophobia that prompted the imposition of limits on the numbers of incoming Europeans also led to increasing numbers of Greeks acquiring U.S. citizenship. Panayotis was way ahead of his time. He became an American citizen in 1908 and changed his first name to Peter, which Greeks considered to be an acceptable anglicization of Panayotis. Many Greek immigrants were anglicizing their first and very often their last names in that era to make themselves sound less foreign. The Tsibouris family was also ahead of their time in the way Calliope joined her husband in America after almost twelve years, in 1914. Very few women, even those who were married, left Greece to settle in the United States that early. It was only when immigration restrictions were going to be implemented by Congress that many Greek immigrants either sent for their wives or invited picture brides to join them in America around 1920.

Calliope would describe her journey to her grandson Peter many years later. She left Tripotamo and went to the port of Piraeus and traveled to Le Havre, France where she boarded a ship with about 800 Greek immigrants that would take them across the Atlantic. By that time the passage to cross the Atlantic was between eight and twelve days. Those in steerage, like Calliope, had to bring their own bedding with them. The process of receiving immigrants in Boston was less well organized compared to that in Ellis Island, but Calliope made her way to Boston's South Station and traveled by train to Chicago, a trip that took over 24 hours at the time. In Chicago she boarded another train for the last leg of a long trip to Sheboygan.

According to her memory the fare for the boat trip cost $8 and the entire journey lasted three months. She recalled the hardships she endured while traveling in steerage, sleeping below deck on the bedding she brought with her. She also heard that one in four of the 800 or so steerage passengers died during the trip across the Atlantic. That is surely an exaggerated number, but indicative of the fears instilled in all who made the difficult crossing. She arrived in Sheboygan in May, 1914 to find her two children had become young adults.

Panayotis' choice to head to the small manufacturing town of Sheboygan was unusual even though the Greeks who settled there found work quite easily. At the time Sheboygan was a bustling manufacturing town whose size grew from 26,000 inhabitants in 1910 to 31,000 in 1920. The original settlers were mostly German immigrants. In April, 1916 The Sheboygan Press extolled the virtues of the Wisconsin town in a front-page article titled 'Sheboygan and her promise for the future'. Proclaiming that the stability of a city, its growth and future rested on its industries, the article declared "no city of a similar size has a more promising future than Sheboygan." Moreover "Contentment reigns supreme. It is a city that has made no boasts yet harbors within her midst quality institutions with quality goods as an offering in the sales end. It is unquestionably the greatest furniture center in the northwest and enjoys the proud distinction of having three of the greatest enamelware plants in the world."

The biggest of those enamelware plants the newspaper referred to belonged to Kohler Co. where Tsibouris got a job. The company was founded by an Austrian immigrant, J. M. Kohler in 1887 in Riverside, a section of Sheboygan which was renamed Kohler and became a company town. Following a chance encounter with a Greek immigrant from Arcadia who impressed him with his work ethic, Kohler asked him to bring over as many compatriots of his as were willing to move to Wisconsin. By the time Panayotis Tsibouris was planning to immigrate therefore, there were already Greeks working for Kohler, and others were finding work in the city's furniture factories, tanneries and railroads so for him, Sheboygan was an obvious destination. After working at Kohler Panayotis opened a billiard hall and later on worked for the Sheboygan-based Northern Furniture Company.

IMMIGRANT LIFE IN SHEBOYGAN

The Greeks settled on the south side of Sheboygan around Indiana Avenue, forming a little Greektown. Among them were maybe as many as 250 families from the

region of Arcadia. One estimate suggests that three out of four of the Greeks in Sheboygan lived on or around Indiana Avenue between 7th and 14th streets. Almost all those Greek immigrants were young, unmarried men who lived in "cooperative housekeeping arrangements" or boarding houses. The city records mention a boarding house owned by Nicholas and Barbara Leider on Indiana Avenue, confirming that its boarders were predominantly Greek until 1915, when Leider's son sold it to a Greek, George Velonis. The property was eventually transformed into apartment units and for short stints it also operated a tavern after it was resold to other Greeks. The Greek occupancy of the building ended in 2002. Tsibouris' name does not appear among the list of boarders, although he lived initially on Indiana Avenue before acquiring his own house at 1126 Indiana Avenue.

It was on or around Indiana Avenue where one could also find Greek-owned stores, barber shops, saloons, tailors and most importantly, coffee shops. The coffee shop was where the Greek men socialized, exchanged news from home, and relaxed playing cards. Very often a back room was where customers played cards for money. Gambling was for many Greeks a form of entertainment and unlike in the workplace they could display traditional masculine traits such as bravado and risk-taking. Unlicensed gambling of that sort was of course illegal. The earliest news item reporting Greeks being arrested and fined for playing cards in a coffee house on Indiana Avenue appeared in the Sheboygan Press in November, 1909. But the news about the local Greeks was not always negative: the same newspaper had reported the Greek community was presenting a play in January, 1908. Sheboygan was also a venue for fights by Greek immigrants who had become professional wrestlers touring the country. The earliest such occasion was when Demetral the 'Terrible Greek', who toured the country, stopped in Sheboygan for a wrestling match. His real name was Vasilios Dimitrelis, and he was from Arcadia in Peloponnesos. The Sheboygan Press reported that "The Greek colony in Sheboygan have a pool of $500 to bet on their countryman and are very enthusiastic."[5] Because the bout was to take place on a Sunday it was stopped by the police, and the newspaper reported that there were 300 Greeks including women in attendance and they were obliged to return to their "settlement" which indicates the existence of a small Greektown around Indiana Avenue. The fight took place the next day in front of 400 spectators and Demetral won to the delight of the Sheboygan Greeks.

Celebratory moments such as those following the victory of touring Greek wrestlers were far and few between in an era that witnessed the rise of xenophobia in the United States and Wisconsin. When the Greeks first started settling on

Indiana Avenue some referred to it as "garlic boulevard," a misplaced pejorative because garlic does not feature as prominently in Greek cooking as it does, for example, in Italian recipes. Yet in Sheboygan xenophobia was relatively muted because the city's establishment was well aware that the enamelware, furniture, and other manufacturing plants relied on the labor of the Austrian, Greek, Jewish, Lithuanian, Russian, and Slav immigrants. Appreciation of the immigrants grew, and negative newspaper items became rarer. An article in 1910 offered the immigrants a backhanded compliment when it mentioned that Sheboygan was a "good moral city" with relatively low crime even though it had in its midst several immigrant groups that were considered to have "disturbing proclivities."[6] And as the immigrants steadily assimilated into American ways grudging praise was offered.

Panayotis Tsibouris would have probably frequented one or more of the coffee shops and maybe he had also watched one of the Greek itinerant wrestlers, but where he devoted a lot of his free time was at the Greek Orthodox church of St. Spyridon. Religion played a big role in the life of the Greek immigrants, especially those who like Panayotis had grown up in rural parts of the country where traditions ran deep and the church was as important as the school. In the United States the church and its services reminded the immigrants of life in the homeland, it bound them together and was the twin pillar of their identity along with the use of the Greek language. A church was the first thing the Greeks established wherever they settled after establishing a 'koinotita' a community organization. The community council, along with a priest who settled in Sheboygan in 1905, the Rev. Nicholas Velonis purchased, land on 1425 S. 10th Street for this purpose. It was well sustained, being close enough to the center of the Greek neighborhood, and yet far enough away from the factories and business establishments on Indiana Avenue. The church building, excluding the current bell tower, was completed in 1906 and it is one of the oldest standing Greek Orthodox churches in America. The tower was added in 1916. The completion of the church was celebrated on Christmas Day 1906 and two years later the church was officially consecrated. In 1910 it was officially incorporated, and at a meeting held in the summer of that year the church's officers were elected. A new priest, the Rev. James Raggos, was the honorary president, Peter Jumes was president, and the vice-president was Peter Tsimbouris. His last name was spelled slightly differently, but in terms of his first name by then he was going by the name Peter, the anglicized form for Panayotis. Peter would remain active in his church for his entire life. In 1911 the church started a Greek school – the teacher, Christopher Kroustos, had four classes that met in the evenings between 7 and 10 pm. By that time there were about 700 Greeks in Sheboygan and demand for schooling the children in the Greek language was growing. The Greeks may have been anglicizing their names and doing their best to adapt to the new environment, but teaching their children the mother tongue was considered as important as preserving their Greek Orthodox faith.

PETER'S PARENTS ERNEST AND STELLA

In 1916 Calliope, aged 36 by then, gave birth to their third child, a boy, whom they baptized with the name Anastasios Panayotis, naming him after his paternal grandfather as is the custom in Greece. This was a time when Greeks were struggling to become accepted in American society, and frequently changed their first name to an anglicized version. Anastasios became Ernest. When Ernest was one year old, Calliope decided she did not like living in Sheboygan, about 5,300 miles away from Dedebey and considerably colder. She moved back to Greece in 1917, taking Ernest with her, in what turned out to be a short visit: they both returned in 1919. When they entered Greece, Calliope gave her son's place of birth as Greece rather than the United States, probably because she was embarrassed to say he was American-born, a rarity for Greeks in those early years of the twentieth century. This caused an unexpected problem for Ernest because it made him automatically a Greek citizen and consequently eligible for doing national service in the military, which was compulsory for all Greeks. He also feared that his medical qualifications would make him liable to serve for a period even at a later stage of his life. Thus he waited until he turned seventy, which definitively released him from any such obligations, in order to return to Greece without getting entangled in his homeland's legendary bureaucracy.

Calliope's back and forth, though rare in the case of women, was not uncommon at the time. Despite the huge distances and arduous traveling conditions there were many Greeks who returned to the homeland for short stay but most did not find it very welcoming. Beyond the vast differences in living standards and daily amenities, the country was politically polarized over whether Greece should enter WWI. Indeed, transatlantic immigration from Peloponnesos and other areas of the country continued unabated. Calliope made her way back to Sheboygan one more time but this time she would stay there permanently.

Growing up in Sheboygan, Ernest followed the path of many other children of Greek immigrants, yet he also displayed a particular love for performance and music which, later, he would pass on to his son Peter. On the one hand, he took Greek language lessons, dutifully attended services at St. Spyridon church, applied himself at school and became bilingual, and on the other hand he began to appear in school plays. St. Spyridon became as big a part of his life, as it had been for father, and he would become one of the church chanters, a psaltis.

He attended Longfellow Elementary a few blocks away from his home on Indiana Avenue. The original school building, which no longer exists looked impressive, in a handsome Romanesque, style though it was modest, comprising two stories of brick and a high basement of stone. It featured eight large rooms with spacious central halls and an addition was built in 1918. Around the same time, the American Red Cross was sponsoring a school milk program. Milk was provided free for those who could not afford the cost. Students who could afford it would be charged two cents for their milk.

Ernest's acting in the local newspaper was fist mentioned in 1926, when he was in fourth grade and was in a play called 'A Christmas Crazy Class'. His name appears again when he was in a play in sixth grade two years later. In 1929 young Ernest appeared in one of a series of performances staged by the Greek school in honor of Greek Independence Day. He was also a popular and good student. In 1932 Ernest graduated from Junior High School as his class vice-president. He graduated from High School in 1935 and went on to Marquette University, a Catholic university in Wisconsin, from which he graduated in 1941 with a degree in dentistry. His decision about what to major in was almost certainly due to the cause of his father's death in June of 1932, aged 60. Panayotis died at St. Nicholas hospital in Sheboygan after several weeks of illness. He had a bad tooth infection which could not be treated effectively – antibiotics were not yet available – and it spread to his heart and lungs, causing his death

A year after Panayotis' death his eldest son Constantinos died. He was the owner of a billiards hall, married with a son and a daughter, and lived in Antigo, a town about three hours away from Sheboygan. He had changed his name to Gustav upon gaining U.S. citizenship. Switching from a Greek to a German name was an obvious choice if one wanted to blend into a town in which the older established elites were of mostly German origin. And hundreds of 'Constantinos' across America became officially or unofficially 'Gus' for the same reason. There have been at least two U. S. Congressmen with that name, Gus Bilirakis of Florida and Gus Yatron of Pennsylvania.

Ernest enlisted in the Army after the United States entered World War II, as did hundreds of other Greek-Americans. He was commissioned in the dental corps and with the rank of captain was assigned overseas in the Aleutian Islands in June, 1943 while the U.S. and Canadian forces were completing a campaign to eject Japanese forces that had landed there in 1942. The news item about his assignment that appeared in The Sheboygan Press on December 13, 1943 – Ernest's 27th birthday – also carried his photograph in uniform, but the caption misspelt his name as Tribouris. That or some other reason made him decide to change his last name to Tiboris, which is easier to spell. This was in 1946, the year he got married to Stella Menas on November 11th at St Spyridon church. There followed a dinner and reception attended by 300 guests.[7] Ernest had already started a dental practice in Sheboygan, a profession he continued to pursue with great dedication and love through his eighties.

Stella's life story up to that point was in many ways representative of the lives of Greek-American women in the first half of the twentieth century. She was born in Waukegan, Illinois, an industrial suburb of Chicago where her Greek-born father Michael, also known as Mike, was the owner of the Royal Restaurant on Washington Street and the family lived in the same building. Menas purchased the restaurant in 1914, and it enjoyed a very good reputation. A local newspaper described it as clean and neat, and the meals and the service was said to be very good, with short orders being served at all hours.[8] The restaurant business was the most common and visible profession among Greek-Americans not only back then but throughout the twentieth century.

In the 1920s Menas became the owner of a billiards hall. Both businesses had their challenges, with customers trying different ways to avoid payment or simply becoming rowdy and gambling on the premises. Michael and his wife Demetra had eight children, three daughters and five sons. Stella was the third daughter, and she was born in April 11, 1923. The Menas family decided to move away from the Chicago area and move to Sheboygan sometime in the 1930s. Stella's name appears in a list of children in a Christmas play at Longfellow elementary school in 1934 and four years later as a player in a Junior High volleyball tournament.

In 1941 Stella was doing volunteer work for the Greek War Relief Association (GWRA). It was a national organization established by leading Greek-Americans as soon as Greece entered WWII in October, 1940. It did so by going to war with fascist Italy that tried unsuccessfully to invade and conquer Greece. Against all odds the Greek army managed to push the superior Italian forces back over the Greek-Albanian border which they had crossed. While the democratic world hailed the heroism of the Greeks, the GWRA branches across the United States mobilized in order to gather funds and materials to send to Greece to help the war effort. It would continue its work after Greece was eventually occupied by German and Italian forces from 1941 until it was liberated in 1944. As was the case in many such instances of volunteer work aiding the homeland, Greek-American women, including young women, played a crucial role even though the Greek-American community leadership was all male and Greek-American families maintained a traditional patriarchal structure, keeping young women sheltered at home. Stella also joined a Red Cross knitting group with several other young Greek-American women in Sheboygan. Such activities continued throughout the 1940s because the GWRA was also concerned with aiding Greek post-war reconstruction. In the decades that followed Stella was active in the Ladies Philoptochos of St Spyridon, something that was made easier after she got married because her husband Ernest was involved in the life of the church. The Philoptochos was responsible for organizing and running the church's philanthropic initiatives and its social events.

Ernest would remain a psalti in his church for sixty years, with a break when he was away at college and in the medical corps during WWII. He served for many years on the board of St. Spyridon church, including several as president and as the director of the choir. He was active in the Greek community's affairs, such as the commemorations of the anniversary of the Greek revolution of 1821. He also played the clarinet, though never publicly. He practiced and played only at home, for his own pleasure as he told his sons. He had a big collection of records and played classical music and opera both at home and at his dental office. Ernest, whom both his sons describe as a dignified and modest man whose life was focused on his family, his church, and his profession, would have had a profound influence on both his sons. And he passed on his love of music to both of them and especially Peter.

Stella gave birth to two boys soon after her marriage to Ernest. Peter was the eldest and was born on October 31, 1947. As was the Greek Orthodox custom, Peter was baptized six months after he was born, in March, 1948. His brother Gust, named after his late uncle Gustav, was born the next year, in December. A third boy, Michael was born in 1951 but died when he was only four years old because he was hydrocephalic. Two years later Stella gave birth to a fourth boy who however was stillborn.

FAMILY MATTERS

It would be hard to overstate the significance of the family in the life of the Greek immigrants in America. The family and the strong bonds that keep it together was a cultural trait that ensured survival in rural Greece in an environment in which government and social services and other institutions were almost non-existent, resources were scarce, and those outside the immediate social networks of family and village were considered a potential threat. The immigrants to America preserved strong family bonds as a means of survival in the new, strange, and sometimes hostile environment. The family, in alliance with the church, preserved Old World values and traditions and Greek identity, expressed through language, religion and a pride in the legacies of Ancient Greece. The Greek immigrant family in America was also a patriarchal family. The father was the breadwinner and role model for the hard work ethic the entire family was expected to embrace and was its undisputed head. Mothers could wield influence as long as they stayed within their assigned roles for the sake of appearances. Sons were allowed much more freedom compared to daughters whose 'honor' had to be protected at all costs. But the freedom and privileges the sons enjoyed were contingent on the loyalty they displayed towards both parents.

The Tiboris family was no exception to this generalized picture, but to his credit, Ernest truly earned the respect of his sons through setting an example of dedication to his work and his family. Peter and his brother recall their father valuing their education very highly, something that was another Greek immigrant trait. Ernest's family took very few vacations because he preferred to spend the money he gained as a dentist on his sons' education rather than going on holiday or on other forms of entertainment. He worked hard all day from Monday to Saturday and devoted his meager free time to playing the clarinet and doing work for St. Spyridon Church. On very few occasions he went to Milwaukee to attend a Braves baseball game, and of course, Sunday morning was devoted to the weekly Greek Orthodox liturgy at the church. Stella went along with this way of doing things, participated actively in the church's activities, and supported her sons as they developed their own ambitions and visions of their future.

Grandmother (or yayá as she was called in Greek by her grandsons) Calliope was also very much part of the tightly-knit Tiboris family unit, and she was especially caring and protective of Peter, her oldest grandson. She lived on the first floor of the family house on 1126 Indiana Avenue and Peter used to sleep there, while Gus, along with their parents, was on the second floor. Peter was spending more time with his yayá downstairs rather than with his parents and this did not always sit well with his mother and there were some moments of family tension. Then in 1960, the entire family moved to a new one-story house near Sheboygan's South High School and the separation issues were resolved.

What remained a constant for both brothers was the quiet, determined presence of their father in their lives. It is not that odd that Gus chose to follow his father's profession and become a dentist. Peter, in contrast, chose to follow his father's love of music and choral singing and do it professionally. Both sons strove to live up to the high standards their father had set, Peter probably more so because of the choice he made to make a career in music, which came second to dentistry in his father's life. This motivational drive instilled in Peter would stay with him his entire life.

BROTHER GUS

In 1964, when Gus was only sixteen years old, he and Michael Sweeney, a fellow student, won an award at a County-wide fair for a project on internal tooth changes due to external stimuli. He went on to study dentistry at Marquette University exactly as his father Ernest had done. Gus opened his own practice in Sheboygan in 1973, the year he received his degree.

Now retired, Gus retains the soft-spoken demeanor that must have been so comforting for his patients. The deep affection the brothers have for each other is obvious. Gus was smiling, as he often does, when we spoke about Peter's career choice. Peter is all about performances, Gus said, whether he is on the stage or off the stage. Gus was also musically inclined as a young boy. The first performances Gus remembers was a band called 'The G-Sharps' made up of himself, Peter and a cousin. The band played Greek music at St. Spyridon Church's facilities. They were ten years old – Gus played the drums, Peter played the accordion, and George Brett their cousin the clarinet, which he played very well. Gus, Peter and George also played the piano at a school recital held in the Ebenezer Evangelical and Reformed church in October of 1957, and Peter, along with George and John Rezevoulis, also played "several Byzantine numbers." Peter, at ten was already the organist at St. Spyridon church.[9]

Gus married Linda Lukovsky in 1978 and the ceremony was held at St. Spyridon church. Throughout the next decade Gus followed in his father's footsteps not only by being a dentist in Sheboygan but also becoming very active in the life of the church. He became one of the organizers of the annual Greek food fair that raised money for the church, and he also became a member of its board of directors. Gus' wife Linda was also very involved. Peter was of course present at his brother's wedding, and the newspaper announcement described him as "Peter Tiboris of Urbana." That was because he was at the University of Illinois at Urbana-Champaign pursuing a doctorate in choral music education studies. For him it was a natural evolution from playing the organ at St. Spyridon, which he did until he graduated from high school in 1966.

Peter harbored a warm, affectionate respect for his brother Gus that stayed with them all their lives. The older brother's respect was due to Gus' devotion to dentistry and the fact that he worked closely with their father Ernest, caring for him and smoothing the way for his retirement from dentistry. Even though Peter had moved far away, he made a point of visiting his brother frequently in Sheboygan or organizing travel with their wives. An important part of the visits back to Sheboygan was playing golf with his brother and their father at Riverdale Golf Course just south of Sheboygan. This was a frequent occurrence, and they often had an evening start to the game, after Ernest closed his dentist's office at 6 pm.

PETER TIBORIS, ORGANIST AT ST. SPYRIDON

Greek Orthodox churches are designed to engender a sense of awe and respect. Austere-looking figures painted on icons stare down on you, and there is a strong smell of incense and of burning candles. The Orthodox relate to God in the first instance through the senses, not through trying to understand the written word. It was in that atmospheric ambiance that Peter had assumed the duties of the church's organist at a very young age – a little before his tenth birthday in 1957. The announcement in the local newspaper noted "a fourth-grade student at Longfellow School, the youthful organist has a acquired a satisfactory knowledge of Byzantine music under the guidance of Father Peter Murtos. He has been active in church affairs as an altar boy since he was four years of age and always likes to participate in church activities. For the past two years he has been a piano student of Mrs. Eugene Meyer."[10]

Peter vividly recalls the sense of community the parish of St. Spyridon provided and the commemorations of religious and Greek national holidays as well its regular activities: the Greek language school, Sunday (religious) School, the bake sales, the annual fundraising food festival, the dance festival in the summer and of course the choir. He remembers having to memorize poetry for the celebrations of Greek Independence Day, March 25th, including verses about the Greek revolutionary hero Theodoros Kolokotronis. There were traditional Greek dancing classes for boys and girls where he learned two of the best known Greek dances, the syrto and the tsamiko, and these were performed in the many events organized by the church.

Peter held on firmly to the identity instilled in him by his parents and the church. He has always been conscious of his Greek roots and told me that "from the time of my birth even until now I am always fully cognizant of my Greek roots that were planted from the moment I first heard and then started learning Greek." His life in the church, especially his involvement as an organist, and the typically Greek strong family bonds around him along with the national and religious commemorations served to reinforce his ethnic identity. Peter remembers all this as a constant and long-drawn-out process that ultimately bore fruit. He enjoyed it – loved it in fact – and all the while it made him feel being special as a Greek-American because that identity also entailed an invocation of the continuity of Greek culture from antiquity to the present. He became an avid reader of classical Greek texts, especially plays and the writing of ancient philosophers such Aristotle, Plato and Socrates.

Playing the organ in the church was Peter's entry point in the world of music. Traditionally, the Orthodox Church in the Old World does not use musical instruments during church services. It is uncertain why organs were introduced to Greek Orthodox churches in America, but it may represent an attempt to 'westernize'. Numerous Greek Orthodox churches installed organs. Archbishop Athenagoras, who took over the Greek Archdiocese in 1931, was a major advocate of organs and he encouraged their usage in America. While he encouraged this, however, it is likely that they had already become relatively common even earlier. In the early 20th century, priests and others in America had begun to compose new Greek Orthodox liturgical music that abandoned the traditional Byzantine modes and single vocal line. The new music with European scales was often presented in a westernized style through choirs accompanied by an organ. Among those associated with the progressive style was George Anastasiou, who arrived in the U.S. from Cyprus in 1920. He settled in Tarpon Springs in 1924, where he became the principal of the Greek Parochial School, organized the Byzantine Choir and served as head chanter at St. Nicholas Greek Orthodox Church from 1931 to 1941. Currently, the National Forum of Greek Orthodox Church Musicians, in its position on the usage of organs in church, says that the organ's main purpose is to assist the choir and the congregation in "maintaining accurate intonation," as many parishioners and volunteer choir members may not be very musically inclined or have a musical background.

FATHER PETER MURTOS

The significance of the organ for Peter cannot be exaggerated. Peter becoming the church's organist while his father was in charge of the choir confirmed the close relationship of the two and Ernest's musical influence on his son. But as he grew up, there were other mentors ready to guide him forward. Peter learned how play the organ at St. Spyridon under the guidance of the priest, Fr. Peter Murtos. Born in Amaliada in the Peloponnesos in 1922, Murtos followed an unusual path to the cloth. He fought with the communist resistance during World War II and then switched sides and fought with the Greek Army during the Greek civil war against the communists between 1946 and 1949. He also served as a member of the Athens police force, during which time he enrolled at the University of Athens as a student of Theology. He later moved to the United States and graduated from Union Theological Seminary in New York and also received his Masters in Theology in the History of Religions. St. Spyridon was his first parish in the United States, and he arrived there in 1954. Fluent in English and able to sing and compose, he quickly became a strong and active parish and community leader who was outspoken against racial injustice. As is usually the case with strong-willed priests, Murtos alienated some of his parishioners and there were tensions as well as dissent among some members of the church. Murtos and Ernest Tiboris, who were the same age, became close friends and spent a lot of time together – Ernest was the chanter in the church and choir director and that cemented their friendship. Peter remembers Murtos as a strict and disciplined musician who taught him not only how to play the organ but also how to sing based on Greek Orthodox neumatics, a form of musical notation that predated the invention of the five-line staff notation of western music. Murtos had learned this in the seminary he attended in Greece.

It was not only in church that Peter practiced and played the organ. He was able to practice on the huge organ at Sheboygan Theater, because the janitor, Christos Spanomihos, a Greek immigrant from Kalamata, let him in and allowed him to play while he was sweeping the floors. The large three manual vaudeville pipe organ was a remnant from the silent movie era when thousands of movie houses depended on live musical accompaniment for the screenings of those films. It was far more affordable to have a 'Mighty Wurlitzer' with a few house organists on staff than to pay for a full orchestra or even modest band to perform in the orchestra pit every day. The appearance of the 'talkies' in film gradually reduced the use of these organs in the entertainment world but, several survived in theaters such as the one in Sheboygan. The theater is presently known as the Stefanie H. Weill Center for the Performing Arts.

Peter and his father attended the first Greek Orthodox Choir Federation convention in Chicago in 1958, where Peter was the organist. In 1964 they were both named as Sheboygan delegates to the second convention of Greek Orthodox Choir Federation that met in St. Louis in October, 1964. Peter played the organ not only during church services but at several other church, community and school events, including weddings and music concerts. At most of those events Peter played the organ, but not always. He also appeared as a member of the G-Sharps. Their repertoire included a range of Greek dances and Peter's own performances often got mentioned in the local newspaper. In 1961 at the annual luncheon of medical auxiliaries in Sheboygan it noted "Peter Tiboris, the son of Dr. and Mrs. Ernest Tiboris, delighted the audience by beautifully playing selections on an electric organ."[11] There would be many more audiences Peter would delight in the future.

CHAPTER TWO

A MUSICAL EDUCATION

Put all of your soul into it, play the way you feel. — Fredrick Chopin

Peter Tiboris first entered the world of higher education in music as a student in 1966. Instead of going to the University of Wisconsin as he had planned, he went to Oshkosh State University, which soon after became the University of Wisconsin Oshkosh. The reason was his doctor's advice after driving into a tree on the night of his high school graduation. Staying closer to home and going to Oshkosh – less than sixty miles away – rather than Madison which was much further away was considered the prudent thing to do. The car accident would not set him back, however. Indeed, going off the road that night was only the first of many twists and turns Peter's life would take as a student and later as a professor of choral music education. Being at Oshkosh enabled him to go back to Sheboygan in September and play the organ at a ceremony at the Masonic Temple where his brother Gus

was installed as Master Councilor of the Sheboygan Chapter of the Order of De Molay in September, 1966. Peter joined De Molay at the same time. After a year at Oshkosh, Peter transferred to the University of Wisconsin-Madison, where he would receive his bachelor's degree in music education in 1970.

University of Wisconsin at Madison, 1967-70

The sprawling 906 acre campus of the University of Wisconsin-Madison on which Peter arrived was located a mile from the state capitol on a series of hills overlooking Lake Mendota, and gathered on those hills was a conglomerate of classic and modern buildings: the Colleges of Letters and Science, Agricultural and Life Sciences, Engineering, Business, Education, Family Resources and Consumer Sciences, Natural Resources, Nursing, Students Pharmacy, Graduate, Law and Medical schools, which housed 130 Departments in total. There were 34,388 students enrolled at Madison for the 1970-71 academic year. Peter would be overwhelmed, not only by its size but also by the academic challenges the institution posed to the Sheboygan High School graduate. He came face to face with the need to study and acquire knowledge and analytical skills. At first he frequently felt a little lost and unsure of himself. Luckily for him, there were his cousins, three brothers, and fellow Greek-Americans who were his childhood friends who were also students at Madison, and they generously offered guidance and support and were his role models. As second generation Greek-Americans, the three Kotsonis brothers took their studies seriously and pursued successful careers – George as a lawyer, Jimmy in the insurance business as an executive and Frankie as a toxicologist and researcher who became an expert on the artificial sweetener aspartame.

One thing at Madison that did not appear to distract Peter Tiboris too much was the brewing student discontent that had begun in earnest on campus, a reflection of the era and of events on other university campuses including Berkeley, Columbia and Kent State. But he does remember the unrest caused by student activists, and that classes were often canceled because the police and National Guard were called in to quell the demonstrations. Peter's apartment was near Mifflin Street, which became the site of a major student protest event, the Mifflin Street Block Party, so when the police sprayed tear gas the entire neighborhood was affected. The ongoing unrest and the uncertainty about what the next day would bring made it hard to focus. During Peter's time at Madison the biggest conflagration came when a bomb went off in the Stirling Building in the early hours of August 24, 1970, killing one researcher. Student activists had set the bomb off because they deemed the Army Math Center which was housed in that building was connected to the war in Vietnam. Tiboris' cousin, Frank Kotsonis, did research in that building as a graduate student but was not in it when the blast occurred. Tiboris himself had just graduated and was driving back home at that time.

The situation on the Madison campus would become even more fraught just after he graduated, but even if he had been there, his conservative upbringing and the values instilled in him by his father and life in the Church would have precluded even the thought of becoming remotely involved in protest movements. Instead, he had become enchanted with the university's music program. It inspired him and he became completely engrossed in his studies with an eye to the possibility of a life in music. In his own words, he found the program challenging, gripping, fascinating and intense; it was an experience that shook him up. At times he felt left behind, but he persevered with success at the end. He had been like the proverbial dry sponge that soaked up everything that came its way.

One of Peter's qualities is that he remembers all those who mentored him, and he does so with fondness and gratitude many decades later. The faculty member that shaped his undergraduate studies was Roger Folstrom, who had joined the University of Wisconsin as a music professor a year earlier. He spent his entire career there, mentoring hundreds of music students. After his death in 2011 Jeanne, his wife of 47 years, described her late husband as someone whose life was music, his family and his church. One can see why Roger and Peter were able to connect so easily.

The other professor who had a great influence on Peter was Donald Neuen, who at the time was the new choral director at the University of Wisconsin's School of Music. Neuen became a very well-known choral conductor and educator who ended his teaching career as the Distinguished Professor of Conducting and Director of Choral Activities at the University of California at Los Angeles. There is a Donald Neuen Appreciation Society Facebook page with over 500 members. Neuen had formed the University Singers upon his arrival in Madison in 1967 and they quickly developed into an acclaimed and popular group. One of the first big steps in his career a little later on was being appointed director of choral activities for the Atlanta Symphony Orchestra, as well as choral director at Georgia State University in 1970. In an interview at the time, he explained his views on choral singing, saying that one of the great things about it was "its total involvement, the way that the individual, though he's a member of a group puts all of himself into his singing, and yes, he usually performs much better than if he were singing alone."[12] As we will see further on, Peter would remain in touch with Neuen and years later would invite him to conduct at concerts organized by MidAmerica Productions at Carnegie Hall.

At Madison, Peter was able to maintain his attachment with his Greek Orthodox faith and music. Madison's Greek Orthodox Assumption church had a strong choir directed by Wisconsin University history professor Michael Boro Petrovich, who was also a member of the Philharmonic Chorus of Madison. Petrovich was born in Cleveland in 1922, of Serbian and Croatian parentage, and like many Serbian Orthodox in America who did not have their own ethnic church where they lived, attended instead a Greek Orthodox Church. The same was true of his wife Dushanka, who was very active in the ladies Philoptochos of the Assumption Church and was also involved in a series of Christian interfaith projects in the area. Petrovich's career at the University of Wisconsin began in 1950. His rise through the faculty ranks was studded with awards and distinctions, campus and professional, for his scholarship and teaching, and culminated in his designation as the Evjue-Bascom Professor of History. His campus service was extensive and included the organization of a Russian area studies program. With the Cold War entering a crucial stage in the 1970s, Petrovich was very much in demand as a public speaker, but he managed to balance his professional duties, his faith and his stewardship of the church's choir.

Petrovich belonged to a generation of Byzantine music practitioners who believed it needed to be updated to make the melodies become more accessible to contemporary worshippers. Petrovich conducted the singing of a new form of the Divine Liturgy of St. John Chrysostom based on the Byzantine original at the 10th anniversary conference of the Midwest conference of Greek Orthodox choirs in Madison in October 1967. He was supported in this by one of his History Department colleagues, the Byzantinist John W. Barker, who was also involved in the church choir. Barker was an ardent and deeply learned connoisseur of classical music, especially opera and oratorio, with a particular devotion to the oratorios of Handel. He was a reviewer for the American Record Guide for 62 years and collected over 110,000 classical music recordings. His interests in history and music combined in a post-retirement career as a music historian who published several book-length studies, primarily on the music of Richard Wagner.

During his time with the Assumption choir Tiboris wrote some choral compositions including Se Imnoumen (We Praise You) and Eisai Agios (You Are a Saint). He composed a few more but soon realized that composing was not what he wanted to do – he wanted instead to conduct. Those short works are still sung in many churches in the Midwest.

GREEK ORTHODOXY

Ernest and his wife Stella instilled a deep-rooted faith in God and the Greek Orthodox religion in Peter and his brother Gus from a very young age. They took their sons regularly to Sunday's church service. Peter served as an altar boy from when he was four years old until twelfth grade. As we know, he also played the organ at church, with his father at his side singing and chanting during both the early morning 'Orthros' service and the regular liturgy. These experiences under the guidance of his father but also other friends neighbors and fellow parishioners such as John Tony Dovas who was also a church chanter instilled a deep sense of faith in Peter. He can feel the influence of the St. Spyridon community to this day, yet, as he puts it, he is not outwardly demonstrative about Greek Orthodoxy – instead, he has a quiet reverence and relationship with his faith, which comes from his parents, who he says guided him in a soft and gentle manner. For him, his Greek Orthodox spirituality is very personal and inwardly oriented. For about twenty years, between the ages of 25 and 45 his interest and involvement in the church diminished as he focused on building his career, but that gradually changed over time and Peter has reconnected with his spirituality – and his religious upbringing.

Recently, in 2022, there was an unexpected honor for Tiboris, an invitation to become an Archon, a member of the Order of St. Andrew, a prestigious organization committed to supporting the 'mother church' of Greek Orthodoxy, the Ecumenical Patriarchate of Constantinople. With an annual budget of over one million dollars and a program of funding various initiatives the Patriarchate undertakes, the Order relies on the contributions of its members, many of whom are wealthy Greek-Americans of the Greek Orthodox faith. The Patriarch awards members with honorary titles that are derived from the Church's history and go back to the Byzantine era. Among past members who were chosen because of their services to the Church rather than their wealth was Peter's father Ernest.

FIRST TRIP TO GREECE

In the summer of 1968, while still a student, Peter made his first visit to Greece, which was memorable for more than one reason. He landed first on the island of Corfu and

then went on to Athens to visit the Kotsonis family. From there he made his way down to Peloponnesos and his ancestral village, Tripotamo. While in Athens he took a tour bus trip to nearby Cape Sounion, where a famous Ancient Greek temple to Poseidon the mythological god of the sea is located. As it happened, just ahead of the bus was the motorcade of Greece's dictator Georgios Papadopoulos, who was traveling to his summer residence which was on the way to Sounion. Papadopoulos has seized power in a military coup in 1967. On that particular day, August 13, 1968, Alexandros Panagoulis, an anti-junta activist, made an assassination attempt on the dictator. The plan was to ignite a roadside bomb at a sharp turn of the road where the motorcade would have to slow down. The bomb went off but did not harm Papadopoulos. Naturally traffic came to a standstill and the tour bus was searched, as were its passengers who were also questioned before it was allowed to proceed to Sounion. Papadopoulos would remain in power until he was ousted by an internal coup in 1973, but the dictatorship collapsed the following year and democracy was restored in Greece. Panagoulis was arrested and brutally tortured. In the first elections after the end of the dictatorship he was elected as a deputy to the Greek parliament.

LAW SCHOOL, 1970-72

After graduating from the University of Wisconsin, Madison with his B.MSc. in choral music education Peter went on to spend one and half years at the John Marshall Law School in Chicago. With his cousins studying law and his brother becoming a dentist Peter felt the need to study something more 'practical' than music. The school, founded in 1899, was one of the few that one could go to with Peter's music education credentials. Studying law was a short-lived experience for Peter, and one that persuaded him to go back to the study of music. Peter remarked quite simply that law was not for him, but his wife Eilana Lappalainen believes that those years had an important influence on her husband. She sees in him someone whose training in legal studies, albeit for only two years, equipped him with a feel for the law and the ways it enables as well as it limits. That helped his career immensely, especially when it grew into presenting and staging music concerts and festivals worldwide.

Rather than return to law school for the Spring 1972 semester, Peter went back to Madison in order to pick up his music studies again. Because he had to wait until September, Peter took a job in Madison, and a most unlikely one at that: he worked as a bartender at the Left Guard, one of the steakhouses owned by two former Green Bay Packers football players, Max McGee and Fuzzy Thurston. They ran the Left Guard steak houses in several cities, including Madison, where it was located on East Washington Avenue. It would be Peter's only exposure to the world of sports. Both players had been on the Packers teams that had won the Super Bowl in 1966 and 1967 and their steakhouses were popular with former players and fans across Wisconsin.

THE M.Sc IN CHORAL MUSIC EDUCATION 1972 TO 74, UNIVERSITY OF WISCONSIN

Back at the University of Wisconsin Peter was able to connect with another instructor who would take him under his wing. Robert Petzold, who was born in Milwaukee in 1917 and received his Doctor of Philosophy at Wisconsin in 1950. He was a professor of music education and was in charge of the master's program in music education that Peter entered in the Fall of 1972. It was an unlikely coupling, because Peter wished to eventually gain a doctorate and teach at a college or university. He was much less interested in gaining an experience teaching music at a public school, something that was a requirement for the degree he was studying for at Madison. Petzold had spent twelve years as a public-school music teacher from 1938 to 1950, but he did not seem to mind Peter's different perspective. Petzold had graduated from high school at the height of the Great Depression, and he had originally wanted to become a mineral engineer and even applied to a school in Colorado, but the tuition and the costs of traveling there were prohibitive, so he stayed closer to home and went to the Milwaukee State Teacher's College. Perhaps that was one of the reasons he sympathized with Peter's determination to try and become a teacher in higher education without spending too much time gaining experience teaching at the public-school level. Petzold encouraged Peter to obtain some experience teaching at public schools, but only gently, and Peter did some teaching, but not enough – something that would become an issue when he applied to a doctoral program after completing the MSc in music education at the University of Wisconsin, Madison.

A teaching position opened at the Madison Area Technical College (MATC), a public technical and community junior college in Madison which, quite uniquely, had a Department of Music with a 2-year College division program in music. It was and still is one of the largest in the state-wide technical college network in Wisconsin.

The College was looking for an instructor who could also serve as choir director, and Petzold encouraged Peter to apply which he did, and he got the job. He would teach college credit classes in basic and advanced music theory, music appreciation, music history and music in performance while studying for his master's degree.

As was the case wherever he had gone to study, Peter encountered another mentor and supporter, a person with whom he says they hit off "in a big way." It was Roland Johnson, a charismatic music professor at MATC who had assumed the position of Music Director and Conductor of the Madison Symphony Orchestra in 1961 and the position as Artistic Director for and founder of Madison Opera in the same year. In October of 1970 Johnson had embarked on his tenth season amid much acclaim. The Madison Capital Times noted "the orchestra has grown steadily since 1961. Its stature in the Midwest has increased considerably; great artists who have appeared with the orchestra have come away not only impressed by the musicians but with a great respect for maestro Johnson. His talent as an artist's accompanist is not often mentioned, but his sensitivity to his soloists is one of his great strengths." The same article praised Johnson's work as conductor of Madison's Civic Chorus and his role in bringing about an exponential growth of MATC's music program: "Johnson has increased the musical program at the Technical College, adding another orchestra and adding more music classes both in day and night schools. He has gained the respect and cooperation of the MATC faculty and has made music an important part of the Technical College. The cooperation of the College with the Civic Music Association has broadened the base of the orchestra to a greater Madison area organization. Johnson likes to feel that the orchestra belongs to the community."[13]

Johnson and Tiboris were alike in many ways, entrepreneurial types, as Peter recalls. As he settled in at MATC Peter would come up with extra-curricular projects that Johnson would support. Tiboris recalls it was in October, 1978 that he was deeply impressed by the power of Johnson's musicians and his conducting in a performance of Tchaikovsky's Romeo and Juliet. "When seeing that performance in the second balcony of the theater where I was teaching, I was struck by the experience and I said to myself, at that time: 'I can do that. I want to do that.'"

Another important source of approval and encouragement was the MATC president Norman Mitby, who had assumed his post in 1967 and who would eventually serve at the College effectively and successfully in various capacities for twenty-eight years. He was known euphemistically as "work-oriented" and also for answering his own phone and eating lunch in his office.

Now back in Madison, Tiboris was able to reconnect with the Assumption Greek Orthodox Church and Michael Petrovich the choir director. In October, 1972, a Greek Orthodox Choirs conference was held in Madison, hosted by the Assumption Church and its choir. Among the several events that were part of the conference, including a Sunday service with a Liturgy arranged by Petrovich, was a workshop for young composers. Singers would have the opportunity to listen to and sing the works of four young composers who had adapted traditional music "to the modern idiom." The four were Thomas Bozikis of Hammond, Ind., Dr. Nicholas E. Maragos of the Mayo Clinic in Rochester NY, John Rezevoulis, a graduate student in Comparative Literature who grew up with Peter in Sheboygan, and Peter himself, who was listed as a graduate student in music education at the University of Wisconsin, instructor in music at MATC and president of the Christian Orthodox Fellowship.[14]

At MATC, Tiboris would soon show both his commitment to classical music but also his entrepreneurial spirit. After the conference, he went back to teaching as well as organizing his first classical music concerts with the choir, held on weekends and open to the public. His wish was to expose MATC students and the general public to highly qualified performers as well as explanations of their work. Within a few months, in April, 1973 it was announced that MATC's first pop-rock-jazz ensemble, 'The New College Singers' would present their first public concert under the direction of Peter Tiboris. The choreographer for the 28-member New College Singers was Tom Terrien of Kenosha, Wisconsin, who had worked closely with Peter on the New College Singers several other projects. The New College Singers toured Wisconsin performing choreographed popular and musical theater songs as well as jazz vocals in designed costumes.

The group had already performed at colleges, area high schools and dinner events and the proceeds from this first public concert would go towards student scholarships. By way of encouraging the public to attend, the local newspaper noted that "the group's attainment of professional quality in its first year of existence can be credited to the skill and determination of its director, Peter Tiboris."[15] One of the first places that the New College Singers visited was Lakeland College in Sheboygan. The local newspaper commented the next day that the group almost blew the roof off Lakeland's Campus center with their torrid top tempos and the high decibel levels of their slick entertainment package. The reviewer praised everything, the singing, the way the show was seamless, the choreography and even the costumes. Peter's former teacher Vito Intravaia was beaming when he described the performance as "fantastic" while Peter himself said "concert choirs should concertize, swing choirs should entertain."[16] The key student performers were Jeff and Kris Von Holzen, Debbie Lange and Diane Ritchie. Robert Monschein was the assistant music director.

THE FIRST METING WITH CHARLES LEONARD, 1974, UNIVERSITY OF ILLINOIS

When Tiboris completed the master's program at the end of the 1974 Spring semester, he met with Petzold at the University of Wisconsin at Madison to discuss what came next. The conundrum remained: Peter wished to gain a doctorate in music education in order to gain a position as a music professor at the university level, but he still did not want to gain the required experience teaching at public school. Professor Charles Leonhard laughed out aloud on the phone after he asked and was told how many years teaching experience Peter had. Petzold had called to ask his good friend to consider taking on Peter as an Ed.D. student despite his limited teaching experience. Petzold thought that Leonhard was the only person who could take on Peter as his doctoral student and Peter's idiosyncratic determination was about to encounter and learn from Leonhard's pedagogic brilliance.

Charles Leonhard was one of the most influential educators in American music history. During his 35 years as professor of music and chairman of the graduate committee for music education at the University of Illinois, he guided more than 200 doctoral dissertations. When they met in 1974, Leonhard was 59 years-old and had been professor of music and education, and chair of the graduate program in music education at the University of Illinois at Urbana-Champaign from 1951. Tiboris recalls shaking in his boots when he met Leonhard, but the meeting went well. The professor told Peter that if he could pass a set of summer courses, he would be accepted in the Ed.D. program and start in September, 1978, and that his policy was that any student accepted would be given every support in order to receive their doctorate. All of his many doctoral students had a university scholarship. Over the course of his long and distinguished career, Leonard, who earned his doctorate at Columbia University, authored a variety of books, including Foundations and Principles of Music Education (McGraw-Hill) and Contemporary Perspectives in Music Education (Prentice-Hall). He contributed more than 100 articles and book chapters to such publications as Music Educators Journal, Music Journal,

Journal of Research in Music Education, and Educational Digest. His awards are many, including the Distinguished Alumnus Award from Teachers College, and Distinguished Alumni Fellow, School of Music, University of Oklahoma. He earned a national citation from the Phi Mu Alpha Sinfonia fraternity in 1994. His assignments included National Recordings Chairman, Editorial Committee Journal of Research in Music Education, Editorial Committee Music Educators Journal, and Commission on Basic Concepts, to name a few.

At their first meeting in 1974, Peter came face to face with Leonhard the person, and over the course of the next few years he would interact with the full force of Leonhard's intellect and his aesthetic approach to music – it would have a profound influence on him, as we will see further on. But to imagine the first impression Leonhard made on the young Tiboris in 1974, we have a wonderful passage from an homage to Leonhard offered by another one of his protégés, University of Massachusetts at Amherst music professor Roger Rideout. The text is from a presentation he made at an event held in remembrance of Leonhard in 2005, three years after his death, organized by Tiboris. Rideout, who described Leonhard as a father to him, provides a wonderful description of his no-frills demeanor: "His annual Christmas party that year was held on December 8, his sixtieth birthday, but he made no mention of it. With his wife, Pat, he stood at the entrance to their living room and received the graduate students like a general welcoming junior officers to a mandatory social event at the officers club. At the time he seemed patriarchal, the very image of the senior professor in full control of his own destiny and, as I feared then, the destiny of all of us in the doctoral program. His greeting was informal yet reserved; not haughty, but you always felt the distance, as if he had deigned to give you his attention, to admit you to his private club where your behavior was being scrutinized before full membership would be recommended."[17]

Beyond the gruff exterior, as Peter quickly found out, was a first-class music educator who helped his students excel. He remembers his encounters with Leonhard and getting to know him was an amazing experience which made going to the University of Illinois the most important music decision of his life. Peter describes Leonhard as a music educationalist and philosopher and most important, aesthetician who knew the inner workings of the arts and music and opened up his mind to a new world. He recalls that students in his classes wrote down every word when he spoke on the subject of musical aesthetics. Peter also recalls his professor was a "raving liberal" and never apologized for it. Once he told his doctoral class of 55 students that he watched conservative news programs, and seeing everyone was shocked he explained that as a staunch liberal he wanted to know what the 'enemy' was thinking and talking about. The two of them would not have agreed politically, but Leonhard displayed an obvious liking towards his Greek-American student. Their relationship was always friendly and warm but at the same time business-like.

CHORAL MUSIC IN AMERICA IN THE 1970S

After Peter passed the summer test that Leonhard set him in their first meeting he began his doctoral coursework while continuing to conduct the New College Singers.

To fully appreciate what Tiboris was able to achieve with the New College Singers one should consider the changing landscape of American choral music in the 1970s. Many of those who worked closely with Tiboris, such as Gene Carr, Terre Johnson, James Redcay and Tim Sharp made it clear to me that Tiboris and his work have to be considered in the broader context of choral music in America and recognized as having a profound influence on its course. Tiboris has been nothing if not an innovator over his entire career, but his initiatives have been shaped by and in turn shaped the bigger picture cultural trends. When Tiboris was starting off, the churches remained the main venue of choral singing, but choral singing was finding other places and ways in which to perform, as well and gaining broader audiences. There had already been such signs in the 1960s, for example with the creation of the Young Americans, a non-profit performing group based in Southern California, which is considered the first show choir in America, mixing choreography with choral singing. The Young Americans would make a string of appearances on television, a medium that naturally encouraged a different type of choral singing. In 1976, the group performed in an outdoor theatre at the foot of the Washington Monument for the United States bicentennial celebration. Also, in 1976, The Young Americans performed their first national Broadway tour performing The Music Man and Oklahoma. They then went on tour across the United States.

The success of the Young Americans can be attributed to a set of broader changes in the 1970s that led to an increase in choral activity throughout the world and benefitted professional as well as amateur choirs that were able to broaden their repertoire and produce new choral sounds. These included a range of new trends, the emergence of new vocal techniques, the inclusion of choral music in films, a new wave of interest in reviving early music and even new ways of listening to music thanks to the ascent of the cassette tape as a playback medium.[18]

JESUS CHRIST SUPERSTAR, 1977

By October 1974, the New College Singers were receiving a great deal of acclaim and were becoming increasingly popular. The local press lavished praise on Peter, both because of what it described as his energy and missionary zeal and also for the skill and facility with which he worked with opera, symphony and choral works along with popular music. "The aesthetic demands are different than for Mozart, Beethoven or Stravinsky but they are there and – let's face it – this is the music that the majority of the public relates to and certainly what most young people respond to" he was quoted as saying. [19]

The contemporary repertoire of the group would include Jesus Christ Superstar, which would be performed for the first time by a local group in the state of Wisconsin. Jesus Christ Superstar is a sung-through rock opera with music by Andrew Lloyd Webber and lyrics by Tim Rice. Loosely based on the Gospels' accounts of the final days of Jesus Christ, it was very controversial when it appeared on Broadway in 1971. There was a range of criticisms levelled against it, including objections that Christ was depicted as a mere human and not as God, that there was no reference to his resurrection, and that the Jews were depicted as villains. The musical met with world-wide success, however, throughout the 1970s and 1980s.

The Madison premiere of Jesus Christ Superstar was scheduled for May 9th, 1975 at the Capitol City Theater and it would be followed by two more evening performances. There was a buzz around the production and the local press paid great attention to the ongoing rehearsals. There were 50 persons rehearsing, all the main roles were double cast, and two separate production units would alternate during the three days of performances. Also rehearsing was an orchestra of 40 pieces and a 4-piece rock band. There were also 20 antiphonal trumpets ready to go. Tom Terrien, the choreographer with whom Peter collaborated, and Peter were the center of attention. A reporter noted "the energetic Tiboris, who radiates enthusiasm and keeps vibrating even when seated almost shouts: "You know we had 129 people audition for what are essentially nine roles. With that kind of interest, we decided to double cast the show and protect ourselves against the problem that sometimes arises when someone drops out at the last minute, or an illness is involved... the casts are very equal in quality – either could open."[20] By May 1st the media hype was in full swing. Peter, entirely in his element, was happy to feed the fires. He confirmed the existence of bolts of actual lightning and heavy rumbling sound effects that would "send a shake through the audience" and added "people are going to be running for the doors. I hope in exhilaration. We are sparing no expense to make this production right. We have opted for some pretty unusual and dramatic effects." On a more serious note, and reflecting his religious upbringing and Christian faith, Tiboris spoke about how the performers were undergoing a special sensitivity session in order to be able to understand the significance of the last days of Christ and how to depict him with integrity even though the script treated him as a human, not as God.[21]

There was a long interview with Peter published on the eve of the premiere. Its purpose was to convey to readers Peter Tiboris the person. The theme that emerged was that Peter was a go-getter with very great skills at motivation and persuasion of those around him. "What he wants, he goes after. Nothing stands in his way" and if need be, the article noted with a touch of exaggeration, he cajoled, bribed and bullwhipped people to do things for him. Peter's dedication to his work was described as his work being nearly his life, with skipped meals, inadequate sleep, long phone calls and little private life. Peter himself explained that it was all worth it because the students were trying hard and he saw his role as helping them perform beyond their capabilities, something the reporter expressed as "Tiboris gives his blood and expects his students to give theirs too." But he himself had a slightly different assessment, saying he gave more than anyone else, adding "that's because I am a maniac. I couldn't expect the New College Singers to do what I do all day. I'm just a bit insane. Peter went on to say he was warned that staging Jesus Christ Superstar would be far too much work, but he thought it was the right moment, and he explained, pounding his fist into his palm, "I'm a very practical person. I like things happening immediately. I think that's important. I think that is how I do things. If you go through life waiting for the right girl or business opportunity, I think you are going to wait all your life. Sometimes it's a matter of seeing an opportunity that is only mediocre and making it work to your benefit."[22]

The performances were a huge success. "The most ambitious locally-produced stage show in Madison's history" had quickly become "the show to see" and the six performances drew an audience of about 7,500 that rewarded the performers with five-minute standing ovations. A key contributor to the show's success was Tom Wopat, who played the role of Judas and was a graduate of the University of Wisconsin School of Music in voice. He was a huge success because, in Peter's words he was handsome, he could sing, and he could act – and he took the show to another level. After performing in Jesus Christ Superstar, he went off to Hollywood where he achieved television fame on the series 'Dukes of Hazzard' and then embarked on a successful music career on Broadway and in recordings.

Reviewers praised the sensitivity with which the topic of Jesus Christ's last days was treated, the acting and the sound and light effects on stage. Booking agents and promoters were so impressed by the quality of the show that there was talk of taking it on the road. Rather than bask in his newfound fame, Peter pointed out the huge publicity that the MATC music program had received. In fact, both he and MATC emerged from this event enjoying widespread admiration and praise. By raising Peter's profile in Madison, it enabled him to do other things, including classical music events, with Ronald Johnson's enthusiastic approval.

With his entrepreneurial spirit always following his artistic talents, Peter decided to take Jesus Christ Superstar on the road as a non-MATC production, which meant he had to incorporate the group as a private company. He chose the name MidAmerica Productions, a name he would return to after as few years. But with the prospective tour not materializing, in February of 1976 Peter announced he would be taking a year's leave from teaching at MATC beginning in the summer. The reason was to be able to complete major portions of his doctoral program, and he would thus be producing the last of his shows with the New College Singers, the group he created when he began teaching at MATC in 1972.

The last show would entail a day-long competition among 12 Midwest swing choirs culminating in a 'Supershow' with the University of Michigan aMazin' Blues, the New College Singers and the winner of the Midwestern competition. The following month, in March, Tiboris coordinated Madison's first Swing/Show Choir Invitational Festival with the aim of showcasing different performing styles and techniques. What was an especially interesting contrast was the Michigan aMazin' Blues, whose style was highly polished with low emphasis on visual extravaganza while Tiboris' choir was known for its splashy and colorful presentation. In his words, it was a contrast between smooth silk and hyper-kinetic energy.[23]

FAMILY MATTERS

In October of 1975 Peter rushed back to Sheboygan to attend his paternal grandmother's funeral. Calliope Tsibouris died aged 95 at the Heritage Nursing Center. The funeral was the first time Peter had seen his grandmother not wearing black because she had observed Greek tradition and wore black in mourning for her husband and son who had died in 1932 and 1933 respectively. Peter asked the priest at St. Spyridon Greek Orthodox Church, the Rev. Basil Apostolos, why she was wearing white instead, and he answered that was because she was now going to meet her husband in heaven. During Calliope's long life that spanned almost a century, her family, her homeland and the country she immigrated to had inevitably changed dramatically. She had outlived her husband, all her eight sisters and her brother and one son and daughter. Surviving her were her son Ernest, who had changed the last name from Tsibouris to Tiboris, six children, including Peter and his brother Gus, and eight grandchildren. The village in which she was born, Dedebey, had its name changed to Tripotamo (three rivers) by a commission tasked to 'hellenize' names of villages that dated back to the time when Greece was part of the Ottoman Empire. And Greece itself had undergone a century of political and economic changes, most recent was the collapse of a military dictatorship that had ruled the country between 1967 and 1974, followed by the re-establishment of a democratic political system. When Calliope had arrived in the United States in 1916, most Greek immigrants had menial jobs and were often the target of xenophobia. But by the time of her death the children and grandchildren of the original immigrants were fully integrated into American society and were one of the most respected, well-educated and wealthy European ethnic groups in the United States.

Marriage to Susan Joy Lindsay

Peter met Susan Lindsay when they were students at the University of Illinois, and they would marry on September 3, 1978 in a church ceremony officiated by the Rev. Anthony Coniaris at St. Mary Greek Orthodox church in Minneapolis. The couple had already announced their plans in January of that year. The Sheboygan Press reported that "Parents of the couple are Mr. and Mrs. William C. Lindsay of Wayzata Minn. And Dr. and Mrs. Ernest P. Tiboris, 2903 S. 11th St. Apparently even in the late 1970s the wives, Dorothy Jean Lindsay and Stella Tiboris, did not have their first names included in newspaper reports of the weddings of their children.
Susan Lindsay, Peter's future wife, was a graduate of Homestead High School in Thiensville, a town north of Milwaukee, and received her bachelor's degree in applied piano otherwise known as piano performance from Lawrence University in Appleton, Wisconsin. She then went to the University of Illinois Urbana-Champaign where she met Peter and completed a Master's Degree in Music in piano and accompanying.
St. Mary's church in Minneapolis in which they married was the first Greek Orthodox church to be built in Minneapolis, as early as 1900. It moved location twice before the cornerstone was laid for the current site of the church on the eastern shore

of Bde Maka Ska (formerly Lake Calhoun) at 35th St. and Irving Ave. in the Spring of 1956. The first services in the new building, a distinctively modern structure, were held at Easter in the spring of 1957, and the church was formally consecrated in early May, 1961. At the wedding for once Peter was not playing the church organ – the honor went to John Rezevoulis, while Peter's father Ernest was one of the chanters. Father Anthony Coniaris, the parish priest who officiated, was known nationally for his extensive authorship, lectures and retreats. On an international level, he would make his greatest contribution by forming the publishing company Light and Life, which disseminated Orthodox literature to countries worldwide.

Ed. D. in Choral Music Education, University of Illinois 1980

By the Fall semester of 1976 Tiboris had completed his doctoral studies course work and embarked on writing his doctoral thesis under Leonhard's guidance. His original choice of topic proved to be too ambitious. It entailed an investigation into the ways the quality of singing could be improved through the use of real-time headphone feedback being used by singers. This raised questions of how exactly the improvement through this 'real time headphone' method could be measured. Another problem was the requirement of establishing criteria along with a rating scale for different, voices which would mean engaging with the tools of audiology and statistics. At the end of two years' work on this topic, Leonhard decided that it would be impossible for his student to successfully defend such a thesis before a University of Illinois committee that would necessarily have included professors of statistics and audiology. "It would have been my Waterloo" Peter reflected. He agreed with Leonhard that he should "chuck the topic" and with Leonhard's advice find one that would not lead to complications. They were soon able to find a more feasible topic and the research and writing resumed.

In 1979, during the course of Peter's doctoral studies Charles Leonhard arranged for him to conduct Cole Porter's 1953 musical 'Kiss Me Kate' for five performances at the University of Illinois' Opera Theater. Thus Tiboris became the first choral education student to cross over from choral music education to the Opera Theater as a conductor. It was an occasion to meet Nicholas Di Virgilio, who had a stellar international career as a tenor and was a professor at the University of Illinois teaching voice to the top singers at the music program. They became friends and several years later Di Virgilio went to Greece to help create a music studio. The high point of their relationship would come when Tiboris conducted Verdi's 'Requiem' with the Royal Philharmonic in London's Royal Festival Hall and Di Virgilio sang the tenor role in the solo quartet. It was a way Tiboris wanted to honor Di Virgilio. A member of that quartet was mezzo-soprano Sharon Munson, a student of Di Virgilio's whom he later married.

A year later, in April, 1980, Tiboris successfully completed a doctoral thesis titled 'A Study in the Feasibility of Constructing a Performance Difficulty Assessment Scale for Musical Theater'. The committee members aside from Leonhard were Professors Frances Crawford, Daniel Kohut, Robert Smith and Roman Tymchyshyn. Peter's acknowledgements included thanks to Nicolas DiVirgilio, Harold Decker, Dorothy Gunsalus, Gil Lazier, William Olson, and Leonard Rumery. The oral defense that took place on August 1, 1980 lasted two hours and went very smoothly, and the process was finally completed. Tiboris recounts what followed: "Professor Leonhard then escorted me out of the conference room and bid me a warm farewell since the process for my Ed. D. began in June of 1976 and now was ending. He and I joked a bit and then he said the following which has stayed with me all these years 'Tiboris... you are a talented conductor and you have a keen instinct for business. I say this to you.....take care of the music and the business will take care of itself.' These words still resonate with me I have never forgotten them. They have, indeed, guided my development by keeping music as the center focus of MidAmerica Productions and MidAm International."

What also stayed with Peter was Leonhard's emphasis on the significance of aesthetic education within music education, and his intellectual mentorship that has been described by his collaborator Richard Colwell as multifaceted: "As a musician he demonstrated to his students the power of an expressive musical line; as a scholar his written and spoken word carried a genuine message... and his unique teaching style, inspiring and colorful, can only partially describe Charlie, the music educator."[24] Peter also retained the core messages of the many thinkers that had shaped Leonhard's own intellectual formation. The first was the philosopher Susanne Langer, whom Leonhard had as an instructor as a graduate student at Columbia University. Langer was known for her theories on the influences of art on the mind. Her 1941 study Philosophy in a New Key, which was required reading for Leonhard's graduate students, put forth the notion that has become commonplace today, namely that there is a basic and pervasive human need to symbolize, to invent meanings, and to invest one's world with meanings. After completing his doctorate at Columbia, Leonhard joined the faculty at Columbia's Teacher's College, which already had a strong history in aesthetics. The philosopher John Dewey had written his seminal work Art as Experience in 1934 while he was there and the emphasis on aesthetics helped Leonhard build on what he had gained from Langer's work.

Monroe Beardsley, a philosopher of aesthetics, also had a great impact on Tiboris, especially his criteria for aesthetic value: unity, complexity and intensity. Beardsley based his understanding of aesthetic value on aesthetic experience that "(1) allows one's mental states to be controlled by the qualities and relations presented by the art object; (2) feels a release from prior concerns and a sense of harmony with what is presented; (3) feels the power of the emotions projected by the object while retaining an ability to rise above them; (4) experiences an exhilaration from the cognitive act of making conflicting stimuli cohere and finding connections between percepts; and (5) has a sense of integrated wholeness and a sense of coherence in the diverse mental acts and events constituting the experience."[25]   Those principles, expressed in an academic language but clearly denoting an aesthetic rather than technical or cerebral connection to music would become a driving force in Tiboris' career.

When Petzold had sent Peter to see Leonard he had told him that he thought Peter was less about academic study and more about performance. That was going to be borne out in the years that followed, even though Peter was already an Assistant Professor of Music at Plymouth State College in New Hampshire. There would be other academic positions, but the bright lights of performance and New York City would soon beckon. And performance, in his mind, what was not only what attracted him but, he assumed, many others. Before he could share his love of performance with others, however, he had to jump through the hoops of academic life.

Village of Tripotramo, Peloponnesos, Greece

Where the grandparents of Peter immigrated from in late 1880's

St. Demetrios Greek Orthodox Church, Village of Tripotamo, Peloponnesos

COLONEL YAMASAKI

Yamasaki, a Colonel in the
Japanese Army, was killed in action
near this point. Colonel Yamasaki
commanded all Japanese Troops
on the Island.

Dad
Attu, Alaska 1943

ERNEST TIBORIS, PETER'S FATHER,
ON THE ISLAND OF ATTU, ALEUTIAN ISLANDS, ALASKA, DURING WORLD WAR II, 1943

PETER'S PARENTS ERNEST AND STELLA IN 1950

PETER AND HIS FATHER ERNEST 1948

PETER VISITING ST SPYRIDON CHURCH, SHEBOYGAN

CHAPTER THREE

FROM LECTERN TO PODIUM

To play a wrong note is insignificant,
to play without passion is inexcusable.
— Ludwig von Beethoven

There are not many persons who would give up an Associate Professorship at a university, let alone when they do not have a ready position to go to as an alternative. But then again, Peter Tiboris has never belonged to the 'many persons' category. What for most people would have been a promising start in a lifelong academic career, was for Peter a professorial interregnum, a stepping-stone on the way to a career outside the ivory tower, towards what would be much more challenging, more public, more international, and what he would describe as being "more about the music."

NEW HAMPSHIRE & THE BIRTH OF ERNEST PETER

His first position in academe, Assistant Professor of Music at Plymouth State College in Plymouth, New Hampshire, which he began in the 1978-79 academic year, was exciting as well as hectic for both Peter and his new wife Susan. They had arrived there in September, 1978 only a day after getting married. The College, which is now Plymouth State University, still has a strong music program. But for Peter and Susan moving to rural New Hampshire and having to adapt to a new environment far away from their families was not easy. Aside from teaching music courses, Peter also conducted the Plymouth Choral Union; the Spring, 1979 concert included Mozart's Coronation Mass. His full title at the time was Director of choral activities and choral music education and Assistant Professor.

The second year was also challenging but a happy one, because their son, Ernest Peter was born on December 8, 1978. Susan gave birth in a hospital in the small New Hampshire town of Laconia, named after the province in Greece, next to that of Arcadia from where Peter's grandparents had emigrated. Peter had a concert that night and rushed from the hospital to the concert venue and then back to the hospital. 'Pete' as the young boy would become known, turned out to be a gifted student as well as a talented athlete. After graduating from Montclair Kimberley Academy he went on to Cornell University on a sports scholarship. The 1998 Cornell Football roster lists him as 6'-2" tall and weighing 240 lbs. and playing as a tight end. Ultimately, his college football career was cut short by an injury, but academically he excelled as a finance major, which was officially known as Applied Economics Management. It was at Cornell where he met his future wife Christy Ely, who would go on to become a lawyer. The roundabout way they eventually decided to get married was interesting enough to merit an article in the New York Times which mentioned Pete's dating skills as follows: "Despite being a jock, he had grown up in a somewhat strict, churchgoing household and felt awkward when it came to dating."[26]

UNIVERSITY OF SOUTHWESTERN LOUISIANA AT LAFAYETTE, 1980-84

At the end of the 1979-1980 academic year, Peter returned to the University of Illinois to receive his doctorate, which was awarded on August 1, 1980. At the same time Robert Smith, the Music Department chair at Plymouth State College, retired, and Peter was named interim chair of the department, a position that sounds like a promotion but as all academics now entails a great deal of additional work. He was the youngest member of the faculty and that made his responsibilities awkward, and inevitably his relationship with the other department members became difficult. He felt he was awarded 'status' without having the necessary stature, something he believed one earned through experience – which he clearly lacked at Plymouth State College. A bright spot during what turned out to be a two-year stay was Peter's creation of the Madrigal Dinner. It was a two-hour event held around Christmas with the choir dressed up in Rennaissance-era dress and performing at a formal and festive dinner.

Concerned about his future prospects at Plymouth, Peter asked Leonhard to pull some strings and find him a position at another institution. Leonhard managed that most effectively because Peter was offered the position of Associate Professor of Music at the University of Southwestern Louisiana in Lafayette, Louisiana, which was renamed the University of Louisiana at Lafayette. He did not interview prior to receiving the offer; Leonhard's word was evidently enough. His starting salary was $25,000, which was twice as much as he was receiving in New Hampshire only a year earlier.

Peter recalls that the University of Southwestern Louisiana at Lafayette had a strong and creative music program and a serious faculty, and that he was much happier there. The family settled in Carenco, a suburb of Lafayette, where they bought a house for $70,500. A year later, Susan joined the faculty at the Academy of the Sacred Heart, a Catholic School for girls as the music and theater teacher. The Academy had been established in 1821 and, remarkably, was the second oldest institution of learning west of the Mississippi.

In October, 1980 a local newspaper carried an interview with what it described as "Lafayette's Singing Pied Piper." A pipe-smoking Tiboris effusively outlined plans to create a "mammoth" choir and also introduce vocal jazz singing and shared his approach to choir directing, saying, "I get a tremendous thrill in working with people. I'm inspired by people who give their time and sing heartfully," adding "I pour everything I know into them." He also acknowledged the challenges of choir singing and noted that "it takes a lot of gall to stand in front of an audience and say listen to me. You'd better be good at what you do. You better be able to hold their attention." The interviewer concluded by stating "the enthusiastic conductor" demanded one thing from his students, namely concentration, through which 95% of all musical mistakes could be avoided. His singers, he demanded, should flush out their minds and give him all their attention. [27] Confirmation of Peter's wish to expand the horizons of the university's 34-voice vocal chamber ensemble Les Clairs-

Matins Acadiens came soon when they staged a concert that covered five centuries of classical choral music. Soon after it was announced that a new 48-member group, the USL singers, would present a selection of pop and jazz-based songs. By April of 1981 the University Chorus had grown to 135 members and was performing along with a full orchestra made up of members of the Baton Rouge Symphony Orchestra. For the 'town and gown' choir's summer performance, Tiboris chose the Gilbert and Sullivan comic opera The Pirates of Penzance because it was being presented at the time on Broadway by the singer Linda Ronstadt, a performance for which she received a Tony nomination.

Stephanie Joy

On December 29, 1982 Susan gave birth to their second child, a girl, named Stephanie Susan. She would go on to Syracuse University in 2002, where she was a Dean's List student. Stephanie graduated with a Bachelors of Fine Arts and Acting in 2005. She would work for a while with her father at MidAmerica Productions in NYC before going into the real estate business.

Peter Tiboris' New York Conducting Debut at Lincoln Center, January 7, 1984

Peter was getting restless in Louisiana. As he began his third year in Lafayette and even though he was adding more and more ambitious and diverse programming to the repertoire of the choirs he was in charge of, he felt the growing need for a much bigger musical challenge. So, when the possibility arose of taking his choir to New York City to perform he jumped at the opportunity. The occasion was a concert that would be held in honor of the 25th anniversary of the appointment of His Eminence Archbishop Iakovos, the Greek Orthodox Archbishop of North and South America.

The Archbishop had already proved to be a dynamic leader of the Greek Orthodox church in America and was also considered as the de facto leader of the Greek-American community. Since assuming his position in 1959 he had guided the church from what in his own words he described as an immigrant church to a mainstream American church. He had marched side by side with the Reverend Martin Luther King, Jr. in the famous march in Selma, Alabama in 1965; he had worked towards allowing the use of the English language in the Greek Orthodox Sunday liturgy; he had become involved in the Greek-American community's mobilization that aimed to shape U.S. foreign policy in the Eastern Mediterranean after Turkey invaded and occupied part of Cyprus in 1974 and he had gained frequent access to the White House and the office of the prime minister in Greece. The Archbishop, who was not shy about self-promotion, planned several events to mark his 25th anniversary, and one of them was a concert. At the time, one of the members of his senior staff was Fr. Alexander Doumouras, a native of Sheboygan, where he had been ordained as priest in 1981 when Iakovos had visited Sheboygan on the occasion of the 75th anniversary of St. Spyridon church, an event at which Iakovos presented Peter's father Ernest with the St. Paul medal of honor in recognition of his services to the church. In 1983 Doumouras, who was serving as Director of Inter Church relations at the Archdiocese and working with Fr. Alex Karloutsos, Iakovos' aide, invited Peter to organize the concert that was being planned, as long as he could raise the money to take his choir to New York.

In October of 1983 Lafayette's newspaper the Daily Advertiser reported that the members of the Southwestern Louisiana School of Music choral members would be performing at a concert scheduled on January 7, 1984, in Lincoln Center's Alice Tully Hall in New York. Invitations were being issued to everyone within the university and the local community to join the choir. A five day-visit was being planned, including sightseeing, and anyone wishing to take part in the trip was invited as well. The concert's program would include a performance of the not-often-heard Rossini's Stabat Mater and a world premiere for a work for soprano and tenor written by Dinos Constantinides. The premiere work was based on the Ancient Greek play Antigone by Sophocles. Performing with the orchestra would be the American Symphony Orchestra and the soloists included Mariana Christos, a Greek-American soprano and mainstay of the New York City Opera and Sharon Munden of New York, Giorgio Aristo Mikroutsikos of Hanover Germany, and Sam Jones of Madison Wisconsin. Among them were another two Greek-Americans, Constantinides who had been born in Ioannina in Greece and taught at the University of Louisiana at Baton Rouge and was Peter's close friend. Christos, who was born in Pittsburgh and had made her debut in the New York City Opera production of Turandot in 1975, was replaced for the concert by another Greek-American soprano, Phyllis Demetracopoulos. There would soon be another occasion for Peter to collaborate with Christos, however.

What was not known at the time was that the trip almost did not happen and that ultimately it did only due to the generosity of a choir member, Carol Boudreaux. When Peter had announced to the choir in early September 1983 that there was a possibility that they could perform at Lincoln Center "the place went berserk." But by the end of the month, the 150 members of the choir had been unable to raise the $50,000 that the trip and the event would cost. Then, at the last moment, Carol Boudreaux, a choir member and wife of a physician in Lafayette, asked to speak to Peter in private. It was brief, but it was one of the most important conversations in Peter Tiboris' musical life. Carol began by saying that she had been a member of the choir for four years and that the experience had changed her life. She was the mother of 11 children and had little time of her own, but the weekly Monday night choir rehearsals had enabled her to get away from home on a regular basis. Now, she wanted to give back, and wished to help change the lives of the choir members. She wanted to cover the costs of the event and write a check for $50,000, so long as the donation remained confidential. Peter, stunned by her generosity, refused at first, then said he needed time but realized it was an offer he could not refuse. The lives of the choir members would indeed be changed. Many of them had not even flown ever before, let alone visited New York or sung at Lincoln Center. At the same time, he would have the opportunity of having his debut there with a 150-voice choir!

For Tiboris, it was an occasion hard to forget: "I remember clearly my nervousness in the rehearsal space of Carnegie Hall, rehearsing with the 70 piece orchestra, the American Symphony Orchestra whose members were all professionals and unionized. I was very nervous. I never had conducted such a group of professionals having just arrived from Louisiana, but I had to prepare the orchestra for my debut performance. They knew I was new, and they were cordial and understanding. I remember just trying to show that I knew what I was doing, but inside of me I really didn't understand what to say to them or what to do except, keep conducting and listening. Ron Sell, the orchestra's manager who was also one of the horn players, guided me, saying that I should remain calm and collected and the orchestra would follow by gestures – and they did. Of course, to me, on the first run-through of the Rossini and Constantinides works, they played it without stop... something to which I was unaccustomed, coming from the university level. It sounded and felt glorious and I knew that this was the first high step for me. All in all, it was a marvelous first experience. And there was much much more to come."

Respected Greek-American composer and conductor George Tsontakis also assisted Tiboris greatly at that event. His chorus participated in the performance of Rossini's Stabat Mater. Tsontakis was born in New York and studied music at the Julliard School and at the Accademia Nazionale di Santa Cecilia in Rome. His music has been performed and broadcast by major orchestras, chamber ensembles and festivals throughout North and South America, Europe and Japan. In 1995 Tsontakis was honored with the 'Academy Award' from the American Academy of Arts and Letters and was the fourth recipient of the coveted Ives Living Fellowship, in 2007.

The concert was a great success – it was a grandiose opening for the series of events that year that would commemorate the Archbishop's twenty-fifth anniversary. The New York Times described the rendition as "vigorous but unpolished" and noted "Mr. Tiboris' alert, energetic conducting."[28] The applause at the end was the crowning moment for what had been an ambitious project that Peter had envisioned and successfully completed. For the choir members it was the highlight of their singing careers, and for Peter, it would be the beginning of a new stage in his life.

GENE CARR

The orchestra that Peter engaged for that event was the New York City-based American Symphony Orchestra whose director of operations at the time was Eugene (Gene) Carr, and Moshe Aaron and Giuseppe Pattane were the music co-directors. Tiboris had met Carr in New York in the Fall of 1983 and asked him about engaging members of the American Symphony Orchestra for the upcoming concert in January. Carr agreed to this, along with the Symphony's manager, Ron Sell.
Carr had studied music at Oberlin and played the cello, but like Peter, also had a business streak. After serving as managing director of several orchestras, he founded CultureFinder.com a groundbreaking website for arts and culture at the dawn of the worldwide web. CultureFinder created a nationwide cultural events calendar combined with an online ticketing system. CultureFinder was a trailblazer in online ticketing and was the first to sell live event tickets on AOL. He continued to combine business entrepreneurship with his music career, very much the way Tiboris would also do, and this cemented the bond between the two men. They produced the first recording of a choral concert that was made available on the internet. The chorus was made up of 250 singers from 40 different states. Tiboris was told that six couples from that group eventually married.

Carr remembers standing with Peter on the corner of 57th Street and 7th Avenue in Manhattan, across from Carnegie Hall, and Peter telling him that he would resign his position at Southwestern University of Louisiana at Lafayette, come to New York and start organizing choir concerts. And one of the reasons that Peter was sharing his plan with Gene Carr was that he foresaw he would be hiring the

American Symphony orchestra to collaborate with the choirs he planned to bring to New York – though at a later stage he would form his own orchestra, called the Manhattan Philharmonic. When Peter talks about his life, he often mentions how he met someone with whom he managed to hit it off. It speaks to an ability to relate to people, to find common ground and common goals and collaborate. That was the case with Gene Carr, who in looking back to their first meetings noted they both shared a love of music and something of an entrepreneurial kindred spirit.

Even as the move to New York was materializing and Peter was finishing up his obligations as Choral director at the University of Southwestern Louisiana at Lafayette, he was also involved with a new company, he created, Madison's Capital City Opera Ltd, of which he was general manager. The company held an opera competition for young artists in July, 1984, and Peter was promoting it energetically: "We are excited at the level of artistry of the contestants" he said, adding "I can assure those in attendance that they will be treated to a tremendous evening of opera arias."[29] In September Peter announced that Madison's opera chorus would be touring in Greece and Italy in July, 1985. The repertoire would include the premiere of a new opera, Constantinides' Antigone featuring soprano Marianna Christos. By February 1985 Peter was preparing to direct the Oratorio Society of New Jersey in a tour of Yugoslavia and Greece.

NEW YORK & NEW JERSEY

The decision to resign from the University of Southwestern Louisiana at Lafayette and move to New York with his family with a plan but nothing concrete – and the hope that presenting choir concerts would work out – was risky to say the least. Susan, as she had done since they had met, supported Peter fully. He had gotten cold feet and even interviewed at the University of Arkansas at Little Rock for an academic position, but it was Susan who stood firm and encouraged him to "take a chance" and ended up playing an instrumental role in the move and career change.

At the end of the 1983-84 academic year his entire family left Lafayette, Louisiana and settled in Montclair, a town in North New Jersey. Montclair is an affluent suburban commuter town within metropolitan New York City, about seventeen miles away from Midtown Manhattan via the Lincoln Tunnel. It is one of several artsy and progressive suburbs that Manhattanites who can afford it consider moving to when their families begin to outgrow the size of their apartments. These, including Montclair, have been described as "the least suburban of suburbs, each one celebrated by buyers there for its culture and hip factor, as much as the housing stock and sophisticated post-city life. They are places where you can easily score a slice of gluten-free banana bread, spend an afternoon at a local farmers' market, and board a train with as many people dressed in jeans and sneakers as in suits."[30] The town the Tiborises moved to, Montclair, is home to several parks and nature reserves, it hosts many art institutions, theaters and art venues and has its own art museum and research university. In 1971 actor Louis Zorich and his wife, Greek-American actress Olympia Dukakis, a future Academy Award winner for her role in the film 'Moonstruck', founded the Whole Theater that had a distinguished two-decade run. Tiboris, who would reside in Montclair for the next thirty-eight years, would meet Dukakis and that was to be the beginning of a fruitful artistic collaboration between those two Greek-American artists.

At first Peter believed the company he established, MidAmerica Productions, and the possibility it offered to choirs to perform in Manhattan would be in great demand, but he soon realized he had to do the work of creating that demand. One of the ways that Peter would get MidAmerica Productions up and running was through his business association and then lifelong friendship and cooperation with New York City travel agent Barry Liben, the owner of Tzell Travel. The two men took to each other – they were both starting their business projects at roughly the same time and that along with their shared sense of business acumen and similar character traits created a very close bond between them. Common business projects were followed by shared family gatherings. All travel arrangements relating to choirs and youth orchestras flying to New York City were made in the form of a gentleman's agreement and no contracts were signed over the 40-year period that ensued – there was no need for that because the two of them hit it off so well. It was another case of making a great choice of a business partner, one of many. Liben himself had a successful career as a travel agent. At the time of his initial investment in 1977, Tzell Travel Group employed three people, but Liben grew Tzell Travel Group to become one of the industry's largest luxury travel agencies with over 700 agents, staff and managers. Liben's philosophy was to create an environment conducive to initiative and hard work, encourage a sense of fun, then let people do their best and recognize it. When he passed in 2020, he was described as an icon in the travel industry, a loyal and honest friend and a generous philanthropist. Peter, a person who forms strong attachments to persons, felt a deep, heartfelt sadness at the loss of his friend.

The first big advantage of their relationship came when Liben offered Peter a

tiny space, not much more than a cubby hole, at his offices on 45 West 34th Street
in Manhattan. That was crucial, because now MidAmerica Productions had "a New
York City address with all the prestige that it entailed." The cubby hole was next to
an old style xerox machine with a sliding top, and Peter had to duck each time it was
being used. Thankfully, he soon moved to a somewhat more comfortable spot. Peter
and Barry's first major event would come in early 1985.

Among the persons that offered Tiboris support in New York was the choral
conductor, educator and radio host David Randolph. When Tiboris arrived in
the city Randolph was an important and longstanding conductor with the NJ
Masterworks Chorale and they became close friends. Randolph mentored him on
several issues regarding doing concerts in New York City. Ron Sell, the manager
of the Manhattan Philharmonic and the American Symphony Orchestra – and an
excellent horn player – was another person who mentored Tiboris on the ways
and means of conducting in New York City. Tiboris began by working for Elliott
Ritter's company Cultural Omnibus. Ritter had already enabled Tiboris to conduct
in Greece for the first time in the town of Patras in 1982 with an American choir and
Russian orchestra. Tiboris learned a great deal from Ritter's promotional activities,
and it was an experience that helped him develop MidAmerica.

MidAmerica's first "All-American choral gala benefit concert" took place on
Sunday May 5, 1985 at Lincoln Center's Avery Fisher Hall. The 'guest conductor'
was Peter Tiboris, the guest soloists Marianna Christos (soprano) and Nicholas
Karoutsatos (baritone) with the American Symphony Orchestra and the
chorus consisted of 400 members. The program included the world premiere of
Constantinides' Byron's Greece and works by Verdi, Dvořák and Barber. There was
a return to Avery Fisher Hall in March, 1986. The New York Times music critic
Allen Hughes did not quite know how to react to the performance. He wrote that
in view of "the astonishing expense of putting on a concert involving the American
Symphony Orchestra involved in bringing pianist James Tocco, the bass Joseph
Tate, hundreds of choral singers brought from far away as Iowa, Minnesota and
Arkansas and an ensemble of brass players from California the event put on at
Avery Fisher Hall on Wednesday night was simply mind boggling" and concluded

by saying "Mr. Tiboris coordinated the performances pretty well on the whole but nothing was really outstanding to make the evening seem reasonable logistically."[31] Hughes, who considered himself more of a dance rather than a music critic, had seen nothing yet. Over the next years MidAmerica Productions would make 'mind boggling' productions and appearances of massed choristers from all over America a familiar occurrence in Midtown Manhattan.

CARNEGIE HALL

Carnegie Hall – "America's Epidaurus theater" in Peter's words – was, and still is, the most historic and prestigious concert venue in the world, in the same way the 4th century BCE theater in Epidaurus, in Peloponnesos, is considered to be the most perfect ancient Greek theatre with regard to acoustics and aesthetics. As the Carnegie Hall website notes, "Since it opened in 1891, Carnegie Hall has set the international standard for musical excellence as the aspirational destination for the world's finest artists. From Tchaikovsky, Dvořák, Mahler, and Bartók to George Gershwin, Billie Holiday, Benny Goodman, Judy Garland, and The Beatles, an honor roll of music-making artists representing the finest of every genre has filled Carnegie Hall throughout the years. The Hall's unique history is rooted in its stunning acoustics, the beauty of its three concert halls, and its location in New York City, where it has played a central role in elevating the city into one of the world's great cultural capitals." However, in the 1970s Carnegie Hall began to deteriorate due to neglect, and the corporation faced fiscal deficits. By the mid-1970s, the venue suffered from burst pipes and falling sections of the ceiling, and there were large holes in the balconies that patrons could put their feet through. At the same time, operating costs had increased from $3.5 million in 1977 to $10.3 million in 1984, and the deficits had also risen accordingly. A major renovation plan began being put in effect in the 1980s, and soon after Tiboris' debut in April of 1986 the Hall was closed for several months to permit the necessary work to be done. It was completed, and MidAmerica Productions would be back the following year and would remain there in the years to come.

Carnegie Hall's website, which lists all the events held there, records Tiboris' debut as follows:

A CONCERT IN CELEBRATION OF YOUTH:
WEDNESDAY, APRIL 30, 1986 AT 8PM MAIN HALL

Presented by: MidAmerica Productions, Inc.
DIMITRIS SGOUROS WITH THE AMERICAN SYMPHONY ORCHESTRA

American Symphony Orchestra Peter Tiboris, Conductor
Zoltán Kodály (1882-1967)
Budavári Te Deum (1936)
Eileen McDaniel, Soprano
Lisa Miller, Mezzo-Soprano
Jeffrey Mosher, Tenor
Stephan Kirchgraber, Bass
Carl Nielsen (1865-1931)
Hymnus amoris, Op. 12 (1896-1897)
Eileen McDaniel, Soprano
Jeffrey Mosher, Tenor
Keith Lynch, Baritone
Stephan Kirchgraber, Bass
Frederic Chopin (1810-1849)
Piano Concerto No. 1 in E Minor, Op. 11 (1830)
Dimitris Sgouros, Piano
[Participating Choirs]:
Anchorage Community Chorus, Choir
Mars Hill University Choir, Choir
Memphis State University Chorus, Choir
Morehead State University Chorus, Choir
University of Tennessee at Chattanooga Chorus, Choir
Western Kentucky University Chorus, Choir
Cincinnati Boy Chorus, Boys Chorus
Dimitri Sgouros

DIMITRI SGOUROS, PIANIST, APRIL 30, 1986

The appearance of 17-year-old pianist Dimitri Sgouros was the highlight of the evening and he brought the house down with his performance. He was barely able to push the piano pedals because of his size but he played beautifully. Describing that night and Sgouros' remarkable performance, Tiboris speaks of the young pianist's "maturity, his amazing artistry and the genius level playing of a Chopin concerto #1 which was executed beautifully and without any hesitation or error," which was met by the audience's thunderous standing ovation. Bernard Holland, the leading New York Times music, critic wrote that Sgouros' solos "were the work of a remarkably talented 17 year old. Vigor usually won out over delicacy, but Mr. Sgouros has a natural feel for melodic lines and seemed to rejoice in his rich, ringing instrumental sound." Holland also had good things to say about the conductor, noting "Mr. Tiboris held his singers together unusually well. He was also a skillful accompanist in the Chopin piano Concerto in E minor that followed."[32]

Sgouros' appearance foreshadowed the many appearances of young artists at Carnegie Hall that would occur over the next decades thanks to MidAmerica Productions. Born in Athens, Greece in 1969, Dimitris Sgouros began his career as an 8-year-old prodigy at the Athens Conservatory, by which time he completed his studies he had received every award offered. He then continued his studies at the University of Maryland and the Royal Academy of Music in London, from which he graduated with the highest mark ever granted by the Academy. In 1982 at the age of 12, Sgouros made his Carnegie Hall debut with the National Symphony Orchestra of Washington, DC, under the direction of Mstislav Rostropovich, performing Rachmaninoff's Piano Concerto No. 3. He was back at Carnegie Hall with MidAmerica Productions in 1986, and he and Tiboris would perform together again for a Mozart piano concerto at Avery Fisher Hall. Sgouros was embarking on an impressive career.

Also getting ready to move forward was Peter Tiboris and MidAmerica. Looking back, Tiboris describes the transition from academe to the world of professional conducting and presentations of classical music as "rather easy," although he adds that, "in retrospect, had I known over the past forty years how many ups and downs were ahead of me, I would not have made the transition. But, in 1983, what did I have to lose? I had a young family and Susan was pushing me to stay-the-course and resign

USL Lafayette and move to New York City – which I did." The rest would follow, in his words relatively smoothly: "No one in the choral concert world was venturing to NYC and the main halls because they did not know how to operate within that environment. Because of my intense experience with Jan 7, 1984, I quickly learned how to do this. My sole objective at that time was to be in a great city, making great music with great music collaborators and 'learning a lot' along the way.

Upon coming to New York City and that particular challenging music environment I knew I would drop to the bottom of the musical barrel, but I loved the challenge of moving up – which over 40 years it appears I have." In addition, reflecting back on his career trajectory, Tiboris asserts: "have I achieved all that I set out to do from 1984? The answer is an unequivocal yes and aside from the music performances, I had a chance to impact thousands of amateur and semi-amateur young musicians who would have never had an opportunity to be in that environment and that, gives me enormous gratification. After all, I started in choral music education and in many ways I stayed there despite my heavy leanings toward high level music associations on a high professional level internationally, much more than I have anticipated and much more than I expected."

CHAPTER FOUR

TIBORIS AND MIDAMERICA PRODUCTIONS, INC.: THE FIRST TWO DECADES

If at first the idea is not absurd, there is no hope for it. — Albert Einstein

Forty years after Peter Tiboris created MidAmerica Productions in 1984, the organization's website is chock full of the numbers of concerts it has organized, their prestigious venues and their prominent conductors. Behind those numbers is the story of a risky venture that became a huge artistic and business success. That success did not come easily, Terre Johnson assures me during one of the breaks in the choir rehearsals before a MidAmerica sponsored concert at Carnegie Hall in June, 2022. The music business in New York operates in a very tough artistic environment he says, and Peter managed to create an industry by being tough himself. So everyone has a story about Peter throwing a tantrum or even firing someone, but it was he who was able to succeed. Johnson, of Clayton University and a Life Member of the American Choral Directors Association, has served as National Chair for Music in

Worship and is currently National Chair for Lifelong Singing. He began bringing choirs to New York in 1989 and continued to do so, and also became one of the guest conductors. Johnson went on to become one of MidAmerica's in-house conductors for a while and then even got to conduct his own compositions in New York and at their New York and world premieres.

PETER'S SECRET

Johnson noted that there was another aspect to the business side of MidAmerica, told in the gleaming eyes of tens of thousands of choral singers who had the once in a lifetime opportunity to sing in hallowed venues such as Carnegie Hall and Lincoln Center that had to do with the opportunity it offered to choirs, orchestras and wind ensembles and their conductors. While not all of the concerts were a musical success – though in many cases, the level was qualitatively very high – the participants experienced the extraordinary thrill of having sung in such an iconic venue. One could be cynical and describe the choir singing at Carnegie Hall as something akin to "pay to play," but as Johnson noted, money changes hands whether the world's most accomplished symphony orchestra is performing, or a small out-of-state church choir is singing there. But when he stood at the back of the Hall next to Norman Dunfee, MidAmerica's longstanding production manager, what they saw when the choristers come down off the stage was a mixture of awe and excitement at having sung on that stage at the center of the music world in Manhattan. And throughout Johnson's long association with MidAmerica that has been the feeling that all choristers conveyed to him. The thrill of being able to sing at Carnegie overshadowed any other thoughts, such as the cost, the travel, the practice times. That, Johnson said, is "Peter's secret": his understanding that the thrill of singing at Carnegie is valued above everything else by thousands of choristers across the country.

These choirs, moreover, don't just arrive and start singing at Carnegie Hall. MidAmerica has a robust vetting process in place. The initial invitation is extended providing a choir meets certain standards, and secondly, it is required to arrive in New York City musically prepared. One of Johnson's duties was to tour the country and monitor the progress of the choir practices prior to their arrival in the city for a five-day residency culminating in the performance in Carnegie Hall. Tiboris also traveled throughout the country for the same purpose in the early years.

CHOIR CULTURE IN AMERICA

The significance of singing at Carnegie Hall goes well beyond the experiences of the thousands of choristers that MidAmerica has brought to New York City. It is something even greater if we consider the role choral singing plays in the United States. A study published in 2009 by Chorus America (the advocacy, research and leadership development organization that advances the choral field) reported that: Choral singing continues to be the most popular form of participation in the performing arts. Chorus participation remains strong in America. Overall, 18.1% of households report one or more adults currently participate in a chorus, an even higher rate of participation than found in Chorus America's 2003 research. When children are added to the equation, participation jumps to 22.9% of households. When the total number of choral singers per household are tallied, there are an estimated 32.5 million adults regularly singing in choruses today and 42.6 million Americans overall (including children), both numbers up substantially from 2003, although some of this increase could be due to changes in methodology. There are nearly 270,000 choruses nationwide. This total includes about 12,000 professional and community choruses (which includes the independent choruses that comprise most of the Chorus America's membership), at least 41,000 K-12 school choruses, and 216,000 religious choirs. These estimates are believed to be conservative, based on the methodology used to calculate these figures.[33]
Additional findings were that adults who sing in choirs were remarkably good citizens and that children that sung in choirs had academic success and were learning important life skills.

This remarkable spread of choral singing throughout America notwithstanding, there was no way a good but ordinary choir would have the opportunity to sing in New York, let alone Carnegie Hall, if it were not for MidAmerica Productions. Tiboris' project, his business, had the effect of democratizing the world of choral music. No longer were those who got to sing in New York City, the nation's cultural capital, only the most accomplished and deserving top-tier choirs. Instead, the high school, college, community and church-based choirs that made choral singing such a core element of American life were rewarded by gaining their proverbial "fifteen minutes of fame." And in doing so, many of those choirs rose to the occasion and performed at their best.

The experience of going to New York within the parameters set by MidAmerica is beneficial to choirs in a pedagogic sense, beyond simply challenging them to do their best conductor Lee Kesselman told me. Because these choirs are too small to perform in the vast space of Carnegie, they are merged in rehearsals days before the actual performance with the other participating choirs, and the rehearsal is often conducted by one of the conductors of those choirs. This exposes choir members to a different set of methods and styles which can be beneficial to them, either as a group or as individuals. It might be something about the music, or the singing or the particular musical piece. This opening of the minds is a way that these amateur and semi-professional groups of singers are gradually professionalized, and their performances improved. And this operates both ways because it exposes the conductors to choirs that might do things differently. It helps both sides get out their silos, Kesselman told me. He is one of those conductors who is also a composer, and he had choir members come up to him and mention how interesting, how novel, how helpful they found something they had encountered earlier in their singing careers. Kesselman served as Director of Choral Activities at the College of DuPage in Glen Ellyn, a suburb of Chicago, since 1981. He is Founder and Music Director of the New Classic Singers, a professional choral ensemble. He also directs the DuPage Chorale and College of DuPage Chamber Singers.

But there is another side to all of this. Carnegie Hall also benefitted. This was what Kesselman emphasized in our conversation. You can't run a music performance hall, he said, all the more so an establishment such as Carnegie Hall, by staging only a few major concerts a year, he noted, and indeed Carnegie's history has been one of continuous efforts to sustain its existence. Thus MidAmerica has performed an important service to Carnegie and New York's musical world writ large by using the Hall so regularly and helping it continue as one of the nation's more iconic cultural landmarks.[34]

MidAmerica Makes its Mark

They say that writing one's second novel is much more difficult than writing the first. Maybe because one's own life experiences can drive the first one to completion, one's biographical information provides rich material, and a life's twists and turns provide the basis for the unfolding of a plot. And the sheer writing from the beginning to the middle and through the end can sometimes happen because it has been a life's dream. But without all this the second time, one has to invent those ingredients and that is more difficult and challenging for an average writer. And writing, at least at this stage, gets no easier and can lose its initial freshness. For many, the second novel proves a bridge too far. 1987 can be considered the year during which Peter Tiboris had to achieve the equivalent of writing his second novel, proving the viability and long-term prospects of his project. He had to demonstrate that his vision could be sustained following its very successful first full year in 1986. MidAmerica had to show it would continue to bring choirs to New York and that a high quality of conducting and singing would be maintained. As successful as 1986 had proven to be for MidAmerica, it had relied on many of the elements that drive a first novel: the newness of the experience and the excitement of achieving a goal. Following the concert for Archbishop Iakovos at Lincoln Center's Alice Tully Hall in 1984, MidAmerica had organized three concerts in 1985 and the number had doubled in 1986 and had included Carnegie Hall as a venue, along with Avery Fisher Hall at the Lincoln Center.

The prospects for the city of New York from the mid-1980s were improving, and this was a reward for the risks Peter Tiboris was undertaking. The city was recovering from the dismal 1970s, which had earned the reputation for crime, disorder and dirty streets. Mayor Ed Koch successfully balanced the city's budget ahead of schedule, allowing the city to re-enter the bond market and raise cash, effectively ending the city's financial crisis by 1981. Gentrification brought new businesses to decrepit neighborhoods and converted low-end rental housing into co-ops and condos that attracted young upscale professionals and businesspeople. Koch's successor mayor David Dinkins continued the trend of curbing the city's crime rate. In the mid-1990s the city's image improved further thanks to the country's economic growth, a stock market boom on Wall Street, and mayor Rudolph Giuliani's clean up and revitalization of Times Square and other initiatives. All this made New York more attractive to out-of-town visitors, including the choirs that MidAmerica hoped to bring to Carnegie Hall. They say you make your own luck, but Tiboris' vision certainly benefitted from all those trends. By the time the 1990s were over, New York was a safer place than it had been at any point since the 1960s. And it showed. By the time the 1990s ended, the city's population began to grow for the first time in decades and it was pulling in 7 million more tourists a year. Many of them, as we shall see, were choristers.

In March 1987, MidAmerica Productions was back at Carnegie Hall. The event was a concert devoted to the music of Dinos Constantinides, the fellow Greek-American and composer that Tiboris had first met back in his University of Southwestern Louisiana days in the early 1980s. Constantinides conducted the Louisiana State University New Music Ensemble performing his own works which included the world premiere of *Genteel Dialogue*. The *New York Times* critic thought that most of the performance left a favorable impression, noting that "the Louisiana State University New Music Ensemble offered proof that there is skillful and idiomatic music making to be heard in bayou country." And added, "All of Mr. Constantinides' works – Reflections IV, A Rhapsody for Flute and Harp, Four Songs on Poems by Sappho, Four Greek Songs and Genteel Dialogue – were expertly made, a few of them eloquent. Mr. Constantinides is at his best in music when he determines to speak simply, often combining Greek modes with traditional Western harmony."[35] MidAmerica would bring Constantinides back to Carnegie Hall in October of that year, in a concert titled '20th Century Music for Violin, Oboe, Piano and Voice'.

Earlier in March 1987 the *Corpus Christi Caller* newspaper reported that Peter Tiboris had visited the South Texas town to rehearse with the Corpus Christi Chorale in preparation for their concert in New York the following month. The event was the 1987 Masterworks Choral Series, the event he had begun in 1985 with three concerts. There would be a time when Tiboris would have his own conductors travel in order to rehearse with a choir, but in 1987 he himself had to make that 1,800-plus mile trip if his project was going to succeed. He made the most of his visit, describing how challenging it was to stage choral performances in New York and also heaping praise on the Corpus Christi singers. Tiboris said the chorale came to his attention because it kept coming up on everyone's list of good choruses. They would be joining another five choirs to make a 250-voice chorus in performing Wolfgang Amadeus Mozart's *C Mass in C Minor* as well as *Five Mystical Songs* by the British composer Ralph Vaughan Williams and *Psalm 150* by the Austrian composer Anton Bruckner.[36] Tiboris had to hurry back to New York because on March 9th he was conducting the American Symphony Orchestra in a concert which included children's choirs. As he would do regularly for at least the next ten years, Tiboris would write to the hometown newspaper of each of the choirs, in this case newspapers in Wyoming, describing the event and offering his congratulations. It was a way of expressing his appreciation and gaining some publicity for MidAmerica Productions. Another way Tiboris attracted publicity was by not holding back when he communicated his future plans. Speaking to a reporter from a newspaper in Jackson, Tennessee he mentioned that MidAmerica's plans included holding forty concerts in 1988, something which, he would discover made it difficult to hold concerts both at Lincoln Center and at Carnegie Hall, and this led him to concentrate the productions at Carnegie Hall. Tiboris was visiting to conduct rehearsals with 108 singers from the Lambuth College and Union University choirs of Jackson, a town about mid-way between Memphis and Nashville who were preparing for a May 31st concert at Avery Fisher Hall that would involve 600 singers from California, Florida, Indiana, Kansas, Michigan and Ohio.[37] The day after the rehearsal, The *Jackson Sun* described Tiboris' conducting style by noting that "he uttered demands jovially but he planted at least one message. This was no ordinary concert. 'I'm here to set the stage for you – so you will not be alienated from the importance of the performance. You're in the Lincoln Center for two hours – just two hours – you are going to be in the world spotlight. Is that important? If you are alive – that is important." The report added that he coaxed, he guided, he cajoled saying, "It's tough, huh? You were doing it the easy way before."[38]

These newspaper reports provided proof that MidAmerica Productions were surging ahead in 1987 and they also reflect a widespread acceptance of the organization's business plan and model. There were no negative insinuations of a pay-to-play strategy. Quite the opposite: there was an appreciation of Tiboris' efforts to ensure the quality of the participants and assist them in their preparations. And the reports conveyed an excitement and pride that a local choir would have a once-in-a-lifetime opportunity to perform in New York City. There was also mention of the cost per student, $586 in the case of the choirs from Jackson, Tennessee and descriptions of each choir's fundraising efforts and how this was a wonderful way of learning the skills of raising money for themselves. In one case, the South Panola high school band hoped to be the first in Mississippi to play at Carnegie Hall, but it was unable to raise the funds to travel the following year, 1989. When director Ken Lewis called Tiboris to cancel, the answer he got was, "I won't let you do this, why don't you shoot for next year," which triggered an enthusiastic resumption of the fundraising campaign. [39]

The last important part of the jigsaw puzzle that underscores MidAmerica's success in this important coming out year was the positive evaluations by music critics. The first review that appeared in the *New York Times* confirmed that MidAmerica had arrived. The review opened by stating "MidAmerica Productions, a new organizational idea for large scale concerts, has established itself in New York and presented an impressive event at Avery Fisher Hall." It mentioned a conductor named Peter Tiboris adding "Mr. Tiboris' idea is simple: adult, college and church choruses all over welcome the opportunity to perform in Fisher Hall, Carnegie Hall and even exotic foreign climes. Mr. Tiboris invites choruses he is interested in, and they pay their way to the location. Mr. Tiboris, in turn hires a local orchestra and puts on a concert – often as not with himself conducting – that makes use of the grandiose forces available." Then came praise for how the simple concept was operating effectively: "The idea seems to be working, since the organization has steadily expanded its activities since its founding in 1983. This season there are 26 scheduled concerts in New York with nearly an equal number in London, Athens, Moscow and Haifa, Israel."

There followed praise for the music and the conductor, when the review noted that "the program was an imaginative one: three *Te Deums* by Walton, Bruckner and Berlioz...Mr. Tiboris led strong, secure performances, with solid playing from the orchestra and sure singing from the nine, count 'em nine choruses involved."[40] That same month, May of 1987, another effusive review appeared, explaining in a nutshell MidAmerica's achievements: "amateur choruses can make up in fervor what they lack in tonal focus, and when they are well conducted in the right repertory, the results can be pretty exciting. That seems to be the secret of Peter Tiboris' success. Mr. Tiboris' MidAmerica Productions has perfected a policy by which choruses from all over the country are invited to New York to perform in monster concerts under Mr. Tiboris' baton. The whole idea seems like a prescription for vanity excess, except that Mr. Tiboris picks interesting programs, hires topflight musicians and conducts with considerable authority."[41]

MidAmerica's successful year also included Tiboris' creation of the Manhattan Philharmonic. Rather than use the American Symphony Orchestra, Peter created his own orchestra and named it Manhattan Philharmonic. The orchestra's Carnegie premiere came that summer with the American premiere of Tchaikovsky's *Ode to Joy with* seven hundred choristers. The *New York Times* critic wrote "It is no easy task to keep all those musicians in line and Mr. Tiboris did the best he could" and that "he relished every opportunity to turn his chorus loose. Throughout the program he worked his singers and instrumentalists to a fever pitch."[42]

SAME FORMULA, SAME SUCCESS

One of the first things Tiboris tells you about MidAmerica Productions is that the company has used the formula he started with, and aside from some necessary tinkering over the years it stuck with it. If one thinks of the risks the company took by bringing untested choirs to the big stage, as well as Tiboris' willingness to choose pieces that were unusual and not part of the regular repertoire, one strikes a nice balance between the continuity the business model provided and the bold and innovative program the company has kept on producing. After 1987 and for the following years we can see this pattern being repeated. While some concerts still took place at Avery Fisher Hall, the numbers held at Carnegie Hall began growing and becoming all the more frequent. There had been three choral music concerts in 1987, the next year, 1988 there were twelve between March and November. Four were part of MidAmerica's Youth Music Debut series, three were of the Manhattan Philharmonic, and the others were standalone concerts, including a 'Fanfare for Christmas' on Thanksgiving weekend. In 1989 there were thirty choral concerts presented at Carnegie Hall, including two featuring jazz music. One concert was by the newly formed Nouvelle Ensemble Moderne based in Montreal, which soon became one of the world's premier chamber orchestras specializing in contemporary classical music.

Norman Dunfee

MidAmerica's success has relied greatly on a number of close collaborators that Tiboris enlisted over the years. He believes that engaging Norman Dunfee, "a pianist and a gentleman" with whom there was a close and personal association for thirty-three years was one of the most important moments in the life of MidAmerica Productions and had a direct impact on its growth and development over the years. Norman Dunfee served as executive director and personally managed and directed more than 550 residencies in Carnegie Hall when concerts were being held. He established a personal contact with all incoming artists and created a professional atmosphere which was memorable for every one of them. Thanks to his musical background he was foremost a musician and knew precisely and exactly the nature of MidAmerica's mission. His last concert residency was on July 8, 2023 in Carengie Hall and it was a gala event dedicated to him. Tiboris brought him on the stage at the conclusion of his conducting Beethoven's *Symphony No. 6,* the Pastoral, and Mozart's *Ave Verum Corpus* with the New England Symphonic Ensemble and the entire audience and orchestra stood and cheered – an emotional night for both men. Among the accolades sent for Dunfee was one from English Composer and conductor John Rutter, one of MidAmerica's mainstays, who stated "Every one of us that has stepped on to the stage of Carnegie Hall at a MidAmerica concert during the last thirty-three years owes you an enormous debt of gratitude. You have been the rock on which our performances have been built." Preston Hawes, artistic director of the New England Symphonic Ensemble, which performed at the farewell concert was also full of praise, stating "Iconic doesn't even begin to encompass the magnitude of your presence and the indelible mark you have left on the thousands of musicians who, through your tireless work, have made music on this storied stage."[43]

JOYCE HOWARD

Another one of the important pillars in MidAmerica's operations is Joyce Howard. Tiboris remembers very clearly when a retired army sergeant, Joyce Howard came for an interview in an accounting position which had opened up. Of the candidates on the short list, she was the only one without an extensive accounting background. Yet she came across as bright, eager, energetic and spoke well. Tiboris immediately felt she was adaptable to the MidAmerica Productions model, the other two were much older and set in their ways. In his own words, he took a chance on hiring Joyce Howard and now, 25 years later, she has become and is one of the true and lasting pillars of MidAmerica Productions and its growth.

SOLOMON KAUFMAN

In 1987 Barry Liben, the owner of Tzell Travel who became Tiboris' travel agent, introduced him to Solomon Kaufman, a Certified Public Accountant (CPA) who had opened an office in New York a few years earlier. Kaufman became Tiboris' CPA and the two men developed a warm personal relationship, which is not surprising given Tiboris' ability to do just that with most persons with whom he worked closely. Kaufman called Tiboris his "Jewish brother" and he took a personal interest in the growth of MidAmerica Productions. Tiboris describes Kaufman's help as being "way beyond what normal CPAs do with their clients." Kaufman's advice was especially important during the economic recession of 2007-2008 and also during the Covid-19 pandemic.

JOHN RUTTER

The conductor of four of those concerts in 1989 which was such an important year for MidAmerica was John Rutter, the well-known English composer, conductor, editor, arranger and record producer, mainly involved with choral music, who was born in London in 1945. He was 'discovered' by the legendary English conductor and educator Sir David Willcocks, a fellow of King's College, Cambridge University and director of the legendary King's College Choir. Rutter, who studied at Clare

College Cambridge, was taking a class with Willcocks who one day asked to see some of the choral music his student had been writing. In a strange way, Rutter's early opportunities as composer and conductor of choral music came not in the United Kingdom but in America beginning in the mid-1970s and especially the 1980s. Peter Tiboris came into the picture, he recalls, because Peter is very curious and likes investigating things, and when he learned more about Rutter, he envisioned they could collaborate. He invited Rutter to be a guest conductor at one of MidAmerica's concerts at Carnegie Hall. For Rutter this came at the right time in his career because he was growing tired of crisscrossing the United States to conduct and lecture at universities, choral festivals, church events and denominational choral retreats.

Rutter's first concert at Carnegie Hall, which was labelled as the 'Big Apple High School Choral Festival' came on April 24, 1988. He conducted three of his own compositions, *Gloria, Three American Folk Songs* and *Requiem*. In November, Rutter was back at Carnegie to conduct at MidAmerica's 'Fanfare for Christmas'. The New York *Daily News* described the concert as "pure musical exuberance," and the critic mused "there must be a bigger role for Rutter in America."[44] Prophetic words, because there would follow over 130 concerts by Rutter sponsored by MidAmerica since that time. Rutter was extremely impressed by the acoustics of Carnegie Hall and relished the challenge of conducting there. And over the years the chemistry and mutual respect between the two men has grown exponentially. Rutter describes Tiboris not only as a brilliant, instinctive businessman but also a teacher like himself, someone who derives satisfaction from enabling young people to learn and do their best. Tiboris the man, he stresses, is impulsive and brilliant and sometimes he can be hot tempered but that often goes with having a generous nature, which Rutter suggests may be a Greek trait, sharing with your neighbor in what was once an impoverished society. And Tiboris has never lost sight of that ethos, Rutter went on to say, adding that he can be a difficult collaborator and some people cannot weather that storm, but most have come out the other side with great admiration for him.

Rutter was back at Carnegie Hall in May, 1989 to conduct his own composition, *Requiem* and he impressed the *New York Times* critic: "On the evidence of the performance, Mr. Rutter is an able craftsman who has estimated the market shrewdly. His Requiem is not difficult to sing and play; it contains agreeably mild echoes of 19th-century classics, Leonard Bernstein and Andrew Lloyd Webber; it sounds good with a huge choir and full orchestra but is also available (the program note said) in a version for organ and six instruments. He knows where to sound briefly portentous and where to break into generous pop-tune banality. His score exudes reassurance.

Following what has been standard practice since Britten's *War Requiem* of 1963, he mixes the Latin liturgy with other texts, including, in this case, the 23d Psalm. He has also left out certain portions of the Mass for the Dead: in particular the 'Dies Irae' and the 'Libera Me', with their possibly upsetting allusions to damnation. The hour of death, Mr. Rutter tells us, is a time when people get into positive feelings, and the afterlife is a place where everyone has a nice day, forever." [45]

Yet Rutter's biggest fan may be Peter Tiboris, whose artistic assessment of John Rutter and their professional and personal relationship he cannot overstate and is brimming with superlatives. They have become very close friends and colleagues. He recalls that he was seeking a major connection with an important person and in 1988 Rutter's name came up as he was beginning to make an impression in the American choral music world, something that led to him acquiring a vast following in the United States. Rutter has made the most appearances of anyone else in MidAmerica's programs, but even more importantly Tiboris considers his presence iconic, noting it has always been at the highest artistic level. Tiboris considers Rutter without equal in choral music, his music writing serves a great array of choral musicians and brings them to musical heights which are not attained by other contemporary composers. Yet Rutter, in Tiboris' eyes, remains grounded, congenial as well as warm and open to new ideas.

LEONARD BERNSTEIN

Peter Tiboris admired the composer and conductor Leonard Bernstein and considered him as one of his most important mentors. As it happens their paths crossed more than once. Tiboris met him on the Avery Fisher Hall stage in mid-April 1988 and Bernstein offered him advice about how to treat Handel's biblical oratorio *Israel in Egypt,* which Peter was conducting the next day. Tiboris described the moment in an interview years later: "As he stepped onto the elevator to leave, following his recording of Copeland's *Symphony No. 4,* he put his hand in the door to stop it and said, 'Maestro, do the locusts movement in four, not eight,'" Mr. Tiboris recalled. "I rushed to my score and changed it immediately to do four beats to the measure, and, of course, it worked beautifully." Two years later, almost to the day, Tiboris saw him at what turned out to be his last performance of *Mahler's 2nd,* for which Bernstein was famous. He attended that concert at Lincoln Center's Avery Fischer Hall along with two fellow conductors, Weston Noble and Hugh Sanders. Tiboris went backstage to the maestro's suite to congratulate him, and Bernstein looked up, recognized Tiboris and asked him if in his performance of Handel's *Israel in Egypt* two years earlier, in the Locust's fourth movement of the oratorio, whether he took his advice and conducted it in four beats per measure instead of eight beats per measure. Tiboris indicated that he took Bernstein's advice and did it in four beats – Bernstein gave a thumbs up and smiled. And so did Tiboris, who described the moment in an interview with the *New York Times* as follows: "There he was wearing a robe, collapsed in a chair, cigarette in one hand, Scotch in the other," he recalled. "He looked up and said, 'Peter Tiboris, MidAmerica Productions.' I was speechless. He launched into a huge discussion of esthetics with me," Mr. Tiboris said. "As I walked away, he called, 'Maestro, did you do it in four or eight?' I put four fingers up, and he did a thumbs-up with a huge grin. The tears were streaming down my face, and it took my breath away."[46]   Five years later Tiboris went to Bernstein's apartment at the Dakota building on Manhattan's Upper West Side to listen to the score of *Trouble in Tahiti,* the one act opera Bernstein had composed. Tiboris was being interviewed because he was about to conduct the Brooklyn Philharmonic at Carnegie Hall in January of 1997 using a baton once owned by Leonard Bernstein. For him, the ivory baton with an amber lion's head, *Bernstein* Yiddish means *amber*, was more than a piece of musical equipment to him, and the purchase was a homage to the great Bernstein – the conductor, music educator and great American musician – who influenced him so hugely.

MidAmerica Reaches its 10th Anniversary

A decade after the January, 1984 concert in Alice Tully Hall, MidAmerica was not only firmly established but also enjoying a growing reputation. At the mid-way point of that early period in the life of MidAmerica, prior to reviewing the opening concert of the 1989 season, *New York Times* music critic John Rockwell looked back on how and what Tiboris' organization had already achieved "with gathering momentum," noting that in the coming year it was presenting 43 concerts in New York along with European tours. He provided a good description of the business model, mentioning that "Mr. Tiboris and his staff organize the series and repertory, select the visiting choruses and orchestras, rent the halls and hire vocal soloists and instrumentalists. He says he is selective about his choices, rejecting groups that are not suitable. Those that do come pay their own way and a minor appearance fee to MidAmerica Productions. The reward is a trip to New York and a chance to sing in a glamorous hall." He also mentioned the way some people regarded the venture, stating "This apparatus evokes a withering cynicism in some observers, with Mr. Tiboris portrayed as an exploiter of naive provincials. In fact, the choirmasters know the rules before they accept, and presumably decide that the rewards make it worthwhile... As it happens, Mr. Tiboris himself has displayed a good deal of vigor and skill on the podium, and he has been venturesome in his choice of repertory..."[47] If anyone needed confirmation about how much the amateur choir members valued their experiences with MidAmerica Productions, one only had to read a number of statements of appreciation that MidAmerica received, expressing thanks for the opportunity and the experiences it had provided. Here are just some of them, which appeared in a full-page advertisement in the December, 1992 issue of the *Choral Journal:*

> MidAmerica Productions is first and foremost about providing and major choral/orchestral performance opportunities of choral singers ... one takes home a life experience. MidAmerica probably the most significant development in choral music decade." Donald L. Trott, Director of Choral Activities, and members of the Long-wood College Alumni Farmville, Virginia [May 26, 1991 -- 1875 Critical Edition of Verdi *Requiem;* Peter Tiboris, conductor]: "Singing in Carnegie Hall was a thrill of a lifetime!" Peggy Joyce Barber, music director, and members of the Nova University Community Singers of Fort Lauderdale, Florida [May 26, 1990 -- Rutter's *Requiem;* John Rutter, conductor]: "...this musical experience has enhanced [the choir members'] awareness of the beauty of music and its aesthetic value in their lives." Timothy Ahem, Director of Choirs, and members of the Allen County Community College Concert Choir of Iola, Kansas [November 25, 1990 - Mozart *Requiem;* Willard Kesling, conductor]: "The experience at Carnegie Hall was the most rewarding one my choir has ever lived through in performance." Betty Lou Hubbard, Director of Music, and members of the First United Methodist Church Chancel Choir of Waynesville, North Carolina [May 28, 1990 -- Brahms *Requiem;* Peter Tiboris, conductor]; "I take pride in knowing that my students have performed on the[se] stages...and that they have been exposed to such musical giants as Sir David Willcocks. I do not believe this would have been possible without our association with MidAmerica Productions." George Murphy, Choral Director, and members of the Lone Oak High School Choir of Paducah, Kentucky [March 23, 1989 - Faure *Requiem;* Sir David Willcocks, conductor]; "The participation in the MidAmerica concert season will indeed be remembered by all of us as

an educationally, culturally, and personally rewarding experience...It was a time of magic." Charlene Larson, Choral Director, and members of the NE Alabama State Jr. College Chorus [November 1990 - Mozart Coronation Mass & Sir David Willcocks' *Ceremony of Psalms;* Jonathan Willcocks, conductor].

To list all the expressions of appreciation and excitement by conductors and choristers at the opportunity they were given to perform in New York would require one to compile an entire book. Everyone I have spoken to reports a uniform feeling that the visitors to New York were aware they were undergoing a once-in-a-lifetime experience. It is likely there were exceptions to the rule, and it is also true that not all managed to perform at their best. It is also true that maybe there were days or concerts which were overcrowded with too much going on. But to assess MidAmerica's contributions, Gene Carr, one of Tiboris' closest friends and advisors during this period, pointed out one should not dwell on one concert let alone one performance. It had to do with understanding the full scale of MidAmerica's project writ large and the tremendous experience it offered to hundreds of singers.[48]

MIDAMERICA MAKES ITS MARK, AGAIN

1989 was also the year when MidAmerica added a Fall season to the Spring season of concerts it had been staging up to then. This move, thanks to the careful vetting of the choirs, served to maintain the high standards of singing. The opening of the Fall season that year elicited praise:

Peter Tiboris, a conductor with an entrepreneurial streak, has made a business of bringing young choruses from around the country and abroad to New York for concerts in the city's large halls. Typically, these are mammoth affairs in which several choirs join forces for Victorian-scale performances, usually accompanied by Mr. Tiboris' freelance Manhattan Philharmonic. Evidently, the idea has caught on. In past years, Mr. Tiboris' MidAmerica Productions concerts were grouped together in the spring. Now the conductor has a fall season too, and on Monday evening, he presented 14 choirs from 4 states in a program of works by Haydn, Puccini, Howard Hanson and Liszt at Carnegie Hall. The musicality of these presentations varies, naturally, according to the preparation of the groups on hand. On

Monday, the performance level was consistently high – and surprisingly so, since the likelihood of a smooth choral blend usually decreases as the number of collaborating choirs increases. The first third of the program featured six choirs from Georgia and one from North Carolina in Haydn's *St. Nicholas Mass.* By today's lights, a choir of about 250 and a modern symphony orchestra at full strength may seem unduly bloated for Haydn. But John Jennings, a conductor from Sam Houston State University, in Huntsville, Tex., drew a precise, polished sound from these forces, and at times – in the Agnus Dei, for example – he elicited a truly sublime sound.[49]

MIDAMERICA'S CHORAL CONSORTIUM

In 1991 Peter Tiboris had the idea of organizing a choral consortium which would enable amateur choirs to study, rehearse and perform in a session with one of several major figures of the choral world at Carnegie Hall. They included, in the order the program listed them, Margaret Hillis, the founder and first director of the Chicago Symphony chorus; Daniel Pinkham, a composer, organist and harpsichordist who taught at the New England Conservatory of Music; Gregg Smith, a noted conductor and gifted composer who contributed greatly to the development of contemporary music through the formation of his chamber choir the Gregg Smith Singers and other musical activities; Karel Husa, the Czech-born American classical composer and conductor who had won the Pulitzer Prize for Music in 1969; John Rutter; Robert de Cormier the musical conductor, composer and arranger of music for many artists including Harry Belafonte and the group Peter, Paul and Mary; Sir David Willcocks, the British choral conductor, organist, composer and director of the renowned Choir of Kings College, Cambridge University; and Jonathan Willcocks, composer and conductor. The program was successful and lasted for six months, bringing together many people of the choral world. It was yet another contribution to educating young singers and promoting amateur choir singing across America.

THE NEW ENGLAND SYMPHONIC ENSEMBLE,
PRESTON HAWES MUSICAL DIRECTOR AND CONCERT MASTER

The New England Symphonic Ensemble (NESE) is a professional orchestra established in the late 1980s. The birth of the ensemble occurred when MidAmerica Productions invited the Youth Ensemble to perform with John Rutter at Carnegie

Hall in New York City in May, 1991. It was Rutter himself who suggested to Tiboris that he form an association with the New England group which was led by its founder Dr Virginia Gene Rittenhouse – a concert violinist, pianist, composer, and conductor who was born in Canada and spent her early years in South Africa. Rittenhouse began her teaching career at Walla Walla College, now University, in the fall of 1945, a year after graduating summa cum laude with a music degree from the University of Washington. She taught for one year before going to Atlantic Union College, where she taught violin and piano until the early 1950s. She had founded the New England Youth Ensemble in 1969 with a group of five students and made their first international trip in 1973 to the World Youth Congress in Edinburg, Scotland. With Rittenhouse as its artistic director NESE grew. In collaboration with MidAmerica Productions, the New England Symphonic Ensemble has been led by a roster of guest conductors including John Rutter, Sherrill Milnes, Helmuth Rilling, Simon Carrington and Jonathan Willcocks, and regularly hosts international guest soloists, more than 650 in total. The New England Symphonic Ensemble's world premieres include Dinos Constantinides' *Byron's Greece, Hymn to the Human Spirit,* and *Midnight Fantasy II* for wind ensemble; John Rutter's *Cantate Domino, Distant Land, Magnificat,* and *Mass of the Children* and John Leavitt's *A Christmas Garland.* It also boasts multiple U.S. premieres, including Mozart's *Die Schuldigkeit des ersten Gebots,* Reimann's *Concerto for Violin and Cello,* Tchaikovsky's *Ode to Joy,* and René Clausen's *Hellas: In the Name of Freedom.*

The relationship between the NESE and MidAmerica blossomed under the baton of John Rutter. From 1991 to the present the Ensemble has performed over 500 times in MidAmerica Productions, 380 of them at Carnegie Hall. A pivotal figure in those performances was the Canadian concertmaster and violinist Dr. Preston Hawes, a Rittenhouse protégé.

Tiboris considers MidAmerica's relationship with the NESE and Preston Hawes as having been pivotal to the success of its programming. Hawes, a graduate of Yale and Johns Hopkins Universities, has certainly gained wide recognition and praise. He has been described by the European Academy of Arts and Sciences as an "electrifying and virtuosic" performer with "exquisite taste and rare talent." He is a laureate of the Concours de musique du Canada, the Andrews International Music Competitions, and the Prix de Musique de Chambre à Fontainebleau, and is a recipient of the J.C. Van Hulsteyn Award and Peabody Career Grant. He is currently an associate professor of music and director of strings at Washington Adventist University in Takoma Park, Maryland, as well as being the artistic director of the New England Symphonic Ensemble.

TWO DECADES CONDUCTING IN NEW YORK AND BEYOND

A decade after his first appearance in New York City Peter Tiboris had become a respected conductor in the United States and abroad. His first concert abroad was in Greece and took place in the town of Patra, a large port city on the northwestern tip of Peloponnesos. It was in Patra where opera was performed for the first time in Greece, due to the city's proximity and ties with Italy. Tiboris' first in Patra was with the help of a Russian orchestra and an American 100-voice choir. A great deal of the conducting appointments came through networking and exchanges. For example, thanks to Christian Catena of the Rome-based organization IUMA management that promotes classical music events, Tiboris conducted in Italian cities with great orchestras, all in all about fifty concerts in 18 Italian cities. This is what the 'exchanges' were all about. Catena did not 'have' Carnegie Hall and Tiboris had no contacts in Italy. Those exchanges went on for 15 years and were essentially a two-way street that brought Italian artists to Carnegie Hall and Peter Tiboris to Italy.

Memorable international experiences were Tiboris' concerts in London. His first performance in the Royal Festival Hall was in July of 1987, conducting Verdi's *Requiem* with the Royal Philharmonic Orchestra presented by Raymond Gubbay with 300 voices from choirs from New Jersey, New York, Pennsylvania, Texas and Wisconsin. They were led by Gary Ebensberger, who was a distinguished musician and conductor, Tiboris recalls. But above all he remembers his amazement at being conducting "this monster work" only six years after leaving Louisiana. A year later, in 1988, he was back in London, this time at the Barbican Center conducting Dvořák's *The Water Goblin*. The following year brought another unforgettable experience, this time in Greece, conducting Carl Orff's *Carmina Burana* for the first time with an American choir of 150 voices and the Moscow Radio and Television Orchestra led by Alexander Michailov. The concert occurred at the foothills of Mount Penteli, just north of Athens.

By 1994 Tiboris had conducted 22 concerts at Carnegie Hall. In 1987 he once again conducted the Royal Philharmonic Orchestra in Verdi's *Requiem* and the following year he was back in the United Kingdom to conduct at the Barbican Hall. He conducted Verdi's *Requiem* again at Carnegie Hall in 1989 eliciting critical praise: "Mr. Tiboris was clearly at home in the score, and the quality of choral tone in the fortissimo climaxes was thrilling. Throughout the concert, the choruses seemed strikingly well prepared for such a large and heterogeneous group."[50] There was more praise later that year for another concert at Carnegie Hall: "Mr. Tiboris conducted his orchestra in Liszt's symphonic tone poems inspired by Dante's 'Inferno' – or at least, by the first two books, since the composer gave up on the idea of musically portraying 'Il Paradiso'. Mr. Tiboris gave a taut, dramatic reading of 'Inferno', and if the 'Purgatorio' performance meandered and seemed less tightly knit, all was put right in the 'Magnificat' at the end. For this, a setting for women's voices, Mr. Tiboris put the sopranos and altos from all 14 choirs in the second balcony (there were enough of them to fill it). The idea was inspired, and the effect was heavenly."[51]

Among other notable performances he conducted in New York was a concert given by the Niedersächsisches Staatsorchester, the Lower Saxony State Orchestra from Hanover, Germany which traced its history back to 1636, making its New York debut in July 1990 with two performances. On the first night, at Carnegie Hall, it was conducted by Georg Alexander Albrecht, its music director since 1965. On the second night at Avery Fisher Hall "the Hanoverians gave the American conductor Peter Tiboris the same alert lush-toned playing they had given Mr. Albrecht the previous evening. The players also seemed fully at home with the pre-war Romanticism of the three Samuel Barber works" the *New York Times* critic noted, but added it was less comfortable with American composer Phillip Glass' Canyon which was given its New York premiere, acknowledging the piece charted some unusual territory. Following that, "Mr. Tiboris closed the concert with a sizzling and precise if sometimes overheated performance of Tchaikovsky's *Fourth Symphony*."[52]

There was another significant occasion for Peter in April, 1991 when he led a 40-player chamber orchestra and five singers in what was billed as the United States premiere of Mozart's *Die Schuldigkeit des Ersten Gebots (The Obligation to Keep the First Commandment)* at Alice Tully Hall. Mozart was 11 years old when he composed the 90-minute didactic oratorio with a text by Ignaz Anton Weiser in which personifications of Compassion, Justice and Christian Spirit wonder at the disinclination of mortals to free themselves from sin. They then wrangle, somewhat inconclusively, with Worldly Spirit over the soul of a Christian. "Mr. Tiboris led a trim performance and had a fine group of young soloists at his disposal. Erin Windle, a lyric soprano, sang Compassion with beauty and fluidity. Leah Anne Myers brought a slightly darker soprano timbre to Justice, and Andrea Adkins was an alluring Worldly Spirit. Gregory Mercer sang firmly yet conveyed the Christian's confusion when confronting the choice between spirituality and worldliness; and Jeffrey Francis gave a lyrical reading of Christian Spirit's music."[53]

Lovers of classical music as well as music critics repeatedly showed appreciation for the way Tiboris kept on finding works that were rarely played and then staging and conducting them with considerable flair and success. And this gained the attention of the critics.

A Rossini opera performed in 2003 drew special praise:

These days, *Ermione*, Rossini's operatic tale of shattered love and violence in the wake of the Trojan War, is like an exotic bird. Sightings are rare, but when they occur, the viewer is often taken by the brilliant plumage, or in this case, the opera's dramatic scope, finely drawn characters and exquisite music... Peter Tiboris' MidAmerica Productions presented a concert version with Mr. Tiboris leading the Manhattan Philharmonic, a combined chorus featuring the Arcadian Chorale and the Richmond Choral Society, and an able set of soloists... Rossini's score has no shortage of vocal high jinks, but it also abounds in sensitive arias and subtle characterizations that make this opera much more than a mere star vehicle for its title character... The cast on Tuesday evening was strongly anchored by the Greek soprano Irini Tsirakidis, who sang Ermione with a generous mix of dramatic commitment, tonal richness and sheer diva power. Barry Banks was a superb Oreste, creating the wonderful illusion that his cascading roulades were not some artificial vocal preening, but the organic expression of emotion boiled over. Victoria Livengood was a sensitive, dusky Andromaca, and Bruce Ford brought a warm and pliable tenor to the role of Pirro. The other soloists and chorus were uniformly solid, and the orchestra, notwithstanding a few untidy moments, rose to the occasion."[54]

CONDUCTING INTERNATIONALLY

John Rutter praises Tiboris for being one of the very few conductors who ventured into Eastern Europe before and after the collapse of communism. It is another sign of his adventurous spirit, and his wish to bring music to as wide an audience as possible that Rutter feels is so important. Music, of course, has always been international. Mahler told Sibelius in 1907 that the symphony must be like the world, it must be all-embracing. In communist Eastern Europe classical music experienced a somewhat different embrace, state support for the purposes of propaganda, but all that collapsed soon after the fall of the Berlin Wall brought the end of communism. With state support also in ruins, classical music artists in Eastern Europe found themselves buffeted by the vagaries of the free market. This only serves to underline the significance of Tiboris venturing into Eastern Europe by inviting artists to

perform in New York and in Greece and spending time there conducting and interacting with composers and musicians. [55]

Tiboris explains why he was drawn to conducting in Eastern Europe:

> As a newcomer to the New York City music scene in the 1980s to early 2000, I did not have the experience of conducting difficult choral and symphonic works, and due to the very short rehearsal periods in New York City this was a problem for me. At those times, I wish I had had rehearsed and performed them at a previous time so that the preparation and concert in New York could be done within budget and expeditiously. It was then that I made myself available to Eastern European orchestras in Poland, Czechia, and Bulgaria where I went to do that repertoire in a much more open and relaxed atmosphere where I could work out the musical details in preparation for New York some months later. I was a welcome American conducting guest of many Eastern European orchestras and I went often to prepare and conduct the very same repertoire I would do later in New York.

Tiboris' conducting had yielded critical praise in both Eastern and Western European music capitals after his over forty performances in Austria; in Canada with the Société Philharmonique de Montréal; in Greece; in the Czech Republic with the Brno Philharmonic; in Poland with the Philharmonics of Szczecin, Gdansk, Poznan and Warsaw; in Russia with the Glinka Cappella Symphony Orchestra and Moscow's Radio and Television Orchestra; in Ukraine with the Kiev Opera Symphony Orchestra; in the United Kingdom with the Royal Philharmonic and Philharmonia; in Yugoslavia with the Dubrovnik Symphony.

The Eastern European venues reflect Tiboris' willingness to widen the horizons of his music performances. Inevitably the presence of Tiboris and his musicians coincided with the upheavals in the region. For example, a summer residency in July of 1991 with American choral singers had been planned to take place in the city called Leningrad, but in the meantime, in June a referendum decided the city's old pre-communist name St. Petersburg should be restored. It was an example of the ongoing collapse of communism in that country and its transition from the Soviet Union to post-communist Russia that was the backdrop of the music Tiboris was conducting.

Among his many international connections, Tiboris the relationship with the classical music world in Poland was especially strong. It was enabled by the excellent management skills of Anna Lazowska, which enabled Tiboris to conduct in ten cities in Poland in the late 1980s and early 1990s. This was a valuable launch of Tiboris' European career and a training ground for his growth as a conductor. Tiboris also established a recording relationship with the Warsaw Philharmonic, and with John Barker's guidance he recorded several CDs. There was another important Eastern European connection, this one with the Martinů Philharmonic of Zlín in the Czech Republic, where Tiboris served guest conductor for 10 years and did 25 or more concerts. There, the manager of the Philharmonic was Malek Obruzalek, who became close friends with Tiboris. It was another wonderful experience and the orchestra eventually traveled to the United States to perform at Carnegie Hall.

A fascinating international engagement came in 1992 in connection with the Summer Olympic Games that were held in Barcelona that year. Tiboris conducted the Moscow Orchestra and 150 singers at an outdoor concert the night before the opening day of those Olympics. They performed Vivaldi's *Gloria* and Beethoven's *Symphony No. 9.* Spain is known for keeping late night hours. Accordingly, the concert started at 11:30 pm and ended at 1:30 am on the day the Olympics would open. While the audience was probably used to such a late night performance, the American singers and Moscow Orchestra members were exhausted at the end.

UKRAINE INDEPENDENCE CELEBRATION, NOVEMBER 1991

The most sensational international engagement for Tiboris came in Ukraine in 1991. He landed in the capital Kiev in late November of that year. The country was in considerable political and social ferment. It had already declared its independence from the Soviet Union in August, and on Sunday December 1st it had scheduled a referendum to approve of that move and also presidential elections. Tiboris was there to rehearse and conduct Mahler's *Symphony No. 2,* known as *The Resurrection Symphony,* with the Ukraine National Orchestra and Opera Chorus and soloists from Kiev. The arrangements were made by Paul Davidovsky, a music impresario of sorts from Russia who had been living in the United States working with artists like Tiboris. He describes the situation he found as follows: "I arrived in Kiev one week before the performance and on the first rehearsal day a private driver picked me up from the hotel and drove me to the opera house where the rehearsals and the concert were to take place with an orchestra of 90 and chorus of 150 and four great soloists for this 90 minute work (which I had planned to perform in NYC some months later). Going to Kiev was a chance for me to work-out other music issues in an Eastern Bloc Country." He soon found out that being in Kiev just as Ukraine was shaking off decades of communist misrule would make his visit memorable in many ways. First came what he witnessed when he arrived at the opera house: "When my private car drove up to the theater entrance, members of the orchestra had also been arriving to enter the theater for the rehearsal. What I then saw before they went into the theater was amazing and extraordinary... they were siphoning gas from their cars into a metal container and carrying the 3-4 gallons of gas into the theater." Tiboris was in shock. His driver explained, telling him "unless these drivers took the gas from their car into the theater (for safe keeping) the gas would be stolen by vandals." It was a lesson about how "the economy in Ukraine was such a wreck that the musicians had the gas cans in the rehearsal so the gas would not be stolen. At the end of the rehearsal the musicians took their gas cans and put the gas back in their cars and drove away. This is how bad it was in Soviet-dominated eastern bloc countries."

There was more to come in Kiev later that week, and Tiboris remembers it well:

Six days later on the day before the performance with these great artists, scheduled for November 29th, I was relaxing in my hotel room and Paul Davidosky (who was with me as an escort) knocked on my door and there were 3 or 4 police officers with him. I was in shock, not knowing what had happened. Paul explained that they came to escort me to the theater for a news conference. I had no idea what this was all about, but I got dressed and went. Once I arrived at the theater there was a news conference and it was announced that Ukraine was declaring freedom from the Soviet Union the next day, and that the concert would be the focal point of the celebrations." Tiboris was also informed that President Leonid Kravchuk and the entire government would be attending the concert. Clearly the move was designed to rally support for a vote in favor independence which was going to take place on December 1st, two days after the concert. It turned out to be a memorable concert night, with political speeches delaying the proceedings until the audience settled down to listen to Mahler's Symphony No. 2 and look forward to their country's resurrection.

REFLECTING ON THE TRANSITION FROM CHORAL TO ORCHESTRAL CONDUCTING AND OPERA AS WELL

Tiboris was trained in conducting choral music at the University of Wisconsin from 1967 to 1970 and firmly believes that being schooled and trained as a choral conductor paid him handsomely as he graduated to opera and symphonic conducting. He explains the way his initial training enabled that transition by saying, "as a choral conductor you have four basic voices occurring at the same time: soprano, altos, tenors, basses – so you are accustomed and trained to hear the blend and balance in these four voice types. You could have 20 singers on each voice part and getting them to blend and sound like one voice in each section is the key to great choral singing... this was my 'life' for many years, but then when I started moving into orchestral music I found that the four choral voice types enabled me to listen to the orchestra in terms of a 'choir of winds', 'a choir of brass' and a 'choir of strings'" not, for example, to listen to individual wind players who happen to be playing together. There is a significant difference to listening and coaching orchestra sections to play as a unit rather than individuals, and my decades-long experience conducting choral music helped me greatly to have my orchestra players think as a 'choir' of players, not as individuals. This ability has been often noticed and remarked upon by my colleagues when I turned into an orchestral leader. It is a great compliment and owe it entirely to my choral training."

TIBORIS FAVORITES

In reflecting on his career as a conductor, Tiboris cannot resist identifying his favorite pieces that he has conducted, starting with one that introduced him to classical music when he was still very young. It was the Risë Stevens recording of Bizet's *Carmen*, the first recording that his father introduced him to when he was twelve years old. Stevens was internationally renowned mezzo-soprano who had a 23-year career with the Metropolitan Opera, where she practically monopolized the role of Carmen during the 1940s and '50s,

Peter played the record over and over, enchanted both by the music and the provocative cover that depicted a negligée-clad Carmen – Risë Stevens.

In terms of the pieces he went on to conduct, the list is one of classic works. His number one favorite is Beethoven's *Third Symphony,* the *Eroica*, and especially with Herbert von Karajan conducting the Berlin Philharmonic. He describes the work as a simply astonishing piece music in an equally astonishing performance with the first three chords changing music history – forever. The second in the list is Mozart's *Requiem*. He recalls Professor Charles Leonhard at University of Illinois discussing Bernstein's recording in a graduate student class. Leonhard took the work apart, movement by movement, measure by measure, with emphasis toward structure, harmonic progression, and aesthetic. Without these analytical and aesthetic insights Tiboris feels he would have left the music field. He retook the same class several times. Third comes Tchaikovsky's *Romeo and Juliet Overture* in the live performance with the Madison Symphony Orchestra by the late Roland Johnson. Tiboris was 25 years old when he watched and listened to the performance and was so moved that he said, "I can do that. I want to do that." Then comes Mozart's *C Minor Mass,* which Tiboris conducted at Carnegie Hall. He was overwhelmed by its beauty and considers it, arguably, the greatest musical achievement of an incomparable genius.

Beethoven's *Symphony No. 6, the Pastoral* - Karajan's recording – comes fifth on the list. When Tiboris conducted it in Vienna he wondered how is such magnificence possible from a mortal? This is followed by Tchaikovsky's *Fourth Symphony,* which he witnessed Leonard Bernstein conducting with the New York Philharmonic at Lincoln Center in 1989, only fourteen months before his death. In Tiboris' words, it was muscle music of over-whelming drama. He conducted this work in Carnegie Hall twenty-five years later. Seventh come two works, Beethoven's *Missa Solemnis* and Bach's *Mass in B Minor,* two towering masterworks which are on his conducting life's 'bucket list'. He believes that after an entire life of performances he finally feels confident and assured enough to rehearse and conduct them. Next comes the fourth movement of Beethoven's *Ninth Symphony* followed by Mozart's *Don Giovanni,* which he considers as the perfect opera, combining Mozart's varying emotions and personalities supported by Lorenzo da Ponte's brilliant libretto. Ranked tenth in this list is Mahler's *Symphony #1 - The Titan.* Tiboris' first performance was in Carnegie Hall, and he looks back on it as a wild and memorable music experience of conducting a powerful work with its deeply moving largo section. This is followed by a work of immeasurable beauty, Mozart's *Piano Concert #17* (K)453. Twelfth is Mascagni's *Cavalleria Rusticana,* which he regards one of his favorites although he does not consider Mascagni a 'first-rank' composer but "profoundly Southern Italian," deeply loved and appreciated. Then comes Verdi's *Rigoletto,* which Tiboris conducted for the first time in Syros and describes as Verdi at his best with soaring and memorable melodies. Fourteenth is the music of Grieg's *Peer Gynt.* For Tiboris this was a novel experience. He conducted a danced performance at the Rome Opera Theater, Renato Zarella directing and choreographing the ballet. Tiboris notes that Grieg was a master at melody and had his own composer's 'voice'. Next comes Samuel Barber's *Prayers of Kierkegaard,* which Tiboris conducted in 1988 in the Lincoln Center in a thrilling performance with the American Symphony with three antiphonal choirs on stage and in the balconies. Next are others of

Beethoven's symphonies, *the Fifth, Sixth, Seventh* – and the *Ninth* as a whole, which rest forever in Tiboris' imagination due to their inventiveness, brilliance and depth. He conducted and recorded them frequently over a fifty-year period and each performance remained rooted in his imagination.

PHILLIP GLASS

Ranked seventeen on the list is Phillip Glass' *The Canyon*. Tiboris met the American composer and pianist Glass in his New York City apartment in 2003. By that time, Glass who was in his mid-sixties, was widely regarded as one of the most influential composers of the late 20th century. Glass occupies a distinct position in the music world. His work has been associated with minimalism, namely a form that is built up from repetitive phrases and shifting layers. In Glass' own words, a music with repetitive structures which he had developed stylistically over time. The National Endowment of the Arts has described him as the first composer to win a wide, multigenerational audience in the opera house, the concert hall, the dance world, in film, and in popular music."

Tiboris visited Glass to discuss the possible inclusion of one of his shorter works on one of his upcoming concerts in which he would conduct the Staatsorchester Hannover on their first American tour. He recalls that "It was remarkable meeting this 20th century contemporary music giant. He was cordial and very interested in me and what I had proposed: for me to conduct one of his works with the Hannover State Orchestra in its New York premiere in the United States, at performances at Carnegie Hall, in Hannover and at Wolf Trap National Park for the Performing Arts near Washington, DC." Tiboris would share the concerts with George Albrecht, the orchestra's conductor. Glass response was positive, "he proposed a work of some 20 minutes called *The Canyon,* which he had written a short time earlier for string orchestra, two pianos and percussion – about 50 players. It sounded very unique and interesting, so I agreed to program the work in Washington first as the U.S. premiere." Following that very cordial and straightforward meeting, Tiboris would discover that things were a little more complicated than he anticipated: "I took the music with me to study and when I opened the score I noticed the 20 minute work was only 12 to 14 pages long – strange. Why so little music for a twenty-minute work? What I found out was that there were dozens and dozens of repeats within the score which made it very very difficult for the orchestra and myself to decipher and follow. Repeat after repeat after repeat, which meant that the orchestra had to back-track and the music did not have a continuous start and finish! It proved to be very difficult to rehearse because these very good players kept getting lost on the repeats. And it was troubling for me as well." Thankfully, things would work out well: "By the time we got to Washington we had not had a rehearsal where we played the work from start to finish without a breakdown to start over. Once we got to Washington there was no way for us to start and re-start, and when we did the performance it all went well much to the relief of the orchestra and myself!"

THE LIST CONTINUES...

The list continues with Handel's epic oratorio *Israel in Egypt,* for which Tiboris conducted the American Symphony Orchestra, a great work for a chorus. (We earlier met Leonard Bernstein giving him advice at his dress rehearsal at Lincoln Center.) Haydn's *The Creation* follows, and Tiboris considers it Haydn's crowning achievement. Then comes Carl Nielsen's *Hymnus Amoris,* a great work which is not very well known, Schubert's *Symphony No. 9* known as *The Great C Major,* a stunning masterpiece. The remaining composers and works on the list are Bruckner's *Tantum Ergo* (motet of 1845); Tchaikovsky's *Sixth Symphony* known as the *Pathétique,* Mahler's revision of Beethoven's *Ninth Symphony;* Cherubini's *Requiem;* Chopin's *Piano Concerto No. 2,* especially the second movement; Dvořák's *New World Symphony No. 9*, and his *Serenade for Strings;* Haydn's *Paukenmesse;* Kodály's *Te Deum;* Liszt's *Faust Symphony* and his *Dante Symphony;* Mahler's *Symphonies Nos 1, 2* and *5;* Mozart's *Die Zauberflöte (The Magic Flute)* and his *Symphonies No. 35, 36, 40* and *41;* Nielsen's *Little Suite for Strings;* Puccini's *Tosca;* Rossini's *The Barber of Seville;* Rutter's *Gloria;* Alfred Schnittke's *Concerto for Piano and Strings;* Strauss' *Four Last Songs;* Tchaikovsky's *Symphonies Nos 4* and *5;* Verdi's *Four Sacred Songs,* the original version of his *Requiem,* his *Stabat Mater;* and Vaughan Williams' *Five Mystical Songs.*

THE FIRST RECORDINGS

In 1993, Tiboris released his first compact discs (CDs) through Bridge Recordings, a high end CD producer based in New Rochelle, NY. The inaugural disc was Gustav Mahler's reorchestration of Beethoven's *Symphony No. 9* with the Brno Philharmonic Opera and the Janáček Opera Choir. Tiboris had already directed the U.S. premiere, at Lincoln Center's Avery Fisher Hall on May 19, 1988. *The Daily News* critic had said at the time: "At the risk of committing heresy, 1 really feel Mahler has… made a great masterpiece even greater… Tiboris' performance was one of the most exciting and inspiring I've ever heard of this masterwork, whatever the edition." As the description of the CD on the Amazon page mentions: "Mahler's grand expansion of Beethoven's *Ninth Symphony* employs an extra 4 horns and an extra set of timpani, revoicing many passages of the venerable masterpiece. Mahler adds occasional counter-melodies and thickens the scoring in order to create his own heightened dynamic scale. Of his own performances of this re-scoring, Mahler wrote: 'Far from following any arbitrary purpose or course, but also without allowing himself to be led astray by tradition, (this conductor) was constantly and solely concerned with carrying out Beethoven's wishes in their minutest detail and ensuring that nothing the master intended should be sacrificed or drowned out amid the general confusion of sound.'"

The second CD featured Schubert: *Symphony No. 9 Great C Major* and *Beethoven: Overture For the Consecration of the House,* again incorporating Mahler's revisions, played by the Warsaw Philharmonic Orchestra, which was also another world premiere release. The third was Sergei Taneyev's *Symphony no. 4* with the Moscow Radio and Television Orchestra and sopranos Jelena Shkolnikova and Stella Zambalis and tenor John Daniecki.

FAMILY LIFE

In 1992 Peter and Susan divorced in an amicable way and remained in touch with each other. Throughout their marriage Susan had been extremely supportive of Peter's plans and projects and she continued to be so whenever possible. She moved to Charlotte, North Carolina, and their daughter Stephanie went with her, attending Charlotte Country Day School. Susan remarried in 1996. Their son Ernest Peter stayed in Montclair with Peter in order to go to Montclair Kimberley Academy. Meanwhile, back in Sheboygan, Peter's father Ernest continued to direct the choir at St. Spyridon church, and he also continued to be the chanter. In addition, he was one of the organizers of the church's successful annual festival which involved Greek food and music. His wife Stella was a member of the church's Ladies Philoptochos Society. In December 1996 Peter would go to Sheboygan, where he and his brother Gus hosted a dinner to celebrate their parents' fiftieth wedding anniversary at Blackwolf Run, a golf course complex in Kohler, a suburb of Sheboygan. Gus, who continued his career as a dentist, had become vice-president of the parish council of the church of St. Spyridon a year earlier; he had already served on the organizing committee of the church food festival for several years.

Peter would return to Sheboygan for family visits several times and in October, 2001 he arrived in the capacity of guest conductor in a concert that was being held to mark the opening of the renovated Sheboygan Theater. Peter wrote to the local newspaper to thank everyone for their hospitality, saying he had a grand, memorable and inspirational time during his visit. He found the new theater stunningly beautiful and acoustically vibrant.

MARRIAGE TO JENNIFER JO MCELRATH

On May 20, 1994 Peter met Jennifer Jo McElrath, who was a violinist with the Ridgewood Symphony Orchestra. The meeting took place on the stage at Lincoln Center's Avery Fisher Hall. Jennifer was concertmaster at a performance of Rimsky-Korsakov's *Scheherazade*. On June 26 1994 they married at St. George's Greek Orthodox Church in Clifton in New Jersey, next to Montclair where Peter lived. The 29-year old Jennifer was born in La Grange, Georgia to Richard Elsworth and Donna Gail McElrath and after graduating from Glen Rock High School in Glen Rock, New Jersey in 1983 she studied at Rutgers University from which she graduated in 1986 with a B.A, degree in English. She played in the Ridgewood Symphony Orchestra from 1983 for over a decade, serving as concertmaster between 1990 and 1993. She then went on to play for several years with the Elysium String Quartet, a group that Peter helped create. Their marriage lasted for ten years after which Jennifer embarked on a six month sailing adventure throughout the Pacific Northwest before moving to Hilo Hawaii, where she resides to this day. She continued her involvement in music playing in various orchestras, musical theater productions as well as numerous chamber music concerts.

THE WEILL HALL CHAMBER MUSIC SERIES AT CARNEGIE HALL

In the 1990s Tiboris decided to explore presenting soloists and chamber groups – that is, professional musicians, not youth or adult amateur or semi-professional musicians – in Weill Hall, the 285-seat auditorium in Carnegie Hall, in order to expand the musical base of MidAmerica productions. Weill Recital Hall was and still is the premier chamber music facility in New York City, elegant and beautiful with a small stage. It turned out to be a successful project. By presenting top professionals

(singers, soloists, pianists, small groups in that 285 seat hall) the program added lustre to the overall image of MidAmerica Productions and offset the giant Carnegie Hall and Lincoln Center concerts where hundreds of singers and orchestras appeared for significant major works. And it was an opportunity for piano soloists, duets, and trios to appear in such a prestigious venue and gain publicity. The response from soloists – who found their own sponsors – was so great that Tiboris had to create a company within his company to manage and foster these solo/duet/trio concerts. They were very sophisticated events and always sold-out. The revenues in this small hall were meager, but the project was done not to create 'wealth' but to show the public that Tiboris had a vision which included sophisticated performers and soloists beyond the standard type of concerts MidAmerica had been producing at Carnegie Hall and Lincoln Center. The very earliest performers, that helped the series become established, included pianist Eleonor Bindman, clarinetist Stanley Drucker, soprano Maria Zouves and the Elysium Quartet. It lasted for 15 years, eventually taking a toll on the staff and MidAmerica's resources, so the chamber music concerts came to an end. By that time, however, over 350 artists had participated and the 650 or so concerts at Carnegie Hall and Lincoln Center and the concerts at Weill Hall put MidAmerica Productions at over 1000 presentations in New York City, a record number.

LUKAS FOSS & THE NATIONAL YOUTH ORCHESTRA

In the mid-1990s Tiboris got to know the composer, pianist and conductor Lukas Foss when he provided his new music for MidAmerica Productions' Weill Hall Chamber Music Series. Foss lived in Manhattan, and he had recently stepped down from his position as music director of the Brooklyn Philharmonic, which he had transformed into one of New York City's most vital ensembles. Tiboris found him congenial, warm, funny and knowing all the 'inside' stories about Bernstein. Foss was born in Germany and while still a teenager he moved to the United States with his family in 1937. He studied music at the Curtis Institute of Music in Philadelphia where he met Leonard Bernstein and with whom they became close friends. In assessing the place of Lukas Foss in the American classical world, New York Times music critic Allan Kozinn wrote he was "considered an important voice in the burgeoning world of American composition, along with Aaron Copland, Samuel Barber, Elliott Carter and Leonard Bernstein. And like Bernstein, he enthusiastically championed the works of his colleagues. But where Bernstein, in his compositions, melded jazz and theater music with a lush symphonic neo-Romanticism – or wrote theater music outright – Mr. Foss preferred to explore the byways of the avant-garde, focusing at different times on techniques from serialism and electronic music to Minimalism and improvisation. But as he moved from style to style, his voice remained distinctive, partly because he distrusted rules and never fully adhered to those of the approaches he adopted, and partly because a current of mercurial wit ran through his work."[56]

Tiboris came up with the idea of creating what was called the National Youth Orchestra and asked Foss to lead it. He loved the idea and did so for a decade, every January at Carnegie Hall. The first such performance Foss conducted was Dmitry Shostakovich's *Symphony No. 5* in January, 1997. Tiboris recalls that because of Foss's reputation and stature as a composer and because of his conducting skills the response from young performers was overwhelming, and they were able to assemble the best 100 players through audio auditions. They all went to New York City for five days and studied and rehearsed with Foss. In his seventies he bore a lifetime of great talent and experience – he was kind and not pushy, demanding but also understanding, as well as humorous. He occasionally chose his own music but more often chose classic works by composers such as Brahms, Mahler, Tchaikovsky and Shostakovich which, the orchestra members were not doing at their orchestras at their home locations. The concerts that took place over a decade ended with bursts of appreciation from the audiences and elation among the performers. For Tiboris it was another worthwhile project that changed lives of young musicians and demonstrated that MidAmerica Productions were "all about the music."

H. ROBERT REYNOLDS & THE NATIONAL WIND ENSEMBLE

Another Tiboris creation around the same time was the National Wind Ensemble, which was conducted by H. Robert Reynolds, the Henry F. Thurnau Professor of Music/Director of University Bands and Director of the Division of Instrumental Studies at the University of Michigan. Tiboris' idea of forming a highly auditioned National Youth Wind Ensemble came about in 1995 because of his association with Reynolds, who was an icon in the wind ensemble music arena. He thought it would be a great idea to have a national auditioned youth wind ensemble for those between 16 to 24 years of age which would be assembled after extensive auditions with musicians selected nationally. Many, many students sent in audition tapes because Reynolds had a national reputation in wind music – in fact the interest was overwhelming. It was an extraordinary experience for those selected who went to New York for five days to work exclusively with Reynolds. The program lasted for ten years through 2005.

Reynolds spoke about his involvement with Tiboris in a testimonial that was published on MidAmerica Productions' website, saying, "MidAmerica has been in my life since 1997 when I brought the University of Michigan Symphony Band to Carnegie Hall as part of the '100th Anniversary of bands at The University of Michigan'. That concert was sponsored by MidAmerica and my longtime friend, Peter Tiboris. Peter and I first became acquainted in Madison, Wisconsin in the early '70s – long before the dawn of MidAmerica Productions. Following that first Carnegie concert in 1997, I began conducting the National Wind Ensemble in 1998 and have been a yearly guest of that MidAmerica ensemble each year since. I embrace my association with MidAmerica, Peter, and all the wonderful people who make up that terrific organization. Some faces change, but the same caring is a constant. Prior to stepping on the stage each time for a concert in Carnegie Hall, I realize how lucky I am to be given this privilege of conducting in such a great hall. It's almost a religious experience – so many of the world's great musicians have mounted that very podium, and I am humbled by the opportunity. I never take it for granted."

The first National Wind Ensemble concert that Reynolds conducted at Carnegie Hall was in May, 1998 and the groups played pieces by composers William Schuman, Percy Grainger, Rolf Rudin and Gustav Holst.

BY AND ABOUT GREEKS

During this period, and as MidAmerica approached its 20th anniversary, the Greek connection – a reflection of Peter's ethnic and religious identity in his creative work and his business pursuits – became more pronounced. There had always been such a bond, exemplified by his New York City debut which was thanks to an invitation to organize and conduct a concert in honor of the 25th anniversary of the enthronement of Greek Orthodox Archbishop Iakovos of North and South America. The help of his Greek-American friend and colleague Dinos Constantinides had been important in the early years in New York, and in the concerts MidAmerica organized in the 1980s and the 1990s one notices a sprinkling of Greek and Greek-American names among the performing artists.

In collaboration with the New York branch of the Hellenic Foundation of Culture Tiboris and MidAmerica organized a series of six classical concerts titled 'By and About Greeks: Hellenism and Music' between 1999 and 2001. The first was with the Louisiana Sinfonietta and its conductor, Dinos Constantinides. The program included works by Greek composers Manos Hadjidakis, Nikos Skalkottas, Athanasios Zervas and by Dinos Constantinides himself. That year, 1999, was the fiftieth anniversary of Greek composer Nikos Skalkottas' death, and the second concert of the series, in December, was dedicated to his music. He was only 44 when he passed away and it was only after his death that Skalkottas' music began to be played, published or critically esteemed to any great extent, partly due to the efforts of friends and disciples. The third of the series was held in January, 2001 and was a concert given by Greek-Cypriot pianist and composer Christos Tsitsaros. Tsitsaros is currently Professor of Piano Pedagogy at the University of Illinois in Urbana-Champaign. He also serves as Piano Chair for the Illinois State Music Teachers Association. There would be a fourth and final concert in the series later on that year that took place soon after the terrorist attack in New York on September 11, 2001.

As part of his activities surrounding this series, Tiboris had given a lecture on the contributions of Greek musicians worldwide at the Center for Macedonian Studies, a Greek-American organization based in Queens, New York in 1999. There he announced publicly that MidAmerica Productions would stage Mikis Theodorakis' opera Electra at Carnegie Hall in 2000.

MIKIS THEODORAKIS, COMPOSER AND GREEK MUSICAL ICON

Sometime in 1998 an academic based at Cornell University took a bus from Ithaca, NY and traveled down to New York to show Peter Tiboris the music score of an opera written by the Greek composer Mikis Theodorakis. Gail Horst-Warhaft had published a book on Theodorakis and translated his poems and lyrics into English. She had just given a talk about Theodorakis' operas at the Cornell Music Department, and after the talk, Professor David Rosen, a noted Verdi and Puccini scholar asked to see the score of the opera Electra that she had talked about, and he suggested that Gail should try and get the opera staged in America. When she responded that she had no connections with the opera world in the United States, Rosen said the only person he could think of who might be interested was Peter Tiboris, whom he had taught as an undergraduate student at the University of Wisconsin at Madison in the 1970s. A few days later Tiboris contacted Gail and asked where he could see a performance of the opera. She answered that would be hard, but it happened the opera would be performed at the great Megaron Mousikis – The Athens Concert Hall the following week. Peter flew to Athens, told her he thought the opera was a masterpiece, and that he would like to put on a performance at Carnegie Hall.

Theodorakis was a household name in Greece and throughout Europe, known for his hugely popular music as well as his left-wing political activism. Several of his songs became unofficial anthems of the Greek Left. In the United States he was known as a composer of music for film soundtracks, most notably *Zorba the Greek, Serpico* and *Z*. He had a classical music training, having studied composition in Paris with Messiaen, but after a success with Antigone, a ballet, he became disillusioned with what he regarded as the limitations of the classical music world and became captivated by the idea of combining high and popular art. He began writing art songs with bouzouki accompaniments, as well as overtly popular and political songs, some of which found a life in translation outside Greece. In the 1980s Theodorakis' interest in classical forms was rekindled, however, and although his works are rarely performed in New York, he was fairly prolific. Among his last projects was a trilogy of operas based on ancient Greek drama, one of which was *Electra*. The opera had its premiere in Luxembourg in 1995 and the following year it was performed at the Herod Atticus open air theater at the foot of the Acropolis under the direction of the distinguished Greek film director Nikos Koundouros. Also in 1996, the opera had its premiere in Germany. The premiere in the United States brought even greater recognition.

Mid America's staging of *Electra* in New York ranks as one of the many highlights of Peter Tiboris' career. The American premiere on June 11, 2000 was an extraordinarily important event not only for Theodorakis but also for the Greek music world because it demonstrated the breadth and depth of modern Greek culture well beyond its stereotypical image of traditional popular music forms based on the bouzouki. The significance of *Electra* coming to Carnegie Hall was not lost on New York's music critics or the Greek-American community and the General Consulate of Greece. There was extensive coverage – a photograph of Mikis and Peter was featured on the front page of the *Ethnikos Kyrix*, the largest circulation Greek language newspaper in the United States. There was a press conference hosted by the General Consulate of Greece at which Peter spoke about meeting Theodorakis and the mutual respect and warm friendship that quickly developed between the two of them. Following this, Mikis and Peter were received by Demetrios, the Greek Orthodox Archbishop of America, and had a very cordial and engaging conversation. Mikis told the press afterwards he was impressed because he found the Archbishop to be very down to earth.[57] Both those important figures certainly shared that characteristic.

On the evening of Saturday, June 10, the eve of the performance, a Washington, DC-based Greek-American advocacy organization, the American Hellenic Institute, honored Theodorakis with its Hellenic Heritage Lifetime Achievement Award. The gala dinner, held at the Grand Hyatt in New York, drew over 200 distinguished guests and featured Greek-American Thalia Assuras, anchor of the CBS 'Saturday Early Show', as Master of Ceremonies. Assuras opened the evening's proceedings with a short account of Mikis Theodorakis' life, highlighting his work as a composer and political activist. She went on to note the work of American Hellenic Institute in its pursuit of the same ideals of justice, democracy and the rule of law. Dinner Chairman, Mr. Peter J. Pappas, CEO of P.J. Mechanical Corp., congratulated Mikis Theodorakis and congratulated the American Hellenic Institute for its 26 years of dedication to the Greek-American community in consistently voicing the concerns and positions of Greek-Americans to policymakers in Washington. Following Pappas' remarks, Peter Tiboris presented remarks on 'Classical Music Among World Hellenes: Myth or Reality. What is the Future?'

Following the speech, the guests were treated to a musical presentation of Theodorakis' songs. Performing the selected works were Stephanie Chigas, mezzo-soprano, accompanied by Kathy Olsen on piano. Chigas, the daughter of Greek immigrant parents who owned a restaurant, was a young aspiring opera singer who would be taking part in a MidAmerica production in Greece that summer. The presentation of the Hellenic Heritage Lifetime Achievement Award to Mikis Theodorakis, followed the performance. Presenting the award to Theodorakis, the American Hellenic Institute's founder Eugene Rossides spoke of the composer who had become "a symbol of democracy and resistance to the 1967-1974 junta in Greece." In his acceptance speech, Theodorakis spoke of the many contributions of Greek-Americans to Hellenism and expressed his gratitude for the warm welcome he has received from so many in the Greek-American community since entering the United States.[58]

The performance of *Electra* the next day was a tremendous success, and its conclusion was met by a prolonged standing ovation. Music critic Allan Kozinn lavished praise on the opera itself and the performance:

> The story, based on the Sophocles version, is familiar from the more venerable Strauss opera, although here Orestes makes short work of slaughtering Clytemnestra and Aegisthus, to the general celebration of the Mycenaeans.

Electra does not have an ecstatic dance and does not die, and Orestes is not tormented by the Furies. A more telling musical difference between Strauss' 'Elektra' and Mr. Theodorakis' opera, though, is that where Strauss used the story as a canvas on which to paint a thoroughly Straussian opera, Mr. Theodorakis' score seeks to evoke the spirit of Greek antiquity – or at least a cinematic version of that spirit. The vocal writing is generally slow and stately, with melodies that convey the character of grand pronouncements. The orchestration is large and lush, with percussion writing that often gives the music a ritualistic solemnity. And a chorus comments on what has been said, or on what the character who has just finished singing actually feels, adding a slightly oracular touch to the proceedings. All told, this talky opera is a succession of monumental gestures: a listener was tempted to envision the action being performed in slow motion by eyeless bronze or marble statues. That had a certain exotic charm although, at nearly three hours, the rich orchestral fabric began to seem slightly oppressive. Another image that came to mind was of being marooned in a seemingly bottomless tub of chocolate mousse. The work was sung in Greek, with supertitles, and for the occasion, Mr. Tiboris imported a cast of Greek singers. The most powerful of the singers were Greek-American Reveka Evangelia Mavrovitis, the mezzo-soprano who sang the title role, and Tassis Christoyannis, the baritone who sang Orestes. Both projected well over the full-throttle orchestra and did much to create a sense of their strong-willed characters. Much the same can be said for Ioanna Forti, whose dark contralto gave Clytemnestra's music a sinister edge. Medea Iassonidi was a generally appealing Chrysothemis, but occasionally had trouble making herself heard. There were also fine contributions in the smaller roles from Yannis Christopoulos (Aegisthus), Angelo Simos (Pylades) and Pavlos Maropoulos (the tutor). There were a few orchestral mishaps, but for the most part he drew a polished and unflaggingly energetic performance from the Manhattan Philharmonic.[59]

Another review of the performance appeared in the *American Record Guide* a magazine devoted to reviews of classical music. The reviewer noted:

The cast was strong. Mezzo-soprano Reveka Evangelia Mavrovitis never tired in the demanding role of Electra, projected strongly in the upper register and gave out smooth, vibrant tones in the lower. Tassis Christoyannis' vaulting baritone, with its distinctive metallic timbre, made a riveting, well-defined presence of Orestes, and Angelo Simos as Pylades seconded him ably. Tenor Yanni Christopoulos' contribution as Aegisthus was brief but effective, and the remaining women – soprano Medea Iassonidi as Chrysothemis and contralto Ioanna Ford as Clytemnestra – brought as much drama to their work as the music allowed. The composer took bows at the end, to a warm welcome from an almost full house."[60]

There was a humorous note during Theodorakis' visit to New York. He and Tiboris were in a car on the Major Deegan expressway traveling to a promotional event and they were passing the old Yankee Stadium where the Yankees were playing the Red Sox. The driver happened to be listening to the game on the car radio, and right at that moment a Yankee hit a home run the stadium's loudspeakers blared out the tune of *Zorba the Greek* in celebration. When both men stopped laughing at the coincidence Tiboris asked Theodorakis if he received royalties for such use of his music. Theodorakis, who barely knew about baseball, let alone the use of organ music during the game, shook his head.

The connection between Tiboris and Theodorakis would continue both in the United States and in Greece. In 2001, only year after the *Electra* performance, and almost to the day, Tiboris conducted the Manhattan Philharmonic in the U.S. premiere of Theodorakis' *Rhapsody for Cello and Orchestra*. The cellist was Nicholas Canellakis, a New York-born Greek-American and a graduate of the Curtis Institute of Music in Philadelphia and the New England Conservatory. In 1997, aged 12, he had appeared as guest soloist with the Queensborough Orchestra of New York, which was directed by his father, Martin. Less than a decade later he was being described as one of the most charismatic virtuosos on America's music scene. The other music piece on the program that day in 2001 was Beethoven's Symphony No. 9, with Marianna Rigaki, Soprano, in her Carnegie Hall debut. That same year, she became the first Greek artist to win an award in the category of opera at the International Maria Callas Grand Prix. The rest of the cast included Angelica Cathariou, Mezzo-Soprano; Dorji Ciren, Tenor; Ricardo Herrera, Bass and six choirs: the Richmond Choral Society, the Riverside Choral Society, the SUNY Buffalo Chorus, the Windsong Southland Chorale, the Westchester Oratorio Society and the Arcadian Chorale.

9/11

On Sunday June 16th 2001 MidAmerica's Spring season concluded with a concert at which the last piece that was played was Mozart's *Requiem*, which he composed in 1791. It was unfinished at his death on December 5th of that year. A completed version dated 1792 by composer Franz Süssmayr was delivered to Count Franz von Walsegg, a German aristocrat who had commissioned the piece for a requiem service in commemoration of the first anniversary of the death of his wife Anna at the age of 20 on February 14, 1791. Death on a mass scale, however, was about to happen before MidAmerica would stage another event at Carnegie Hall.

As MidAmerica was stepping up its preparations for the Fall season of 2001 the terrorist attack on 9/11 occurred, plunging New York City into a climate of fear and uncertainty. With the collapse of the Twin Towers of the World Trade Center nearly 2,800 people died, including civilians, firefighters and police officers. Hundreds of thousands of people were exposed or potentially exposed to dust, particulates and other environmental contaminants on that day as they endured or witnessed deeply traumatic events. Fires burned and smoldered at the site for months. Many who lived, worked or attended school in the area found their lives upended and their livelihoods damaged or completely destroyed; thousands of the city's residents were temporarily displaced. In late September efforts turned to an unprecedented recovery, cleanup, and restoration of New York City's infrastructure. As the pain and confusion raged on, it became clear to Mayor Rudolph Giuliani and Schuyler G. Chapin, his commissioner of cultural affairs, that something had to be done quickly to restore at least some sense of continuance to the city, to avert a potential economic crisis that might cost artists and technicians their jobs and, in doing so, declare that the terrorist attacks had not done permanent damage. And so the word went out from city leadership to Broadway imploring them to restore normality as best they could by reopening the shows that had suddenly closed down. Remarkably, on Thursday, Sept. 13, just 48 hours after the attacks, all 23 Broadway theatres were up and running. It was – by any historical standards -an extraordinary public and private achievement and a crucial cog in the wheel of the city's recovery. Giuliani quickly expressed his thanks, announcing at a press conference that if anybody wanted to help New York, a really good way to do so would be to go and see a Broadway show. On that night all those shows featured a moment of silence prior to the performance. And, as is traditional in times of loss, all of the Broadway marquees dimmed their lights in tribute to all those who had lost their lives. Carnegie Hall was naturally part of this effort to help the city overcome the trauma.

Normal scheduling resumed in late September and at the end of the month there was a 'Concert of Remembrance' honoring the victims of the tragedy.

Tiboris and MidAmerica were also committed to resuming full operations. Its office staff in Midtown Manhattan had witnessed the attack but they returned to work as soon as possible. Peter remembers he was sitting in his home in Montclair in New Jersey when the news broke that fateful Tuesday morning. Fortunately, the next MidAmerica concerts scheduled would not be until November.

Nonetheless the immediate problem was that outside New York there were fears about the security in the city, and school boards for example were forbidding their students to travel there. In Terre Johnson's words, "Peter had to put on his businessman's hat on and tell them the concerts were going to take place safely and therefore there would be no refunds." Ultimately, there were only two groups that withdrew from the several concerts that were scheduled and did take place.[61] The first MidAmerica event that took place at Carnegie Hall that Fall was on October 8th. It was the fourth in the 'By and About Greeks' series and was almost entirely made up of Greek performers and compositions by Greeks with Theodore Antoniou, a Greek composer and conductor based in the United States, as the conductor. The music was from composers Skalkottas, Ianis Xenakis and Jani Christou and the artists included the Alea III music ensemble that Antoniou had established at Boston University, pianists Nelli Semitekolo and Konstantinos Papadakis, percussionist Dimitris Dessylas, mezzo-soprano Maria Karagevreki La Vita and actor Gregoris Semitekolo. There would be twelve more concerts held through the end of the year creating a momentum that saw MidAmerica approach its twentieth year growing stronger.

The continued growth was due to many factors: the popularity of MidAmerica's programs of bringing choirs to Carnegie Hall, the expert way that MidAmerica's staff handled the process and Tiboris' leadership, which included his ability – when required – to "put his businessman's hat on" to use Johnson's expression. There would be other occasions in the future, most notably the financial crisis of 2008 and, later on, during the Covid-19 pandemic, when Tiboris protected the interests of MidAmerica Productions by taking hard-nosed business decisions. And his associates who spoke to me about those moments, including James Redcay, a graduate of New York University who joined MidAmerica in 2015 and witnessed the company's response to the pandemic first-hand, used similar euphemisms to describe Tiboris' response. This is probably because Redcay and others saw no inconsistency in the changing of hats – they recognized it was the same head wearing them. Tiboris, constantly motivated to achieve success, was always combining his artistic persona with that of charismatic leader along with that of businessman, and thus there was nothing surprising of seeing him suddenly order the drawbridge to be pulled up in order to defend MidAmerica Productions and its budget from outside forces.

MidAmerica at Twenty!

In 2002 MidAmerica staged 60 concerts at Carnegie Hall and the next year it staged 57 – the numbers speak for themselves and point to peak seasons enjoyed by the organization, but they don't tell the whole story. A closer look demonstrates the diversity of MidAmerica's music programs, continuity in terms of bringing amateur choirs from all over America to New York, and an increased outreach to musicians and singers from other countries. For Peter himself, continuity in staging rarely played music and strengthening his ties with Greece and its music was also important. This included the conclusion of the 'By and About Greeks' concerts with separate performances from guitarist Elena Papandreou and pianist Jenia Manoussaki. In March, 2002 Tiboris was in California at a conference of the members of the Archbishop Iakovos Leadership 100 Fund, a group of wealthy benefactors of the Greek Orthodox Church in America. He organized an event titled 'Opera-Fest by the Sea', a performance by Greek and Greek-American opera singers.

MidAmerica's publicity mentioned that the organization was starting its twentieth season but only in passing. One gets the sense that it was too busy adding concerts to focus too closely on itself, and that if anything was an achievement in itself. The concept of 'Continuity and change' is a very apt lens through which to study Peter Tiboris' career and his MidAmerica Productions. The successful formula was repeated, but the range of activities steadily expanded. And that combination had brought success.

Matters of the Mind

Success, nonetheless, is often achieved at a cost. Back in 1986, Peter felt he needed help in coping with the new life he was facing in New York and his transition from academe into the real world. He began having sessions with a psychologist, Robert Siroka. Dr. Siroka is well known in his field and beyond. He is the founder of the Psychodrama Training Institute and has years of experience in counseling and psychotherapy. Since 1968, he had given training and supervision in Psychodrama,

Sociometry and Group Psychotherapy to many of today's leading teachers and practitioners. Tiboris' sessions with Siroka were in the form of regular counseling

Tiboris recalls that while the transition he was experiencing was a one-way street in his mind, the process of adaptation to the new environment had its bumps and ups and downs in terms of success and failures and he required professional advice and help. The move to New York created great uncertainty about the future. Going through a second divorce with Jennifer McElrath, which also created bumps, added to the stresses Tiboris was experiencing.

The weekly sessions with Siroka at which he listened and responded carefully turned out to be extremely helpful and this continued over the next fifteen years. Tiboris recalls that the most important lesson he learned from him, and which he still remembers clearly and uses regularly, was "If you want a happy life, don't try to change the other person in line with what you want; accept people as they are and if you can't do that, then separate calmly from them." Those principles lay at the heart of the achievements that Tiboris and MidAmerica could justifiably celebrate twenty years after the journey in New York had begun.

CHAPTER FIVE

TIBORIS AND MIDAMERICA'S GLOBAL REACH

Music produces a kind of pleasure which human nature cannot do without. — Confucius

MidAmerica Productions went past its 20th anniversary and entered its third decade by continuing with the same winning formula which had guaranteed success and riding a wave of an increasing number of jubilant choral singers in America coming to Carnegie Hall. What changed was that Peter Tiboris and his dual career as conductor and presenter of concerts went global. Tiboris founded MidAm International, a company that did internationally what MidAmerica did domestically, namely, to send choirs on short ten-day singing engagements in European cities, described as residencies. Tiboris himself conducted many of those concerts and his presence in Europe resulted in invitations to conduct concerts given by European-based orchestras. MidAmerica's domestic programs remained the mainstay of his operations by far, about 85% he estimates, but he stepped back from conducting at Carnegie and focused more on international engagements. This allowed more space for younger conductors to experience Carnegie Hall and allowed

him to expand in Europe, a new and exciting prospect. His focus as a conductor in international events can be seen by the numbers of concerts he conducted at Carnegie Hall. Between 1986 and 2003, the period covering MidAmerica's first two decades, he conducted on 32 occasions at Carnegie Hall, but over the next two decades only on 12 occasions.

From the early 2000s through the arrival of the Covid pandemic which halted music concerts the world over, one can discern four main strands in Tiboris' relationship to music. First was his leadership of MidAmerica and its programming at Carnegie Hall which enabled all his other projects. The second was his international activities that were expanding throughout Europe. Third and fourth are Tiboris' growing engagement with his roots, his Greek Orthodox background and his ancestral homeland Greece, where he established what is now an acclaimed summer music festival on the island of Syros and is important enough to consider in a separate chapter.

The first two decades also brought big changes to Peter's family life. First came his marriage to Eilana Lappanainen, which was followed a few years later by the passing of both his parents. This is a turning point for most people as it was for Peter, especially because of the ways his father inspired and motivated him throughout his life. A few years later, Peter would become a grandfather. A grandfather who by his own account trusted his children's parenting abilities and would only offer advice when asked.

MARRIAGE TO EILANA LAPPANAINEN, 2007

Peter's international outreach which gained momentum in the early 2000s included having an agent in Rome, Italy. The agent, as professional courtesy suggested that Tiboris consider soprano Eilana Leila Lappalainen as a potential performer in a MidAmerica concert. Lappalainen was born in Toronto, Canada where her parents emigrated from Finland. Eilana grew up in Toronto, Tampere, Finland and Rochester New York, and eventually the family settled in California where she started her first music lessons, violin, piano and voice. After 20 leading roles in local Musical Theater productions in the Silicon Valley, at age 17 Eilana auditioned for the former Metropolitan Opera star mezzo-soprano Irene Dalis, who was of Greek and Italian parentage. Ms. Dalis built a training program for young opera singers in the late 1980s guiding and training young artists such as Eilana. This relationship was an inspiration for the young soprano. Along with her 30 leading roles with the company, Eilana was also awarded the position of first full-time Resident Artist for the company, Opera San Jose. She left California, moving back to Canada and then on to Germany, while she began her international work in Mexico, Finland, Israel, Canada, Germany, the Czech Republic, Poland, new cities in the USA, Japan and Italy, singing repertoire from operas by Verdi, Puccini, Bizet, Strauss, Donizetti, and Wagner. She was building a distinguished international career and also venturing into difficult works by new composers, even bringing her to debut in the title role of Tatjana by Azzio Corghi at Milano La Scala. Aside from singing her Italian repertoire with Puccini and Verdi roles, she sang the title role of Jenufa by Janacek, Ellen Orford in *Peter Grimes,* as well as numerous operettas. While living and working in Germany, she became noted for German repertoire singing noted roles including Elsa, Senta, Arabella, Agathe, Marie in Berg's *Wozzeck,* and the title role in Berg's *Lulu*, which she sang at San Francisco Opera. Her name grew, becoming a respected interpreter of Strauss' *Salome* on the international opera scene, where singing, acting and dancing gave Eilana the opportunity to display all of her talents. This role took her around the world, opening doors for debuts in countries from Norway to Japan, cities like Montreal to Seattle, and eventually to Lincoln Center for her New York City Opera debut.

While we can only guess at the thinking of the person who introduced Eilana and Peter to each other in 2007, the logic between the proposed match was clear. Peter, who became 60 that year was an internationally acclaimed conductor and presenter of music concerts and Eilana was an internationally acclaimed soprano whose career was continuing on an upward trajectory. She had made her name becoming a respected interpreter of challenging roles. She was also successful in a number of other major roles such as the title role in the operas Tosca, *Madama Butterfly* and as Mimi in *La Bohème.* Critics described her *Salome* with phrases such as "best ever" and "don't miss it." She sung the title role in a *Salome* performance in 2002 "that churned emotions" in which she demonstrated her ability to act, dance and sing on stage according to music critic Roy Wood, who added: "Lappalainen is an attractive stage presence and moving actress. Lappalainen even did her own, very energetic, dance. I realized that sopranos who perform their own dance, especially one as 'moving' as Lappalainen's, must have a hard time vocally after it. Surely, the dance must wear them out physically and they still have the soprano's showcase to sing! Also, Lappalainen's revelry with... [John the Baptist's] head bordered on the filthy – I loved it."[62] She also proved accomplished and skilled in other roles as well such as the title role in Franz Lehar's *Merry Widow,* which she performed on one of her returns to Canada with the Opera of Ontario, eliciting warm praise from the website Stage Door.com: "In the title role Eilana Lappalainen, a fine actress, gives us a Hanna by turns elegant, folksy, sentimental and wild. She certainly must be one of the few opera singers who can hold her own in a can-can line! The 'Vilja-Lied' in Act 2 is her finest moment."[63]

Eilana Lappalainen's first appearance at MidAmerica Productions was in November, 2005 at Carnegie Hall where she sang Mozart's *Requiem*. There followed four more appearances between April, 2006 and June, 2007 featuring works by Handel, Chilcott, Poulenc and also the Verdi *Requiem*. By that time the professional relationship had taken a romantic turn, and Peter and Eilana were married on September 1, 2007 in the Greek Orthodox Church of Agios Dionysios in Athens. A honeymoon in Italy and France followed as well as, as we will see, an important music engagement in Rome.

Peter and Eilana's union is the story of how two musicians of considerable professional stature who shared an intensity and drive for success built their marriage in the arena of international music. In Peter, Eilana saw the immigrant work ethic that had motivated her parents in Canada. Because of her background she could easily relate to Peter's drive, the way he wished to live for the moment as well as plan ahead, and also the way he built a team of collaborators around him, acknowledging that "it takes a village to succeed."[64] In Eilana, Peter saw someone who could be his life's companion but also his partner professionally. Eilana soon was able to broaden her presence in the musical world by undertaking teaching and mentoring as well as work as an artistic director. Both Eilana and Peter shared a deep commitment to whatever project they were pursuing. Eilana would continue her singing career while becoming more and more involved in MidAmerica's and MidAm International's programming, and in a very significant way in the Festival of the Aegean as well. Neither of them were afraid of confrontation when dealing with a range of obstacles in their way, whether these were local bureaucrats or underperforming artists or employees. Peter and Eilana would very quickly became a formidable duet on and off the stage.

EILANA LAPPALAINEN

But above all Eilana's career as a soprano continued to define her and to impress. One important performance followed the other. In 2008 she was in Leonora's role in a production of Verdi's *Il Trovatore* and music critic William Thomas

Walker wrote in the *Classical Voice of North Carolina:* "I caught part of dramatic soprano Eilana Lappalainen's vocal warm up in the huge assembly room under the auditorium, and I was astonished at the sheer sustained power she could wield. As the tormented Leonora, the Finnish-Canadian singer easily filled Landmark Theater's large auditorium, and her high notes, hit precisely, were spectacular. Her refined, quiet singing was just as impressive."[65] Eilana's career involved a dizzying and very demanding schedule of performing and traveling internationally. She sang in Verdi Galas and recitals in Espoo, Finland, and performed the Verdi *Requiem* in the Czech Republic. She had also sung at a Verdi gala in Japan in 2005. She had done recitals in Germany and California, made her New York recital debut with the Sibelius Society, and also made an Italian Aria performance at Roy Thompson Hall in Toronto. She also sang the Four Last Songs by Strauss with the Romanian Radio Symphony Orchestra and the Filharmonie Katowice with Tiboris conducting. The same city heard her with the Radio Symphony Orchestra in Salome and in June, 2014 she was presented in a DVD in Warsaw singing Beethoven's *Ah! Perfido* with Tiboris conducting in both. In Bari, Italy, Lappalainen sang Wagner's *Wesendonck-Lieder* and in Mexico Mahler's *Fourth Symphony.* She returned to Mexico in 2015 to sing Arabella and Tatjana from *Eugene Onegin* in concert with the State of Mexico Symphony Orchestra of Toluca.

The 2016-2018 seasons brought Eilana Lappalainen to celebrate another debut in Macau, China singing Beethoven. Additionally she sang Haydn's *Mass in Time of War,* Dvořák's *Te Deum* and Vivaldi's *Gloria* at Carnegie Hall. In Florence Italy she performed, Johnson's Song of the Captive, and Beethoven's *Ah! Perfido.* In Vienna she performed the Austrian debut of Mullholland's *Missa Romantica,* Poulenc's *Gloria,* and Mozart's *Requiem.* She was the soprano soloist in Rossini's *Stabat Mater* in Florence & Belluno Italy and Greece. Other concerts included Rossini's *Stabat Mater* and Kodaly's *Te Deum,* as well as her debut in Athens in a grand Opera Gala at the Megaron Mousikis. She also sang the role of Nedda in *I Pagliacci* and the title role in *Madama Butterfly.*

It was an energetic artistic output that would continue, and, importantly, match that of Peter Tiboris.

There was also the administrative and leadership dimension of Eilana Lappalainen's career that developed. She assumed responsibilities such as General Director of the Greek Opera Studio, Berlin Opera Studio, Artistic Director (Opera Division) for the Young Artists Festival Bayreuth, Stage director and vocal teacher for the Young Artists Programs, Festival Manager and Artistic Director Opera Division for the International Festival of the Aegean and the Artistic Administrator for MidAmerica Productions.

STELLA AND ERNEST

Peter's parents moved into Terrace Estates, an assisted living facility in Sheboygan in 2007, while continuing to be members of St. Spyridon Greek Orthodox Church. Stella passed in 2012 at the age of 89. She had been very active in the life of the church, and her obituary notice also mentioned that Stella adored her five grandchildren, Pete, Stephanie, Michael, Deno and Kallie, indulging all five with little gifts in the mail and teaching them Greek words and traditions. When they were little, they made up a silly song called 'YiaYia the Bee' to celebrate how their grandmother (*YiaYia* in Greek) was always keeping busy with those she loved. Peter's father Ernest passed two year later in 2014, at the age of 97. His obituary notice naturally mentioned the significant service he had offered St. Spyridon church, where he had been a member and president of the church board, and that he had been named an Archon in the Order of St. Andrew the Apostle. It also mentioned he had led his sons Peter and Gus by example, which was an understated way of saying that he had played a profound role in shaping their characters and their lives.

PETER TIBORIS IN THE GRANDFATHER'S ROLE

Tiboris was soon to become a grandfather. His son (Ernest) Pete married Christy Ely in 2013. They had met years earlier at Cornell University, and their marriage was a reunion which, as we have seen, was recorded in an article in the *New York Times*.[66] Pete, a Wealth Management Advisor and Christy, a lawyer with the Securities and Exchange Commission, have four children, Dessa, Ernie, Susanna and Selene. Tiboris has two more grandchildren, Stella and Kalliope, the children of his daughter Stephanie, who became a real estate agent and is married to Jon Marotto, a financial analyst.

CHORAL SINGING IN AMERICA IN THE 21ST CENTURY

Undergirding the continued success of MidAmerica Productions was the growing popularity of choral singing in America and the continuing role of New York City as a cultural and tourist destination along with the enduring mystique of Carnegie Hall. We have seen that Chorus America, an advocacy, research, and leadership development organization that advances the choral field, noted, in its '2008 Chorus Impact Study' a significant increase in choral singing across America. It was important for MidAmerica Productions that New York City's popularity would show similar trends.

Luckily, New York City recovered fairly quickly from the effects of the terrorist attacks of 2001 in terms of the number of tourists, especially domestic visitors. Within a few years the number of tourists from America and abroad surpassed the pre-9/11 figures and continued rising steadily. Inevitably, MidAmerica's success in organizing visits by out-of-town organizations to New York in order to perform found imitators. One of the earliest was formed by two former MidAmerica employees, and other companies followed, a backhanded compliment underlining the success of MidAmerica's model. But as Tiboris stresses, MidAmerica's knowledge and exclusive emphasis on music and its outsourcing of the travel and other logistics involved in the visit of the choirs to New York makes it retain its unique character and leadership in its field.

Carnegie Hall's reputation as an iconic venue remained intact throughout this period, which was another advantage for MidAmerica productions. Underneath the main auditorium, the Isaac Stern Auditorium/Ronald O. Perelman Stage which seats 2,804, it created a second venue, the underground Zankel Hall, which opened in in 2003 and seats 599. There is also the intimate and salon-like Weill Hall, with 268 seats. National Public Radio's correspondent Anastasia Tsioulcas, writing in 2012, described Carnegie Hall as one of the most prestigious performance facilities in the world and noted that being able to say you've played at Carnegie Hall might just be one of the ultimate badges of musical honor.[67]

ACADEMY AWARD WINNER OLYMPIA DUKAKIS

It was very appropriate that MidAmerica's third decade began in 2004 with an unusual and unique concert – the kind of event which had become one of the recognizable features of Peter's work. The concert also involved well-known Greek-American film and stage actress Olympia Dukakis and attracted a great deal of media attention. New York Times music critic Allan Kozinn wrote that while Tiboris and MidAmerica were known for big spectacular productions, "huge choral jamborees," nonetheless, Tiboris:

has also presented concerts built around unusual works, particularly huge, neglected choral pieces from the Russian Romantic repertory. Often, a listener leaves with a fair understanding of why the music is rarely heard, but they have been pieces that deserve an airing now and then. And for anyone interested in the odd corners of the repertory that are often ignored, Mr. Tiboris' adventures are worth following... this year, the grand novelty, offered at Carnegie Hall on Wednesday evening, was Agamemnon, a work that Mr. Tiboris billed as an opera by Sergey Taneyev. Actually, it was both less and more than that. Taneyev wrote only one opera, Oresteya, a compressed but still vast setting of Aeschylus' 'Oresteia' trilogy, completed in 1894. 'Agamemnon' is the first act of Oresteya, roughly a third of the work. But Mr. Tiboris offered a bonus. In addition to a slate of vocal soloists, no fewer than three choirs (some arrayed in the balconies) and his Manhattan Philharmonic, Mr. Tiboris invited a handful of actors, including Olympia Dukakis, to read parts of the Aquila Theater Company's version of the Aeschylus text, in a translation by Peter W. Meineck."

Kozinn had mixed views of the way the readings were interpolated into the music, but he concluded his review by stating "Mr. Tiboris moved the performance along ably, drawing some fine playing from the Manhattan Philharmonic, and a robust choral sound from the combined forces of the Russian Chamber Chorus of New York, the Connecticut Choral Society and the New Jersey Choral Society."[68] What the critic did not know was that Olympia Dukakis had appeared very nervous prior to her performance, so much so that Tiboris was concerned, only to be reassured by her agent that when she went on stage she would excel – which was what happened.

Tiboris had met Dukakis by chance and discovered that they both lived in Montclair, New Jersey and subsequently they would stay in touch. They discovered that her mother was born in Megalopolis, in Peloponnesos, near Tripotamo, the village where Peter's grandparents were born. In 2021, when Olympia passed away at the age of 89, Peter issued a statement recalling the performance in 2004:

I presented Olympia at a MidAmerica Productions concert in Carnegie Hall some sixteen years ago, where she ... [was] part of the U.S. premiere of Taneyev's Agamemnon. She was a trifle nervous about doing the reading in Carnegie Hall in the midst of a 200-voice chorus with the Manhattan Philharmonic behind her in this 90-minute concert production, but she overcame this stage situation when she gave a dramatic reading of the role of Clytemnestra. Her 20-minute speech at the end of Act I stole the show. It was, in short, simply overwhelming and captivating. I clearly remember standing on the podium facing the orchestra and chorus with Olympia to my right, and watching and listening to her deliver the role, shaping each word in compelling tones without any musical sound or movement. It was consummate and unforgettable. The audience understandably went wild, and the *New York Times* praised the event as "a significant musical presentation." Several years later, Olympia – with her entire family, including her grandchildren – came to the island of Syros, Greece, and the historic Apollo Theater at my invitation, where she gave two performances of *Rose,* a one-woman play, as part of the Festival of the Aegean. *Rose,* by Martin Sherman, who was also present at the performances, is a monologue. The story is about an 85-year-old Jewish woman who has recently lost her husband. Olympia was sitting shiva on a couch facing the audience; she spoke about her life during the Holocaust, then moving to the U.S. with her husband and raising her family. Olympia and her husband, Louis Zorich, who was also a well-known TV and theater actor, both lived in Montclair, New Jersey, where I also lived. I first met Olympia at the baggage carousel of Newark International Airport as we both arrived at the same time late one Sunday night, two decades ago. From that time, partly because we were both Greek-American, we became good friends. Over the years, I found her to be magical, memorable, dramatic and intense as a performer, as well as a great and captivating artist. On a personal level, we had a warm and engaging friendship. She will be missed.

MidAmerica at Carnegie Hall

MidAmerica Productions continued to be very active in the early 2000s both in terms of bringing choirs to New York and also presenting classical music concerts. In 2004 the company presented 43 classical music and choral concerts at Carnegie Hall and Weill Hall, and 58 the next year with several notable big names appearing, such as the composer Lukas Foss and the mezzo-soprano Jennifer Larmore. The year ended on Thanksgiving weekend with John Rutter conducting the New England Symphonic Ensemble in his own *Mass of the Children* and Handel's *Messiah*. In 2006, the first choral concert presented by MidAmerica was on Martin Luther King weekend and typically involved a number of choirs: Davidson College Concert

Choir, Nyack College Chorale, Charleston County School of Arts Chorale, Seahawk Voices, Perham High School Concert Choir, Forest City First Baptist Church Choir, Cookeville First Baptist Church Choir, Voices of the Mountains, Memphis Christ United Methodist Church Choir and Bluefield College Variations.

With MidAmerica's concerts typically not being considered newsworthy, and with newspaper coverage of classical music concerts being drastically reduced, reviews had become infrequent. A rare performance of Cherubini's French-language opera Medea in the summer of 2006 attracted some attention and praise from *New York Times* critic Bernard Holland: "Maria Callas made much of the title role; our chances to hear the piece, especially in French, are rare. It is a working proposition in this city that those with enough enterprise to put on operas like this will never have the resources to do them properly. Mr. Tiboris' effort – with a good orchestra and the strong Russian Chamber Chorus of New York in front of him – brought us something literate, comprehensible if not always terribly elegant. It is a seller's market. Listeners take what they can get and are grateful. The singers came from Greece, Romania, Spain, Italy, Belgium and the United States. None were household names, and all were probably happy to add Carnegie Hall to their credits... In the title role, the Greek singer Irini Tsirakidou had the good sense to finish strong. Her soprano made the big sound when asked. The top notes are astringent, but they carry and do so with a presence the quieter singing can't quite manage. One was grateful for the passion and forgiving of occasional waywardness."[69]

SURVIVING THE 2008 RECESSION

The entire choral world was naturally impacted by the 2007-2009 economic crisis which was deep and protracted enough to become known as 'the Great Recession' and was followed by what was, by some measures, a long and unusually slow recovery. The recession had a negative impact on attendance at movies and live performances. Art organizations saw budget cuts, endowment losses and in some cases had to close. Classical music was hit hard because it relies on donations and ticket sales. MidAmerica was deeply affected by the recession, because that type of so-called discretionary expenditures choirs would incur in order to travel to New York City would be one of the first to be eliminated in such times. The organization survived by cutting down on expenses and doing fewer concerts. About half the number of concerts that were previously done annually were lost.

Peter recalls the years between 2007 and 2010 as ones that began with drastic

reductions in staff followed by a successful effort to build the company back. The years 2005 to 2007 were the biggest years in the history of MidAmerica Productions, with some 14,000 artists appearing in 40+ concerts – then the recession hit. It had a direct impact on the number of participants in the 2008 series, the total dropping to 3,800 in just one year. It was necessary to reduce the MidAmerica Productions staff from 42 to 6 persons. Peter clearly remembers having an office meeting with the remaining staff and announcing that, despite the global recession, the company was not going to change its business model or its music model. The way he saw things was that his company had become a leader in 15 years and the manner in which it operated would remain the same. It was the only way he and his team knew how to do what they did. Everything of course was scaled down, but the company recovered by 2010 – almost all of the staff who were laid off in 2008 were brought back.

The 25th Anniversary 2009

MidAmerica celebrated its 25th anniversary with a gala performance in Carnegie Hall's Stern Auditorium on Sunday, November 29, 2009. The program featured Peter Tiboris conducting The New England Symphonic Ensemble and the two winners of that year's prestigious Maria Callas Grand Prix, held in March in Athens, Greece – soprano Yun-Jeong Lee and tenor Jaesig Lee. They sang solo works and duets including Donizetti's 'Verrano a te sull'aure' *(Lucia di Lammermoor),* Mozart's 'Der Hölle Rache' *(Die Zauberflöte),* Donizetti's 'Una furtiva lagrima' *(L'elisir d'amore),* Gounod's 'Ah! Je veux vivre' *(Roméo et Juliette),* Donizetti's 'Favorita del re...spirito gentil' *(La favorita),* Rossini's 'Una Voca poco fa' *(Il Barbiere di Siviglia),* Donizetti's 'Ah mes amis...pour mon âme' *(La fille du régiment)* and Rossini's 'Tutto apprendi' *(Guglielmo Tell).* On the same program, John Rutter celebrated his 100th performance with MidAmerica, leading his own *Magnificat* with Sarah Mattox, soprano, and a chorus composed of Columbus East High School Choir, Indiana; First Congregational Church Choir, Fall River, Massachusetts; Columbia Union College Chorale, Takoma Park, Maryland; Hannibal-LaGrange College Concert Choir, Hannibal, Missouri; Woods Chapel Church Choir, Lee's Summit, Missouri; Raytown High School Concert Choir and Camerata, Missouri and Oak Harbor High School Choir, Ohio.

To mark its 25th anniversary MidAmerica proudly produced a brochure with letters of appreciation from important figures in the classical music world. Simon Carrington, Professor of Choral Conducting and Conductor of the Yale Schola

Cantorum at the Yale School of Music wrote: "I remember with particular affection my first concert with MidAmerica when I was rather 'green' and had taken my first position in the U.S. as Director of Choral Activities at the University of Kansas not long before. In addition to the choir, Peter had kindly agreed to allow me to feature a quartet of marvelous Kansas University soloists (two of whom were still undergraduates) in our performance of the Mozart *Coronation Mass* – what a fantastic opportunity for them and for us all. I was beginning to have some success in building the Kansas University program at that time and our trip to Carnegie under your auspices was a huge boost."

Stanley Drucker, Principal Clarinetist, New York Philharmonic, wrote on behalf of himself and his wife Naomi Drucker, also a clarinetist: "What a joy it is to work with our dear friend and colleague Peter Tiboris and to share with him the joy of making music together in some extraordinary events and places. When you start out in a work relationship which becomes a valued friendship, you know that something rare and wonderful has happened. Some highlights of our 14 years together include traveling to the Czech Republic to record the *Krommer Concerto for Two Clarinets on Music for Doubles* (Elysium Recordings, 1998) and performing that concerto in Carnegie Hall with Peter conducting (2000); touring the beautiful Greek islands playing chamber music (1998, 1999, 2000) where we had the most fun of our lives; and [performing in] Weill Recital Hall where I presented an all-Weber program (2003) and we gave a duo recital (2000). MidAmerica Productions has a staff of great people, among them Norman Dunfee, Betsy Stein and Molly Waymire who do a fantastic job in all areas. We wish Peter and his MidAmerica Productions continuous success in all endeavors and send congratulations for 25 years and their many accomplishments!"

Naomi Drucker sent a separate letter, signing as American Chamber Ensemble Co-Director, American Chamber Ensemble Adjunct Assistant Professor of Music, Hofstra University. Her message included words of great appreciation and warmth:

> "Meeting Peter Tiboris changed my life! In addition to the many concerts and special events Stanley and I shared with Peter, my American Chamber Ensemble entered a new chapter under his auspices... I have been very fortunate to have three angels in my life helping to make my lifelong dreams come true, my father Monroe E. Lewis, my husband Stanley Drucker, and my friend Peter Tiboris."

L. William Kuyper, a retired French Hornist of the New York Philharmonic wrote: "In the spring of 1993, I approached Peter Tiboris with my idea for a recording of Robert Schumann's complete works for Winds and Piano, which would feature musicians from the New York Philharmonic. Our mutual friend, Oscar Ravina, a new York Philharmonic violinist, had suggested that I share the idea with Peter, who graciously invited me to meet with him in the old 36th Street offices of MidAmerica Productions. I had heard of MAP and Peter's Manhattan Philharmonic, but I was unprepared for the energy that seemed to overflow from that tight little warren of manic activity. It was a fortunate coincidence that my proposal came at about the time that MAP had launched a new venture – Elysium Recordings, Inc. Peter showed me some new recordings and an impressive plan for others. As the Schumann project developed, I realized that I was involved with a significant company consisting of an efficient, dedicated staff."

THE 30TH ANNIVERSARY SEASON

MidAmerica marked its 30th anniversary season in 2012 with a total of 29 concerts presented at Carnegie Hall, nine of them featuring the New England Symphonic Ensemble. The first was in February, and it included a characteristic mix of high school, college, church and civic choirs. There was also a special anniversary concert held at Avery Fisher Hall, with the New England Symphonic Ensemble with three guest conductors, Daniel R. Alfonso Jr., Patrick K. Freer and Stefan Fraas.

THE 2018 SEASON IN CARNEGIE HALL

MidAmerica Productions' 2018 season, which opened in February in Carnegie Hall, featured MidAmerica's mix of choral and instrumental music along with guest artists and Ensemble Spotlight performances. The season featured such modern classics as Dan Forrest's *Requiem for the Living* and Ola Gjeilo's *Sunrise Mass,* as well as staples that included Handel's *Messiah,* Mozart's *Solemn Vespers* and *Requiem,* Rutter's *Magnificat* and *Requiem,* Orff's *Carmina Burana,* Bach's *Magnificat* and Fauré's *Requiem.* Most importantly, British composer and conductor John Rutter returned to Carnegie Hall and presented the New York premiere of his new work,

Visions, while Candace Wicke conducted Stephen Edwards' *Requiem for My Mother;* her company Continuo Arts collaborated with MidAmerica Productions.

John Rutter made a huge impression on the participants, and they conveyed that in their messages of thanks to Tiboris. Sandy Errante, Conductor, Girls' Choir of Wilmington, was one of the most effusive:

> I want to thank you all for an uplifting and amazing opportunity. My choir members and families were 100% thrilled with the experience this past weekend at Carnegie Hall. Candace did such a wonderful job preparing the children for the rehearsals with John Rutter – she was strict, engaging, and professional. Those kids' eyes did not leave her for a second, and she skillfully united all the voices and pulled the music right out of them. The organization, logistics and facilities were spot on... John Rutter was so gracious and kind to all of the children and their families. If it is possible to communicate this to him, that would be wonderful. His warmth and willingness to sign autographs, and even pose for selfies was such a bonus. The children, of course, wanted to live up to his musical expectations. They were enthralled with the opportunity of working under his direction. They were prepared to work hard and try their best to please the Maestro. But I don't think they were expecting him to embrace them and smile on them as much as he did. They will remember this forever as a musical endeavor and achievement like no other. But, for the many more times that they sing *For the Beauty of the Earth, The Lord Bless You and Keep You, Candlelight Carol, All Things Bright and Beautiful* and so many of the other Rutter pieces in our choral library, they will remember him as the person who composed this music. They will remember his enthusiasm, the 'ding' moment, the Christmas story about wishing for low notes, and the sincerity with which he communicated and connected with them. If music is meant to be the food of love, then surely we had our fill this weekend."

ON THE EVE OF THE PANDEMIC

The calendar year 2019 was very active for MidAmerica Productions. The New England Symphonic Ensemble performed in 14 concerts at Carnegie Hall. The year ended on December 13 with the appearance of the Central Conservatory of Music

Symphony Orchestra of Beijing at Carnegie Hall. With Feng Yu as the conductor, the Symphony performed pieces by Chinese composers Guoping Jia, Wenchen Qin, Weiya Hao, Xiaogang Ye, Jianping Tang, Danbu Chen, Ping Chang, Wenjing Guo – several of their pieces had their U.S. premiere.

Each composer in his own way brings Chinese traditions to symphonic forms, sometimes incorporating folk elements, sometimes in concertos for traditional Chinese instruments.

Composer Feng Yu, who was also the president of the Central Conservatory of Music, expressed the hope that the concert would display the artistic accomplishments of the Central Conservatory of Music and exemplify its creative concept, an artistic philosophy rooted in national creation, embracing the world, and embracing the future. He wished for a great success that would promote contemporary Chinese music and advance a healthy dialogue between musicians and audiences in China and the United States. The next day, MidAmerica began looking ahead to the opening concert which was scheduled for mid-March, 2020.

GOING GLOBAL

Under the rubric 'Appointments and Positions' on his website, Peter Tiboris includes a number of posts he held in orchestras across Europe for various periods since he created MidAm International Inc. in 2004. The listing includes Principal Guest Conductor, Direttore Ospite Principale, Orchestra da Camera Fiorentina Florence, Italy; Founder, Music Director and Conductor, Pan-European Philharmonia Warsaw, Poland; General Music Director and Conductor Symphonisches Orchestra Wien, Vienna, Austria; Principal Guest Conductor Direttore Ospite Principale Collegium Symphonium Veneto, Padova, Italy; Vienna, Austria and Principal Guest Conductor and Honorary Conductor Bohuslav Martinou Philharmonic Zlin, Czech Republic.

This impressive list was the tip of the iceberg of what was an interrelated and overlapping range of activities that consisted of MidAm residencies of choirs abroad, and Tiboris conducting some of their concerts but also being invited to conduct orchestras in the same countries as the residencies took place or in other countries.

The international trips for the choirs MidAm International organized usually involved a ten-day stay. It is widely acknowledged that touring abroad has many benefits for American choirs. These include building camaraderie and unity, collaborating with choruses in foreign cultural environments, gaining perspective by seeing how other cultures do things differently – from serving food to organizing rehearsals and concerts. Traveling together can build a choral program through intense shared artistic experiences. Touring can also generate publicity for a chorus, which helps in recruiting and retaining members, and can raise an ensemble's stature nationally or internationally.[70]

Concurrently with the growth of MidAmerica Productions and MidAm International Tiboris continued his conducting career on a global scale. His performances garnered widespread acclaim from one end of Europe to the other. For example the *Gazetta del Nordebarese*, a newspaper in Barletta, Italy, proclaimed in a January 2009 headline, that Tiboris' music held the public "spellbound" while in February 2009, the *Oxford Times* in England said of his performance of Tchaikovsky's *Fifth Symphony:* "Tiboris drew an open, transparent sound from the Philomusica (not always an easy thing to do in the Sheldonian), and expertly tying march tempi, so that woodwind solo passages had time to breathe."

It is difficult to pinpoint the residencies concerts in Europe which were the most special, given Tiboris' commitment to engage in as many countries as possible. But a few stand out in his memory:

ITALY

Soon after his honeymoon with Eilana the Fall of 2007, Peter traveled to Rome where his agent there had arranged for him to conduct an orchestra in a ballet performance based on *Peer Gynt*, the incidental music to Henrik Ibsen's 1867 play of the same name, written by the Norwegian composer Edvard Grieg in 1875. It was the first ever time he would conduct such a performance, but he accepted the challenge and began rehearsals earlier than normal. A few days into the rehearsal, a distinguished-looking woman arrived on the set, at which point the entire cast stood up and burst into applause. The agent had not told Peter that the role of Peer Gynt's mother would be played by the legendary ballet dancer Carla Fracci, the so-called "Maria Callas of dance" and an Italian cultural icon. Peter considered meeting and working with Fracci, with whom he became close friends, as a welcome reward for accepting the challenge of conducting *Peer Gynt*. The performance was so successful that it was named as the best ballet performance in Italy that year. Offers to Peter poured in from other ballet companies, but he restricted his venture into that type of conducting to two or three more occasions.

There would be many happy returns to Italy, as for example in June, 2015 when Tiboris conducted Beethoven's *Coriolan Overture* and *Symphony No. 7* plus Schubert's *Mass in G* at Auditorium di Santo Stefano di Ponte in Florence as part of MidAmerica Productions' 'Great American Choirs in Firenze Series'. Back in Florence in 2019, Tiboris led the Orchestra da Camera Fiorentina in Beethoven's *Fidelio* Overture and *Pastoral* Symphony, and the Schubert *Mass in G* with visiting choirs from the United States. One return to Italy that was almost not as happy as the rest was when Tiboris was invited to conduct in the town of Bari on Italy's Adriatic coast by Marco Rienzi. He went there to do a performance of orchestra music which featured Chopin's Piano Concerto No. 1 – or so he thought. He arrived in Bari at the hotel and as he was checking in he saw the poster advertising the concert of music, and it listed, not the Chopin first piano concerto, but Chopin's *Piano Concerto No. 2* – which he had never conducted. Evidently his office had assumed he was doing the first piano concerto which he had done often. Maestro Tiboris had brought the wrong music with him! He quickly overcame his shock, delayed the rehearsals for a day and began reviewing the *Piano Concerto No. 2*. He found its second movement astonishingly beautiful and it was one that has always stayed with him.

Austria, Czech Republic, Poland and Portugal

MidAm International could not but be associated with Vienna, the city considered as the world capital of classical music. More famous composers have lived in Vienna than any other city in the world including Austrians such as Mozart, Haydn, Mahler and Bruckner; others, such as Beethoven, Gluck and Brahms came from other countries in Europe. Events organized in that city by MidAm International included music tours to Vienna by American conductors at the Peterkirche (St. Peter's), an early 18th century church with an impressive baroque interior which is known for its classical Viennese concerts and concerts. In 2017 there was a concert at the Votivkirche church in Vienna, when Tiboris conducted the Vienna Symphonic Opera which performed Mozart's *Requiem* and his *Symphony No. 40* in G minor. The program informs us that the singers included soprano Eilana Lappalainen, mezzo Melody Wilson, tenor Walker J. Jackson, bass/baritone Falko Hönisch and choirs from Arizona, New Jersey, New Mexico, Omaha and Oregon. In 2019, at another of Vienna's historic venues, the Minoriten Church, Michael J. Glasgow gave the European premiere of his *Requiem*; Mark W. Bartel led Mozart's *Coronation Mass*;

and R. Paul Crabb conducted Poulenc's Gloria. Tiboris conducted Beethoven's *Pastoral* Symphony and the Mozart *Requiem*.

In 2017 Tiboris and Eilana Lappalainen gave guest performances with the Moravian Philharmonic in Olomouc, Czech Republic. Their repertoire included works by Verdi, Puccini, Catalani, Ponchielli and Tchaikovsky.

Warsaw, the city in which Frédéric Chopin grew up, became a very important base of operations for Peter Tiboris. In 2008 he founded the Pan-European Philharmonia which a plays throughout Europe, records and is the resident orchestra of the Festival of the Aegean in Syros, Greece each summer. Jakub Fiebig served as the Philharmonia's executive director. Among its many performances, one that stands out was in Warsaw in 2018 and was titled 'Tiboris at 70' and at which Tiboris conducted the orchestra playing Tchaikovsky's *Symphony No. 5*. The following year also in Warsaw, Tiboris led the Pan-European Philharmonia in Tchaikovsky's *Symphony No. 4*.

Following a concert in Bulgaria, Tiboris got to know music presenter Nikolay Lalov, and Tiboris established another beachhead, this one in Lisbon, Portugal for the purposes of establishing residencies. In 2019 he conducted the Orquestra de Câmara de Cascais e Oeiras in Beethoven's *Symphony No. 7* at the Basilica Estrela in Lisbon.

Tiboris ventured beyond Europe as well. He made his Asian conducting debut in Macau in 2016, leading the Macau Symphony Orchestra, the Taipei Philharmonic Chorus; and soloists Songmi Yang, mezzo-soprano; Dongwon Shin, tenor; and Yoo Ji Hoon, baritone; in Schubert's *Stabat Mater* and *Tantum ergo*, and Beethoven's *Mass in C*.

THE GREEK AND GREEK-AMERICAN CONNECTIONS

Aside from the Festival at Syros, Tiboris' contacts and presence with Greece multiplied, as did with his involvement with the Greek Orthodox Church in America. Tiboris had always collaborated with fellow artists who were Greek or of Greek origin, not favoring them over others in any way but instead being there to help their careers. One of his closest Greek associates was the composer Dinos Constantinides. Asked to comment on MidAmerica's 25th anniversary, he recalled he had been connected with Peter from the beginning: "In the first concert on

January 7, 1984, at Lincoln Center, Peter included on the program two works of mine with the theme 'Antigone of Sophocles'. They fit the occasion as both Peter and I share Greek heritage. Since then, I have always been a witness and sometimes participant in the admirable achievements of Peter and MidAmerica. Recently, with the inclusion in his activities of opera performances in my native Greece, my interest and approbation are even stronger."

Other Greek-Americans tried to show their gratitude with more than words. On Peter Tiboris' first performance of Verdi's *Requiem* at Lincoln Center, he engaged the wonderful Greek-American contralto Yeorgia Magremis. Born Georgia Magrames in Mishawaka, Indiana, in 1935, to parents who had both emigrated from the Peloponnese region, she studied at De Pauw University and graduated from the Indiana University School of Music with a B.A. She continued her studies at the National Conservatory of Music in Athens. When she began her musical career in the 1960s, she changed her name to Yeoryia Megremis, a transliteration she considered more faithful to the original Greek, and moved to New York City, where she lived in the Ansonia Hotel near Lincoln Center for many years. The historic Beaux-Arts building, once a haven for musicians, became a landlord-tenant battleground for many years, and Yeoryia told stories about her role on the front line of the activists in the days of lawsuits and rent strikes. Highlights of her career included a 1966 debut recital at Carnegie Hall and a benefit concert she presented in South Bend, Indiana for the Valley of Promise Foundation for handicapped children. For several summers she performed in summer productions in Rome, New York., playing such roles as the Mother Abbess in *The Sound of Music*.

Tiboris became friends with Yeorgia and respected her talents, noting that "she brought dramatic flair to the quartet of singers." But on the very day of that performance at 8 pm everyone had come to the stage to perform the Requiem except Magremis, and this made Tiboris extremely nervous especially when it was 5 minutes prior to 'curtain' and the orchestra and chorus were on stage and the quartet was waiting for him to walk on together with Yeorgia. Tiboris describes what happened next: "All of a sudden, we all hear her coming up the stairs from the street to the stage saying loudly, 'I am here, I am here!'" Why was she late? Because she was bringing a large tray of baklava, the traditional Greek pastry she had been preparing as a gift for Peter. It had taken longer to bake than she anticipated! At the time, Tiboris did not think it was very funny but now, looking back he has fond memories of Yeorgia and of that particular incident.

AN OPERA ABOUT THE PARTHENON MARBLES

Tiboris' international engagements included an increasingly strong Greek dimension. In May, 2012 he was the conductor of a very original opera with a theme very dear to the Greeks. It was titled *Opus Elgin: The Destruction of the Parthenon* a two-act opera by Theodore C. Stathis. The performance was in the Megaron Mousikis, the new Athens concert hall. It was described as an original work concerning the story of the plundering of the Parthenon and Greece's demand that the Parthenon marbles be returned. The work was directed by Christophoros Christofis, the set designer was Yiannis Varelas and the choreographer, Ersi Pitta. The soloists were Nina Lotsari soprano, Eleni Davou mezzo-soprano, Dionisis Sourbis baritone and Dimitris Kavrakos bass. *Opus Elgin: The Destruction of the Parthenon* portrayed the story of looting and of the Parthenon Marbles by Lord Elgin in the early nineteenth century. The composer, Theodore Stathis, had also composed the opera *Antigone*, which had premiered the previous year at the Megaron Mousikis, receiving rave reviews. *Opus Elgin* was made up of ten successive scenes, most of which take place on the Acropolis. The last scene begins in the hall of the British Museum, where the marbles are displayed, and ends with a teleconference between the British Museum and the brand new Museum of Acropolis in Athens. The event was organized by Imeros, which is a non-profit organization for Cultural Development created for the purpose of raising awareness of Greece's demand that the marbles be returned to their place of origin. The date of the performance, May 29th, 2012, coincided with the date officials from the organizing committee of the London Olympics of 2012 would participate in the official lighting of the 'Olympic Flame' in Olympia, Greece.

AT THE ATHENS CONCERT HALL

The first big concert in Athens that MidAmerica organized at the Megaron Mousikis was a grand gala with arias from works by Verdi, Bizet, Giordano and Mascagni, taking place in July, 2018. The arias were among the finest of the operatic repertoire: *Un ballo in maschera, La forza del destino, Rigoletto, Nabucco, Tosca, Carmen, Les pêcheurs de perles, Turandot* and *La Traviata*. The international cast consisted of soprano Eilana Lappalainen, tenor Gian Luca Pasolini, bass/baritone Carry Perrson, more than 300 choristers from the United States and Greece, and in its first appearance in Athens, the Warsaw Pan-European Philharmonia conducted by Peter Tiboris, with guest conductor Giovanni Pacor and chorus master David R. Thye. Wishing to familiarize Greek choirs with the choirs from America that were performing, Tiboris offered a number of free tickets to members of choirs who belonged to the Hellenic Choirs Association. The association was established in 2002 as a non-profit organization aiming to represent amateur choirs and promote choral song in Greece. Currently it has 116 member-choirs.

THE ARCHBISHOP IAKOVOS LEADERSHIP 100 FUND

Considering that Peter's career as a conductor began in earnest following his New York City debut at a conference in honor of Greek Orthodox Archbishop Iakovos, it was fitting that he became a member of the Archbishop Iakovos Leadership 100 Fund. It is a non-profit organization whose mission is to advance the Orthodox Faith and the life-giving legacy of Hellenism in America through support of the National Ministries of the Greek Orthodox Archdiocese of America. Members contribute a total of $100,000 over a period of ten years. Peter became a fully-paid-up member in 2008. As part of the 24th annual Leadership 100 Conference, in Orlando, Florida in 2014 Tiboris conducted the Orlando Philharmonic Orchestra in 'Symphony at Sunset', featuring Eilana Lappalainen. The special program included the University of Central Florida Choir of 60 members in a performance of the Mikis Theodorakis *Zorba Suite Ballet* 'Finale'. The highlight was Eilana's performance of Beethoven's *Ah! Perfido*. Other selections conducted by Tiboris, in addition to the Greek National Anthem and the *Star Spangled Banner,* were the Overtures of Verdi's *La forza del Destino,* Mozart's *The Marriage of Figaro*, and *B*eethoven's *Symphony No. 9*. Tiboris conducted a concert the following year as well at the organization's conference in Arizona.

REFLECTIONS AT 70

In 2016 Peter was a year shy of his 70th birthday and in a position to reflect back on his life and his career. He shared his perspectives with Choral Net, which is the website of the American Choral Directors Association.[71] Following some introductory remarks he outlined his reflections in eleven points to which he would add a twelfth later on, along with a quotations from Fernando Pessoa, the Portuguese poet and modernist writer:

> I began looking back on my 60-plus years of music study and performance, which began in 1952 when I first took piano lessons from Mrs. Meyer at age 5, and then, two years later, when I became church organist at the St. Spyridon Greek Orthodox Church in Sheboygan, Wisconsin (my father, a dentist, was the choir director). Why I began this exercise on this subject, I am not sure. What, after all, did I learn over a lifetime of thinking about, studying, preparing and performing music?
>
> I began writing down these 'essentials' of my music world, which began in that Lake Michigan town and continued at the University of Wisconsin (BM and MS) and the University of Illinois (Ed. D.). Thereafter, for the next 10 years, I taught music at a piano studio and at public middle and high school, junior college, and university levels – all of which contributed to my decision in 1983 to move to NYC and create MidAmerica Productions and MidAm International; the move was prompted by my desire to find greater diversity and challenges than I had previously experienced. Now, after 35 years in New York City and a thousand-plus concerts in NYC and world-wide as a conductor and presenter, I am writing about what I have learned as I have grown and evolved as a musician and conductor. Here are some of my thoughts:
>
> 1. **Know Thyself:** Attributed to Socrates and inscribed on the Temple of Apollo in Delphi, Greece. Why is music important? Why is one a musician? Why did I feel this was the only road I wanted to take in my professional life?
>
> 2. **Before You Conduct,** Have the Entire Score 'In Your Ear': Know in advance what you are expecting to hear. You cannot rehearse or perform any work unless you 'own it' prior to the first gesture.
>
> 3. **Understand What Makes for a Great Work of Music:** I learned that there are six important and critical aesthetic factors: Unity, Complexity, Intensity, Proportion, Blend, and Balance (all attributed to American

aesthetician Monroe Beardsley, 1915-1985). When these notions work together, there is a deep, unforgettable and satisfying feeling. A composer attempts to achieve these in a composition and a conductor attempts to bring these characteristics to light through his artists. This was the most important idea I learned while at the University of Illinois.

4. **Choose Music to Perform that is Worthy of Your Precious Time.**

5. **Conduct Your Music, as Much as Possible, from Memory:** Doing so will free up your hearing. Looking at a score while you conduct cuts down dramatically on what you are hearing. As the great conductor Herbert von Karajan said, "There is nothing to look at except your performers, so listen with your eyes."

6. **Learn the Basics of Latin, Italian, German and French:** The vast majority of the most important western vocal music is in these four languages.

7. **Lead Your Music Performances, but Let the Composition Dictate Your Gestures.**

8. **Learn to Conduct by Watching and Listening to Other Conductors:** I recommend familiarizing yourself with the Berlin Philharmonic's digital concerts live, in archives and interviews. This became, for me, an invaluable tutoring source for all repertoire provided by the great orchestra and all their guest conductors going back to the 1930s. I highly recommend viewing on YouTube, 'The Art of Conducting: Great Conductors of the Past'.

9. **Don't Over-Conduct:** Let the artists sing. Let them play. Conductors make no sound, but they can make music. Make gestures when you need to guide the interpretation, create the drama, and mold the tender moments.

10. **Every Time One Conducts it is an Audition,** either in rehearsal or in concert.

11. **Know the 'Form' of the Work You are Conducting:** Form dictates everything and is dictated by the composer. The composer's intentions are central to understanding and conveying a performance.

12. **There is no greater collaboration between conductor and ensemble than when the performers under your direction want to perform for you:** When that happens, there is no limit as to what the conductor can ask of his or her performers and musical magic will occur.

And, finally, listen to these words from Fernando Pessoa (1888 to 1935), Poet, Author, Writer, Philosopher: "The value of life is not in the time it lasts, but in the intensity in which it is lived. Make life about unforgettable moments, unexplained events and incomparable people."

ON THE GREAT COMPOSERS

In discussing the greatest composers, Tiboris starts by saying that along with Mozart and Haydn, Beethoven is the most important classical composer in the history of music: "I am a great lover of his music. I perform it often and each time it is a revelation. The depth of Beethoven's musical understanding was and is simply astonishing and ever-lasting. He was an historic music radical smashing the door of the historic period of Romanticism wide open and he changed music, forever. Among his most revered and loved collection of works are his nine symphonies. Each of them is a jewel of extreme musical power and understanding. They are loved throughout the world and will never cease to be loved and played and studied. It is said that of the nine symphonies the ones which are the most popular are the 1st, the 3rd, the 5th, the 7th and the 9th (Ode to Joy). I have conducted most of them and consider them all to be gems, giant works by a musical giant."

Yet in Tiboris' case the work he has conducted – and recorded – and which he found the most intriguing is Beethoven's *Symphony No. 6*, the Pastoral. He loves and has the highest regard for the 1st, the 3rd, the 5th, the 7th and 9th symphonies, but for Tiboris:

The 6th is unique because it is a 'programmatic' work, meaning, it is the only symphony of his which is based on depicting the natural world. Beethoven was a musical purist and wrote music for it's own sake and own sounds. But here, he had nature in mind and the five movements in this work depict it

in sound. This was what classical composers such as Beethoven have always avoided but in this case he made an exception and what he did in doing this was historic and monumental because it pointed towards the Romantic Period of music making, which followed his death in 1827. From that year forward, programmatic-music took center stage for all composers. So what did he do with this programmatic idea in the sixth symphony? The music in this symphony tries to make one feel he or she is in nature, in the forest, among birds and animals; the sounds of the orchestra are written to give you that feeling. Movements 1, 2 and 3 are about beautiful walks in the forest and what you see and feel about being alone on such walks. At the same time, it is beautifully written with grace and elegance. One hears the mimicking of birds and other animals sounding from within the orchestra in beautiful fashion – memorable. Then, what happens in the fourth movement is simply extraordinary... a gigantic storm occurs with thundering timpani and brass and aggressive playing from everyone for about 10 minutes. It is absolutely frightening. Swirling wind sounds from the piccolo, aggressive thundering from the timpani, and on and on and on... washes of wind and rain and on and on. It is what you would hear and feel if you were actually in a real storm in a forest, and he turned that feeling into musical form. Those ten minutes for a musician can be life-changing, and for me they were. What happens in the fifth movement, which ends the 55-minute symphony? Calm and sweetness are reinstated, telling you the "storm has passed," and you are back to the world described in the first three movements. The entire experience is astonishing and this *Symphony No. 6* is very difficult to play and, therefore, not heard often. I love it and perform it often, and when I do, audiences and symphony players find it dramatic and a revelation.

Aside from the nine symphonies, Beethoven's body of music is astonishing and large, including string quartets, trios, piano sonatas, concerti and so forth, Tiboris notes, however: "The works which stand out for me are his piano concerti, especially the fifth and his mid-boggling 90 minute choral/orchestral work *Missa Solemnis*. *The Fifth Piano Concerto* is one of the great masterworks of all time and the second movement (largo) is among the most beautiful of all musical compositions. I can't hear it enough, and I have conducted it with Dimitri Sgouros in Syros as part of the Festival of the Aegean. It is mesmerizing and very difficult to play for the pianist. Sgouros, at 17 years of age, played it in magnificent and memorable fashions. The *Missa Solemnis* for large chorus, large orchestra and four incredible soloists, is a towering 90 minute work akin to Bach's *Mass in B minor.* I heard if for the first time in 1980 in New Orleans at the National American Choral Directors convention with the choral icon Robert Shaw conducting the New Orleans Symphony Orchestra. It was simply over-powering. Never to be forgotten."

Wolfgang Amadeus Mozart, Tiboris goes on to say, is a genius in a class of his own. He notes that Mozart was coached and guided by his father Leopold and adds, "in an incredibly short life he composed 626 works, including 41 symphonies and 27 operas, and hundreds of chamber works and choral works – the most prolific classical composer who ever lived and most beloved. In the same 'class' as Beethoven and Haydn. I am a great Mozart lover. I can't say enough. I have conducted his greatest works and am always astonished at their beauty and complexity and long-lasting effect on me. He was essentially a composer for voice and even his instrumental music has that quality of elegance. In conducting his operas, as I have done, I sometimes will think as I am conducting, 'how does a mortal make such beauty and artistry and make it alive? How can this happen?' But it does – with him. The works I admire most are *Requiem, Così Fan Tutte,* the Symphonies nos. 35, 40 and 41 and *Don Giovanni.*

Johann Sebastian Bach, in Tiboris' words, is "clearly one of the greatest and most towering music figures in the Baroque period. Oddly enough, I have not conducted a great deal of Bach's towering works such as his *St. Matthew Passion* or his *Mass in B Minor* or the *St. John Passion* or his *Magnificat.* He was a prolific composer and a giant like Beethoven, Mozart, and Haydn, most of his music being religious in substance. What I do remember about my student days is Professor Robert Monschein in music history at the University of Wisconsin-Madison taking the Mass in B Minor apart over the period of a semester and, as a graduate student, being transfixed on the complexity of this composer's towering work, hoping some day that I would conduct this two- hour masterpiece, which, as of today, I have not done. It is on my bucket list."

Tiboris concluded his reflections on the great composers by saying, "My personal music conducting has always been classical. I think the reason for less Bach compared to my conducting Beethoven, Haydn and Mozart is that it takes extraordinary musicians of high caliber and I just was too young to grapple with this work at the university level."

In what would be yet another big step in his career, Tiboris would bring the music of these and other major composers to his ancestral homeland when he created the Festival of the Aegean. It would be a return to his roots armed with decades of musical experience.

Peter conducting in 2015 in Carnegie Hall

PETER IN OXFORD UK GUEST CONDUCTING THE OXFORD PHILHARMONIC,
BEETHOVEN'S SYMPHONY #6 "PASTORAL"

PETER AND ELIANA IN MONTCLAIR, NEW JERSEY

PETER AND ELIANA AT DINNER IN PARIS

PETER IN THE APOLLO THEATER, ISLAND OF SYROS GREECE

JOHN RUTTER, CBE

GUSTAV MAHLER'S
1895 re-orchestration of
BEETHOVEN
SYMPHONY No. 9

Leah Anne Myers, soprano
Ilene Sameth, mezzo-soprano
James Clark, tenor
Richard Conant, bass-baritone

Brno Philharmonic Orchestra
Janáček Opera Choir

conducted by
Peter Tiboris

BRIDGE ®
BRIDGE 9033

PETER'S FIRST CD

CHAPTER SIX

THE FESTIVAL OF THE AEGEAN

Music isn't what I do, it is who I am — Raquel Castro

To understand the significance of the Festival of the Aegean that Peter Tiboris created one has to consider its place in the long tradition of musical and theatrical performances in Modern Greece. It began with the creation of the Athens Festival by the Greek government in 1955 for the purpose of promoting artistic and theatrical creation, and by extension promote tourism in the summer months. In the first year the festival featured conductor Dimitri Mitropoulos and the New York Philharmonic. Since then summer festivals mushroomed throughout Greece, over a third of them on one of the islands like Syros that were tourist attractions. Several of these were focused on classical music (referred to by some as western art music) and over the years their number increased despite an economic crisis that Greece experienced for about a decade beginning in 2009. Writing during the crisis, a scholar noted "the explosion of festivals of western art music in contemporary Greece as well as their persistence under unfavorable circumstances over the last

few years should undoubtedly be viewed in association with the main functions these festivals serve. Indeed, in a country where the familiarity with this musical tradition and its popularity are even lower than in most other European countries, the blossoming of such festival is less about satisfying an existing large demand than a question of increasing the supply in order to serve the key purposes these festivals serve, namely education, networking and tourism."[72]

The Festival of the Aegean served all three of those purposes effectively and did much more. In terms of education, one could argue that the Tiboris artistic and business model already had an inherent emphasis on education in that it enabled amateur choirs to perform on a grand stage and encounter new conductors and new ways of doing things. This would also apply to the choirs Tiboris would invite to Syros and the many young singers from Greece and elsewhere who had the opportunity to sing in the operas staged on Syros. And as we will see, Tiboris' partner Eilana Lappalainen, while maintaining her focus on her career as an internationally known soprano, would establish a type of workshop that offered young singers training and new opportunities.

The networking of the music world at festivals is a win-win for everyone involved. Tiboris himself benefitted through being invited to conduct in other places in Europe, but at the same time his invitees were able to connect with each other and Greek artists. With regard to tourism, while there are no exact figures, when one sees that in one year four hundred choristers arrived to participate in the festival, the benefits to the local tourist industry and the island as a whole are obvious. The Municipality, cognizant of the significance of the festival, did not charge for the use of public spaces or the work that was involved for its staff. A respondent to an academic survey stated that in July, Syros lived off the Festival of the Aegean, which attracted so many participants from around the world. Moreover, one of the reasons that festival was more popular than another one that existed on the island, the International Music festival of Cyclades, was that Tiboris' festival focused on opera and symphonic music but the other one on chamber music.[73]

That said, there are considerable risks in staging a classical music festival on a small Aegean island with a population of 20,000 and which in the peak year of 2019 saw 200,000 arrivals during the June-September tourist season. The risks involve local administrative support and permits in a country with a notoriously byzantine bureaucracy, the strengths and weaknesses of the local infrastructure and the attitudes of the local population in a country in which there is an ingrained suspicion towards entrepreneurial innovation. And then, to get more specific, there is the need to stage the type of music that will be accessible to the broader public and will be attuned, literally and metaphorically, to a public that is enjoying a summer vacation on the beaches and is not likely to gravitate to more sophisticated forms of evening entertainment.

These multiple demands, difficult as they were, all fell within Tiboris' wheelhouse. If there was one person who believed that the phrase "If you build it, they will come" could apply to an Aegean island during the height of the summer tourist season, that was Peter Tiboris. Tiboris' legendary stubbornness combined with his charisma were tailor-made for dealing with the Greek bureaucracy and the frustrations that this encounter could generate, which were tempered by his love of Greece and determination to bring classical music to the land of his ancestors. One thing that works in Greece is knowing the right people in the right places and, if not, getting to know them and getting them on your side, something that was one of Tiboris' strengths. And as for presenting an appropriate repertoire, Tiboris was well aware of what would work. There would be none of the somewhat marginal or forgotten composers or compositions with which he often treated the more sophisticated audiences in New York City. The names that would appear in the Festival of the Aegean programs were all familiar ones, from Beethoven to Puccini and from Mozart to Rossini. Tiboris' preference for the classics rather than the more modernist twentieth century composers was a perfect fit for the Festival of the Aegean on Syros.

"A MAN WALKED INTO A THEATER ONE DAY..."

"Tiboris' plans, which we considered to be ambitious at first and, to a degree, pipe dreams, nonetheless were realized and were successful. The festival turned into a widely acclaimed cultural event and became an international cultural magnet that brought many friends of the musical arts to our island."[74] Those are the words of longtime mayor of the town of Ermoupolis on the Cycladic island of Syros. In a sense, Dekavallas was confirming that he had joined the group of persons to whom Peter Tiboris had confided ambitious 'pipe dreams' and who were happily surprised to witness their fruition. The earliest members of that group that was born back in the 1980s were Gene Carr, who was then the executive director of the American Symphony Orchestra, and fellow Greek-American composer Dinos Constantinides. Dekavallas was referring to his first meeting with Tiboris in 1999 in the mayor's office in Ermoupolis, Syros. At that particular moment in his career, Peter had conducted in several venues in Greece over the years but was now looking for somewhere where he could acquire a base and remain there organizing music events every summer. He was on the island of Mykonos, and met the mayor of Mykonos, Christos Veronis and the well-known art collector and hotelier Dimitri Tsitouras who would become a very close friend and advisor. Tsitouras had introduced him to several key persons on Mykonos who helped in connection with those concerts. They included hotel owner Stavros Gladzis, Tassos Stamboglis and Dimitri and Alexandra Oluf. At that point Tiboris had done six concerts in eight years, four chamber music concerts in the *Pnevmatiko Kentro* (Cultural Center) and two at the Laka outdoor theater. By then Mykonos was already established as a high-end destination tourist island in the Aegean known for its nightlife and gay-friendly culture. There was no local infrastructure nor the ability of the local authorities to devote resources in supporting the type of bigger and more regular classical music festival Tiboris had in mind. This group of people he connected with on Mykonos encouraged him to go to the nearby island of Syros and explore the possibility of doing concerts at the Apollo theater in Ermoupolis, the island's capital.

He chose Syros, which turned out to be another good decision, encouraged by Dimitri Tsitouras, who had tried to set something up for Tiboris on the island of Mykonos which had not worked out. By then Mykonos was already established as a high-end destination tourist island in the Aegean known for its nightlife and gay-friendly culture. There was no local infrastructure nor the ability of the local authorities to devote resources to supporting the type of classical music festival Tiboris had in mind. Syros is an island that belongs to the same cluster of whitewashed Aegean islands, known as the Cyclades. Although Syros could not compete as an international tourist destination with Mykonos or Santorini it possessed its own version of Cycladic island beauty and it also had its own homegrown cosmopolitan character because of the presence of a Catholic community, a legacy of Venetian rule in the medieval period. And back in the nineteenth century Syros in the age of sailing ships was one of the wealthiest commercial and shipbuilding ports in the Eastern Mediterranean.

In the meantime, Dimitri Tsitouras remained a close friend and a mentor of sorts, interpreting Greek reality for Peter Tiboris and encouraging him in his venture on Syros. A lawyer by training, Tsitouras had come into contact with Greece's literary elite when, as a student, he worked at a major bookstore in Athens. He would subsequently because a major figure in the Greek world of art collecting. Initially, he followed his father's footsteps into the law profession but at the age of forty he decided to become a designer and hotelier on Santorini, achieving international prominence. Tsitouras soon became one of the most respected experts in home decoration in all of Greece. He took a liking to Tiboris and became his unofficial advisor and guide on issues of local etiquette and good taste in Peter's professional and personal life.

THE APOLLO THEATER, SYROS ISLAND

Mayor Dekavallas evidently thought there was something in Tiboris' enthusiasm about the possibility of establishing a regular presence in Syros and went with him to see the Apollo Theater, right next to Ermoupolis' grandiose square in front of the imposing neoclassical municipal building. Peter Tiboris had been overawed – stunned – when he saw the building earlier and even more so when he entered the Apollo Theater. He made up his mind there and then that Syros was going to be his artistic summer home in Greece and told Dekavallas as much when he returned to visit the theater again with him. He added that one day he would be performing an opera again in that very space because an opera house is not an opera house without hosting performances. Years later he wrote the following words in the 2014 program of the Festival of the Aegean: "I remember coming to Syros from Mykonos some years ago, wondering if it was really possible that there was a great opera theater on this small but important Cycladic Island. But from the moment I walked up the eleven steps and through the doors and into the theater, my doubts were blown away. This was the same feeling, I might add, that I had experienced when I entered Carnegie Hall for the first time on November 24, 1983. How was it possible that there was such a magnificent theater on this Cycladic Island? I consider myself so fortunate to have arrived at the theater at that particular time in my life." And this was thanks to the encouragement he had got from Dimitri Tsitouras.

The building was befitting an island that had witnessed such great prosperity and the comings and goings of European and Greek merchants. It was constructed between 1862-1864. Designed by the Italian architect Pietro Sampo, it is an architectural jewel of Syros and remains to this day one of the oldest indoor theatres of modern times as well and the eleventh oldest opera house in Europe.

It is widely believed that the Apollo Theater was modeled after the famous La Scala di Milano Opera House in Milan – it is known as La Piccola Scala – however, other influences are evident as well. The auditorium and the double arch of the proscenium with Corinthian columns trace their influence to La Scala in Milan, the restored Teatro San Carlo di Napoli, the theater at Castelfranco near Venice and the Teatro della Pergola in Florence. The dome and its support follow the French architectural traditions of the 19th century. The inaugural performance at the Apollo Theatre appears to have been the opera *La Favorita* by Gaetano Donizetti on October 3, 1864, although other sources claim the first performance was *Rigoletto* by Giuseppe Verdi on April 20, 1864. Opera and theater performances became the center of the cultural life in Ermoupoli; contemporary reports of foreign travelers remark on the sumptuous staging of the operas and plays, and the well-dressed and 'chic' audience. The Apollo Theatre played host to numerous Greek and Italian theatrical and operatic troupes.

The slow decline of Ermoupolis' economy when steamships began replacing ships with sails brought a steady reduction of opera performances, and they were replaced by performances featuring Greek theater companies. During World War II, the building suffered damage and ultimately in the 1950s the theatre was deemed unsuitable for performances. Attempts to renovate it stalled, but reconstruction work began in the 1980s and the theater reopened in 2000 after a long period of careful restoration with a team headed by architect Petros Pikionis under the auspices of the Ministry of Culture, with the assistance of the Municipality of Ermoupoli.

THE FESTIVAL OF THE AEGEAN IS BORN, JULY 2005

Greece, despite the fact that is it a modern nation that belongs to the European Union, is not a country known for its openness to new ideas and new projects. A certain complacency and satisfaction with the ways things were always done and an unwillingness to take risks are all common in Greece, in sharp contrast with the openness to taking chances and trying something new which is a characteristic of many diaspora Greeks. In a famous anecdote from Herodotus' *Histories* of the 5th century BCE, a messenger from Periander, the tyrant of Corinth, asks Thrasybulus the tyrant of Miletus for advice on ruling. Thrasybulus, instead of responding, takes the messenger for a walk in a field of wheat, where he proceeds to cut off all of the best and tallest ears of wheat. The message, correctly interpreted by Periander, was that a wise ruler would preempt challenges to his rule by 'removing' those prominent men who might be powerful enough to challenge him. It is a story that modern

Greeks are fond of reciting to illustrate contemporary dislike on the part of the status quo of a proposal out of the ordinary.

Tiboris himself does not like to dwell on the obstacles he faced on the way of creating the Festival of the Aegean. The only thing he says in that respect is that if he were not Greek-American, of Greek descent in other words, he would have stopped trying long before the project was completed.

Conductor Zoe Zeniodi suggests that next to Tiboris' unique combination of utter stubbornness and disarming charm another of his qualities is his ability to forgive and move on. She wrote in an email: "There was an incident at the Festival and Peter was very fair. But other people had not been fair to him. He was always fair and always understanding and always trying to find solutions and make things work. That was a difficult incident. The day after, we had a concert at the Church, and I went to find him just before the dress rehearsal. I found him alone, sitting on one of the benches. He had tears in his eyes. I sat next to him, and I asked him if I could help somehow. He looked at me and smiled and he said: No, I am patient, and I forgive..."[75]

Tiboris and Dekavallas began working closely and each summer after his first visit in 1999 Tiboris organized performances in Syros. It was not all uphill because many people on the island realized the importance of what he was trying to do and offered their support. An important ally was Babis Koulouras, a native of Syros, composer, lyricist and performer known internationally as the director of music and Greek poetry ensembles that have performed world-wide with a special emphasis on the poems of the Alexandrian Greek poet C. P. Cavafy.

Prior to the festival on Syros, Tiboris established Opera Aegean, though which 21 artists from around the world, and an artistic and administrative staff of 15 arrived in Greece in July, 2000 for a visit that involved performances, rehearsals, attendance at concerts and a meeting with Placido Domingo in Athens as well as sightseeing trips. Headed by Tiboris, the artistic staff included Sherrill Milnes, Artistic Director; Carol Castel, Staging Director; Nicholas Di Virgilio, Master Teacher and Coach; Maria Zouves, Artist-in-Residence and Manolis Papasifakis, Principal Coach and Accompanist. There were performances in Athens, the islands of Andros and Paros, and the Peloponnesos.

THE FESTIVAL OF THE AEGEAN TAKES OFF

The Festival of the Aegean kicked off in 2005. The first opera performance in the Apollo – after a hundred years of no opera performances - was Rossini's *Il Barbiere di Siviglia,* (The Barber of Seville) produced by the Festival of the Aegean, Peter Tiboris conducting, on July 14, 2005. Gianmaria Romagnoli was the stage director and the cast included Figaro: Pietro Masi, baritone; Rosina: Maria Francesca Mazzara, soprano; Almaviva: Amedeo Moretti, tenor; Dr. Bartolo: Carmine Monaco, bass; Don Basilio: Raffaele Costantini, bass-baritone; Fiorello Stefano Viti, baritone; Berta: Takako Horaguchi, mezzo-soprano, The Rome Philharmonic Orchestra soloists and pianists Yannis Xylas and Tania Panayanopoulou. Dekavallas wrote that the emotions of the audience witnessing that performance was indescribable especially, those native to the island.

The following year, 2006, the Festival expanded its scope and was held over three days and celebrated the 250th anniversary of Mozart's birth. Tiboris conducted Mozart's Don Giovanni with baritone Armando Mora in the title role, Eilana Lappalainen as Donna Anna and Antonio Stragapede as the Commendatore. The next two days featured an All-Mozart classical music program as well as selections from *West Side Story, Oklahoma!, My Fair Lady, Candide, South Pacific, Carousel, The King and I* and *Porgy and Bess.* The Broadway songs performance also took place on the neighboring island of Paros. A website about events on the island was full of praise: "The evening of Broadway Music presented by Opera Aegean on July 13 at the Hotel Paros Agnanti was one where the great confident songs of mid-century America were given an outing with verve, style, panache. In fact, just the right tone was struck, where style and parody meet in a form of homage. Melody Kielisch, Eilana Lappalainen, sopranos, Giorgio Aristo, tenor, Antonio Stragapede, bass, and Yannis Xylas on piano all complemented each other with great elegance. It is impossible to single one out because all were exemplars of strut, pout, preen and posture that go with Rogers and Hammerstein, Sondheim, Lerner and Lowe, Gershwin, Bernstein, Andrew Lloyd Webber et al. All that remains to be said is congratulations to all."[76]

Back on Syros, with Mayor Dekavallas' support the following year, 2007, witnessed another successful summer festival. The prestigious Athens newspaper Kathimerini reported the excited anticipation of the opening of a new Festival of the Aegean: "Rising above the role of a typical summer tourist destination, the town of Ermoupolis on Syros is emerging as a cultural capital, with a history dating back to the founding of modern Greece. This is the third year the Festival of the Aegean is being held on the Cycladic island, but this year's event boasts a longer run and more varied and international productions than ever before. Peter Tiboris, general director and artistic director of the Aegean Festival, remarked at a press conference yesterday that the festival has grown from being a child to a young adult. A third-generation Greek-American, the acclaimed conductor and head of MidAmerica Productions also admitted that Syros is an extraordinary place, having become in a few years' time his second musical home."[77]

The Gala Opening of the Festival had Tiboris conducting the Czech Republic's Bohuslav Martinů Philharmonic with mezzo soprano Irini Tsirakidis. This was followed by three nights in which Tiboris conducted the Martinů Philharmonic in opera pieces with Eilana Lappalainen, Jennifer Larmore, mezzo-soprano, Todd Geer, tenor and William Powers, bass-baritone. The program also included three performances of Pietro Mascagni's opera Zanetto, never before performed in Greece. And in an innovative move, aside from classical music it included performances by Greek saxophonist Stratos Vougas and his Jazz quintet and traditional Greek rebetiko with Taximi, a Greek folk music group based in Stockholm, Sweden preforming in Ermoupolis' central Miaouli square.

The festival kept growing exponentially every year both in numbers and in its international scope and in 2008 featured members of the Manhattan Philharmonic of New York, the Columbia Collegiate Chorale of Maryland and the Choir of the Podlasie Opera and Philharmonic from Bialystock, Poland. In 2009, the fifth annual festival included Raymond Hughes as Principal Guest Conductor; Peter Meineck, Director, Aquila Theatre of New York; Renato Zanella, Dance Director and Choreographer, as well as the Pan-European Philharmonia Orchestra, the Southwestern College Concert Choir, Chula Vista, CA directed by Teresa Russell, singers from the Greek National Conservatory with chorus master Spyros Klapsis, the Athens Singers and members of the Ionian University Department of Musical Studies.

Dance director and choreographer Zanella would return to the festival for two more summers. In 2011 he was appointed artistic director of the Greek National Ballet in Athens and remained in that position for four years but continued to take part in the Festival of the Aegean. Born in Verona, he began his artistic career as a dancer and moved on to become a choreographer of opera and ballet performances.

A NIGHT IN A SYROS JAIL

Tiboris' commitment to Syros and his determination to overcome local obstacles was not put off when he had to spend a night at the Syros police station and a few hours in a jail cell. It happened due to the narrow minded application of the letter of the law by provincial policemen who would have treated a Greek person with the right political connections quite differently and much more leniently. Following a performance at the Festival of the Aegean on Syros, Tiboris was driving to the Hotel Ploes, which was hosting its annual reception for the Festival participants, accompanied by his close friend and colleague Christos Papageorgiou. While trying to overtake them, a motor bike struck Tiboris' driver's door and the rider was knocked on the ground. Fortunately, he was unhurt, the motor bike was on its side but not damaged and the car was slightly scratched. The incident occurred in the central square and a police car appeared on the scene and asked the motor bike rider and Tiboris for their driver's licenses. The motorbike driver's had expired, Tiboris had a valid Florida driver's license but no international permit. Only a few weeks earlier the European Union had enacted legislation requiring Americans to have an international driving permit, but Tiboris had not gotten one since he was already in Greece when that law took effect.

This meant that both drivers had to be taken to the police station to be processed and this is where things got farcical but not at all funny. The police said that Tiboris had to wait at the police station to be released by the local prosecutor, who would arrive in the morning at around 9 am. By the time all this had taken place it was about 2 am and Tiboris had missed the reception. The policeman did not accept Papageorgiou's explanation that Tiboris was in charge of the Festival of the Aegean and that he had a rehearsal the next day or his assurances that Tiboris would return first thing the next morning to sort things out with the local prosecutor. The police captain on duty said he could not let Tiboris go, but instead of being held in a cell he could wait in the reception area. Tiboris, exhausted, remained in the reception area until 6 am when the policemen was relieved by a colleague who proved to be over-officious and demanded that Tiboris be placed in a cell downstairs. Everyone at the police station was in shock. Tiboris recounts what followed: "They escorted me to the lower level, and I picked a jail cell where I sat inside locked from 6:15 am until 9 am, when the prosecutor said I should be released. They brought me upstairs to the main entrance and I was leaving the police stationary when the captain who had incarcerated me for three hours said, Mr. Tiboris, my family's and I look forward to seeing you conduct tomorrow night in the Apollo Theater as we are great supporters of the Festival and what you are doing for Syros.

Of course, I didn't say a word to the fool. I just left and went to a rehearsal at 10 am in the Apollo Theater after that incident, not having gone home. I was exhausted. Months passed and our Syros friend Attorney Manthos Manthopoulos appeared in the court hearing and got the ticket dismissed."

There was a humorous note associated with the incident after all, however. While Eilana was teasing Peter about not following the rules, which would have avoided all the trouble, she was informed over lunch by Manthopoulos that she was also given a ticket. Peter said, "because the car was I was driving was registered under her name and she was as culpable as he was for the incident. Ultimately, the judge said to Manthopoulos that both tickets (hers and mine) would be dismissed. But she was included in the post-jail offense proceedings because the judge said that she should not have allowed me to drive her car since it was registered under her name and not mine."

The Syros judicial system's performance of the theater of the absurd thankfully ended well, but the story is a reminder of the narrow bureaucratic approach of Greek civil servants that makes enacting any new project especially challenging.

The 6th Festival in 2010

The sixth Festival of the Aegean in 2010 opened with Tiboris conducting Bizet's opera *Carmen*, with Zanella as stage director. The Bulgarian-Mexican mezzo-soprano Carla Dirlikov Canales, currently an internationally acclaimed performer and recognized as an advocate for arts and culture, sang the title role. The Cuban-American tenor Raul Melo was in the role of Don José and significantly there were several Greek singers in the cast. The breadth of the festival was evident in the long list of participants, the variety of the offerings, which included sunset concerts at St. Nicholas church and a concert with the legendary singer Maria Farandouri, known internationally through her close and longstanding collaboration with composer Mikis Theodorakis. There were also several choirs from Canada, Greece and the United States: the Birmingham Alabama Concert Chorale directed by Philip Copeland, the Vocal Ensemble of Mira Costa High School from Manhattan Beach, California directed by Michael Hayden, the Michael O'Neal Singers from Georgia directed by Michael O'Neal, the King College Symphonic Choir from Tennessee directed by W. Patrick Flannagan, the Kamloops Choristers from British Columbia directed by Margaret Brown and three choirs from Greece, the Camerata Vocalis from Corfu directed by Rosa Poulimenou, Members of the National Conservatory's Choir of Athens directed by Spyros Klapsis and the St. Nicholas Greek Orthodox Church of Syros Men's Chorus.

FRANCIS BARDOT OF PARIS

Also performing in 2010 at the Festival of the Aegean was an important children's choir from Paris, the Choeur d'Enfants d'Ile-de-France directed by Francis Bardot. It was their first appearance and subsequently they would perform at the festival every two years. Bardot had been bringing his children's choirs to Syros for several years already, with the support of the Catholic church. Bardot is somewhat of a renaissance man with a deep love and respect for Ancient Greece, Modern Greece and its people as well as for Greek Orthodoxy. A tenor soloist specializing in oratorios from the age of 18, he gave 2,000 concerts in France and abroad, and producing some twenty recordings under labels including RCA and Deutsche Grammophon. Nurtured by a deep passion for the humanities, he has taught Latin, Ancient Greek, classical French literature and Philosophy and became at the age of 24 a professor at the Institut Supérieur de Pédagogie (college of education science) of the Institut Catholique de Paris, where he founded his first choir school for children. He then decided to dedicate himself entirely to conducting choirs and orchestras and founded several such choirs in France and as choirmaster has toured the world.

Bardot and Peter first met on Syros in 2009, and as Bardot recalls there was an electric current that courses between them and by now Bardot considers Tiboris as a brother. That is not surprising because they discovered they had many commonalities, starting from their age: Bardot was born in 1946 – a year before Tiboris – they were both religious, Francis a Catholic and Peter Greek Orthodox, and both had devoted their lives to music. Bardot was impressed with Peter's organizational skills, hiring administrators with a musical background, and by his extraordinary abilities as a conductor, which he first noticed when Peter was conducting Beethoven without the help of the music score.[78]

THE GREEK OPERA STUDIO AND EILANA LAPPALAINEN

Another 'first' at the festival was a gala performance of the Greek Opera Studio in 2010. Eilana Lappalainen, as part of the deepening of the activities and initiatives she was undertaking in Syros, founded The Greek Opera Studio in 2010, in conjunction with the festival and ELArtists, based in the United States, Greece and Germany. ELArtists supports three summer Opera Studios (Greek Opera Studio, Berlin Opera Studio, and Hamburg Opera Studio) and the new Palm Beach Vocal Arts. These organizations with the mission to build young artists' professional solo careers, is directly connected to a production company presenting performances at Carnegie Hall. European concerts are also presented, where young artists are sometimes selected to make debuts in important cities. This summer performance/ study program based on the classical vocal art form and suited for entry-level young artists focused on a career in the world of opera. The program offers intensive training and stage development for young singers interested in preparing for future opera auditions and advancing to the regional and international stages in this vocal profession. Eilana Lappalainen has supported the growth of young talented vocal artists specializing in classical voice and opera throughout her entire opera career.

The Opera Studio performed again in 2011 and in 2012 as part of the festival kickoff, the first event of that year's festival. This was also the case in 2013, and in 2014 it performed as part of the festival's finale. By then it had become a regular and central feature of the opening and closing of the Festival of the Aegean.

MUSIC AT A TIME OF CRISIS

Two months before the 6th Festival of the Aegean opened in Syros, Greece's capital city Athens erupted with violent demonstrations that cost the lives of three people after demonstrators threw firebombs at a bank. Greece had entered what was to be an almost decade-long economic crisis from which it would emerge in 2018. The protests in 2010 were against the first of a series of austerity measures which negatively affected wages and salaries, pensions and taxes, plunging many Greeks into poverty. Across-the-board cuts in government spending affected the arts in Greece, which are funded mainly through the government rather than private donations. Government grants to some of the largest Greek cultural organizations (such as the Megaron Mousikis in Athens), were decreased by 75% compared to their funding prior to the economic crisis.[79] But cultural organizations with funding from abroad, or those with low budgets survived. Arguably, meanwhile, the crisis triggered a growing interest in the arts especially locally at a time when people were traveling less. The reduction in ticket prices in Athens and elsewhere that also occurred contributed to that trend.

The Aegean islands, including Syros, were obviously affected by the crisis as was the entire country, but income from tourism over the summer blunted the sharper edges of the austerity measures. And in this sense, the presence of the Festival of the Aegean every summer had a hugely beneficial effect economically and also in terms of morale, given how music can inspire, connect and unite people.

A 7-YEAR ANNIVERSARY IN 2011

One very consistent pattern in Peter Tiboris' life is that he is very conscious of anniversaries, and he always staged concerts commemorating anniversaries of births or deaths of great composers. Tiboris also had an eye for the anniversaries in his own professional life, as for example MidAmerica's foundation, which he dated back to 1983 which was a year before his New York debut. Most anniversaries were marked when they fell on a round number of years but not always. For example, the program of the 2011 Festival of the Aegean included an open letter to "friends and festival lovers" that spoke with considerable emotion of the festival's 7th and also in typical Tiboris style generously thanked and recognized all his collaborators. He wrote:

> It is difficult to believe that this year's Festival of the Aegean has now grown to 7 years, as it seems like only yesterday that Mayor Dekavallas and I signed a 'letter of understanding' regarding the ten-year mission of the Festival. At the time, these were modest goals but goals of substance. Who would have thought that we would have eclipsed those goals, and [are] now heading into new performance frontiers which make these series of events special for anyone and everyone world-wide. It was on July 14th 2005 that our first opera occurred, Rossini's *Il Barbieri di Seviglia* – the first staged opera with orchestra in Apollo Theater in more than 105 years – with an all-Italian cast and orchestra!!!

> Since then... *Cavalleria Rusticana, Zanetto, Don Giovanni, Carmen, Tosca* and this year, Verdi's timeless masterwork *La Traviata*. There has been world-class ballet with Dance Director Renato Zanella, Shakespeare and Homer with Aquila Theater and Director Peter Meineck, Symphonic works, concerti, folk music, Greek music, sacred music in St. Nicholas Greek Orthodox Cathedral and the newest festival component, Greek Opera Studio founded by Eilana Lappalainen, soloists of international acclaim and

choruses from the USA, France, Canada and Greece (this year featuring guest directors Tim Sharp, Earl Rivers and Janet Galvan). There have been master choral works featuring hundreds of singers and memorable concerts at St. Nicholas Church. And this year, we move to Miaoulis Square for the first time to present *Carmina Burana* and works by Mikis Theodorakis. And if that were not enough, this year... the great theater and cinema actor, Olympia Dukakis... all in the glorious Aegean, grace this special island as well! There are just too many people to thank, so for fear of leaving anyone unmentioned I will say to all of you: a passionate and heartfelt thank you... With your enthusiastic support, this Festival has grown to something very special throughout Greece and beyond... All of this is pointing to a special gala year of events in 2014 when the Theater celebrates its 150th anniversary... It was on April 20th, 1864 that the theater opened for the first time with Verdi's *Rigoletto*. We will do the same in 2014... which will be the Festival's tenth anniversary. It should be noted that April 20th, 2014 is Easter Sunday, no less! I cannot close without mentioning the supporters and friends of the Festival (Mayor Dekavallas and the Council – Yiannis Keranis and Yiannis Pitaoulis) and especially the sponsors in America who provide 90% of the funding for the festival. And, of course, the professional staff of MidAmerica Productions in NYC which this year celebrates 29 years in the historic Carnegie Hall...

CARMINA BURANA UNDER THE STARS

When Tiboris told Dekavallas of his plan to stage an open air performance of Carmina Burana, Carl Orff's operatic cantata with twenty four songs, the mayor got very worried about what interest there would be on the island. It's one thing to hold such a performance in an indoor space where music lovers will go knowing what to expect, and another thing exposing the performance to an audience with very little musical education. The venue was going to be the vast Miaoulis Square (Plateia Miaouli) at the center of Ermoupolis, which is framed by the imposing neoclassical municipality building. Tiboris, naturally, was not going to be stopped. The performance took place at 10 pm on July 17, 2011 in the square, with Babis Koulouras' cameras recording the event. In the main roles were Greek soprano Myrsini Margariti and male counter-tenor Paul Zachariades and American baritone Frederick Burchinal, and they were supported by the Pan European Philharmonia and choirs from Canada, Greece and the United States totaling 400 singers. The choir members were placed on the fifty-foot-wide stairs of the municipal building and the orchestra was arrayed just below them. The conclusion was met with a standing ovation from the audience, which as Dekavallas notes had enjoyed a once-in-a-lifetime experience justifying Tiboris' vision.

Syros-based journalist Litsa Charalambous remembers that people from the entire town of Ermoupolis went to the square. There was not enough seating, so they went back to their houses and brought their own chairs or stools. Charalambous is a great admirer and supporter of Tiboris' efforts. There was an immediate connection between the two of them when they met on Syros. She describes him as a giant with an angelic face, moist eyes and a broad smile. She believes Tiboris put Syros on the map and contributed mightily to the island but always maintained a humble and humorous outlook.

What made the plan to stage *Carmina Burana* outdoors even more ambitious was that the festival that year was the biggest ever and included several other major events. That same evening's concert included highlights from Mikis Theodorakis' Zorba Suite including Asteraki' 'Hasapiko Dance', 'Strose to Stroma Sou' with mezzo-soprano Marissia Papalexiou. There was a concert commemorating the 100th anniversary of Gustav Mahler's death in 1911 with Tiboris conducting the Pan-European Philharmonia with Eilana Lappalainen on stage, and there was also a stage reading by Olympia Dukakis of *Rose*, the one-woman play by Martin Sherman, an event that Tiboris had described in his tribute following Olympia Dukakis' death. The play is about the postwar story of a member of the Jewish diaspora, as told by an immigrant woman who has traveled from the Ukraine to Miami Beach. While sitting shiva for a loved one left unnamed until the final moments of the play, Rose tells of her childhood in a Russian shtetl, marriage and terror in the Warsaw ghetto, the Exodus to the new nation of Israel, a second marriage in Atlantic City, success as a hotelier in Miami, and, finally, disillusionment with contemporary Jewish culture. Dukakis had performed the role in London and on Broadway and had elicited rave reviews.

THE PAN-EUROPEAN PHILHARMONIA

The Warsaw-based Pan-European Philharmonia that performed in Syros that year was already well-known and had gained widespread recognition and acclaim for its performances of operatic, symphonic and chamber works across the globe. It was founded by Tiboris in 2008, and he served as Music Director and Conductor. The orchestra, which is made up of young musicians from Poland and other European countries, has performed at many renowned venues across Europe and has collaborated with many leading artists. Jakub Fiebig was the Executive Director of the Pan-European Philharmonia, responsible for the administrative leadership of the orchestra. He has been instrumental in helping to develop and execute the organization's strategic vision. Fiebig has played a crucial role in the *Philharmonia's* continued success since its inception, working closely with Tiboris and his team to ensure that the orchestra delivers exceptional musical experiences for audiences across the globe. Immediately following its appearance at the Festival of the Aegean, the Pan-European Philharmonia, conducted by Tiboris, performed in Athens on July 18th at a concert under the auspices of the Embassy of the Republic of Poland in cooperation with the Michael Cacoyannis Foundation, to mark Poland's Presidency of European Union that year.

THEODORAKIS AT THE FESTIVAL OF THE AEGEAN

For the people living on Syros, the most exciting event of the Festival of the Aegean that summer was the arrival of Mikis Theodorakis himself. He was there for the screening of two documentary films by Asteris Kutulas (a Greek documentarist and event and music producer who grew up in Romania and Germany) and German documentarist Klaus Salge. Both films, 'Mikis Theodorakis. Composer' and 'Mikis Theodorakis. Sun and Time' examined the life and work of the great man. Following the screenings and for three nights the Festival of the Aegean featured a world premiere ballet presentation of Theodorakis' *Medea's Choice*. It was a dance performance in one act, choreographed by Renato Zanella with Maria Kousouni (a prima ballerina with the Greek National Opera) in the role of Medea, and with Danilo Zeka, Franziska Hollinek, Eno Peci, Sofia Pintzou and Nicky Vanoppen in supporting roles along with the Akropoditi Dance Theater of Syros. Theodorakis was visibly moved after the performance, which made a huge impact on the entire audience. Kutulas made a film based on that performance and he released it in 2013 with the tittle 'Recycling Medea'. The film won the Cinema for Peace Most Valuable Documentary Award 2014 at the Berlin International Film Festival.

FESTIVAL OF THE YEAR!

Inevitably perhaps, but certainly justifiably, the Festival of the Aegean's 2011 program was recognized for its quality. It received the award 'Festival of the Year Award in Greater Greece' from the Hellenic Music and Theater Critics Association of Athens. Mayor Dekavallas had received it in December of 2011 in Athens, and he presented to Tiboris on the opening night of the 2012 festival at the Apollo Theater on Syros. That evening Tiboris conducted the Symphony Orchestra of the National Theater of Opera and Ballet, Tirana, Albania, in Beethoven's *Symphony No. 9* and his *Piano Concerto No. 5*. The pianist was Dimitris Sgouros in his festival debut. The others on stage were mezzo-soprano Maria Ratkova, tenor Keith Ikaia-Purdy and bass Dimitri Kavrakos and choruses from Canada, Greece and the United States. The other concerts held in the summer of 2012 included Eilana Lappalainen in one of her signature roles, Salome in Richard Strauss' opera, and John Rutter's appearance as a conductor in another open-air concert on Miaouli square.

By that time, the Festival of the Aegean was being noticed throughout Greece. Announcements of its program were appearing all over the internet. Critic's Point, a Greek-language electronic magazine focused on music, theater, dance and art sent someone to observe two nights of the festival. The reviewer, Constantinos Karambelas Sgourdas, heaped praise on the Albanian performers, Rutter's "sensitivity and rhythm," Tiboris' conducting, Zanella's choreography and the choirs. He was also very complimentary of pianist Christos Papageorgiou.[80]

HONORARY CITIZEN TIBORIS

On the same evening in July, 2012 Mayor Dekavallas presented Tiboris with the best festival award he also awarded him with the award of Honorary Citizen of the Municipality of Syros. In his speech Dekavallas spoke about how the municipality felt it was both an honor and an obligation to honor Tiboris and he went on to list the benefits that the Festival of the Aegean had brought to the island and its people. He also noted the way the Festival of the Aegean organization cooperated with the municipality and its department of cultural affairs. He concluded by saying, "Syros honors Peter Tiboris this evening with a big thank you to him for all he has done for the cultural life of our island and all that he plans to do in the future." Tiboris graciously responded that his life and that of his family had changed for the better since he arrived on Syros and hoped his efforts had meant the same for the people of the island.[81]

THE 150TH ANNIVERSARY OF THE APOLLO THEATER
APRIL 20, 1864-APRIL 20, 2014

The tenth festival of the Aegean in the summer of 2014 coincided with the 150th anniversary of the Apollo Theater. The exact date of the anniversary was April 20th and Tiboris happened to be in Ermoupolis on that date. Dismayed that nothing official was being done, he invited Yannis Rotas and his wife to share a bottle of champagne with him on the steps of the theater that evening, which was Greek Easter Sunday. A more public celebration would have to wait for the summer. In that year's festival program Tiboris reflected on what the Festival had achieved: "ten years and more than a hundred performances later, with the support of the Friends of the Festival, we have presented thousands of world-class artists, including 55 choruses, 10 orchestras, hundreds of soloists, directors, technical support staff, and members of the Greek Opera Studio in 16 operas, Plateia concerts, sacred music concerts, children's concerts, ballet, theater, popular music, jazz, symphonies and oratorios, to appreciative audiences. The Island of Syros, and especially the City of Ermoupolis, has become famous throughout Greece and beyond as a summer destination for the very highest level of cultural programming."

The festival opened in July, 2014 with a Puccini concert in the main square. It was a gala tribute to Puccini by a company of 450 artists from nine countries, including highlights from *Tosca, La Bohème, Turandot* and *Madama Butterfly*. Tiboris along with guest conductor Grigor Palikarov led the Pazardzhik Symphony Orchestra from Bulgaria along with choruses from France, Greece and the United States. The two-week long festival included classical music performances for children and three days of jazz concerts.

2015: A TURNING POINT YEAR

This was the last festival to be held under Mayor Dekavallas, who decided to step down after twenty-four years in that post. Tiboris expressed his thanks in the festival's program: "Special mention must be made of my friend, Mayor Yannis Dekavallas. We met 15 years ago during my first visit, and we have maintained an abiding friendship. Without him, there would be no Festival of the Aegean. He has been supportive both personally and professionally, always kind, always personable, always respectful, and always sincere." The next year's festival program congratulated George Marangos and Thomai Mendrinos on their election as Mayor and deputy Mayor responsible for Culture respectively in 2015, and continued to thank them for their support every year. Ermoupolis-based journalist Litsa Charalambous, one of the most ardent advocates of the festival on the island, believed the new administration could have done more in terms of funding and support and recalls that this reticence resulted in an open-air concert not taking place in 2017.[82]

THE FESTIVAL MARCHES ON

In typical Tiboris style, in the program for the 2016 festival, he mentioned the problems posed by reduced funding but in the same breath stated his commitment to the festival and to Syros. He wrote: "Creating and developing a Festival of this scope is a complicated and intricate endeavor made even more difficult in a climate where there is severe lack of funding in cultural activities. Happily, we have been able, so far, to overcome these difficulties. The Festival is part of the growth and development of Syros artistically, culturally and economically. I will do whatever is necessary to have it a continuing artistic enterprise on this unique and beautiful island. This year the main offering is the great and dramatic opera by Leoncavallo – *I Pagliacci*, as well as the great masterworks – Tchaikovsky's *Symphony No. 6,* Haydn's *Mass in Time of War* and cello concerto, Brahms *Tragic Overture,* Chopin's *Piano Concerto No. 1,* and Beethoven's *Violin Concerto*. Plus, as always, we are presenting the Greek Opera Studio. Syros is our home. Syros is where we have chosen to be. Syros is where we remain. Your continued support, participation and involvement is greatly appreciated and encouraged."

Whatever the obstacles the festival might have been facing, Tiboris was his usual optimistic – one could say enthusiastic – self in the program for the 2017 summer season of events: "It is all quite remarkable that in this most unlikely place, such a series of cultural events could occur and, as many, many have said, put Syros on the cultural map of the world. And why not? Is there any place on the planet more beautiful to be in during July than in the middle of the Aegean, relaxing, enjoying and attending performances of the great musical masterworks of Western Music? I think not. And to this end, it is worth noting that more than 327 performances have taken place since 2005, including 13 operas performed by over 7,500 visiting artists from 43 different countries. The summary of this is simple: the island is changing in dramatic fashion due to leadership in many sectors, but mostly because of Mayor George Marangos – Eilana and I congratulate him for his vision and initiatives. The changes on Syros can be felt and heard throughout the music world; make no mistake, it is real and palpable. It is also important to note that the coordination and development of cultural activities has been guided by Vice-Mayor Thomai Mendrinou, who works tirelessly, not only on the Festival of the Aegean, but also on cultural activities throughout the year from January through December."

And he went on to say: "This year's Festival is grander that any of the previous ones with opera, symphonic works, ballet, Greek Opera Studio, chamber music, folk music, and master classes with collaborators from 26 countries and more than 350 visiting artists. I began this letter by proclaiming it... 'The Salzburg of the Aegean'. Is this an overstatement? I think not. It describes exactly what this Festival has become – one which has made a significant cultural and economic impact on Syros and throughout the Cyclades. The Festival of the Aegean has 'changed lives'. And this follows what has guided our Carnegie Hall productions since 1983: that we are 'changing lives, one concert at a time.'"

The rest of the program listings justified Tiboris' optimism about where the festival had arrived and where it was headed towards. Below Tiboris' name as the founder, general director and music director of the festival, and Lappalainen's as artistic director of festival opera productions and general director of the Greek Opera Studio and festival manager, there was an impressive list of participants that included the Pan-European Philharmonia of Warsaw and its executive director Jakub Friebig, 311 visiting artists and production persons, Giovanni Pacor, the conductor of *Madama Butterfly,* Johanes Weigand, the stage director of *Madama Butterfly,* Renato Zanella who was directing the Ballet of the National Opera of Bucharest, Detlef Soelter Stage Director - *Don Giovanni,* Fortino Ibarra Conductor - *Don Giovanni,* Jens Huebner, Technical Director, Set and Lighting Designer and Marta Kluzynska Warsaw Conducting Associate. Significantly, this impressive roster included Greek names, Christos Papageorgiou Festival Spotlight Artist – Piano, Nicholas Canellakis, Festival Spotlight Artist – Cello, Jenia Manoussaki Festival Spotlight Artist – Piano and conductor and Zoe Zeniodi as Special Music Consultant to Peter Tiboris.

The 2016 Festival was the first of four consecutive summers that Giovanni Pacor took part in the festival as guest conductor, a time he fondly remembers as one in which he forged an "incredible" friendship with Peter Tiboris. Born in Trieste, Italy in 1957 with an Italian father and a Greek mother, he studied violin in his home country until 1980, and soon after moved into conducting. He served as artistic director at the Greek National Opera (2008/10) where his performances staged included first Greek productions of operas by Rossini, Bellini, Zemlinsky, Dvořák, Donizetti, Piazzolla, Xarchakos and Yannis Constantinidis. That was when he met

Peter for the first time – interestingly, he had already met Eilana a few years earlier when she sang Salome in Trieste. Unfortunately, because of the budget cuts at the Greek National Opera and due to the general social unrest, Pacor decided he could no longer work productively in Athens.

At the 2016 festival Pacor took over some of the conducting that Tiboris was supposed to undertake but was unable to because he was in poor health. Pacor was back on Syros for the 2017 Festival of the Aegean to conduct Puccini's *Madama Butterfly,* with Eilana Lappalainen in the title role and Italian tenor Alessio Boraggine as Lieutenant Pinkerton. The *Kathimerini* newspaper gave the performance a rave review, singling out the work of stage director Johannes Weigland, of conductor Giovanni Pacor and Jens Huebner, Technical Director, Set and Lighting Design. The review described Eilana Lappalainen's Madama Butterfly as "excellent" and praised the other singers as well.[83]

The festival had opened with Tiboris conducting pieces by Mozart and Tchaikovsky. The finale was a "Gala Night featuring the Stars from the Ballet of the National Opera of Bucharest" directed and choreographed by Renato Zanella.

HEALTH MATTERS

When Pacor replaced him, Tiboris was suffering from something much more than poor health. A routine medical test in May 2015 had revealed cancerous cells in his stomach, the diagnosis being of stage I gastric cancer. In September 2015 he underwent extensive surgery during which his entire stomach was removed by Dr. Mark Reiner at Mount Sinai Hospital in New York City. The surgery was successful. Aside from dealing with the immediate danger the medical procedures also brought about a dramatic reduction in Tiboris' size and weight. He had unsuccessfully struggled with his weight for decades and ended up being overweight – that was when Charalambous met him and saw a giant with an angelic face. Following the surgery his heavy, wide frame was a thing of the past, but needless to say, Peter's energy remained boundless. And he never stopped thanking Pacor for stepping in and helping that summer.[84]

Tiboris faced another major health issue in 2020 and in September of that year Dr, Steve Xydas repaired two arteries around his heart. Face to face with his mortality, Tiboris changed his lifestyle dramatically and began swimming on a daily basis for forty or fifty minutes without missing a day, surprising his doctors with the speed of his recovery.

A Rossini Anniversary

The 2018 Festival of the Aegean fell on the 150th anniversary of the death of the Italian composer Gioachino Rossini, so the opening night featured a performance of his *Stabat Mater,* based on a Christian hymn about the suffering of Mary the mother of Christ during his crucifixion. Tiboris conducted the Pan European Philharmonia, with Eilana Lappalainen Soprano, Katerina Roussou mezzo-soprano, Alessandro Luciano tenor and Daniel Borowski bass. The participating choruses that crowded the stage at the Apollo theater were from France and the United States. The second half of the evening was a performance of Tchaikovsky's *Symphony No. 5,* and there was more Rossini on offer the second night with a performance of his opera *La Cenerentola* based on the tale of Cinderella. Rossini composed *La Cenerentola* when he was 25 years old, following the success of *Il Barbiere di Siviglia* the year before. *La Cenerentola,* which he completed in three weeks in 1816, is considered to have some of his finest writing for solo voice and ensembles. On that second night on Syros, Principal Guest Conductor Giovanni Pacor was on the conductor's podium. It was the third year in a row that he was taking part in the festival. The 2018 festival concluded with a dance performance of Theodorakis' opera *Electra* choreographed by Renato Zanella with Asteris Kutulas co-director. The dancers were from Albania, Brazil, France, Greece and Romania.

'Ariadne Auf Syros'

Southeast of Syros, at a distance of only thirty miles across the sea lies the island of Naxos. It is one of the cluster of islands in the Southern Aegean known as the Cyclades which includes not only Syros but also Mykonos and Santorini. As we all know, Mykonos and Santorini became world-famous tourist destinations several decades ago, but of all the Cycladic islands it was Naxos that gained worldwide fame the earliest, not due to its undeniable natural beauty but because of Richard Strauss' opera, *Ariadne auf Naxos* (Ariadne on Naxos). It is an opera that includes within it a performance of an opera inspired by the Greek myth about how Prince Theseus of Athens set out for Crete to kill the Minotaur, a creature half-man, half-bull, who was concealed in a labyrinth. Princess Ariadne of Crete fell in love with Theseus and gave him a ball of thread that enabled him to find his way out of the labyrinth after he had killed the Minotaur. When Theseus left Crete, he took Ariadne with him as his bride and during their voyage home, they stopped at the island of Naxos. While

Ariadne was asleep, Theseus slipped away and continued his journey to Athens without her. The opera *Ariadne auf Naxos* begins at that point.

The Greek premiere of the opera was in Athens in February, 1974, and the most recent one was in 2009 with Giovanni Pacor conducting. With the Festival of the Aegean in 2019, Tiboris was bringing *Ariadne auf Naxos* as close to Naxos as the opera will ever be unless somehow it is performed on Naxos itself. Eilana Lappalainen was in the title role and the other main singers were mezzo-soprano Adrian Angelico, soprano Louise Fribo and tenor Ta'u Pupu'a. The festival's rich program included the first-ever appearance of the Greek-Cypriot pianist and conductor Marios Papadopoulos, the founder and music director of the Oxford Philharmonic, Orchestra in Residence at the University of Oxford.

Without knowing that there would be no festivals for the next two years because of the Covid-19 pandemic, Tiboris was in a reflective mood in the 2019 festival program. He offered thanks on the part of himself and Eilana, noted the contributions the festival made to Syros and for the first time mentioned his Greek roots: "What has happened during the past 15 years is extraordinary on any level – hundreds and hundreds of performances featuring thousands and thousands of visiting artists from 50 or more countries world-wide sharing their musical talents in front of countless music lovers. The economic impact on Syros has been significant, and now, Syros has world-wide recognition... As we arrive at this 15th anniversary season it is important that Eilana and I look back and thank everyone for your generous support and encouragement in creating and developing such a grand and important Festival in the most unlikely of places – far from a metropolitan area but in the middle of the Southern Aegean, which is replete with history and beauty. Of course, it is no coincidence or surprise that I would be attracted to this historic place, being Greek-American as my family immigrated from Megalopoli (Arcadia) in the early 1900s. Throughout my life, I have had close ties with the Greek culture, history and people."

A week before the 2019 festival opened general elections were held in Greece and the conservative New Democracy party won and returned to power after four-and-a-half years. This event coincided with the end of the economic crisis, the country having formally exited the foreign financial bailouts in August of 2018. There was a sense of relief that the worst was over, and the country was slowly returning to normal. In that sense, the Festival of the Aegean that had weathered the crisis so well could look forward to the future with even greater confidence. The commitment to Syros that expressed in the 2019 program was genuine and reflected a commitment born from the moment he had set foot on the island in 1999. In 2006, a year after the first Festival of the Aegean was held on the island, Peter and Eilana purchased a beautiful, whitewashed villa in Danì, on the western coast of the island from where one could watch the sun setting in the Aegean sea. When I spoke to Rotas he described how much work the house had needed to shore up its foundations because it was perched on a slope overlooking the sea. But that, like everything about Peter Tiboris' life was symbolic of the patient effort of building something against the odds. Eilana, whose family had been in the construction business, managed to overcome the structural challenges by overseeing the construction of the house in a multilevel form, producing a traditional island home replete with a swimming pool that overlooked the wine dark waters of the Aegean. There was lots more to do on Syros beginning in 2020. The pandemic put things on hold, but as it turned out, thankfully not for long.

THE PANDEMIC STRIKES

On March 15th, 2020 Carnegie hall shut down due to the Covid pandemic. MidAmerica's first concert for the new season had been scheduled to take place five days later. About twenty more concerts were supposed to have taken place through June, but everything was wiped out just as groups were flying in from around the country, about 500 choral artists from six states. What would the cancellations mean in terms of refunds and finances was critical and decisions had to be made in a chaotic and unnerving environment. James Redcay, MidAmerica's Chief Executive Officer, credits Tiboris with protecting the interests and indeed the future of the company by adopting a hard-nosed business savvy attitude. There were no refunds from MidAmerica – the scheduling was moved to 2021, and this remained the policy when Carnegie Hall extended its closure to the entire year. The majority of the groups agreed to this, not knowing that the 2021 season would also be cancelled. One of the performances scheduled during the pandemic that never took place was an opera-oratorio titled *Eleni* by Greek-Australian composer Nestor Taylor. It was based on the best-selling book by the same title written by Greek-American author Nicholas Gage, and it recounts his mother's life and death at the hands of communist guerillas during the Greek civil war in the 1940s. Tiboris had planned the performance for March 25th 2021, marking the 200th anniversary of Greece's independence. Precisely when the pandemic broke out Tiboris and Taylor were to discuss the orchestration, but the uncertainty of whether the 2021 season would take place made planning for such a big event no longer possible.

Three months before the pandemic Eilana and Peter had decided to move to Palm Beach Florida. Palm Beach on the east coast of Florida is known for its luxurious estates and its beaches, upscale boutiques, galleries and restaurants. Its residents have a very high per capita income and its more famous residents have included Presidents John F. Kennedy and Donald Trump. The move came after 38 years of living in Montclair, New Jersey which was a relatively short commute to Peter's office in Manhattan. Peter reflects that it was pure luck that he and Eilana moved prior to the pandemic. Meanwhile, the entire office closed down and everyone worked remotely. At first it felt discombobulating not having a physical office after it closed in March, 2020 due to the pandemic and everyone began working remotely. Soon however, Tiboris discovered that remote work and communications had advantages. He was able to engage these first-rate conductors and business types to work with MidAmerica from their present and home location without moving to New York City, which for many was daunting because of the high cost of living.

For Tiboris, the loss of the 2021 season felt much worse than the loss of the previous year's because the pandemic appeared to be having a long-term impact, and thus the prospects for 2022 were bleak. It looked like the end had come: "we thought we were done with this thing," he recalls. Tiboris reduced the staff at MidAmerica from 24 to six persons, the office was closed, and those still employed were working remotely. The next move would have been to shut down operations completely. Tiboris recalls everyone believed the pandemic measures would be over and finished by early Fall, 2020 and that Carnegie Hall would be reopened, paving the way for a strong 2021 season, but this was not the case, and a second season was lost. Tiboris reflects that the loss of all of 2021 was much more severe than losing 2020 because with the complete loss of 2021 one had to think that maybe 2022 would be lost too. The loss of 2020 concerts was bad; the entire loss of 2021 was scary and dreadful; it raised the prospect of a third season being lost which would have meant the end of his company and many other classical music institutions throughout the country, especially in New York City. Throughout 2021 there was hopeful planning for the 2022 season, with the understanding that there was no other way than going forward. Fortunately the pandemic measures were lifted and about 75% of MidAmerica's normal programming took place beginning in March of that year, and most of the staff was brought back.

2022: The Comeback year

Tiboris and MidAmerica's policies during the pandemic paid off and a full recovery and return to normal began in 2022, underlying the organization's success and popularity. The first concert was on March 19th, and the first piece performed that day was Francis Poulenc's *Gloria*, with Eilana Lappanainen the featured soprano and Clell Wright conducting the Albany Chorale, the Grambling State University Concert Choir, the Huntington High School Choir, the Lee County High School Choir, the Shreveport Chorale, the Texarkana College Choir, the Texarkana Regional Chorale and the Valdosta State University Chamber Singers.

Following its first post-pandemic concert on March 19, 2022 the New England Symphonic Ensemble performed again in April, and then in a series of concerts in late May and throughout June, when MidAmerica's programming also included a performance by the Oxford Philharmonic Orchestra and its conductor Marios Papadopoulos. Things had gone back to normal with one ironic exception. Tiboris tested positive for Covid and was unable to conduct. He sat forlorn in his Midtown Manhattan hotel, with Eilana Lappalainen bolstering his morale with text messages sent from afar. Tiboris' absence from the podium was missed, but otherwise, MidAmerica's staging of concerts was running as smoothly as they had before the pandemic's rude interruption thanks to James Redcay, Eric Spiegel, Sonja Sepúlveda, Norman Dunfee, Joyce Howard, CJ Harden and Matt Harden, to name only a few.

The Festival of the Aegean and the Pandemic

As was the case with the Carnegie Hall programming, the Festival of the Aegean on Syros also lost two seasons. On April 2, 2020 the Festival issued the following statement:

> We are announcing the cancellation of all 2020 Festival of the Aegean and Greek Opera Studio programs and the postponement of all performances and programs to 2021. With all the uncertainty surrounding the coronavirus and plans for the summer, we are unable to book flights, communicate with venues, or ensure that all of our artists will be able to safely make it to Greece. We are very disappointed that we will not be able to make music together this summer, but the safety and wellbeing of all of our wonderful artists is our top concern and we look forward to presenting *Don Carlo* and

La Bohème in July 2021. We are viewing this isolation period as a time for creative growth and are working hard to implement new ideas and programs so that our 2021 Festival will be an even more rewarding experience for all involved. We wish everyone health and safety through these uncertain times, and we look forward to creating art together soon. In times of darkness, music truly is the best healer.

Two years later, in the summer of 2022, the festival was back with its 16th season. The premiere featured an opera gala honoring Peter Tiboris, who was stepping down as the festival's director and being replaced by Eilana Lappalainen. Aside from her singing career, Eilana was taking over the role of General Artistic Director for the International Festival of the Aegean, while also retaining her positions at the Greek Opera Studio and Berlin Opera Studio, as well as being the Artistic Administrator and Director of the Vocal Division at MidAmerica Productions and MidAm International. The gala in honor of Tiboris marking his fifteen years as the festival's director at the Apollo Theater featured Greek & International soloists, pianist Manolis Papasifakis, the Paris Children's Choir, American visiting choirs and a choir from the island of Syros. Speaking at the end of the event Tiboris said his efforts to establish and run the festival in Syros was for the love of doing it and because Greece was his ancestral home, and that ultimately "it's all about the music." The rest of that year's festival included Israeli and Greek music, the Athens Chamber Ensemble, Verdi's opera *Don Carlo,* an evening dedicated to Gershwin's music, the Children's *Bohème* by Puccini, a song night with the Greek Opera Studio soloists, a tribute to the American composer Erich Wolfgang Korngold and a gala performance by the Greek Opera Studio.

2023: THE ODYSSEY CONTINUES

The year 2023 was the year that MidAmerica and MidAm International returned to the normal full set of concerts and Tiboris himself returned to the conductor's podium. The hiatus of the pandemic was well in the back-view mirror. The 2023 season at Carnegie Hall ended with a 40th anniversary season finale performance honoring the work and retirement of our longtime Production Manager Norman Dunfee. At the conclusion of the last performance Tiboris called Dunfee to the stage in order that he could acknowledge the applause in his honor. The other guest conductors that day, Saturday, July 8th were Phillip Morrow and Jeremy Tucker. The participating choirs were the Campbell University Choir, the Deep River

Singers, the Fuquay-Varina Chorale, the Willow Spring High School Chorus and the Winders Ensemble. Later that month Tiboris was in Syros conducting Mozart's *Symphony No. 40* at the 2023 Festival of the Aegean. Earlier that year he was in Athens meeting with Dr. Nicholas Maliaras, the Music Director and Conductor of the Athens Philharmonia, discussing recent and future collaborations. From Athens he had gone on to the United Kingdom to take part in MidAm International's residency there.

In his 75th year, Peter Tiboris realizes he cannot engage in ambitious long term plans. Yet he continues to expand the geographic horizons of his personal and professional Odyssey with plans to be conducting in China in 2024. He passed on the artistic development to Eilana on Syros but remains at the helm of MidAmerica Productions and MidAm International.

While Peter Tiboris is cutting back although also planning future projects, he is taking time to reflect on his life's trajectory. There is a certain mellowing in the personality of the stubborn, uncompromising businessman. He realizes he has to treat friends and colleagues respectfully at all times, and when he is unable to do so he is quick to make amends. The process of having his biography written led him to reflect on his views on music and his life.

As a footnote to his view on music, Tiboris reflected on his life's Odyssey: "Now that I am 75 years old the project of this biography has been revealing and eye-opening and it has brought me back to places I had forgotten about and not thought about for generations. At times, it was very moving and caused me to stop and relive and think about how fortunate I have been to come from Sheboygan, Wisconsin, from a small parish, moving to where I could impact so many young people with the "art of music performances" in heralded places performing music of the highest order in the highest places. I am never forgetful of that. All of this has culminated into what we call 'wisdom', a nebulous word but a word which comes about only when one's life-experiences are so unique and singular that codifying those experiences provides reflective wisdom. I am grateful and I know I am one of the most fortunate persons in any musical circle. I have never forgotten that, and certainly hold these life experiences closely to me now."

E PILOGUE

Peter Tiboris describes his conducting style as one which allows the orchestra to play. He believes a conductor should not over conduct and he should find ways get the musicians to play for him and elicit the best out of them. This may well be true, but it is only the tip of the iceberg that showcases his easygoing charm. To get to that point at which he is on the podium of the concert hall and also at the helm of his business operations and can afford to be easy going, he has worked extremely hard. What lies below the waterline and is Peter Tiboris is what this biography has tried to reveal. The rich trajectory of his life so far had been examined with the help of countless conversations and messages exchanged between the two of us, interviews generously provided by his family members, including his wife, soprano Eilana Lappalainen, his closest associates in both Greece and the United States, newspaper articles and the extensive material available on MidAmerica's website.

Homer's *Odyssey* opens with a characterization of the hero of this epic story which translators have rendered in English in different ways. For example Robert Fitzgerald describes Odysseus as a "man skilled in all ways of contending," Robert Fagles calls him "a man of twists and turns," while in the more recently published and more vernacular translation Emily Wilson has him simply as "a complicated man." All three of those ways of explaining Odysseus are apt in Tiboris' case. Like

Odysseus, Tiboris went on a journey, a metaphorical one as well as a literal one. The metaphorical one was a quest for success and recognition as a presenter of classical music concerts and as a conductor. The second was a journey that took him from Sheboygan, Wisconsin to New York City and from there to Europe and beyond, and finally to acquiring a second musical home in Greece, his ancestral homeland.

To succeed in both those journeys Tiboris mobilized all the qualities which his personality, his upbringing, his training and his life experiences instilled in him. His personality seems to be an almost paradoxical combination of his father Ernest's quiet, faith-inflected modesty and self-effacing charm and Professor Charles Leonhard's self-assured no nonsense gruffness, along with the will to share the knowledge of music and to succeed which drove both those men. Ernest Tiboris instilled a love of music in his son along with a reverence towards the ancestral homeland and its Greek Orthodox religion. He then stood back and supported his son in his choice of career. Leonhard overawed Peter with his presence and his depth of knowledge and truly educated, inspired and motivated him. In a sense Peter never allowed himself to move away from the benign shadows his father and his professor cast over him. In some ways he remained the dutiful son and the studious disciple, something that required a constant effort to do more and more in order that he measure up to their high standards. Well below the surface there continued to be an insecurity about himself, however, his physical and mental being, his intellect and his talent. Tiboris responded with an incessant and continuous and stubborn effort to create and share music with as many people as he could reach. The perpetual flame that propelled him forward is still burning brightly as he reaches the seventy-fifth year of his life. This self-generated momentum is what his closest associates witnessed and describe when they speak of the combination of charm, obsessive energy and stubbornness. Tiboris, as one of them put it, is both "an unstoppable force and an immovable object."

This powerful impetus led Tiboris into the business side of music, where he would thrive despite being a novice. At the conclusion of the doctoral defense, Professor Leonhard told Peter to take care of the music and everything else would follow, which sounds very nice coming from an academic, and it stayed with Peter, who says basically his life is "all about the music." But it also sounds like the advice a respected music professor would give not having to worry about the rough and tumble business side of the music world. Peter was able to build on Leonhard's advice, keeping his focus on the music and its quality, but ensured he would be able to pursue a life in music by creating a solid business foundation. In doing so he forged new ground, becoming involved in a world that lay beyond that of his father and his professor. He had to use his wits and think on his feet because neither his background nor his training had equipped him for the major step he took by leaving the security of academia and entering the world of the music business in New York City.

Yet at the same time as his drive led him to take risks and to innovate – the MidAmerica concept is the epitome of a bold and original idea – Tiboris mitigated the risks by being cautious in the way he implemented his plans. When the formula worked, he explained, there was no need to change it. There was also a conservative approach to classical music, where his preferences remained in the Classical and Romantic periods, with only a few calculated forays into more modern works. Of classical music and in terms of business, as he himself likes to emphasize, once a particular model for MidAmerica's operations worked, it stayed in place and basically did not change in any environment.

In the Odyssey, the enchantress Circe describes the hero of the story as "the man who can adapt to anything."[85] Clearly Tiboris was also able to adapt along the way. He himself mentions family members and many friends and mentors who inspired him and from whom he gratefully accepted advice, and who helped and supported him at key moments in his life and career. In most cases the advice and the suggestions did not stop him moving ahead, they essentially informed and shaped the ways he went forward. MidAmerica Productions and its success were born out of his vision and imagination and the benefits to everyone around him were countless. As we have seen, for thousands of choristers and choir conductors the concerts at Carnegie Hall became the equivalent of witnessing one of Bernstein's televised Young People's Concerts, and arguably even more important. The growing success and growth of MidAmerica productions over forty years and also that of MidAm International have been highlighted in the preceding pages. Tiboris' remarkable range of conducting engagements throughout the world reflect a restless spirit unencumbered by boundaries and able to acclimatize in new environments. And the creation of the Festival of the Aegean and its continued success in a most difficult environment – with Odysseus-like adaptability in full demand – could count on its own as a major life achievement.

We can accept Peter Tiboris' own assessment of his life as being "all about the music" only if we take into account his extraordinary life journey and its rich complexity: One that took him from playing the church organ in Sheboygan, Wisconsin under his father's benevolent supervision all the way to Carnegie Hall as maestro Tiboris, a conductor and founder and general director of MidAmerica Productions, and on to series of other appointments and positions internationally culminating in the establishment of the Festival of the Aegean. A career that touched the lives of thousands of musicians and brought music to thousands around the world. A journey inspired by many and undertaken with a mixture of charm and stubbornness, artistic sensitivities and a sharp business acumen and self-promotion leavened by humility. A journey worthy of Odysseus, "a complicated man," "skilled in all ways contending" and able to deal with life's "twists and turns." But in Tiboris' case, Ithaca, the final destination, was and continues to be to be able to conduct, to produce and to share music the world over.

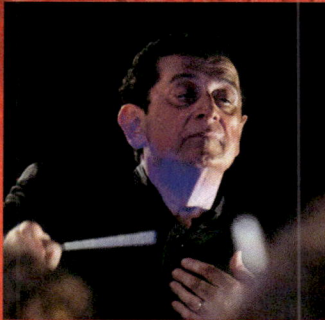

ATHENS CONCERT HALL POSTER

COMPLETE TIBORIS FAMILY OF GUS AND PETER, THEIR CHILDREN AND ALL GRAND KIDS, 2022, ELKAHART LAKE WISCONSIN REUNION

MIDAMERICA STAFF IN MANHATTAN CELEBRATING ON JULY 8 2023
NORMAN DUNFEE'S RETIREMENT AFTER 33 YEARS WITH
MIDAMERICA PRODUCTIONS

PETE, PETER AND STEPHANIE SUMMER OF 2022

PETER PRESENTING JOHN RUTTER WITH A FIRST-GENERATION OF A MOZART QUINTET
FROM EALRY 1800'S. A POST CONCERT GIFT AT CARNEGI H ALL

PETER AND EILANA AFTRER THE FIRST OPERA PERFORMANCE AT THE APOLLO THEATER JULY 10 2005

PETER AND EILANA IN NEW YORK CITY

CLOSE FRIEND DIMITRI TSITOURAS OF ATHENS AND PETER IN ATHENS OUT FOR DINNER

PETER AT HIS MOTHER AND FATHER'S GRAVESITE IN SHEBOYGAN, WISCONSIN

PETER IN SYROS WITH FRUIT DELIVERY FROM SPYROS RAMAS OF ALBANIA

PETER WITH BROTHER GUS IN 2022

PETER WITH CHRISTIAN CATENA OF ROME IN SYROS

Peter with Italian ballet choreographer and director Renato Zanella on Syros

Peter with Italian conductors Giovanni Pacor and Giuseppe Lanzetta after a concert in Florence

Peter with Longtime Friend and tenor Giorgio Aristo Mikroutsikos

PETER WITH NIKOS MALIARAS MUSIC DIRECTOR OF THE PHILHARMONIA ORCHESTRA OF ATHENS

PETER WITH NORMAN DUNFEE, CENTER ON HIS 33 YEAR RETIREMENT ON JULY 8 2023
AND WITH NORMAN'S PARTNER RAYMOND HUGHES IN MANHATTAN

Theodorakis Concert at the Festival of the Aegean

Poster content:

THE 14TH ANNUAL INTERNATIONAL
FESTIVAL OF THE AEGEAN
PETER TIBORIS, GENERAL DIRECTOR

THEODORAKIS
ELECTRA
(DANCE PERFORMANCE)

WORLD PREMIERE: FRIDAY, JULY 27, 2018 - 2030hrs

MIKIS THEODORAKIS, COMPOSER   RENATO ZANELLA, CHOREOGRAPHER

ASTERIS KUTULAS, CO-DIRECTOR
ELECTRA - SOFIA PINTZOU (GREECE)
CLYTEMNESTRA - ALEXANDRA GRAVILESCU (ROMANIA)
CHRYSOTHEMIS - TAMARA ALVES DORNELAS SOUZA (BRASIL)
ORESTES - ELTION MERJA (ALBANIA)
AIGISTHOS - VALENTIN STOICA (ROMANIA)
PYLADES - FLORIENT CADOR (FRANCE)

AND ADDITIONAL PERFORMANCES
JULY 28 & 29, 2018 - 2030hrs

APOLLO THEATER
HERMOUPOLIS, SYROS, GREECE

This performance is made possible with the cooperation of Europaballett

MIDAMERICA PRODUCTIONS, INC.
PETER TIBORIS, FOUNDER, GENERAL DIRECTOR & MUSIC DIRECTOR
JOHN RUTTER, CONDUCTOR LAUREATE
Celebrating MidAmerica's Historic 41st Anniversary
presents

Conductor
Peter Tiboris

*On the 40th Anniversary, to the day, of his New York
conducting debut and the 40th Anniversary of
MidAmerica Productions and MidAm International*

leading a performance of
BEETHOVEN'S
NINTH SYMPHONY, Op. 125
"Ode to Joy"
For adult, university, college choirs & individual singers

also featuring
Special Guest John Rutter
conducting his
Magnificat
For youth choirs, high school choirs & individual singers

with the **New England Symphonic Ensemble
and Distinguished Soloists
SUNDAY, JANUARY 7, 2024**
Stern Auditorium / Perelman Stage at
CARNEGIE HALL

Choral Residency: Thursday, January 4, 2024 - Monday, January 8, 2024
Open to all distinguished American choral singers
Choral Registration Deadline: July 1, 2023

> Tiboris' performance was one of the most exciting
> and inspiring I've ever heard of this master-work.
> B.Zakaraisen, *NY Daily News*

M&AP
MIDAMERICA
PRODUCTIONS
www.midamerica-music.com
www.petertiboris.com

For more information, contact Matthew C. Harden, Program Development Associate
at +1 (646) 248-6443 or at mharden@midamerica-music.com

FOSTER OF JANUARY 7TH 2024 CONCERT AT CARNEGIE HALL

VIEW OF THE TIBORIS-LAPPALAINEN HOME AT DANI ON SYROS

APPENDICES

I. APPOINTMENTS AND POSITIONS

Founder, General and Artistic Director (1984 - present) MidAmerica Productions, Inc. and MidAm International, Inc.New York, NY,

Founder, Music Director and Conductor (1988 - 1999) Manhattan Philharmonic New York, NY,

Principal Guest Conductor (December 2013 - 2018) Direttore Ospite Principale Orchestra da Camera Fiorentina Florence, Italy

Music Director and Conductor (2009 - present) Pan-European Philharmonia Warsaw, Poland

General Music Director and Conductor (March 1, 2014 - April 30, 2021) Symphonisches Orchestra Vienna, Austria

Principal Guest Conductor (2010 - 2012) Direttore Ospite Principale Collegium Symphonium Veneto Padova, Italy

Founder and Artistic Director (2005 - 2020) International Festival of the Aegean Ermoupolis, Island of Syros, Greece

Honorary Conductor (2008) Principal
    Guest Conductor (1992 - 2004)
    Bohuslav Martinou Philharmonic
    Zlin, Czech Republic
Founder, Producer, Elysium Recording
    (2000-Present) with 30 releases
    world-wide
Founder, Producer of "Just Tenors"
    Management Inc., NYC (2002-
    2012)

II. Partial Listing of Conducted Repertoire since 1984

Works Conducted

Operas:
Bizet: Carmen
Cherubini: Médée
Lehár: The Merry Widow
Mascagni: Cavalleria
Mascagni: Silvano
Mascagni: Zanetto
Mozart: Don Giovanni, K.527
Mozart: Die Zauberflöte, K.620
Puccini: Tosca
Rossini: The Barber of Seville
Rossini: Ermioni (NY Premiere)
Theodore Stathis: Lord Elgin
Taneyev: Agamemnon (from the
    Oresteia)
Theodorakis: Elektra (US Premiere,
    June 2000)
Verdi: La Traviata
Verdi: Rigoletto

Ballets:
Adam: Il Corsaro
Grieg: Peer Gynt (Premiere Teatro
    di Roma, October 2007; Named
    Ballet of the Year in Italy, 2007;
    Renato Zanello, Choreographer)
Ravel: Boléro
Ravel: Pavane pour une infante défunte
Ravel: La valse, poème
    choréographique pour orchestre
Ravel: Valse Nobles et Sentimentales
Incidental Music
Grieg: Peer Gynt (complete)

Concert Works
Arriaga: Overture to Los escalvos
    felices
Arriaga: Symphony in D minor
Bach: Lobet den Herren (Motet No. 6)
Bach: Cello Suite No. 1 in G major,
    BWV 1007
Barber: Adagio for Strings
Barber: Overture to The School for
    Scandal
Barber: Prayers of Kierkegaard, Op.30
Barber: First Essay for Orchestra, Op.
    12
Barber: Second Essay for Orchestra,
    Op. 17
Barber: Third Essay for Orchestra, Op.
    47
Beethoven: "Ah, perfido!" Op. 65
Beethoven: Choral Fantasy, Op.80
Beethoven: Concerto for Violin, Cello,
    and Piano in C major, Op. 56

Beethoven: Coriolan Overture

Beethoven: Leonore Overture No. 1

Beethoven: Leonore Overture No. 2

Beethoven: Leonore Overture No. 3

Beethoven: Mass in C major, Op. 96

Beethoven: Overture to The Consecration of the House, Op. 124

Beethoven: Overture to Egmont, Op. 84

Beethoven: Overture to Fidelio, Op. 72

Beethoven: Overture to Die Geschöpfe des Prometheus, Op.43

Beethoven: Symphony No. 1 in C major, Op 21

Beethoven: Symphony No. 3 in E-flat major, Op. 55 ("Eroica")

Beethoven: Symphony No. 4 in B-flat major, Op. 60

Beethoven: Symphony No. 5 in C minor, Op. 67

Beethoven: Symphony No. 6 in F major, Op. 68 ("Pastorale")

Beethoven: Symphony No. 7 in A major, Op. 92

Beethoven: Symphony No. 9 in D minor, Op. 125 ("Choral")

Beethoven: Piano Concerto No. 1 in C major, Op. 15

Beethoven: Piano Concerto No. 3 in C minor, Op. 37

Beethoven: Piano Concerto No. 4 in G major, Op. 58

Beethoven: Piano Concerto No. 5 in E-flat major, Op. 73 ("Emperor")

Beethoven: Violin Concerto in D major, Op. 61

Beethoven/Mahler: Overture toThe Consecration of the House

Beethoven/Mahler: Symphony No. 3

Beethoven/Mahler: Symphony No. 5

Beethoven/Mahler: Symphony No. 7

Beethoven/Mahler: Symphony No. 9 (1895) (NY Premiere)

Bellini: Te Deum in C major

Berlioz: Le mort de Cléopâtre, H. 36

Berlioz: Te Deum, Op. 22

Bernstein: Candide (excerpts)

Bizet: Carmen Suite No. 1

Bizet: Carmen Suite No. 2

Bizet: Te Deum

Boccherini: Sinfonia No. 8 in A major, G. 508

Boito: "Prologo in cielo" from Mefistofele

Brahms: Ave Maria, Op. 12

Brahms: Ein deutsches Requiem, Op. 45

Brahms: Piano Concerto No. 1 in D minor, Op. 15

Brahms: Symphony No. 1 in C minor, Op. 68

Brahms: Symphony No. 3 in F major, Op. 90

Brahms: Symphony No. 4 in E minor, Op. 98

Brahms: Tragic Overture, Op. 81

Brahms: Variations on a Theme by Haydn, Op. 56a

Bruckner: Psalm 150

Bruckner: Te Deum

Bruch: Violin Concerto in G minor,
  Op. 26
Brusa: Adagio for Strings (European
  Premiere, 2011, Firenze)
Catalani:"Ebben? Ne andro lontana"
  from La Wally
Cherubini: Overture to Lodoïska
Cherubini: Requiem in C minor
Chopin: Piano Concerto No.1 in E
  minor, Op. 11
Chopin: Piano Concerto No. 2 in F
  minor, Op. 21
Constantinides: Byron's Greece (World
  Premiere)
Constantinides: Lament of Antigone
  (NY Premiere, January 1984)
Constantinides: Hymn to the Human
  Spirit (World Premiere, May 1985)
Copland: Appalachian Spring
David: Trombone Concerto, Op. 4
Debussy: L'Enfant prodigue (lyrical
  scene)
Dello Joio: Nativity: A Canticle for the
  Child (NY Premiere, December
  1988)
Dohnányi: Stabat Mater (for women's
  voices) (NY Premiere, November
  1989)
Donizetti: "Verrano a te sull'aure"
  (Lucia di Lammermoor)
Donizetti:"Una furtiva lagrima"
  (L'elisir d'amore)
Donizetti:"Favorita del re...spirito
  gentil" (La favorita)
Donizetti:"Ah mes amis....pour mon
  âme" (La fille du régiment)

Dvořák: Carnival Overture
Dvořák: Cello Concerto in B.minor,
  Op. 104, B.191
Dvořák: Scherzo Capriccioso
Dvořák: Serenade for Strings, Op. 22
Dvořák: Slavonic Rhapsody in G
  minor
Dvořák: The Spectre's Bride
Dvořák: Symphony No. 4 in D minor,
  Op. 13, B. 41
Dvořák: Symphony No. 5 in F major,
  Op. 76, B. 54
Dvořák: Symphony No. 6 in D major,
  Op. 60
Dvořák: Symphony No. 7 in D minor,
  Op. 70
Dvořák: Symphony No. 9 in E minor,
  Op. 95 ("From the New World")
Dvořák: Symphonic Variations
Dvořák: Te Deum
Dvořák: The Water Goblin, Op. 107
Effinger: Set of Three (NY Premiere)
Fauré: Requiem in D minor, Op. 48
Gerratana:Edymion Prima
  Escuyzionese Arch (World
  Premiere)
Gershwin: Porgy and Bess Suite
Glass: The Canyon (NY Premiere,
  April 1991; German Premiere,
  March 1991)
Gounod: "Ah! Je veux vivre"(Roméo et
  Juliette)
Grieg: Peer Gynt Complete Incidental
  Music based on Ibsen's play
Grieg: Holberg Suite, Op. 40
Handel: Israel in Egypt

Handel: Messiah

Haydn: Arianna auf Naxos (solo cantata for mezzo-soprano)

Haydn: The Creation

Haydn: Cello Concerto No. 1 in C major, Hob. VIIb/1Hob.

Haydn: Cello Concerto in D , major

Haydn: Paukenmesse

Haydn: "Perchè, se tanti siete" from Scena di Berenice

Haydn: Piano Concerto in D major, Hob.XVIII:11

Haydn: Trumpet Concerto in E-flat major, Hob.XVIIe:1

Haydn: Symphony No. 43 in E-flat major

Haydn: Symphony No. 60 in C major ("Il distratto")

Haydn: Symphony No.104 in D major

Kodály: Te Deum of Budavár

Liszt: Dante Symphony

Liszt: A Faust Symphony

Liszt: Piano Concerto No. 1 in E-flat major, S.124

Liszt: Piano Concerto No. 2 in A major, S. 125

Mahler: "Des Knaben Wunderhorn"

Mahler: Symphony No. 1 in D major

Mahler: Symphony No. 2 in C minor

Mahler: Symphony No. 4 in G major

Magarshak: Piano Concerto in C minor (World Premiere, May 1992)

Martinů: Double Concerto for Two String Orchestras, Piano and Timpani

Mascagni: Intermezzo from L'Amico Fritz

Mascagni: Intermezzo from Cavalleria rusticana

Mendelssohn: Ellijah

Mendelssohn: Symphony No. 3 in A minor, Op. 56 ("Scottish")

Mendelssohn: Symphony No. 4 in A major, Op. 90 ("Italian")

Mendelssohn: Symphony No. 5 in D major/D minor, Op. 107 ("Reformation")

Mendelssohn: Concerto for Violin and Piano in F major

Mendelssohn: Concerto for Violin, Piano, and String Orchestra in D minor

Mendelssohn: Violin Concerto in E minor, Op. 64

Mozart: Ave Verum Corpus, K.618

Mozart: "Ch'io mi scordi di te?" from Idomeneo, K.505

Mozart: Concertante for Violin and Viola, K.364

Mozart: Concerto No.1 for flute and orchestra, K.313

Mozart: Concerto for flute and harp, K.299

Mozart: Concerto No. 5 for violin and orchestra, K.219

Mozart: "Coronation Mass," K.317

Mozart: ""Der Schauspieldirektor" from The Impresario, K.486

Mozart: Die Schuldigkeit des Ersten Gebots, K.35 (NY Premiere)

Mozart: Divertimento in D, K.142

Mozart: Divertimenti for String Orchestra, K.136

Mozart: Ergo Interest, K.143

Mozart: Exsultate, Jubilate, K.165

Mozart: Serenade No. 13 for Strings in G major, K.525 ("Eine Kleine Nachtmusik")

Mozart: Great Mass in C minor, K.427

Mozart: Mass for Archbishop Colloredo, K.337

Mozart: Overture to La clemenza di Tito

Mozart: Overture to Le nozze de Figaro

Mozart: Overture to The Impresario, K.486

Mozart: Overture to The Magic Flute, K.620

Mozart: Piano Concerto No. 12, K.414

Mozart: Piano Concerto No. 14, K.449

Mozart: Piano Concerto No. 17, K.453

Mozart: Piano Concerto No. 19, K.459

Mozart: Piano Concerto No. 21, K.467

Mozart: Regina Coeli, K.108

Mozart: Requiem, K.626 (Sussmayr)

Mozart: Symphony in D major, K.207a

Mozart: Symphony No. 16 in C major, K.128

Mozart: Symphony No. 29 in A major, K.201

Mozart: Symphony No. 38, K.504

Mozart: Symphony No. 40, K.550

Mozart: Symphony No. 41, K.551

Mozart: Violin Concerto No. 3 in G major, K.216

Mozart: Violin Concerto No. 4 in D major, K.218

Mozart: Violin Concerto No. 5 in A major, K.219

Mozart/Mahler: Symphony No. 40, K.550

Mozart/Mahler: Symphony No. 41, K.551

Mussorgsky/Rimsky-Korsakov: "Coronation Scene" from Boris Godunov

Nielsen: Hymnus Amoris (NY Premiere)

Nielsen: Little Suite, Op. 1

Nielsen: String Suite

Nielsen: Symphony No. 3, Op. 27 ("Sinfonia Espansiva")

Orff: Carmina Burana

Ponchielli: "Suicidio" from La Gioconda

Poulenc: Gloria

Puccini: Intermezzo from Manon Lescaut

Puccini: "Un bel di vedromo" from Madama Butterfly

Puccini: "Visi d'Arte" from Tosca

Prokofiev: Cello Concerto, Op. 58

Prokofiev: Romeo and Juliet, Suites Nos. 1 and 2

Ravel: Bolero

Rimsky-Korsakov: Concerto for Trombone and Orchestra in B-flat major

Rossini: Overture to The Italian Girl in Algiers

Rossini: Sonata for Strings No. 2

Rossini: Stabat Mater

Rossini:"Una voce poco fa" (Il barbieri di Siviglia)

Rossini:"Tutto apprendi" (Guglielmo Tell)

Rutter: Gloria

Sarasate: Carmen Fantasy for Violin

Saint Saens: Piano Concerto No. 2

Schnittke: Concerto for Piano and Strings (NY Premiere)

Schubert: Overture to Rosamunde

Schubert: Salve Regina, D.676

Schubert: Stabat Mater

Schubert: Tantum ergo, D. 962

Schubert: Symphony No. 4 in C minor, D.417 ("Tragic")

Schubert: Symphony No. 5 in D-flat major, D.485

Schubert: Symphony No. 8 in B minor, D. 759 ("Unfinished")

Schubert: Symphony No. 9 in C major, D. 944 ("The Great")

Schubert/Mahler: Symphony No. 9 (First NY Performance since 1910)

Schumann: Symphony No. 3 in E-flat major, Op. 97 ("Rhenish")

Schumann: Symphony No. 4 in D minor, Op. 120

Shostakovich: Festival Overture

Shostakovich: Piano Concerto No. 2 in F major, Op. 102

Shostakovich: Sonata for Cello and Piano in D minor, Op. 36

Shostakovich: Symphony No. 1 in F minor, Op. 10

Shostakovich: Symphony No. 5 in D minor, Op. 47

Sibelius: Romance in C major for string orchestra, Op. 42

R. Strauss: Tod und Verklärung, Op. 24

R. Strauss: Four Last Songs

R. Strauss: Salome

R. Strauss: Zueignung, Op. 10, No. 1 ("Devotion")

R. Strauss: Muttertandelei, Op. 43, No. 2

R. Strauss: Wiegenlied, Op. 41, No. 1

R. Strauss: Waldseligkeit, Op. 49, No. 1

R. Strauss: Cacillie, Op. 27, No. 2

Suppe: Poet and Peasant Overture

Taneyev: Symphony No. 4 in C minor (US Premiere)

Taneyev: Duet for Soprano and Tenor after Tchaikovsky's Fantasy Overture Romeo and Juliet (US Premiere)

Taneyev: "Agamemnon" from Oresteia (US Premiere)

Tchaikovsky: Ode to Joy (NY Premiere)

Tchaikovsky: Piano Concerto No.1 in B-flat minor

Tchaikovsky: Romeo and Juliet

Tchaikovsky: Serenade for Strings in C major, Op. 48

Tchaikovsky: Symphony No. 1 in G minor, Op. 13

Tchaikovsky: Symphony No. 4 in F minor, Op. 36

Tchaikovsky: Symphony No. 5 in E minor, Op. 64

Tchaikovsky: Symphony No. 6 in B minor, Op. 74 ("Pathetique")

Tchaikovsky: Tatiana's Letter Scene from Eugene Onegin

Tchaikovsky: Violin Concerto in D major, Op. 35

Theodorakis: Rhapsody for cello and orchestra (US Premiere, May 2003)

Vaughan Williams: Five Mystical Songs

Vaughan Williams: Hodie

Vaughan Williams: Magnificat

Vaughan Williams: Serenade to Music

Verdi: Ave Maria

Verdi: "Ecco L'orindo campo" from Un Ballo in Maschera

Verdi: "La Peregrina-Ballet de la Riene" from Don Carlo

Verdi: Overture to La Forza del Destino

Verdi: Overture to Luisa Miller

Verdi: Overture to Nabucco

Verdi: Stabat Mater from Quattro Pezzi Sacri

Verdi: Te Deum from Quattro Pezzi Sacri

Verdi: Requiem

Verdi: Requiem (NY Premiere of David Rosen's 1874 Critical Edition)

Verdi: Stabat Mater

Verdi: "Triumphal Scene" from Aida

Vivaldi: The Four Seasons

Vivaldi: Gloria

Wagner: The Immolation of Brünnhilde from Götterdämmerung

Wagner: Wesendonck Lieder

Weber: Overture to Oberon

III. ORCHESTRAS CONDUCTED SINCE 1984

New York Orchestras Conducted
Manhattan Philharmonic, Founder, Music Director and Conductor (Since 1988)
American Symphony Orchestra
Brooklyn Philharmonic
New York City Symphony
Manhattan Chamber Ensemble
U.S. Orchestras Conducted
Phoenix Symphony, Arizona
Orlando Philharmonic, Florida
Knoxville Symphony Orchestra, Tennessee
Orchestras Conducted on Recordings
Bohuslav Martinů Philharmonic(Czech Republic)
Brno State Philharmonic (Czech Republic)
Moscow Radio/TV Symphony Orchestra (Russia)
Sofia National Opera Orchestra (Bulgaria)
Virtuosi di Praga (Czech Republic)
Warsaw Philharmonic Orchestra (Poland)

International Orchestras Conducted

ALBANIA
Symphony Orchestra of the Opera and
    Ballet of the National Theater of
    Albania, Tirana
AUSTRIA
Symphonisches Orchestra Wien
    (Vienna)
BULGARIA
Pazardjik Symphony Orchestra
Plovdiv National Opera Orchestra
Sofia National Opera House Orchestra
CANADA
Société Philharmonique de Montréal
CHINA
Macau Symphony Orchestra
CROATIA
Orchestra and Chorus of the Croatian
    National Theater (Split)
CZECH REPUBLIC
Bohuslav Martinů Philharmonic
Brno Philharmonic Orchestra
Czech Philharmonic Chamber
    Orchestra
Moravian Philharmonic (Olomouc)
North Czech Philharmonic Orchestra
    (Teplice)
Radio Symphony Orchestra Prague
    (October 2012)
Virtuosi di Praga
EGYPT
Cairo National Opera Orchestra
ENGLAND
Royal Philharmonic (London)
Philharmonia Orchestra (London)

Oxford Philomusica (Oxford)
FRANCE
Orchestre Bel'Arte (Paris)
GERMANY
Europa Philharmonie, Baden-
    Wurttenburg (2013)
Niedersächsische Orchester Hannover
ISRAEL
Israel Symphony Orchestra Rishon Le-
    Zion (Herzliya)
ITALY
Orchestra da camera di Bari
Il Orchestra del Giglio (Empoli)
Orchestra da Camera Fiorentina
    (Florence)
Orcestra di Teatro di Messina
    (Taormina)
Orchestra Filarmonia Calabrese
    (Lamezia Terme)
Orchestra Filarmonica Della Calabria
    (Amantea, Italy)
Orchestra "I Solisti di Napoli"
Orchestra Sinfonica Abruzzese
Orchestra Sinfonica Città di Grosseto
Orchestra Sinfonica della Provincia di
    Veneto
Orchestra Sinfonica del Mediterraneo
    Messina
Orchestra Sinfonica di Molise
    (Campobasso)
Orchestra Sinfonica della Provincia di
    Bari
Orchestra Sinfonica della Provincia di
    Lecco
Orchestra Sinfonica Siciliana di
    Palermo

Orchestra Sinfonica Trentina (Belluno)
Orchestra del Teatro Regio di Parma
Orchestra del Teatro dell'Opera di
Roma
Orchestra del Teatro Marrucino di
Chieti (Pescara)
Orchestra Sinfonica della Magna
Grecia (Taranto)
Sinfonica di Lecce
Orchestra Teatro del Giglio Lucca
Teatro Filarmonica di Verona
MEXICO
Guanajuato Symphony Orchestra
Orquestra de Bellas Artes Mexico City
Orquesta Sinfonica del Estado de
Mexico
State of Mexico Symphony Orchestra
(Toluca)
POLAND
Pan-European Philharmonia
Opera i Filarmonia Podlaska
(Bialystok)
Silesian Philharmonic (Katowice)
State Philharmonic of Bialystok
State Philharmonic of Bydgoszcz
State Philharmonic of Poznan
State Philharmonic of Rzeszow
State Philharmonic of Wroclaw
PORTUGAL
Orquestra de Camara de Cascais e
Oeiras
Filarmonia de Gaia
ROMANIA
Radio Symphony Orchestra of
Bucharest

RUSSIA
Glinka Capelle Philharmonic of St.
Petersburg
Radio and Television Orchestra of
Moscow
SERBIA
VSO Serbian Symphony (Novi Sad)
SPAIN
Orquesta Sinfonica Ciudad de Elche
(February 2013)
SWITZERLAND
Sinfonieorchester Swiss-Appenzell
(Zurich)
TURKEY
Millî Reasürans Chamber Orchestra
(Istanbul)
UKRAINE
Kiev National Symphony
National Symphony Opera Orchestra

IV. MUSICAL WORKS CONDUCTED SINCE 1980 THAT LEFT A LASTING IMPRESSION ON HIS MUSICAL CAREER

Samuel Osmond Barber II (1910 -
1981)
Prayers of Kierkegaard, Op. 30
Ludwig van Beethoven (1770 - 1827)
Symphony No. 3 in E♭ major, "Eroica",
Op. 55
Symphony No. 5 in C minor, Op. 67
Symphony No. 6 in F major,
"Pastorale", Op. 68

Leonore Overture No. 2 in C major, Op. 72a

Leonore Overture No. 3 in C major, Op. 72b

Piano Concerto No. 5 in E♭ major, Op. 73

Symphony No. 7 in A major, Op. 92

Symphony No. 9 in D minor, Op. 125

Symphony No. 9 in D minor, Op. 125 [Orchestration by Gustav Mahler (1860 - 1911)] (*New York Premiere)

Leonore Overture No. 1, Op. 138

Georges Bizet (1838 - 1875)

Carmen

Johannes Brahms (1833 - 1897)

Symphony No. 1 in C minor, Op. 68

Symphony No. 3 in F major, Op. 90

Symphony No. 4 in E minor, Op. 98

Josef Anton Bruckner (1824 - 1896)

Tantum ergo, WAB 32

Luigi Cherubini (1760 - 1842)

Requiem No.1 in C minor

Frédéric François Chopin (1810 - 1849)

Piano Concerto No. 2 in F minor, Op. 21

Antonín Dvořák (1841 - 1904)

Serenade for Strings in E major, Op. 22 (B. 52)

Symphony No. 7 in D minor, Op. 70, B. 141

Symphony No. 9 in E minor, "From the New World", Op. 95, B. 178

Philip Glass (b. 1937)

The Canyon (*New York Premiere)

Edvard Hagerup Grieg (1843 - 1907)

Peer Gynt, Op. 23

Georg Friedrich Händel (1685 - 1759)

Israel in Egypt, HWV 54

Franz Joseph Haydn (1732 - 1809)

Symphony No. 60 in C major "Il distratto", Hob. I/60

Symphony No. 104 in D major, Hob. 1/104

Die Schöpfung, "The Creation", Hob. XXI:2

Missa in tempore belli, "Paukenmesse", Hob. XXII/9

Zoltán Kodály (1882 - 1967)

Te Deum

Franz Liszt (1811 - 1886)

Eine Faust-Symphonie in drei Charakterbildern, S.108

A Symphony to Dante's Divine Comedy, S.109

Gustav Mahler (1860 - 1911)

Symphony No. 1 in D major, "Titan"

Symphony No. 2 in C minor, "Resurrection"

Symphony No. 5

Pietro Mascagni (1863 - 1945)

Cavalleria rusticana

Felix Mendelssohn (1809 - 1847)

Symphony No. 3 in A minor, "Scottish", Op. 56

Elias, Op. 70

Symphony No. 4 in A major, "Italian", Op. 90

Symphony No. 5 in D major/D minor, "Reformation", Op. 107

Wolfgang Amadeus Mozart (1756 - 1791)

Missa Solemnis in C major, K. 337

Große Messe in c-Moll, K. 427/417a

Piano Concerto No. 17 in G major, K. 453

Piano Concerto No. 21 in C major, K. 467

Le Nozze di Figaro, K. 492

Don Giovanni, K. 527

Symphony No. 40 in G minor, K. 550

Symphony No. 41 in C major, K. 551

Die Zauberflöte, K. 620

Requiem in D minor, K. 626

Carl August Nielsen (1865 - 1931)

Suite for Strings (Little Suite), Op. 1

Hymnus Amoris, Op. 12

Giacomo Puccini (1858 - 1924)

Tosca

Gioachino Antonio Rossini (1792 - 1868)

Il Barbiere di Siviglia

Stabat Mater

John Milford Rutter (b. 1945)

Gloria

Magnificat

Requiem

Alfred Garrievich Schnittke (1934 - 1998)

Concerto for Piano and String Orchestra

Franz Peter Schubert (1797 - 1828)

Symphony No. 5 in B♭ major, D. 485

Symphony No. 8 in B minor, "Unfinished Symphony", D. 759

Symphony No. 9 in C major, "The Great", D 944

Richard Georg Strauss (1864 - 1949)

Vier letzte Lieder, TrV 296/AV 150

Pyotr Ilyich Tchaikovsky (1840 - 1893)

Romeo and Juliet, TH 42, ČW 39

Symphony No. 4 in F minor, Op. 36

Symphony No. 5 in E minor, Op. 64

Ralph Vaughan Williams (1872 - 1958)

Five Mystical Songs

Giuseppe Fortunino Francesco Verdi (1813 - 1901)

La Traviata

Messa da Requiem

Rigoletto

Stabat Mater

Te Deum

V. DISCOGRAPHY SINCE 1984

Recordings: 1992-2023

March, 2023

Pan-European Philharmonia of Warsaw

All Beethoven:

Symphony No. 6 in F major, Op. 68, "Pastoral"

Piano Concerto No. 1. in C major, Op. 15 with pianist Marios Papadopoulos, London UK

Peter Tiboris, Music Director & Conductor

April, 2019
Pan-European Philharmonia of
    Warsaw
Tchaikovsky:
Symphony No. 4. in F minor, Op. 36
Beethoven:
Symphony No. 7 in A major, Op. 92
Peter Tiboris, Music Director &
    Conductor

April, 2018
Pan-European Philharmonia of
    Warsaw
Beethoven:
Symphony No. 3 in E flat major
    ("Eroica"), Op. 55
Tchaikovsky:
Symphony No. 5. In E minor, Op. 64
Peter Tiboris, Music Director &
    Conductor

June, 2015
Pan-European Philharmonia of
    Warsaw
Verdi:
Overture to La Forza del Destino
Beethoven:
"Ah Perfido" Op. 65
Eilana Lappalainen, soprano
Schubert:
Symphony No. 8 in B minor, D. 759
    ("Unfinished")
Peter Tiboris, conductor

2008
Mascagni: Zanetto and
L'amico Fritz—Intermezzo
Cavalleria rusticana—Intermezzo
Elysium GRK726
Bohuslav Martinů Philharmonic of the
    Czech Republic

1998
Music for Doubles:
Peter Tiboris, conductor
Krommer: Concerto for Two
Clarinets and Orchestra, Op. 35
Stanley & Naomi Drucker, clarinets
Saint-Saëns: La Muse et le poète
Charles Rex, violin; Christopher Rex,
    cello
Martinů: Double Concerto for Two
    String Orchestras, Piano and
    Timpani
Elysium GRK714
Jacqueline Schiller, piano;
Gregor Kruyer, timpani
Bohuslav Martinů Philharmonic of the
    Czech Republic

1997
Beethoven:
Symphony No. 5 in C minor, Op. 67
Symphony No. 7 in A, Op. 92
(incorporating Mahler's Retuschen in a
    World Premier Release)
Elysium GRK712 Peter Tiboris,
    conductor
Warsaw Philharmonic Orchestra
(Rerelease by Albany Records)

1996
Mozart:
Symphony No. 40 in G minor, K.550
Symphony No. 41 in C ("Jupiter"),
    K.551
Beethoven:
Leonore Overture No. 3
(incorporating Mahler's Retuschen in a
    World Premier Release)
Elysium GRK710
Peter Tiboris, conductor
Bohuslav Martinů Philharmonic of the
    Czech Republic

1995
Dvorak: The Spectre's Bride
Elysium GRK700
Peter Tiboris, conductor
Jitka Sobehartova, soprano;
Jan Markvart, tenor;
Jiri Kubik, baritone
Bohuslav Martinů Philharmonic &
    Bratislava Chorus of the Czech
    Republic
All Dvorak:
The Water Goblin, Op. 107;
Symphonic Variations, Op. 78;
Slavonic Rhapsody, Op. 45, No. 2;
Scherzo Capriccioso, Op. 66
Elysium GRK701
Peter Tiboris, conductor
Jitka Sobehartova, soprano;
Jan Markvart, tenor;
Jiri Kubik, baritone
Bohuslav Martinů Philharmonic &
Bratislava Chorus of the Czech
    Republic

All Beethoven:
Symphony No. 3 in E flat, Op. 55
    ("Eroica")
Coriolan Overture, Op. 62; Leonore
    Overture No. 2, Op. 72A
(incorporating Mahler's Retuschen in a
    World Premier Release)
Elysium GRK702
Peter Tiboris, conductor
Bohuslav Martinů Philharmonic of the
    Czech Republic
Haydn and Hellenic Antiquity:
Symphony No. 43 ("Mercury"), Scena
    di Berenice, Ariadne Auf Naxos
    Cantata, Aria from
Orfeo, Insertion Aria for Traetta's
    Iphigenia
Elysium GRK706
Peter Tiboris, conductor
Eleni Matos, mezzo-soprano;
Jeff Prillaman, tenor
Virtuosi Di Praga
Bohuslav Martinů Philharmonic of the
    Czech Republic
Mascagni: Silvano
Elysium GRK707
Peter Tiboris, conductor
Joseph Wolverton, tenor (Silvano)
Rachel Sparer, soprano (Matilde)
Bojan Knezevic, baritone (Renzo)
Lorraine DiSimone, mezzo-soprano
    (Rosa)
Pro Arte Chorale (Bart Folse, director)
Bohuslav Martinů Philharmonic of the
    Czech Republic
Verdi: Requiem

Elysium GRK708
(Critical Edition)—Including the 1874
 "Liber scriptus" for fugue chorus
 (World Premier Release)
Peter Tiboris, conductor
Maria Belcheva, soprano;
Stefka Mineva, mezzo-soprano;
Roumen Doykov, tenor;
Dimiter Petkov, bass
Sofia National Opera House Chorus
 and Orchestra

1993
Schubert: Symphony No. 9 in C (The
 Great C Major)
Beethoven: Overture "For the
 Consecration of the House"
(incorporating Mahler's Retuschen in a
 World Premier Release)
Albany 089 World Premiere Recording
Peter Tiboris, conductor
Warsaw Philharmonic Orchestra,
 Janácek State Opera Chorus
Beethoven: Symphony no 5 in C minor,
 Op. 67;
Symphony No. 7 in A, Op. 92
(incorporating Mahler's Retuschen in a
 World Premier Release)
Albany 110
Peter Tiboris, Conductor
Warsaw Philharmonic Orchestra

1992 (Premier Recording)
Beethoven: Symphony No. 9 in D
 minor, Op. 125 "Choral"
(incorporating Mahler's Retuschen in a
 World Premier Release)
Bridge 9033
Peter Tiboris, Conductor
Leah Anne Meyers, soprano;
Ilene Sameth, alto;
James Clark, tenor;
Richard Conant, bass
Janácek State Opera Choir
Brno State Philharmonic of the Czech
 Republic
Tchaikovsky: Romeo and Juliet (Vocal
 Version by Taneyev for Soprano &
 Tenor in a
World Premier Release)
Taneyev: Symphony No. 4 in C minor,
 Op. 12
Bridge 9034
Peter Tiboris, Conductor
Elena Shkolnikova, soprano
Stella Zambalis, soprano
John Daniecki, tenor
Moscow Radio/TV Symphony
 Orchestra

VI. PARTIAL LISTING OF PRESS REVIEWS SINCE 1984

"Elegant Syros once more opened its arms to welcome the International Festival of the Aegean, which, for 15 years, is organized with love and consistency by the Greek-origin conductor Peter Tiboris and his Finnish-Canadian wife, soprano Eilana Lappalainen. For two weeks, each July, Syros is transformed to probably the most musical island of the Cyclades, hosting musicians from several countries world-wide who arrive with a singular aim: to give their best self to their art and their audience. Most of the events take place at the beautiful "Apollo" theater, a real masterpiece, built in 1864. On its stage, that same year, on 20th of April, Rigoletto by Giuseppe Verdi had been performed. This year's Festival of the Aegean opened on 14/7 and ended on 26/7. The opera production of this Festival was Ariadne on Naxos (Ariadne auf Naxos, Op. 60) by the important composer and conductor Richard Strauss, a composer who was born in 1864, exactly the same year that "Apollo" theater opened its doors to the public. There it is that, during this summer, we attended the production of this work. Strauss loved and was inspired by Hellenic culture. He visited Greece twice, in 1892 and in 1926. During that second visit he conducted four concerts in Athens and was awarded the merit of Grand Commander of Order of the Redeemer, while he met great personalities of Greece, among them poet Angelos Sikelianos, who hosted him in Delphi. Later, in 1930, he was named honorable citizen of Naxos, in recognition of his opera, which, in the form we know today was completed in 1916 and premiered in Vienna, at the Imperial and Royal Opera Theater of the Court of Vienna (Vienna State Opera), on October 4, 1916, as a second version of another earlier work (1912) which included music written for the end of the play Le Bourgeois Gentilhomme by Moliere. The first Greek performance took place in Athens, by the National Greek Opera, at Olympia Theater, on 22 February 1974, with the famous soprano Antigone Sgourdas, as Ariadne.

At the Festival of the Aegean Ariadne was sung by Eilana Lappalainen using very well her Wagnerian voice as well as her impressive stage presence. With her experience, knowledge and attention to detail, she brought forward the beauty of Strauss's wonderful melodic writing and collaborated perfectly with the rest of the cast. Next to her, as Bacchus, the talented Polynesian (born in Tonga) tenor Tu'u Pupu'a, a Dame Kiri Te Kanawa protege, convinced us with his very particular color of voice, his very well studied part and his musical sensitivity. He had to sing a dramatic tenor role, with a lot of vocal traps, a high tessitura and many technical difficulties. We hope to hear him again in our country soon. Danish soprano Louise Fribo was a pleasure as Zerbinetta.

The following evening the Pan-European Philharmonia, under the direction of Peter Tiboris performed works by Beethoven. The soloist, the distinguished Cypriot pianist (and conductor) Marios Papadopoulos, who resides and performs in England gave a performance that showed his respect for the classical style of the score, it was musically consistent and interesting throughout. Tiboris and his orchestra gave a careful accompaniment full of meaning and formal sensitivity."

KONSTANTINOS P. KARABELAS-SGOURDAS, "MUSIC DELIGHTS AT THE 15TH FESTIVAL OF THE AEGEAN: STRAUSS'S ARIADNE AUF NAXOS AND A BEETHOVEN CONCERT" JULY 28, 2019.

"The Festival of the Aegean was one of the few organizations in Greece that honored the memory of Gioachino Rossini (1792-1868) this year which marked the 150th anniversary of his death. The Festival of the Aegean decided to present two important works of the composer: the sacred masterpiece Stabat Mater and the charming opera La Cenerentola... Maestro Tiboris led a performance that highlighted the sacred but also the operatic elements of this majestic score. At his disposal he had a well formed quartet of soloists: Eilana Lappalainen, soprano, Katerina Roussou, mezzo-soprano, Alessandro Luciano, tenor, and Daniel Borowski, bass, which brought to the forefront the anguish and agony as the sensitive shades of the high musical inspiration. The choirs that participated took over the stage, placed behind the orchestra and the side balconies, offering a multi-dimensional sound experience. They sang with emotional intensity, great intonation and clarity... a special mention is owed to the Pan-European Philharmonia of Warsaw, which, made of mainly young musicians, pleased the audience with its musical efficiency for the Rossini work, as well for the second part of the concert, Symphony no. 5, op. 64 by Pyotr Ilyich Tchaikovsky, completed in 1888. The members of the orchestra followed Tiboris in an inspiring interpretation, full of drama (First movement, Andante-Allegro con anima-Molto più tranquillo) and lyricism (Second movement, Andante cantabile, con alcuna licenza-Non allegro-Andante maestoso con piano). The conductor built the big phrases very carefully, and the tempi he chose were not hectic at all, and gave to the music the space it needed to develop, becoming epic in dimension. His approach brought to mind the mature interpretation by Leonard Bernstein towards the end of his life."

KONSTANTINOS P. KARABELAS-SGOURDAS, "14TH INTERNATIONAL FESTIVAL OF THE AEGEAN- PETER TIBORIS' DOUBLE SUCCESS" CRITICS POINT AUGUST 9, 2018.

"On the first night at the historic Apollo Theater we heard the Pan-European Philharmonia under the direction of Tiboris. The orchestra is based in Warsaw and consists mainly of young musicians. The program opened with Overture to Rosamunde, written as incidental music for the play by Helmina von Chézy and composed by Franz Schubert. The history of this piece is somewhat complicated: the score saw the light of day in 1890, several decades after the composer's death (1828) and included an introduction older than the one heard during the first performance of the work in 1823. In fact, the introduction came from a work the composer had composed in 1820 for an opera, Die Zauberharfe. Maestro Tiboris' reading was imaginative. It is worth mentioning the excellent and highly expressive contribution of woodwind instruments. Immediately after we heard the Concerto for violin, cello and piano, Op. 56, known as the "Triple Concerto" of Ludwig van Beethoven. The work, created in 1803, received a vigorous interpretation. The solo parts were played by the youthful Trio 92, which has its headquarters in Vienna (Maciej Skarbek, piano, Nadja Kalmykova, violin, and Lucia Loulaki, cello). The three soloists, all enthusiastic and very capable musicians, dived into the depths of the amazing Beethoven score to bring forth all the vigor of the Allegro, volume of the Rondo alla pollaca, and the lyrical romanticism of the Largo. It's really gratifying to see young people playing with such musicality and impeccable technical precision. Maestro Tiboris, both here and in the following work, Beethoven's Symphony No. 6, Op. 68, known as the Pastoral (1808), guided the orchestra with inspiration and attention. He encouraged the musicians of the orchestra to emphasize the descriptive nature of the work and to highlight the many wonderful solo passages...

In the performance of Cherubini's Medea the director Dirk Schattner, partnering with Jens Huebner (set and lighting design) and Eva Sefradiou (costumes), created a neoclassical set and costumes. We believe that this option complemented perfectly the elegant architecture and decoration of the theater. The Finnish soprano Eilana Lappalainen portrayed the leading role with expert knowledge and aural comfort, offering a tragic and dynamic heroine. Her mature dramatic voice, expressive in the high range, gave an integrated musical interpretation. Beside her, as Giasone, stood Ukrainian tenor Konstantin Andreiev, winner of many international operatic competitions and numerous appearances at renowned opera houses. He interpreted the role with attention to the formation of phrases, expressive directness and, where necessary, drama. The young soprano Lydia Zervanos, in the important and quite extensive role Glauce, showed distinct musicality and acting prowess. She sang with respect for the style of the time, immediacy and taste, while her movement was always well aligned with the desired plot...The choir performed its parts consistently, while the orchestra (Pan-European Philharmonia), offered a convincing and fine accompaniment.

Maestro Tiboris led the score with knowledge and respect for the musical text. He supported the singers with real interest and aimed at an interpretation where the dramatic feeling was singled out and held the public's interest undiminished until the end."

KONSTANTINOS P. KARABELAS-SGOURDAS,
REVIEW OF THE 2015 FESTIVAL OF THE AEGEAN CRITIC'S POINT AUGUST 6, 2015.

"This year the eighth festival, from 9 to 22 July, hosted an impressive number of famous artists from around the world... Specifically, with enthusiasm and passion, the Festival presented a series of events that satisfied every taste: opera -- Richard Strauss' Salome -- symphonic and choral music, chamber music, piano recitals, and ballet, theater, and an opera workshop for young opera artists, the Greek Opera Studio...the iconic Bolero by Maurice Ravel followed [which] . . . revealed the immortal music by the important French composer and the imaginative choreography by Zanella. Tiboris conducted the orchestra with care and meaning.

KONSTANTINOS P. KARABELAS-SGOURDAS,
REVIEW OF THE 2012 FESTIVAL OF THE AEGEAN CRITIC'S POINT, JULY 31, 2012.

"Important was the performance of Peter Tiboris who, as music leader of the arena orchestra, was able to provide the perfect sound and choreographic rhythm to the Ravel music."

OLGA SAVENKO, GB OPERA MAGAZINE, VERONA, FEBRUARY 18, 2012.

"He is one of those individuals you never tire of listening to. This Greek American conductor and producer, Peter Tiboris (already acclaimed on the podium for his performance production of Le Corsare and Peer Gynt at Teatro di Roma) is now in Italy for a series of five evenings of an all Ravel Ballet in Teatro di Verona (February 18-23). Tiboris is not only a talented conductor but also a leading entrepreneur who has been producing and conducting classical music for 30 years at historic Carnegie Hall in New York City. He is also the artistic director of a unique festival called Festival of the Aegean that takes place every July in Greece. Tiboris is also a collector of famous batons including those owned and used by Arturo Toscanini, Leonard Bernstein, Frederick Chopin, and Giuseppe Sinopoli and owns the first editions of Don Giovanni (full score) and Rossini's Stabat Mater (choral score).

LORENZO TOZZI, "THE MAGIC OF CARNEGIE HALL" IL TEMPO, VERONA, FEBRUARY 2, 2012.

"As raised glasses heralded the 'Drinking Song,' the signature 'La Traviata' toast set the tone--both on and off stage. Directed by Italian choreographer and newly appointed artistic director of the Greek National Opera Renato Zanella, the popular opera served as the curtain raiser of the 7th Annual International Festival of the Aegean, taking place in Ermoupoli on Syros, the capital of the Cyclades."

ELIS KISS, "AEGEAN FESTIVAL RAISES A GLASS" INTERNATIONAL HERALD TRIBUNE, JULY 16, 2011.

"[The] Organization [of the Festival] was impressive; I can say the team's work was almost flawless. Every year thousands of people visit the island to participate in the festival. Hotel reservations are made weeks in advance, and tickets are sold out quickly. There is a loyal audience of visitors who arrange their holiday plans around this festival. Even though Syros Island is not one of the heavily visited Greek islands, such as Mykonos and Santorini, Hermoupolis can be called the "cultural capital of Cyclades."

SELEN YILMAZ, ARTICLE ON FESTIVAL OF THE AEGEAN ANDANTE MAGAZINE,

ISTANBUL, TURKEY, JULY 2011.

"The Greek-American conductor Peter Tiboris is the founder and general director of the company MidAmerica Productions, the orchestras Manhattan Philharmonic and Pan-European Philharmonia, and the International Festival of the Aegean. The latest is an annual event, which takes place in Syros, Greece, every summer offering the opportunity to visitors and inhabitants of the island to enjoy music, theater and dance performances. While the audience of the Festival has grown through the years, this time we were also amongst the ones who had the pleasure of attending two of its many activities in two different spaces in the city of Hermoupolis... With the right sense for style, and with a distinctive knowledge and respect to the needs of the singing voice, Mr. Tiboris presented us with a fully dramatic, lyric and sensitive performance of Verdi's melodrama La Traviata. Under his guidance, the Pan-European Philharmonia Orchestra, the Tulsa Oratorio Chorus and the University of Georgia Opera Ensemble, rendered brilliantly their parts. The same can also be said for the majority of the soloists... Mr. Tiboris led the American choirs (Taghkanic Chorale, Durango Choral Society, Sardis Presbyterian Church Sanctuary Choir, The Knox Choir of Presbyterian Church, Warwick Valley Chorale, Brevard Community College, Tulsa Oratorio Chorus, Nova Voce) with great effect in the performance of Carmina Burana. The Maestro managed to project the epic as well as the erotic tone of the score... Zorba Suite: The concert was concluded with excerpts from the Suite by Mikis Theodorakis, Zorba, performed cheerfully and passionately by Mr. Tiboris and the orchestra. The excited applause of the audience in the end of the concert was well deserved."

KONSTANTINOS P. KARABELAS-SGOURDAS, "THE IMPACT OF PETER TIBORIS" ELEFTHERIOS NEWSPAPER, ATHENS, AUGUST 5, 2011.

"Grieg: Peer Gynt and Complete Incidental Music Teatro Filharmonica di Verona, Italy.

... Peter Tiboris has interpreted the [music]: meticulous and balanced in tempi, at times a bit exaggerated to emphasize the disturbing and ghostly sweetness of some pages or the grotesque and demonic flavor of others. For this Greek-American director, the world of imagination and poetry seems to be made of light and shadow that alternate incessantly and leave us with a subtle feeling of anguish. One must also applaud the orchestra of the Fondazione Arena, which accompanied him with great skill in his beautiful musical exploration."

GILBERTO MION, TEATRO.ORG - THE PORTAL OF ITALIAN THEATER, MARCH 4, 2011.

"Peer Gynt at Teatro Filarmonico": "The responsibility for the music is with Peter Tiboris. He reaches with Verona's Arenian Orchestra [Teatro Filharmonica] a beautiful, clear sound and shapes the colors so to make you remember 'the forest' of [Grieg's] Great North, 'the morning' which was transparent as the African sky, the very introspective and sad pages of 'the mother's death' and the exuberant, concentrated, and dramatic 'dances.'"

L'ARENA: IL GIORNALE DI VERONA MARCH 7, 2011.

"Before the arias, the Oxford Philomusica played two Cherubini overtures, Lodoïska and the overture to Médée itself. Both lull you into a sense of false security, with a leisurely start before the music whips into a frenzy. Guest conductor Peter Tiboris drummed up lots of dramatic expression and emotion from Cherubini's scores...

The second half of the concert was a completely different kettle of fish in every way. Conductor Tiboris, now working without a score in front of him, seemed liberated by Tchaikovsky's relaxed and optimistic fifth symphony. While the symphony opens with a haunting, mournful clarinet melody (beautifully played by Lorraine Schulman and Julian Farrell), much of the music is in warm, major-key mode. Tiboris drew an open, transparent sound from the Philomusica (not always an easy thing to do in the Sheldonian), and expertly judged the underlying march tempi, so that woodwind solo passages had time to breathe...

The fifth is not without Tchaikovsky's trademark periods of desire and passion, and these, too, were well marked, as were the blazing brass highlights – the orchestra's brass section was in particularly exuberant form. Throughout, ensemble was tight and controlled. "Bravo!" shouted Philomusica music director Marios Papadopoulos, sitting near me in the audience, at the end of the performance. Quite right too."

GILES WOODFORDE, "CHERUBINI: OVERTURE TO LODOISKA AND MÉDÉA (SELECTIONS) TCHAIKOVSKY: SYMPHONY NO. 5 IN E MINOR, OP. 64 OXFORD PHILOMUSICA, SHELDONIAN THEATER" THE OXFORD TIMES, OXFORD, UK, FEBRUARY 4, 2009.

"The Symphony Orchestra of the Province of Bari led by the masterly skills of the great Greek-American music director Peter Tiboris, started the concert with the Ouverture of Fidelio and immediately caught the attention of a public that in Barletta is getting always more competent yet demanding... The penetrating and expressing rhythmic force that Tiboris gave to the execution clearly produced the intent of the great composer of Bonn, and utilized to the fullest the all the sections of the Barese's orchestra....The performance, thanks to the excellent accompaniment of Tiboris, came out charged with meaning yet quite contagious."

"TIBORIS' MUSIC HELD THE PUBLIC AT CURCI SPELLBOUND" LA GAZETTA DEL NORDBARESE, BARLETTA, ITALY, JANUARY 30, 2009.

Mascagni: Zanetto (Elysium Recordings) Bohuslav Martinu Philharmonic Jennifer Larmore (Zanetto), Eilana Lappalainen (Sylvia): "Peter Tiboris guides the piece with style. He doesn't mistake this smaller scale writing for full-blown verismo of the Cavalleria variety, and he allows the climaxes to build steadily and surely. The Bohuslav Martinu Philharmonic... sounds warm and vibrant, without [an] air of swarthiness and heaviness..."

STEPHEN FRANCIS VASTA, OPERA NEWS, AUGUST 2008.

Adam: Il Corsaro Orchestra e Corpo di Ballo del Teatro Dell'OperaTeatro dell'Opera di Roma, Rome "...the dramatic pace remains dynamic and always tight, thanks to the book, here "lightened", and by the lively musical direction of Peter Tiboris ..."

FABIANA RAPONI, NOTI DA LEON, MAY 31, 2008.

Mozart: RequiemBasilica di San Nicola Bari, Italy: "From the beginning, the work that Tiboris had done to obtain the best results was clear. His vision of the oratorio (intended as a creation pervaded by a passionate emotion, a warm humanity, and free from inner excesses) was completely realized, with an involving ardor, that was enlivened again with a sincere guiding of the soloists, chorus, and orchestra. The perfect balance of the artists in playing their role was clearly worthy of the director, who was able to sculpt the phrasing and melodic lines for a passionate and involving expressivity, absolutely worthy of the sublime dramatic tension that animates the score."

NICHOLAS BAISA, LA GAZZETTA DEL MEZZOGIORNO, NOVEMBER 23, 2007.

Edvard Grieg: Peer Gynt Teatro dell'Opera di Roma (Theater Premiere, new ballet production) Rome: "Much attention was paid to detail and a connection with the stage was made by orchestra director Peter Tiboris... The conducting of Peter Tiboris was incisive and tasteful."

IL GIORNALE, NOVEMBER 10, 2007.

Mascagni: Zanetto (Greek Premiere) Arias and duets by Verdi, Ponchielli, Bellini, Cilea, Rossini, and Donizetti, Festival of the Aegean, Island of Syros, Greece

"The gala revealed Tiboris to be a fine conductor. The overtures went with a swing, while he was a considerate colleague to his singers."

THESTAGE.CO.UK

"Mr. Tiboris's effort...brought us something literate, comprehensible..."

BERNARD HOLLAND, "'MÉDÉE': INTRIGUE AND VENGEANCE REVEL IN THE SOUNDS OF CHERUBINI"
NEW YORK TIMES JUNE 5, 2006.

"Mr. Tiboris moved the performance along ably, drawing some fine playing...and a robust choral sound."

ALLAN KOZINN, "TANEYEV: AGAMEMNON" NEW YORK TIMES.

"Tiboris conducted with dauntless energy..."

MARTIN BERNHEIMER, THE FINANCIAL TIMES.

"The Manhattan Philharmonic...played...with great passion and accuracy for conductor Peter Tiboris.... The audience went understandably wild at the opera's close."

ROBERT LEVINE, ROSSINI: ERMIONE CARNEGIE HALL CLASSICSTODAY.COM

"[Peter Tiboris] drew a polished and unflaggingly energetic performance from the Manhattan Philharmonic."

ALLAN KOZINN, "MIKIS THEODORAKIS: ELECTRA" THE NEW YORK TIMES.

"Maestro Peter Tiboris...led the orchestra and singers seamlessly through the work. Directing with crisp, definite cues, he ensured that the singers on stage and the musicians in the orchestra pit stayed right with each other."

BOB BARRETT MOZART: THE MAGIC FLUTE KNOXVILLE OPERA COMPANY THE KNOXVILLE NEWS-SENTINEL, TENNESSEE.

"Under the direction of American conductor Peter Tiboris, the orchestra of La Société Philharmonique de Montréal staged a rather rare event: Beethoven's Ninth Symphony in the edition retouched by Gustav Mahler.... The results were, all in all, spectacular."

CAROL BERGERON DVORAK: TE DEUM BEETHOVEN: SYMPHONY NO. 9, OP. 125 ("CHORAL") LE DEVOIR, MONTREAL.

"Peter Tiboris['s] powerful and highly emotional interpretation had such an emotional impact on the audience.... What became the most important was a vivid action, dramatic narration and well-executed high point of the drama.... The interpretation of the American conductor showed the deep understanding not only of the musical forms of the separate movements, but also in the whole piece...."

ALEKSANDRA KLAPUT, "BEETHOVEN: "CORIOLAN" OVERTURE BEETHOVEN: SYMPHONY NO. 7 SAINT-SAËNS: PIANO CONCERTO BYDGOSZC PHILHARMONY" GAZETA REGIONALNA , POLAND.

"Peter Tiboris...conducted with tremendous impetus and dynamic passion. I must admit it has been a long time since I have heard the introduction to the first movement being rendered in this incredibly dense, collected, undistracted spirit, full of awe, as if a premonition of something tragic and frightful to happen...and then those undescribably passionate outbursts of the tempestuous drama in the otherwise lyrical second movement!"

JOZEF KANSKI, "TCHAIKOVSKY: SYMPHONY NO. 5 RZESZOW PHILHARMONY" RUCH MUZYCZNY, POLAND.

"At Avery Fisher Hall, the [Niedersachsisches Staatsorchester Hannover] gave the American conductor Peter Tiboris...alert, lush-toned playing.... The bright textures of the Overture to 'The School for Scandal' (Op. 5) came through with unusual transparency, and the thematic expansions and elaborations of the 'Second Essay'

(Op. 17) were rendered cohesively.... Mr. Tiboris led the Adagio for Strings...[and] elicited a dignified, tonally rich performance.... Mr. Tiboris closed the concert with a sizzling and precise... performance of the Tchaikovsky Fourth Symphony."

ALLAN KOZINN, "BARBER: OVERTURE TO THE SCHOOL FOR SCANDAL, OP. 5; BARBER: ADAGIO FOR STRINGS, OP. 11 BARBER: SECOND ESSAY FOR ORCHESTRA, OP. 17 GLASS: THE CANYON: A DRAMATIC EPISODE FOR ORCHESTRA TCHAIKOVSKY SYMPHONY NO. 4 IN F MINOR, OP. 36 NIEDERSÄCHSISCHES STAATSORCHESTER HANNOVER (GERMANY) AVERY FISHER HALL" NEW YORK TIMES.

"...a first-rate...conductor.... In...the Overture to 'The School for Scandal,' 'Adagio for Strings' and 'Second Essay for Orchestra,' every measure was alive with love for the music, and the playing was as technically expert as enthusiastic...."

BILL ZAKARIASEN, THE DAILY NEWS, NEW YORK.

"It would have been foolhardy to begin with six scenes from Prokofiev's ballet Romeo and Juliet, because of its exposed brass and often raw sound, but all went exceedingly well. Tiboris led with a thorough understanding of the music and... we had a performance that was virile, lyric, compassionate and lush.... The concert ended with an idiomatic, enjoyable reading of Tchaikovsky's First Symphony, Winter Dreams."

BERT WECHSLER, "TIBORIS AMBITIOUS AS EVER" THE DAILY NEWS, NEW YORK.

"Tiboris' upbeat, bracing conducting of 'Messiah' paid dividends—his tempos... were markedly similar to those of Sir Thomas Beecham."

BILL ZAKARIASEN, "DELLO JOIO: NATIVITY: A CANTICLE FOR THE CHILD HANDEL: MESSIAH (CHRISTMAS PORTIONS) CARNEGIE HALL" THE DAILY NEWS, NEW YORK.

"Mr. Tiboris was clearly at home in the score, and the quality of choral tone in the fortissimo climaxes was thrilling. Throughout the concert, the choruses seemed strikingly well prepared for such a large and heterogeneous group."

WILL CRUTCHFIELD "VERDI: REQUIEM CARNEGIE HALL" NEW YORK TIMES.

"Tiboris' performance was one of the most exciting and inspiring I've ever heard of this masterwork, whatever the edition."

BILL ZAKARIASEN, "BEETHOVEN/MAHLER: SYMPHONY NO. 9, OP. 125 ("CHORAL") AVERY FISHER HALL" THE DAILY NEWS, NEW YORK.

"Mr. Tiboris relished any opportunity to turn his chorus loose .... [H]e elicited from his orchestra a smooth, gentle introduction to the 'Ode to Joy' section, and it was stirring to hear all those singers at full tilt roaring out the symphony's climax."
MICHAEL KIMMELMAN TCHAIKOVSKY: ODE TO JOY BEETHOVEN: SYMPHONY NO. 9, OP. 125 ("CHORAL")
AVERY FISHER HALL THE NEW YORK TIMES JUNE 2, 1987.

"Mr. Tiboris led strong, secure performances, with solid playing from the orchestra and sure singing from the nine...choruses involved. The Walton, with its antiphonal effects, was especially stirring. But the Bruckner took on a nice, almost strident urgency, too, and the Berlioz sounded grand and moving...."
JOHN ROCKWELL "WALTON: CORONATION TE DEUM BRUCKNER: TE DEUM BERLIOZ: TE DEUM AVERY
FISHER HALL" THE NEW YORK TIMES.

"An added plus was the admirably well-paced conducting of Tiboris and the splendid orchestral playing—virtues which would remain constant throughout the program.... The finest performance, though, was granted Berlioz' massive masterwork—not only were the sonics often grand in the extreme, but the vast performing lineup sang and played with amazing alertness and precision."
BILL ZAKARAISEN, THE DAILY NEWS, NEW YORK.

"There was no pretense at instrumental 'authenticity': great choral music was fervently, eagerly, and accurately sung, it proved stirring.... There was life and warmth in the music-making."
ANDREW PORTER HANDEL: ISRAEL IN EGYPT AVERY FISHER HALL THE NEW YORKER.

"Verdi's Requiem as performed by the American Symphony Orchestra...under conductor Peter Tiboris...was sheer fire. Tiboris' execution of the massive score... was alive with such sincerity as must transport any expression.... Polished fire. Great Performance."
EMERSON RANDOLPH, "THE POLISHED FIRE OF VERDI'S REQUIEM"
"THE WORLD AND I," WASHINGTON TIMES.

"Tiboris is far more than a talented maestro...to combine strengths and ameliorate the differences of visiting ensembles; to perform as a united and thrilling whole."

HARRIETT JOHNSON VERDI: MESSA DA REQUIEMAVERY FISHER HALL THE NEW YORK POST.

"Tiboris is a Pied Piper who is able to get hundreds and even hundreds more with a singing heart to follow his baton down an endless line." The Daily News, New York. "Tiboris...proved to be a conductor of decisive authority.... [T]he choruses in two tiers of boxes on either side of the hall contributed to an enchanting effect."

HARRIETT JOHNSON, "KODALY: BUDARVI TE DEUM NIELSEN: HYMNUS AMORIS, OP. 12 CHOPIN: PIANO CONCERTO NO. 1 IN E MINOR CARNEGIE HALL." THE NEW YORK POST

CD REVIEWS

"... widely recognized as the foremost proponent of Mahlerian performance editions. He secures solid and...accomplished performances here.... This release triumphs time after time. I can only commend it to you in the strongest possible terms."

FANFARE MAGAZINEBY MICHAEL JAMESONMOZART: SYMPHONY NO. 40 IN G MINOR, K.550 SYMPHONY NO. 41 IN C MAJOR, K.551 ("JUPITER") BEETHOVEN: LEONORA OVERTURE NO. 3, OP. 72A

"...a fine collection of...Dvořák tone poems and overtures including The Water Goblin, Symphonic Variations, Slavonic Rhapsody and Scherzo Capriccioso. Keep your eye on Elysium; future releases will include Mahler's rearrangements of well-known symphonies and a number of unjustly neglected Romantic and Classical-era masterpieces. This is good news for anyone who has already 'done' the top 100 classics."

"CD PICKS," ON THE AIR MAGAZINEBY RICHARD HALLEYDVORÁK: THE SPECTRE'S BRIDE

"Peter Tiboris conducts the Bohuslav Martinu Philharmonic and Bratislava Chorus with feeling and no little poetry."

GRAMOPHONE BY BARRYMORE LAURENCE SCHERER

VII. THE WORKS HISTORIAN AND PROFESSOR JOHN BARKER RECOMMENDED THAT PETER TIBORIS CONDUCTS

In the Fall of 2002, Professor John Barker, a Byzantinist at the University of Wisconsin at Madison, and a connoisseur and historian of music recommended a list of works to Peter Tiboris. The list appears below. An asterix indicates that Peter either performed or recorded or both that particular piece.

Juan Crisóstomo de Arriaga (1806 - 1826)*
Symphony in D Major
Johann Sebastian Bach (1685 - 1750)*
Magnificat, BWV 243
Samuel Osmond Barber II (1910 - 1981)*
Medea's Meditation and Dance of Vengeance, Op. 23a
Béla Viktor János Bartók (1881 - 1945)
Dance Suite, Sz. 77, BB. 86a
Music for Strings, Percussion and Celesta, Sz. 106, BB 114
Divertimento for String Orchestra Sz.113, BB.118
Alban Maria Johannes Berg (1885 - 1935)
Lulu Suite, 5 symphonic pieces from the opera for soprano & orchestra
Louis-Hector Berlioz (1803 - 1869)

Harold en Italie, symphonie avec un alto principal
Symphonie fantastique, H. 48
Georges Bizet (1838 - 1875)*
Souvenirs de Rome, Symphony in C major, Op. 11
Patrie Overture, Op. 19
Ridolfo Luigi Boccherini (1743 - 1805)*
Symphony No 6 in D minor 'La Casa del Diavolo', G506
Stabat Mater, G.532
Johannes Brahms (1833 - 1897)*
Serenade No.2, Op.16
Ein deutsches Requiem, nach Worten der heiligen Schrift, Op. 45
Edward Benjamin Britten (1913 - 1976)*
Serenade for Tenor, Horn and Strings, Op. 31
Josef Anton Bruckner (1824 - 1896)
Symphony No. 5 in B-flat major, WAB 105
Symphony No. 7 in E major, WAB 107
Symphony No. 9 in D minor, WAB 109
Luigi Cherubini (1760 - 1842)*
Requiem No.1, in C minor
Requiem No.2, in D minor
Chant sur la mort d'Haydn for soprano, tenor and orchestra
Frederick Theodore Albert Delius (1862 - 1934)
Florida Suite
Paul Marie Théodore Vincent d'Indy (1851 - 1931)
Symphony No. 1 'Italienne' in A major

Antonín Dvořák (1841 - 1904)

Symphony No. 4 in D minor, Op. 13, B. 41

"Vanda" Overture, Op. 25, B. 97

Symphony No. 6 in D major, Op. 60, B. 112

"My Home" Overture, Op. 62, B. 125a*

"Hussite" Overture, Op. 67, B. 132*

The Spectre's Bride, Op.69*

"In Nature's Realm" Overture, Op. 91, B. 168*

"Carnival" Overture, Op. 92, B. 169*

"Othello" Overture, Op. 93, B. 174

The Wild Dove, Op. 110, B. 198*

Sir Edward William Elgar, 1st Baronet (1857 - 1934)

Variations on an Original Theme, Op. 36

Mikhail Ivanovich Glinka (1804 - 1857)

Spanish Overture No. 1, Capriccio Brilliante "Jota Aragonesa"

Spanish Overture No. 2, Souvenir d'une nuit d'été à Madrid

Georg Friedrich Händel (1685 - 1759)

Israel in Egypt, HWV 54*

Concerti grossi, Op. 3, HWV 312–317

Twelve Grand Concertos, Op. 6, HWV 319–330

Franz Joseph Haydn (1732 - 1809)

Ouverture da L'isola disabitata, Hob. Ia:13

Symphony No. 60 in C major "Il distratto", Hob. I/60

Symphony No. 91 in E♭ major, Hob. I/91

Symphony No. 92 in G major, Hob. I/92*

Symphony No. 104 in D major, Hob. I/104*

Sinfonia Concertante in B flat major, Hob. I/105

Die sieben letzten Worte unseres Erlösers am Kreuze, Hob. XX/2

Zoltán Kodály (1882 - 1967)

Dances of Galánta

Franz Liszt (1811 - 1886)

Tasso: lamento e trionfo, S. 96

Les préludes, S. 97*

Orpheus, S. 98

Mazeppa, S. 100

Gustav Mahler (1860 - 1911)

Symphony No. 4 in G major for Soprano and Orchestra

Kindertotenlieder

Bohuslav Jan Martinů (1890 - 1959)

Symphony No. 6, H. 343

Felix Mendelssohn (1809 - 1847)

Die Hebriden, Op. 26

Meeresstille und glückliche Fahrt, Op. 27

Die schöne Melusine, Op. 32

Ruy Blas, Op.95

Symphony No. 5 in D major/D minor, Op. 107

Wolfgang Amadeus Mozart (1756 - 1791)

Divertimento No. 2 in D major, K.131

Symphony No. 25 in G minor, K. 183/173dB

Divertimento No. 7 in D major, K. 205/167A

Serenade No. 7 in D major, "Haffner", K.250*

Serenade for Orchestra No. 9 in D major, K. 320

Große Messe in c-Moll, K. 427/417a

Maurerische Trauermusik in C minor, K. 477

Carl Heinrich Maria Orff (1895 - 1982)

Carmina Burana*

Sergei Vasilyevich Rachmaninoff (1873 - 1943)

Symphony No. 2 in E minor, Op. 27

Symphonic Dances, Op. 45*

Charles-Camille Saint-Saëns (1835 - 1921)

Symphony No. 2 in A minor, Op. 55

Franz Peter Schubert (1797 - 1828)

Symphony No. 7 in E major, D 729*

Symphony No. 8 in B minor, D. 759*

Robert Schumann (1810 - 1856)

Manfred. Dramatisches Gedicht in drei Abtheilungen, Op. 115*

Dmitri Dmitriyevich Shostakovich (1906 - 1975)

Symphony No. 7 in C major, Op. 60

Jean Sibelius (1865 - 1957)

Symphony No. 2 in D major, Op. 43

Symphony No. 3 in C major, Op. 52

Richard Georg Strauss (1864 - 1949)

Der Rosenkavalier, suite, TrV 227d, AV 145

Tod und Verklärung, Op. 24

Salome, Op. 54

Josef Suk (1874 - 1935)

Fantastické Scherzo, Op.25

Sir Arthur Seymour Sullivan, MVO (1842 - 1900)

Overture di Ballo

Ralph Vaughan Williams (1872 - 1958)

Symphony No. 2, "A London Symphony"

Symphony No. 5 in D major

Symphony No. 6 in E minor

Symphony No. 8 in D minor

Giuseppe Fortunino Francesco Verdi (1813 - 1901)

Quattro pezzi sacri*

Wilhelm Richard Wagner (1813 - 1883)

Faust Overture

VIII. MOST FAVORITE POP / JAZZ SINGERS

1. Tony Bennett (1926 – 2023)
2. Barbara Joan "Barbra" Streisand (b. 1942)
3. Frank Sinatra (1915 – 1998)
4. Ella Jane Fitzgerald (1917 – 1996)
5. Lou Rawls (1933 – 2006)
6. Joan Chandos Baez (b. 1941)
7. Harry Belafonte (1927 – 2023)
8. Janis Lyn Joplin (1943 –1970)
8. Lady Gaga (b. 1986)
9. Ray Charles Robinson Sr. (1930 –2004)
10. Billie Holliday (1915 – 1959)
11. Charles Aznavour (1924 – 2018)
12. Louis Daniel Armstrong (1901 – 1971)

13. Michael Steven Bublé (b. 1975)
14. Whitney Elizabeth Houston (1963 – 2012)
15. Nat King Cole (1919 – 1965)

IX. List of Current MidAmerica Productions and MidAmerica Employees

Departments, names, years of service, titles.

1. Artistic Management

Peter Tiboris
42 years
General Director and Music Director of MidAmerica Productions and MidAm International

Eilana Lappalainen
17 years
Associate General Music Director of MidAmerica Productions; MidAm International
Artistic Administrator (2005 to 2020); General Director and Artistic Director (2020 to present) of the International Festival of the Aegean, Apollo Theater, Island of Syros, Greece

James E. Redcay III
9 years
Chief Executive Officer

Eric Spiegel
8 years
Chief Operating Officer

Sonja Sepúlveda
10 years
MidAm International Program Administrator & Conductor-in-Residence

Andrea Niederman
3 years
Director of Public Relations, Publications & Audience Development

Cailin Marcel Manson
2 years
Conductor & Artistic Consultant

2. Core Administration

Joyce Howard-Brazel
27 years
Chief of Account Operations

Giovanna Boyd
3 years
Bookkeeper/Account Operations Associate

Julie Kahn
3 years
Principal Administrative Associate to General Music Director and Artistic Director, Peter Tiboris

3. Distinguished Composers/Conductors:

Marc-André Bougie
Texarkana, TX, USA
Distinguished Composer & Conductor

Terre Johnson
Morrow, GA
Distinguished Composer & Conductor

Michael John Trotta
Red Bank, New Jersey, USA
Distinguished Composer & Conductor

Conductors:
Matthew Harden
8 years
Conductor-in-Residence & Program Development Associate

Jack Hill
4 years
Conductor & Program Development Associate

Stephen Pu
4 years
Conductor & Program Development Associate

Adam Stich
3 years
Conductor & Program Development Associate

Candace Wicke
8 years
Conductor & Program Development Associate

4. Program Development

C.J. Harden
5 years
Director of Program Development

George Berry
5 years
Associate Director of Program Development and Assistant Production Manager

Lily Wintringham
3 years
Program Development Associate and Assistant in Concert Production

Sawyer Branham
2 years
Program Development Associate

5. Digital & Social Media

Daniel Wilde
2 years
Social Media, Public Relations, and Publications Assistant

Kristen Butler
3 years
Graphic Designer

Lisette Gonzalez
20 Years
Web Consultant & Development
New England Symphonic Ensemble

Preston Hawes
32 years
Artistic Director and Principal
Violinist, New England Symphonic
Ensemble

X. PARTIAL LIST OF MIDAMERICA PRODUCTIONS AND MIDAMERICA INTERNATIONAL EMPLOYEES SINCE 1984

Ahern, Timothy
Anderson, Jennifer
Anderson, Stacey
Armstrong, Kim
Arnold, Craig
Asprion, Ryan
Becker, Samuella
Berg, Sean
Berry, George
Betzen, Olivia
Biddle, Brandi
Bill, Joseph
Blutner, Amanda
Bong, Sara
Borden, Meredith
Bosque, Erica
Boyd, Giovanna
Branham, Mackenzie (Sawyer)

Brisotti, Katie
Brosseau, Alexander
Budhoo, Barbara
Burgos, Sally
Busch, Mary Ann
Butler, Kristen
Bynog, Shyron
Byrne, James
Case, Susan
Chandler, Sandra
Charlop, Diana
Chen, Royce
Cheng, Cecilia
Chiu, Shih-Han
Conyers, Danyel
Cooper, Bradley Q.
Daugelaite, Jurate
Derke, Iris
Desiano, Nicole
DiMarzio, Rosana
Drohan, Kathleen
Dunfee, Norman
Dutkanicz, David
Economou, Elizabeth
Edwards, Drew
Falkenburg, Julia
Feo, Tiffany
Filpo, Lincy
Frazier, Torbjorn
Frole, Jeffery
Gardner, Eddie
Garneau, Adrienne
Gerstein, Melissa
Gonzales, Lisette
Gotanco, Teresa-Maria
Griffith, Jonathan

Guerrier, Sean

Guss, Daniel

Harden, Christian

Harden, Matthew

Hawes, Preston

Hill, Jack

Holland, Darius

Howard, Joyce

Huitzacua, Peter

Hunt, Kendal

Johnson, Richard

Johnson, Tabitha

Johnson, Terre

Kahn, Julie

Kapilevich, Renata

Knapp, Eric Dale

Kodlick, Johanna

Krawczyk, Alex

Kumar, Jai

Lappalainen, Eilana

Li-Wintringham, Xuan

Liepold, John

Lin, Jenny

Liu, Lu

Lott, Tayrn

Loy, Dennis J.

Majette, Jeri

Maldonado, Kimberly

Manokara, Sharmatha

Manson, Cailin Marcel

Matthews, Britton

McGillicuddy, Kara

McLaughlin, Joseph

McLeod, Emmaline

Messolaras, Irene

Milhizer, Aimee

Mondesir, April

Morin, Jeffery

Moser, Drew

Naylor, Kirk

Niederman, Andrea

Octave, Thomas

Pellegrino, Lauren

Person, James

Polanco, Yenercis

Pope, Sage

Powell, Timothy

Pu, Stephen

Ramswamy, Indrawattie

Redcay, James

Reyna, Lincy

Reynolds, Jeffery

Rivera, Frances

Rosin, Michael

Rousseaux, Andrea Rose

Rubaja, Carina

Sanchez, Lindsey

Scruggs, Edgar

Sepulveda, Sonja

Sharp, Timothy

Shultz, Angela

Simeone, Tracy

Small, Electa

Smyth, Matthew

Spencer, Kellie

Spiegel, Eric

Stark, Turia

Stebbins, Joseph

Stein, Betsy

Stewart, Allyson

Stich, Adam

Suragiat, Jennifer

Tao, Zui

Thomas, Jeff

Thye Cheri
Thye, David
Tiboris, Peter
Tiboris, Stephanie
Tobet, Amanda
Torkelson, Paul A.
Walters-Reinfried, Lesleigh
Waymire, Molly
Welsh, Mary
Wicke, Candace
Wicke, Dallas
Wihelm, Gary L.
Williamson, Barry Scott
Wollett, Caitlyn
Wong, Alexander
Xu, Yifei
Zagorski, Raymond
Zeidman, Dale
Zhang, Xinni
Zilkha, Genan

XI. Guest Conductors on the MidAmerica Productions and MidAmerica International Series since 1984 who made their Debuts at Carnegie Hall

Name, Ensamble, Place, Years
Steven Accatino Band CA, USA 1997, 2001, 2007
Steven Acciani Band CA, USA 1999, 2002, 2006

Julian Ackerley Choir AZ, USA 2016
Randolph Adams Choir AZ, USA 1997
Ray Adams Choir CO, USA 2019
Paul A. Aitken Choir Nova Scotia, Canada 2010, 2023
Kari Ala-Pollanen Choir Espoo, Finland 1990
George Albrecht Choir Germany 1989
Michael Alexander Orchestra TX, USA 2004
Michael Allard Orchestra CA, USA 2000, 2005, 2017
Burt Allen Choir LA, USA 1997, 2001
Neal Allsup Choir KS, USA 1999, 2001, 2005, 2007
Stephen Alltop Choir IL, USA 2007
Bradley L Almquist Choir KY, USA 2010
Jerry Ann Alt Choir NM, USA 1990
Morinobu Amano Choir Hiroshima, Japan 1998
Robert Ambrose Band GA, USA 2005
Cheryl Anderson Choir CA, USA 2007
Michael Anderson Choir IL, USA 2007
Hilary Apfelstadt Choir ON, Canada 2006
Filippo Arlia Orchestra Rome, Italy 2016, 2018
Craig Arnold Choir IA, USA 1997, 1999
Michael Arthur Orchestra PA, USA 2015
Jean Ashworth Bartle Choir Toronto, Canada 1994, 1995(2), 1997, 1998, 2001, 2007, 2009

Dennis Assaf Choir LA, USA 1993

Monte Atkinson Choir CO, USA 2008, 2010, 2013, 2017

Jonathan Babcock Choir TX, USA 2006

Larry Bach Choir MN, USA 2006

Brian J. Bacon Choir TX, USA 2013, 2015, 2019

Peter Bagley Choir CT, USA 1997

Larry Ball Choir CA, USA 1998

Sheridan Ball Choir NY, USA 2001

Mareena Boosamra Ball Choir AZ, USA 2012

D. Brent BallwegChoir OK, USA 2008, 2018

Martha Banghart Choir MD, USA 2018

Francis Bardot Choir Paris, France 2023

Robert Bass Choir New York, NY 1988

James K Bass Choir CA, USA 2019

David Bauer Choir NE, USA 1997

Aimee Beckmann-Collier Choir IA, USA 1998, 2002

Rebecca Bedell Choir FL, USA 2007

John Bell Band NY, USA 1995

Richard Bell Choir MO, USA 2002

Douglas Belland Choir OH, USA 1999

David Belles Choir CT, USA 2011, 2014

Jenny Bent Choir CA, USA 2022

Magdolna Berezvai Orchestra CA, USA 2017

Sean Berg Choir NY, USA

Yaacov Bergman Choir OR, USA 1990

Almeda Berkey Choir NE, USA 2000, 2003, 2005, 2007, 2009

Linda Mack Berven Choir CO, USA 2010, 2018

Thomas R. Best Concert Band TN, USA 2006

Richard Best Wind Ensemble TN, USA 2017

Tucker Biddlecombe Choir TN, USA 2019

Lisa Billingham Choir VA, USA 2019

James Bingham Choir MD, USA 2004, 2006

Dudley Birder Choir WI, USA 1993, 1996

Robert Bode Choir WA, USA 1990

Geoffrey Boers Choir WA, USA 2000, 2003,2007, 2019

Kevin C. Bogen Choir KS, USA 2011

Harrison Boughton Choir KS, USA 2004, 2006

Marc-Andre Bougie Choir TX, USA 2010, 2018, 2022

Sean Boulware Choir CA, USA 2006, 2008, 2014, 2015, 2022

Drew Bradley Choir AL, USA 2022

Paul Brandvik Choir MN, USA 1998, 1999

Mary C. Breden Choir CA, USA 1997

Michel Brousseau Choir Ottawa, Canada 2010

Bruce Brown Choir IN, USA 2001

Bruce Browne Choir OR, USA 2003

David Brunner Choir FL, USA 1999, 2003, 2005, 2009, 2011

Robert Bryant Band TX, USA 2000

Amity Bryson Choir MO, USA 2022

Scott Buchanan Choir IN, USA 2001, 2004

Robert Bucker Choir OR, USA 2000

Jill Burgett Choir CO, USA 2023

Lawrence Burnett Choir TX, USA 1997, 2005

Kerry P. Burtis Choir OR, USA 1996

Paul Caldwell Choir WA, USA 2014

Stephen Caldwell Choir AR, USA 2023

Rodney H. Caldwell Choir NC, USA 2007, 2014, 2017

Bruce Caldwell Wind Ensemble NC, USA 2012, 2016

Charles F. Campbell Jr. Wind Ensemble KY, USA 2006

Edward Cannava Band CO, USA 1998

Lisette Canton Choir Toronto, ON 2019

Kenneth Capshaw Orchestra TX, USA 1998

Simon Carrington Choir Cambridge, UK 1996, 1997, 2000, 2005

William Carroll Choir MS, USA 1993

Kim Carson Choir MO, USA 2017

Giuseppe Cataldo Orchestra Palermo, Italy 2009

Dustin Stephen Cates Choir PA, USA 2013

Bruce Chamberlain Choir AZ, USA 1995, 2005

Deborah Chandler Choir LA, USA 2017

Karl Chang Choir CA, USA 2017, 2019, 2022

David Chase Choir CA, USA 2012

Mei-Ann Chen Orchestra IL, USA 2004

Raymond Chenault Jr. Choir GA, USA 1998

Paul Chiang Orchestra Taiwan 2007

Bob Chilcott Choir Cambridge, UK 2005

Shelby Chipman Orchestra FL, USA 2015

Cynthia Claborn Stevens Choir MT, USA 2016

Kimberly Clark Choir CA, USA 2009

Rene Clausen Choir MI, USA 1995, 1996, 1997, 2010

Jeffrey Cobb Choir MI, USA 2023

Paul-Elliott Cobbs Orchestra WA, USA 2000, 2005

Nick Cobos Orchestra CO, USA 1998

Grant Cochran Choir AK, USA 2022

Christopher M Cock Choir IN, USA 2009

Beth Cohen Choir NY, USA 1991

Maurizio Colasanti Orchestra Italy 2008

David C. Cole Orchestra TX, USA 2014

Drew Collins Choir CT, USA 2007

Mark Conley Choir RI, USA 2009

Warren Cook Choir SC, USA 2023

Britt Cooper Choir OH, USA 2019

Philip L. Copeland Choir AL, USA 2006, 2011

John Cornish Choir MO, USA 2017

Gardar Cortes Choir Reykjavik, IS 2004

Pascal Cote Choir Montreal, QC 2017

Duncan Couch Choir FL, USA 1998, 2004

Thomas M. Council Choir GA, USA 2014, 2016

Dennis Cox Choir ME, USA 2002, 2006, 2017

Andrew Crane Choir UT, USA 2016

Jenny Crober Choir Toronto, ON 2015

Emily Crocker Choir WI, USA 1999, 2001, 2005

Kip Crowder Choir KY, USA 2012

Monica O. Crowder Choir KY, USA 2012

Fabrizio Da Ros Orchestra Italy 2016

Sandra Dackow Orchestra PA, USA 1998

David Dahlquist Choir UT, USA 2019

Leslie Dala Choir Vancouver, BC 2019

Edward Dalton Choir NJ, USA 2002

Terry Danne Choir CA, USA 2005

Theodore Davidovich Choir MA, USA 2003

Kenneth Davis Choir TX, USA 1998

Janet Davis Choir KY, USa 2001

Francisco de Araujo Choir MD, USA 2006

Juan de Dios Hernandez Choir OK, USA 2018

Mark Deakins Choir KY, USA 1999, 2003, 2008

Henley Denmead Choir CT, USA 1998

Francesco Di Mauro Choir Italy 2006

Wendi Dicken Choir MO, USA 2023

Rachel Dirks Orchestra KS,USA 1998

Lawrence Doebler Choir NC, USA 2018

Carlo Donadio Orchestra Italy 2008

Don Donaldson Choir IL, USA 2001

Cheryl Dupont Choir LS, USA 1993, 1997, 2009, 2013, 2017

Ruth E. Dwyer Choir IN, USA 2012, 2014, 2017

Christopher Eanes Choir OH, USA 2019

Jeannette Ebelhar Choir TN, USA 2006

Gary Ebensberger Choir TX, USA 1997

Steven Edwards Choir LA, USA 2007, 2015

Lee Egbert Choir CO, USA 2003

Eph Ehly Choir MO, USA 1991

Giselle Elgarresta Rios Choir FL, USA 2006

Sixto Elizondo Orchestra TX, USA 2014

Bradley Ellingboe Choir MN, USA 2008

Maria Ellis Choir MO, USA 2023

John Emanuelson Orchestra WI, USA 2014, 2018

Arnold Epley Chorus MO, USA 2006

Barry Epperley Choir OK, USA 2005

Jack Ergo Choir MO, USA 2000

Lynne Erickson Choir CA, USA 2013

Judith Evans Orchestra FL, USA 2006

Frank F. Eychaner Choir TX, USA 2018

Charles Facer Choir MO, USA 1994, 1999

Laurier Fagnan Choir Alberta, Canada 2018

Paula C. Ferguson Orchestra WA, USA 2016, 2019

Linda Ferreira Choir TN, USA 1990

David Ferreira Choir ND, USA 2018

Karen Fink Chamber Orchestra CA, USA 2018

C. Myron Flippin Choir AR, USA 2010

Carmen Florez-Mansi Choir NM, USA 2017, 2023

Jennifer Morgan Flory Choir GA, USA 2018

Joseph Flummerfelt Choir IN, USA 1990

Martin A. Follose Concert Band OR, USA 2009

Mindy Forehand Choir GA, USA 2022

Lukas Foss Orchestra NY, USA 1998, 1999, 2000, 2001, 2003, 2004

Marc Ashley Foster Choir NC, USA 2011

Pamelia Foster Choir TX, USA 2011

Jeshua Franklin Choir IN, USA 2019

Cindy Freeman Choir VA, USA 2014

Patrick Freer Choir GA, USA 2010

Karen Frink Orchestra WI, USA 2014, 2023

Greg Fritz Band OH, USA 1997

Brian P. Froedge Wind Ensemble KY, USA 2006

Kenneth Fulton Choir LA, USA 2004

Eric Funk Choir MO, USA 2004

Michael R. Gagliardo Choir AL, USA 2015

Brian Galante Choir WA, USA 2004

Melodie Galloway Choir NC, USA 2012

Janet Galvan Choir NY, USA 1997, 1998, 1999, 2000, 2001, 2002, 2003, 2004, 2006

Derek D. Galvicius Choir IL, USA 2017

Philip Gabriel Garcia Orchestra TX, USA 2016

Eduardo Garcia-Novelli Choir KS, USA 2015, 2017

David Gardner Choir WA, USA 2005

Patrick Gardner Choir NJ, USA 2007

Dirk Garner Choir LA, USA 2009

Gregory Gentry Choir CO, USA 2008, 2010, 2018

Roby George Orchestra IN, USA 2005

Anthony A. Giles Choir NY, USA 2009

Michael J. Glasgow Choir NC, USA 2017, 2022

Scott Glysson Choir CA, USA 2019, 2022

Gregorio Goffredo Orchestra Italy 2010

Gabriel Gordon Orchestra UT, USA 2014

Gerald Gray Choir TN, USA 2014

J. Ernest Green Choir MD, USA 1993, 2001

David Greenlee Choir KY, USA 1999

David Gresham Choir NC, USA 2018

Jonathan Griffith Choir OR, USA 1989, 1996(2), 1997(3), 1998(4), 1999(2), 2000(4), 2001 (6), 2002, 2003(2), 2004(4), 2005(5), 2006(3), 2007

Steve Grives Choir SD, USA 2002

Steve Grussendorf Orchestra WY, USA 2016

Lucille Guarino Choir NJ, USA 2001

John P. Haggard Orchestra AZ, USA 2010

Jacqueline Hairston Choir CA, USA 2012, 2016

Robert Ham Choir KY, USA 1998

Anna Hamre Choir CA, USA 2006, 2009

Craig Hancock Band IA, USA 2003

Chris Hansen Choir SC, USA 2022

Matthew Hanson Band NC, USA 2000

Matthew Harden Choir WI, USA 2011, 2017

Janet Harms Choir CA, USA 2003

T.J. Harper Choir CA, USA 2022

Robert Harris Choir IL, USA 2000

Darryl E. Harris Choir MS, USA 2015

Charles Hausmann Choir TX, USA 2003, 2006, 2011

Mark Hayes Choir MO, USA 2007, 2008, 2016, 2018

James Haygood Choir LA, USA 1997, 2005

Billie Hegge Choir KS, USA 1995

Peter Hendrickson Choir MN, USA 2015

Stephanie A. Henry Choir MO, USA 1996

Kevin Hibbard Choir GA, USA 2022

Les Hicken Orchestra SC, USA 2016, 2019, 2023

Terry Hill Orchestra NV, USA 1998

Thomas M. Hodgman Choir MI, USA 2010

Ernest Hoetzl Orchestra Austria 2008

Shulamit Hoffman Choir CA, USA 2009, 2019

Roy C. Holder Concert Band TN, USA 2006

Ryan Holder Choir AZ, USA 2023

Sandy R. Holland Choir NC, USA 2017

Solveig Holmquist Choir OR, USA 1999, 2002, 2004, 2007

Arthur J. Holton III Choir CA, USA 1991

Paul Hondorp Choir KY, USA 2019

Chyi-Lin Hong Choir Taiwan 1998

Juan Huey-Ray Choir WA, USA 2012

Raymond Hughes Choir WA, USA 2007

J. Edmund Hughes Choir WA, USA 2017

Jon Hurty Choir IL, USA 2011

Jason Iannuzzi Choir MA, USA 2023

Melinda Imthurn Choir TX, USA 2019

Stanley Irwin Choir IN, USA 1998

Doreen Irwin Choir CA, USA 2012

Maria Isaak Band NH, USA 2001

Sean Ivory Choir MI, USA 2014

Thomas Jaber Choir TX, USA 2019

Cora L. Jackson Choir CA, USA 2012

Buddy James Choir CA, USA 2023

John Jennings Choir AL, USA 1991

Dale Johnson Choir WA, USA 2005

Terre Johnson Choir GA, USA 1996, 1998, 2003(2), 2004(2),2007, 2008, 2014

John Paul Johnson Choir TX, USA
    2000, 2002, 2004
Cameron Johnson Weiler Choir AL,
    USA 2017
Ronald Jones Orchestra WA, USA
    1993, 2001, 2009, 2017
Randy Jordan Choir TX, USA 2007
Jerry Jordan Choir MS, USA 1989,
    1991
Douglas M. Jordon Wind Ensemble
    FL, USA 2007
Jerron Jorgensen Choir SC, USA 2022
Clark Wayman Joseph Choir TX, USA
    2023
Lawrence Kaptein Choir CO, USA
    2001
Duane Karna Choir WI, USA 2007
Amir Kats Orchestra MN, USA 2004
John Keenan Choir NY, USA 1988
C. David Keith Choir GA, USA 2006
Ryan M. Kelly Choir PA, USA 2011,
    2018
Donald Kendrick Choir CA, USA
    1995, 2003
Karen Kennedy Choir FL, USA 2003
Will Kesling Choir FL, USA 1990(2)
Lee R. Kesselman Choir IL, USA 2022
Antoine Khouri Orchestra FL, USA
    2005
James Kinchen Choir WI, USA 1998,
    2004, 2006
Allison Lee King Orchestra TX, USA
    2017
Lee Kjelson Choir FL, USA 2000
Kenneth S. Klaus Choir LA ,USA 2018
Nancy K. Klein Choir VA, USA 2017

Kevin M. Klotz Choir TX, USA 2018
Anna Klus Choir MN, USA 2017
Eric Dale Knapp Choir CT, USA
    2001(2), 2003, 2004, 2006
Bruce J. G. Kotowich Choir Ontario,
    Canada 2018
Carol Krueger Choir GA, USA 2010
Patrick Kukes Orchestra WY, USA
    2009, 2016
Paul Kwami Choir TN, USA 2022
David Ladd Choir IL, USA 2006
Po-Wei Lai Orchestra CA, USA 2015
Iris Lamanna Choir CA, USA 2004
Brian Lamb Wind Ensemble OK, USA
    2006
Michael Lancaster Choir NC, USA
    1998
Laura Lane Choir IL, USA 2005
Graeme Langager Choir Canada 2015
Giuseppe Lanzetta Choir Italy 2006,
    2009, 2016, 2017, 2018, 2019
Mark F. Lawlor Choir OK, USA 2006
John Leavitt Choir KS, USA 1998,
    1999, 2001, 2002, 2003, 2004, 2005,
    2007
Henry Leck Choir OH, USA 1990
Richard Lee Choir TX, USA 1996
Frank Lee Choir North Vancouver, BC
    2011
Francesco Lentini Choir 2007
Drew Lewis Orchestra CA, USA 2014
Patrick M. Liebergen Choir IL, USA
    2006
John Liepold Choir NY, USA 2004,
    2006

Roland Lister Choir AL, USA 2015
Helen Litz Choir Winnipeg, MB 1990
Kuanfen Liu Choir CA, USA 2022
Brian LKlenzendorf Concert Band TX, USA 2004
Ed Lojeski Choir CA, USA 2006
Wallace Long Jr. Choir OR, USA 2006
Doug Longman Choir WA, USA 2011
Vicente Lopez Choir TX, USA 2018
Dennis J. Loy Choir NJ, USA 2013
Adam Luebke Choir NY, USA 2023
Robert Lyall Choir TN, USA 1998
Megan Lynch Orchestra TN, USA 1997
Debra Lynn Choir IN ,USA 2022
Toufic Maatouk Choir Lebanon 2015
Terry Maddox Choir AL, USA 2009
Dennis Malfatti Choir IN, USA 2011, 2016
Cailin Marcel Manson Choir MA, USA 2023
Michael Marcades Choir DE, USA 2004
Galen Marshall Choir CA, USA 1989
Ronald Martz Wind Ensemble MO, USA 2009
Lorissa Mason Choir AR, USA 2022
Rui Massena Orchestra Portugal 2007
John Massoro Choir AZ, USA 2005
Robert McBain Choir FL, USA 2003
Kevin McBeth Choir MO, USA 2002, 2006, 2011
Jerry McCoy Choir TX, USA 2001(2), 2003
Pamela D.J. McDermott Choir VA, USA 2023

Albert McNeil Choir CA, USA 2001
James M. Meaders Choir London, UK 2006, 2008
Verotta Means Orchestra SC, USA 2001
Douglas M. Mears Choir VA, USA 2015
Richard Medrano Choir CA, USA 2018
Matthew Mehaffy Choir MN, USA 2009
Michael Meise Choir TN, USA 2014
Stephen Melillo Band NY, USA 1996
James Melton Choir CA, USA 2001, 2003
Kevin A. Memley Choir CA, USA 2016
Cory J. Mendenhall Choir UT, USA 2016
Nancy Menk Choir IN, USA 1999, 2001, 2003, 2005
Dick Meyer Orchestra GA, USA 2008
Alexander Mikhaylov Choir 1991
Todd Randall Miller Choir TX, USA 2007
DaVaughn L. Miller Choir NC, USA 2010
Dale Miller Choir AR, USA 2000, 2004, 2008
Jeremy Mims Choir SC, USA 2019
Eugene Minor Orchestra NJ, USA 2004
H. Vincent Mitzelfelt Choir CA, USA 1999
Joseph Modica Choir CA, USA 2013
Lesley Moffat Wind Ensemble WA, USA 2012, 2016

Robert Molison Choir CO, USA 1995

Jean Montes Orchestra LA, USA 2009

Michael Morgan Choir CA, USA 1988

Jane DeLoach Morison Choir TN, USA 2017

Bob Morrison Choir FL, USA 2019

Phillip Morrow Choir NC, USA 2023

Bryson Mortensen Choir VA, USA 2018, 2023

Metford Mountford Choir TX, USA 1991

Joel Munc Orchestra NV, USA 2000

Chris Munce Choir MO, USA 2022

Wendolin Munroe Choir Canada 2010

Sylvia Munsen Choir UT, USA 2006

Joanna Nachef Choir CA, USA 2005, 2010, 2015, 2018

Nina Nash-Robertson Choir MI, USA 2004

Eric Nelson Choir GA, USA 2002

Kellyann Nelson Choir OH, USA 2019

Carol Nelson Concert Band OR, USA 2004, 2012, 2016

Paul Nesheim Choir SD, USA 2015

Donald Neuen Choir CA, USA 1999, 2004, 2005

Jonathan Ng Choir AZ, USA 2007

Robert R. Nichols Orchestra AZ, USA 2010

Larry Nickel Choir BC, Canada 2016

Weston Noble Choir IA, USA 1989, 1997

Francisco J. Nunez Choir NY, USA 2000, 2001

Michael O'Neal Choir GA, USA 2000

Masahiko Okochi Orchestra Gunma, Japan 2000

Jim Oliver Band MO, USA 1997

Carla L. OliverChoir MO, USA 1997

Kira Omelchenko Choir ON, Canada 2023

David Orcutt Choir NY, USA 1993

Jerold Ottley Choir HI, USA 2001

Richard Owen Choir NY, USA 2002

Gary Packwood Choir MS, USA 2012, 2019, 2022

Kevin Padworski Choir CO, USA 2019

Nick Page Choir MA, USA 2007

Randy Pagel Choir NV, USA 2000, 2002, 2004, 2005, 2006

Timothy Pahel Choir IL, USA 2018

Carlo Palleschi Orchestra Italy 2006

Joel Panciera Choir OK, USA 1997

Jason Paulk Choir NM, USA 2011, 2013, 2015

Denise Murchison Payton Choir NC, USA 2013

Wendolin Pazitka-Munroe Choir Canada 2016

Suzanne Pence Choir TX, USA 2003

Daniel Perkins Choir NH, USA 2014

Pierre Perron Choir Canada 2002, 2015

Susanna Pescetti Choir Italy 2007

Sandra Peter Choir FL, USA 2003

Timothy Peter Choir FL, USA 2003, 2004, 2006

Allan Robert Petker Choir CA, USA 2015, 2018

Nancy Petterson Strelau Orchestra NY, USA 1996

Davin Pierson Torre Orchestra MI, USA 2000

Joanna Pinckney Orchestra CA, USA 2000

Paul T. Plew Choir CA, USA 2007, 2018

Erin Plisco Choir MO, USA 2023

Johnny Poon Choir Hong Kong 2000(2)

Thomas Porter Choir ND, USA 1998

Jo Ann D. Poston Choir NC, USA 1997

Sterling Poulson Choir UT, USA 2019

William C. Powell Choir AL, USA 2006, 2009

Rebecca Prater Choir KS, USA 2016

S. Bryan Priddy Choir ON, Canada 2004

Stephen Pu Choir CA, USA 2019

David J. Puderbaugh Choir IA, USA 2018

Alex Qian Orchestra TX, USA 2016

Edward Quick Band MI, USA 1998, 2003

Elaine Quilichini Choir Canada 2003

Christopher Quinn Choir UT, USA 2018

Susan Quinn Choir Canada 2010, 2014

Khalil Rahmeh Choir Lebanon 2015

John Patrick Rakes Choir IL, USA 2022

David Ramadanoff Orchestra CA, USA 2000

Imant Raminsh Choir BC, Canada 2006

Sharon Ramsey Wilkins Choir MO, USA 1996

Doreen Rao Choir IL, USA 1990, 1991, 1993, 1997

John Ratledge Choir AL, USA 2013, 2019

James Ray String Orchestra WA, USA 2017

Robert Ray Choir MO, USA 1998, 2002

David Rayl Choir MI, USA 2007

James Reddan Choir OR, USA 2022

Tracy Resseguie Choir MO, USA 2007, 2014, 2017

Diane Retallack Choir OR, USA 2022

H. Robert Reynolds Band CA, USA 1998, 2004, 2008

Leonard L. Riccinto Choir MI, USA 1996, 2004

David A. Richardson Choir SC, USA 2022

Kevin Riehle Choir TX, USA 2001, 2003

Giselle Elgarresta Rios Choir FL, USA 2008, 2016

Virginia-Gene Rittenhouse Orchestra MA, USA 1993, 1997, 2001(2), 2002, 2004, 2006

Earl Rivers Choir OH, USA 1998, 2004, 2007, 2010

Ian Robertson Choir CA, USA 1998

Andrew Robertson Orchestra WA, USA 2016, 2019

Russell L. Robinson Choir FL, USA 2006, 2014

Stephen Roddy Choir TX, USA 1995

Jennifer Rodgers Choir IA, USA 2023

Piero Romano Orchestra WA, USA 2008

Peter Rosheger Orchestra IL, USA 2006, 2018

Michael Rossi Choir VA, USA 2010

Rebecca Rottsolk Choir WA, USA 1990

James Rouintree Band 1998

Cornell Runestad Choir NE, USA 1995

Terry Russell Choir CA, USA 2007, 2010, 2016

John Rutter Choir England, UK 1989, 1991(2), 1992(2), 1993(2), 1994, 1995(4), 1997 (5), 1998(5), 1999(4), 2000(5), 2001(3), 2002(4), 2003 (6), 2004(6), 2005(4), 2006(4), 2007(3), 2008(4), 2009 (2), 2010, 2011(2), 2012(4), 2013(2), 2014(3), 2015, 2018, 2019

John Rutter Orchestra/Choir England, UK 2009, 2010

John Rutter Orchestra England, UK 2009, 2010 (2), 2011

Paul Salamunovich Choir CA, USA 1997

Kristofer Sanchack Choir AL, USA 2023

Ronnie Sanders Choir TX, USA 2005

Hugh Sanders Choir TX, USA 1989, 1990

Elizabeth Schauer Choir AZ, USA 2019

Jan Pedersen Schiff Choir CA, USA 2006, 2018

David Schildkret Choir AZ, USA 2018

Irene Schmor Choir NY, USA 1990

Jill Schroeder-Dorn Choir CO, USA 2019

Ralph Schweigert Band MI, USA 1996

Nina R. Scott Choir MI, USA 2012

Sabrina Scruggs String Orchestra WA, USA 2017

Gary Scudder Wind Ensemble CA, USA 2016

Anthony Sears Choir LA, USA 2023

Timothy Seelig Choir CA, USA 2002, 2006

Lester Seigel Choir AL, USA 2016

Sonja Sepulveda Choir NC, USA 1997, 2016(2), 2017, 2022

Elden T. Seta Orchestra HI, USA 2005

Timothy C. Sexton Choir Australia 2018

Kristy Shaffer-May Band OH, USA 1997

David Sharlow Choir MO, USA 2019

Lahonda Sharp Choir TX, USA 2002, 2005, 2019

Timothy Sharp Choir FL, USA 2004, 2006

Tim Sharp Choir OK, USA 2006, 2010

Kirby Shaw Choir OR, USA 2009

Tom T. Shelton Choir NJ, USA 2015

Michael Short Choir CA, USA 2009, 2017

John Silantien Choir TX, USA 2008, 2017

D'Walla Simmons - Burke Choir NC, USA 2008, 2023

Stephen Simons Choir TX, USA 1998

Robert Sinclair Choir IL, USA 2022

Berislav Skenderovic Orchestra Serbia 2008

William Skoog Choir TN, USA 2017

Alfred Skoog Choir AR, USA 1989, 1993

Thomas Sleeper Orchestra FL, USA 2002

Michael Smith Band OH, USA 1996

J. Christopher Smith Band OH, USA 1997

Paul A. Smith Choir NC, USA 2006

Jeffrey R. Smith Choir PA, USA 2009

Byron Smith Choir CA, USA 2023

Justin Smith Choir NC, USA 2012, 2022

Bonnie Borshay Sneed Choir OK, USA 2007

Sandra Snow Choir MI, USA 2007

Johannes Somary Choir NY, USA 1996

Kathy Sorensen Choir UT, USA 1993

Allin Sorenson Choir MO, USA 1999

Bruce Southard Choir CA, USA 2019

Ethelyn Sparfeld Choir MO, USA 1990

Richard Sparks Choir WA, USA 2005

Tram Sparks Choir CA, USA 2023

Randall Speer Choir VA, USA 2012

Linda Spevacek Choir AZ, USA 1999

Raymond Sprague Choir LA, USA 1999, 2006

John Stafford, II Choir KS, USA 2022

Diane Stallings Choir GA, USA 2012

Paul John Stanbery Choir OH, USA 2018

Eric Stark Choir IN, USA 2002

Gabriel Statom Choir TN, USA 2008

Ida Steadman Orchestra TX, USA 1998

Adam Stich Choir AZ, USA 2018

Mary Alice Stollak Choir MI, USA 2003, 2005

Lee Stone Orchestra FL, USA 2002

Jonathan Strasser Orchestra NY, USA 1997, 2001

Z. Randall Stroope Choir OK, USA 2016

Jason Strunk Choir Washington DC, USA 2002

Donald Studebaker Choir OK, USA 2003

David Stutzenberger Choir TN, USA 2002

Averill Summer Choir FL, USA 1993

Giulio Svegliado Orchestra Italy 2009, 2010

Barbara Marble Tagg Choir FL, USA 1990

Miklos Takacs Orchestra Canada 1993, 1994

Jonathan Talberg Choir CA, USA 2007

Mary Tallitsch Choir IL, USA 2011

Amos Talmon Orchestra Israel 2010

Jim Taylor Choir TX, USA 2019, 2023

Pamela Tellejohn Hayes Orchestra MI, USA 1997

Matthew Temple Orchestra IL, USA 2018

Ray Theaux Band LA, USA 1996

Rebecca Thompson Choir KY, USA 1990

Sandra Thornton Choir OH, USA 2013

Stanley John Thurston Choir Washington DC, USA 2018

David Thye Choir AZ, USA 2005, 2007(3), 2008(2), 2009, 2016(4), 2017(2), 2018(3), 2019

Joshua D. Thye Wind Ensemble AZ, USA 2008, 2018

Peter Tiboris Orchestra/Chorus FL, USA 2018

Peter Tiboris Choir FL, USA 2019

Peter Tiboris Choir FL, USA 1986, 1987, 1988, 1989, 1990(2), 1995, 2000, 2003, 2006, 2007

Peter Tiboris Orchestra FL, USA 1989(2), 1991(2), 1993, 1995, 2000, 2005, 2007, 2009, 2016, 2018

Danya Tiller Choir AZ, USA 2016

Alton Wayne Tipps Concert Band TN, USA 2006

Paul Torkelson Choir NV, USA 1989, 2011, 2013

Stephen Town Choir MO, USA 2007

Joel Tranquilla Choir BC, Canada 2023

Lynn Trapp Choir MD, USA 2007

Michael John Trotta Choir NJ, USA 2014, 2017, 2019

Samuel Tsugawa Orchestra UT, USA 1998

Jeremy Tucker Choir NC, USA 2023

Scott Tuomi Choir OR, USA 2018

George E. Umberson Choir AZ. USA 2015

Corrado Valvo Orchestra Italy 2019

Carolyn Vandiver Orchestra TX, USA 2005

Susan Vaughan Choir IL, USA 2006

Miran Vaupotic Orchestra Croatia 2017

Bradley Vogel Choir KS, USA 2019, 2022

Sean Vogt Choir GA, USA 2022

Randi von Ellefson Choir OK, USA 2000, 2003

Andy Waggoner Choir IL, USA 2011

Bill Wagner Symphonic Band CA, USA 2007

Deborah Wales Orchestra ON, Canada 2018

Scotty E. Walker Band LA, USA 1996

Rod Walker Choir KS, USA 2005

Nicholas Walters Orchestra CA, USA 2017

Roger Walworth Choir AL, USA 2005

Ying-Chien Wang Choir CA, USA 2022

Mike Ware Choir TX, USA 2003, 2006

Dale Warland Choir MN, USA 1998

Roger Waters Choir GA, USA 2004

David B. Weaver Choir ON, Canada 2018

Noel Weaver Choir KY , USA 2003, 2011, 2016

Jeffrey Webb Choir PA, USA 2023

Raymond Weidner Choir VA, USA 2016

Shawn Weis Orchestra WY, USA 2009, 2016

Mike Wells Orchestra TX, USA 2000

Jeffrey Wenz Band CO, USA 1999

David R. White Choir GA, USA 2005

Candace Wicke Choir NJ, USA 2002, 2004, 2006(2), 2019

Stanley Wicks Choir CA, USA 2002

Gary Wilhelm Choir IL, USA 1998, 2009

Jonathan Willcocks Choir England, UK 1990, 1996(2), 1998, 1999(2), 2000, 2004, 2013

Ronald Williams Choir OH, USA 2007

Richard Williamson Choir SC, USA 2016

Dawn Willis Choir VT, USA 1999

Judith Willoughby Choir OK, USA 2006

Brent Wilson Orchestra CA, USA 1997

Renee Wilson-Wicker Choir GA, USA 2023

Daniel Wing Orchestra WI, USA 2015

Jeanne Wohlgamuth Choir OH, USA 2023

Stanley Wold Choir MN, USA 2000

Brian T. Wolfe Wind Ensemble OK, USA 2008

Clell Wright Choir GA, USA 2022

Gwendolyn Wyatt Choir CA, USA 2010

Larry Wyatt Choir SC, USA 1990, 2000, 2005

Giselle Wyers Choir WA, USA 2022

William Wyman Choir NE, USA 2009, 2012, 2014, 2018

Rodney Wynkoop Choir NC, USA 2006, 2017

Elizer Yanson Jr. Choir AL, USA 2018

Hanan Yaqub Choir CA, USA 1998

F. Jackson Yonce Orchestra CO, USA 2015

Scott Alan Youngs Choir AZ, USA 2017

Amir Zaheri Choir AL , USA 2022

Craig Zamer Choir TN, USA 2018

Benjamin Zander Orchestra MA, USA 2006

Zoe Zeniodi Orchestra Greece 2017

Kyle Zeuch Choir MI, USA 2017

Greg Zielke Choir NE, USA 2009, 2016

XII. Choral Ensembles which have performed in Carnegie Hall, Lincoln Center's Avery Fischer Hall and Abroad since 1984

Aberdeen High School And Miller Junior High School 4/1/2002

Aberdeen High School And Miller Junior High School 4/15/2001

Aberdeen High School And Miller Junior High School 3/31/2002

Aberdeen High School And Miller Junior High School 5/14/2000

Abiding Hope Lutheran Church 3/5/2001

Abiding Hope Lutheran Church 3/2/2004

Academies of West Memphis High School 3/19/2000

Acalanes High School Choir
12/1/1996
Adrian College Choir/ Lenawee
Community Chorus 3/19/2018
Air Academy High School Choir
6/1/2019
Airline High School 5/14/2000
Alabama State University Choir
5/13/2023
Albany Chorale 3/19/2022
Albany Community Chorus 5/29/1988
Albert McNeil Jubilee Singers
1/18/1999
Albert McNeil Singers 6/3/2001
Albertsons College of Idaho 4/1/2002
Albion College 5/30/1999
Albuquerque Academy Choir
3/23/1997
Albuquerque Academy Choir
3/26/2000
Alden Area Ecumenical Choir
5/28/2011
Aldersgate Chorale 1/18/2004
Aldersgate Chorale 5/19/2001
Aldersgate United Methodist Church
11/25/2001
Aledo United Methodist Church
Choirs 5/28/2018
All Saints' Episcopal School A Capella
Choir 5/27/2019
All Saints Episcopal School 5/30/2011
Allyson Hogan 5/30/2022
Ambrose University 6/14/2019
American Bach Soloists 4/28/2018
American International School of Utah
6/2/2018

American Preparatory Academy
6/18/2017
Ames Chamber Artists 5/29/2023
Ames Chamber Artists 5/29/2023
Amherst Central High School
4/23/2023
Amity High School 5/26/1997
AmorArtis, Inc. 5/12/1996
Anchorage Concert Chorus 4/30/1986
Anchorage Concert Chorus 6/3/2022
Anderson University 6/25/2022
Angelica Cantanti 6/17/2001
Ankeny High School 5/26/2002
Ankeny High School 5/29/1999
Ankeny High School 5/26/2002
Annapolis Chorale And Severn School
11/20/2001
Annapolis Chorale And Severn School
11/20/2001
Antelope Valley Master Chorale
3/2/2004
Antelope Valley Master Chorale
3/2/2004
AOL Chorus 11/30/1997
AOL CultureFinder Chorus
11/29/1998
Apex High School 3/25/2001
Appleby College 5/14/2000
Apple Valley High School 5/26/1997
Apple Valley High School 5/26/1997
Apple Valley High School 4/9/2023
Apple Valley High School 3/19/2012
Apple Valley High School 3/19/2018
Apple Valley High School Wind
Ensemble 5/8/1988
Aptos High School 4/4/2004

Aquila Theatre Company 6/11/2000
Arapahoe High School 3/5/2001
Arapahoe High School 11/22/1998
Archbishop Blenk High School
    2/17/2002
Aria Women's Choir 4/17/2022
Arizona Cantilena Chorale 6/21/2019
Arizona Cantilena Chorale & Friends
    6/1/2018
Arizona Cantilena Chorale & Friends
    6/21/2019
Arizona Masterworks Chorale
    11/25/2001
Arizona State University Choral Union
    6/2/2018
Arkansas High School 6/9/2002
Arkansas State University 3/21/2004
Arkansas State University 1/13/2008
Arkansas State University 3/19/2000
Arlington Heights Methodist Church
    6/22/1997
Arlington High School 11/30/1997
Arrowhead Chorale 5/7/2000
Artios Chorale 6/25/2023
Asheville Symphony Chorus
    4/15/2012
Asheville Symphony Chorus
    7/10/2019
Ashland High School 6/17/2001
Aspen High School 2/18/2008
ASU Choral Union 6/2/2018
Atascadero High School 1/14/2001
Atash And St. Stephen's Global
    Ensemble 4/23/2018
Athens Master Chorale 6/4/2022

Atlanta Master Chorale 4/16/2002
Atlantic Union College 3/2/2004
Atlantic Wind Symphony 3/22/1998
Auburn High School 3/11/2023
Auckland Choral Society 5/30/2011
Augustana College 5/29/2011
Augustana College 5/29/2011
Augustana Lutheran Church
    5/29/2011
Austin Community College
    11/26/2000
Austin Community College
    11/25/2001
Avila University 5/27/2022
Avon High School 4/15/2001
Baldwin County High School
    11/26/2000
Ballard High School 3/22/1998
Ballard High School Concert Choir
    3/14/2011
Bangor Area High School 6/25/2023
Bangor Area High School 6/10/2019
Baptist Voice Children's Chorus
    6/27/1999
Barack Obama Male Leadership
    Academy 6/3/2022
Barren County High School 4/15/2012
Barry University 4/7/2002
Barstow High School 5/29/2000
Bartlesville High School 6/3/2001
Battle Creek Community Singers
    6/6/1999
Baxter Springs High School 4/1/2001
Bayfield Troller Concert Band
    5/9/1999
Bay Port High School 3/21/2004

Bear Creek High School 4/4/1995
Bear Creek High School 4/4/1995
Bear Creek United Methodist Church
    4/16/2002
Beaufort County Choral Society
    6/2/2002
Bedford Junior High School 6/26/2000
Bel Canto Choir & Northern Voices
    1/14/2001
Bel Canto Choir & Northern Voices
    3/21/2004
Bel Canto Chorus 12/1/1996
Bel Canto Chorus of Saint Louis
    1/20/1998
Bel Canto Singers 3/28/2011
Bel Canto Singers 11/23/2012
Bellevue Chamber Chorus 5/14/2000
Bellevue East High School 5/26/2012
Bellevue Newport High School
    5/14/2000
Beloit Memorial High School
    11/30/1997
Belvidere High School 6/1/2019
Bemidji High School 5/30/1988
Bemidji High School 3/11/2023
Bend High School 1/18/1999
Berean Christian Academy 2/17/2019
Bergenfield High School 5/26/2002
Bergen Youth Orchestra 3/31/2002
Bergen Youth Orchestra 3/22/1993
Berrien Springs High School
    6/25/2023
Berryville High School 6/26/2022
Berthoud H.S. 4/15/2001
Bethany College Oratorio Society
    4/7/1997

Bethel College Choir 5/30/1988
Bethel College Choir 11/29/1998
Bethel College Choir 11/29/1998
Bethel College Choral Union
    7/11/2018
Bethel College Choral Union
    5/11/2019
Bible Baptist Christian School
    6/17/2018
Bishop England Chorale 5/25/2019
Bishop Heelan Catholic High School
    5/29/2000
Bishop Heelan Catholic High School
    5/29/2000
Bishop Miege High School 5/27/2022
Bishop Watterson High School
    3/19/2012
Bismarck-Mandan Civic Chorus
    6/14/1998
Bismarck-Mandan Civic Chorus
    6/14/1998
Blackburn College 11/26/2000
Blackburn College 6/25/2023
Black Hills State University 2/16/1998
Blackwell High School 1/14/2001
Blair Children's Chorus/Young Men's
    Chorus 2/17/2019
Blue Mountain College Choir
    5/13/2018
Blue Ridge High School 11/20/2001
Bluestem JR/SR High 1/19/2004
Boardman High School Symphonic
    Band 3/28/1988
Bob Jones Academy 5/21/2001
Bob Jones Academy 6/25/2023
Bob Jones University 6/25/2023

Bob Jones University 6/17/2018
Bolles School 4/1/2001
Bonham High School 5/21/2001
Booker T. Washington High Vocal
    Harmony 4/21/2019
Booneville High School 12/1/1996
Boonville High School 5/30/2022
Bosque School 3/28/2011
Bothell High School 4/16/2000
Bradford High School 5/26/1997
Bradford High School 5/26/1997
Bradford High School 5/27/2001
Bradford High School 5/26/1997
Braintree Choral Society 5/13/2018
Braintree Choral Society 4/15/2012
Branford High School 5/26/1996
Branford High School 6/3/2001
Brass Mosaic Chamber Ensemble
    1/19/1997
Brentwood Palisades Chorale
    5/26/1996
Brentwood School Madrigals &
    Concert Singers 3/19/2018
Brescia University 4/16/2002
Brevard Chorale 6/26/2000
Brevard Chorale 5/28/2012
Brevard College 4/23/2018
Brewer High School 3/31/2019
Brigham Young University - Hawaii
    5/16/2023
Broadmoor United Methodist Church
    5/30/1988
Brooklyn Community Chorus
    6/16/2019
Brooklyn Community Chorus
    5/28/2019

Brooklyn Youth Chorus 1/20/1997
Brookwood High School Orchestra
    4/14/2002
Brown Junior High School 3/31/2002
Brownson Memorial Presbyterian
    Chancel Choir 5/28/2022
Bryan High School Choirs 3/21/2004
Bucknell University 5/9/1999
Bucknell University 5/9/1999
Buena Vista High School 5/19/2018
Buena Vista University 6/10/2000
Burke Chorale/Winston-Salem State
    University Choir 4/9/2023
Butler Phiharmonic Chorus 6/17/2018
Butler Philharmonic Orchestra &
    Chorus 6/17/2018
Butler University-Indianapolis
    Symphonic Choir 5/12/2002
Cabrillo High School 5/14/2000
CACS Chorus 1/18/1999
Cajon High School 5/26/1997
Cajon High School 4/16/2000
California Central Coast Chorale
    4/17/2022
California State University, East Bay
    4/23/2023
California State University, Fresno
    6/2/1996
California State University -
    Bakersfield 6/17/2001
California State University - Channel
    Islands 6/25/2022
California State University -
    Dominguez Hills 6/3/2001
Cal Poly Choirs 7/7/2022

Cal Poly Pomona 3/21/2004
Camden Fairview High School
    6/9/2002
Camerata New York 3/11/2002
Camerata of Los Angeles 6/28/1998
Camerata of Los Angeles 6/27/1999
Cameron University 5/30/2022
CAMMAC 50th Anniversary Chorus
    6/9/2002
Campanella Children's Chorus
    11/23/2012
Campbell County High School Select
    Choir 4/15/2012
Campbell University Choral Soc.
    7/8/2023
Campus High School 6/17/2001
Cantare 6/17/2001
Cantari 5/29/2011
Cantemus Women's Choir 7/10/2019
Canton Symphony Chorus 6/10/2019
Cantores Clestes Women's Choir
    5/28/2018
Canyon Creek Presbyterian Church
    6/26/2000
Canyon Singers 4/28/2019
Cappella Cantorum 5/12/2002
Cappella Cantorum 5/27/2001
Cappella Festiva Chamber Choir
    5/30/2011
Cardinal Stritch University 3/23/1997
Carleton College 1/20/1997
Carleton University - Coro Vivo
    Ottawa 5/25/2019
Carl Junction High School 5/26/2002
Carolina Youth Symphony 4/8/2001
Carolina Youth Symphony 4/23/2023

Carolina Youth Symphony 4/21/2019
Carondelet HS/de la Salle HS
    3/31/2002
Carondelet HS/de la Salle HS
    5/26/1997
Carondelet HS/de la Salle HS
    4/23/2000
Carthage College 5/29/2011
Carthage College 5/29/2011
Caryn Bickel 5/30/2022
Cascadian Chorale 5/28/2022
Cass Technical High School 3/11/2002
Catalina Foothills Advanced Choirs
    4/23/2023
Catalina Foothills Advanced Choirs
    4/28/2019
Cathedral Basilica of St. Francis of
    Assisi 6/3/2023
Cathedral Choir of First Lutheran
    Church 4/23/2018
Cedar Park High School 3/11/2002
Cedar Rapids Concert Chorale
    5/30/2011
Cedar Rapids Washington High School
    Choir 2/21/2000
Cedar Shoals High School 4/8/2012
Cedarville University 4/24/2011
Celebration Community Chorus
    6/7/2019
Celebration Singers of Asheville
    5/27/2017
Centenary United Methodist Church
    5/26/2023
Centenary United Methodist Church
    5/27/2017

Central Arkansas Christian HS
4/12/1998
Central Arkansas Christian HS
4/12/1998
Central Arkansas Christian HS
3/19/2000
Central Baptist Church of South
Dakota 5/30/1988
Central Bucks East High School
5/28/2012
Central Bucks High School East
1/13/2008
Central Bucks West High School
11/24/2006
Central Bucks West High School
4/8/2001
Central Bucks West High School
5/24/1998
Central Bucks West High School
11/30/1997
Central Bucks West High School
5/26/1996
Central Bucks West High School
2/20/2011
Central-Carroll High School
6/30/2022
Central Community College
5/28/2011
Central Conservatory of Music
12/13/2019
Central High School Choir 4/23/2000
Central Kitsap High School 4/8/2001
Central Lutheran Church 3/2/2004
Central Missouri State University
6/14/1998

Central Oregon Mastersingers
6/20/2022
Central Presbyterian Church 3/5/2001
Central Presbyterian Church
5/30/2011
Central Presbyterian Church 4/7/2002
Central Regional High School
6/5/2022
Central Regional High School
6/25/2023
Central Regional High School
6/1/2019
Central Regional High School
5/28/2019
Central Regional High School
6/16/2019
Central Valley Youth Symphony
6/25/2000
Chamber Singers of Iowa City
6/2/2018
Chamber Singers of Southeast Iowa
6/10/2000
Chancel Choir of First United
Methodist Church 3/23/2019
Chandler-Gilbert Community College
4/6/2017
Channel Islands Choral Association
6/25/2022
Chanson de Montagne 4/21/2019
Chantry Singers 6/2/2018
Chapin School 6/17/2001
Charleston County School of the Arts
4/1/2002
Charleston Symphony Orchestra
Chorus 5/8/2021

Charlotte Senior High School
4/6/2017

Chase Collegiate Chorus 5/28/2012

Chatfield Senior High School 4/3/2000

Chattanooga School For the Arts &
Science 5/8/2021

Chelan High School 5/26/2002

Cherry Creek Chorale 5/31/2021

Cheyenne Mountain HS Band
4/24/2011

Chief Sealth High School 5/14/2000

Chief Sealth High School 4/24/2011

Children's Chorus of Carroll County
2/18/2001

ChildrenSong of New Jersey 5/13/2023

Chilton High School 6/17/2001

Choate Rosemary Hall School
11/27/2011

Choctaw High School 2/21/2000

Choir of Athens University 7/7/2022

Choir of the Carolinas 5/28/2022

Choral Arts Ensemble 5/12/2002

Choral Arts of Southern New Jersey
5/28/2012

Choral Arts Society of Utah 3/31/2019

Chorale Saint-Jean 5/19/2018

ChoralSounds Northwest 3/31/2019

Chowan University 3/25/2001

Christ Church, New Brunswick
6/2/2002

Christ Church Episcopal School
11/25/2001

Christ Church Sugar Land 4/16/2002

Christ Church UMC Chancel Choir
3/19/2000

Christ Church United Methodist -
Tucson 5/28/2001

Christopher Dock Mennonite High
School 5/28/2011

Christopher Dock Mennonite High
School 5/4/1997

Christopher Dock Mennonite High
School 5/26/2002

Christopher Dock Mennonite High
School 4/15/2001

Christ the King Catholic Church
5/30/1999

Christ United Methodist Church
4/1/2001

Christ United Methodist Church
6/11/2017

Christ United Methodist Church
11/26/2000

Church of the Resurrection
11/13/2011

Cincinnati Boychoir 4/30/1986

Cincinnati Choral Society 5/30/1999

Cincinnati Choral Society/Mason
UMC 5/30/1999

Cincinnati Christian High School
4/4/2004

City Honors High School 5/27/2023

City of Angels Master Chorale And
Community Choir 11/23/2012

City of Angels Master Chorale And
Community Choir 6/17/2018

City of Angels Master Chorale And
Community Choir 11/23/2012

City of Angels Master Chorale And
Community Choir 6/17/2018

Civic Chorale of Greater Miami
    3/19/2000
Clallam Bay High School 5/14/2000
Clarendon College 1/13/2008
Clarion University 11/25/2001
Clark Atlanta University 11/25/2001
Clark University 3/11/2023
Classen School of Advanced Studies
    4/28/2018
Classical European Music Academy
    Los Angeles 6/18/2017
Classic Choral Society 1/13/2008
Clayton State University 5/26/1996
Clayton State University 6/4/2022
Clements High School 3/26/2000
Clemson University 11/26/2000
Clemson University 11/26/2000
Clermont Chorale 6/8/2018
Clifton High School 4/16/2002
Clifton High School 5/23/1999
Clifton High School 5/27/2001
Coastline Arts Community Choir
    5/28/2022
Cocke County High School 6/25/2022
Coker United Methodist Church
    Chancel Choir 5/27/2019
Coker University 5/27/2022
College of DuPage 6/5/2022
College of St. Teresa Chamber Choir
    5/29/1988
College of the Ozarks Chorale
    6/10/2000
College of the Ozarks Chorale
    5/29/2017
Collegium Vocale 6/7/2019
Collegium Vocale 6/30/2022

Colony High School 5/4/1997
Colorado Chorale 4/1/2018
Colorado Christian University
    2/18/2008
Colorado Christian University Choir
    6/1/2019
Colorado Easter Chorale 4/4/1999
Colorado Mesa University Choir
    2/18/2008
Colorado Mesa University Choir
    6/5/2017
Colorado Springs Children's Chorale
    3/23/1997
Colorado State University 4/4/1999
Colorado State University 4/4/1999
Columbia Basin College DeserTones
    5/19/2018
Columbia College 5/29/2011
Columbia College/Missouri UMC
    3/25/2001
Columbia Collegiate Chorale 3/2/2004
Columbia Collegiate Chorale
    3/24/2002
Columbia Collegiate Chorale
    11/27/2011
Columbia Collegiate Chorale
    4/15/2001
Columbia Union College 1/18/1998
Columbia Union College 12/1/1996
Columbus East High School
    11/23/2012
Community College of Baltimore
    County 5/28/2011
Como Park High School Choir
    5/27/2019

Concord Chorale & Lawrence
    Academy Singers 4/28/2019
ConCordia Sacrae 6/17/2018
Connecticut Children's Choir
    6/27/1999
Connecticut Master Chorale
    3/31/2002
Connecticut Symphonic Winds
    1/20/2002
CONTINUOARTS Symphonic
    Chorus 5/26/2023
CONTINUOARTS Symphonic
    Chorus 6/1/2019
CONTINUOARTS Symphonic
    Chorus 7/10/2019
Contra Costa Children's Chorus
    4/16/2000
Cookeville Master Singers 5/13/2018
Coppell High School 12/30/1999
Coro Lux 6/1/2018
Coronado High School 5/31/1998
Coronado High School 6/2/2002
Coronado High School 5/31/1998
Coronado High School 5/31/1998
Coronado High School 5/12/2002
Coronado High School 6/16/2019
Coronado High School Orchestra
    6/2/2002
Coro Schola Cantorum de Puerto Rico
    1/18/1999
Cosmopolitan Music Society [Chorus]
    5/19/2018
County Classic Chorale 5/19/2018
Cranford High School 3/24/2002
Crescendo: The Tampa Bay Women's
    Chorus 5/26/2002

Crestwood High School 4/28/2019
Crystal Cathedrale 6/25/2000
Crystal Coast Choral Society 6/2/2002
Crystal Ensemble 4/16/2017
Crystal Ensemble 4/21/2019
Crystal Ensemble 4/17/2022
Cuero High School 3/11/2002
Culdee Presbyterian Church 5/28/2022
CUNY Queens College 11/20/2001
Curtis High School 4/6/2017
Cy-Fair High School 4/28/2001
Cypress College 5/19/2001
Dakota Chorale 5/29/1988
Dalhousie University 1/14/2001
Dallas Baptist University 4/4/1999
Dallas Baptist University 4/4/1999
Darlington High School 5/27/2001
Davenport West High School
    2/16/1998
Dayton Philharmonic Youth Orchestra
    5/8/1988
DC Area Chorus 5/29/2023
Decatur Civic Chorale 5/28/2018
Deep River Singers 7/8/2023
Deer Creek Chorale 5/30/2011
Deer Creek Chorale 3/19/2018
DeKalb Choral Guild 6/4/2022
De La Salle High School 5/21/2001
Delavan-Darien High School Choirs
    3/19/2012
Delta Sigma Theta Choraliers
    2/19/2012
Denver Choir League 5/25/2019
Denver Chorale 6/1/2019
DePauw University 5/31/1998

DeQuincy High School 3/23/1997
Derby High School 6/17/2001
Desert Harmony 2/19/2012
Desert Ridge High School 6/27/2023
Desert Vista High Schools Bands
    5/29/2018
Des Moines Choral Society 6/17/2001
Dominguez Hills Jubilee Choir
    1/18/1999
Dominican Academy GIRLS
    5/26/2023
Dominion a Cappella Ensemble
    2/19/2012
Don Donaldson Minneapolis Singers
    11/25/2001
Dorothy Cotton Jubilee Singers
    3/19/2022
Dothan High School Show Choir
    4/24/2011
Douglas Anderson School of the Arts
    5/26/1996
Douglas Anderson School of the Arts
    5/26/1997
Douglas Anderson School of the Arts
    5/26/1997
Douglas County Chamber Singers
    6/23/2023
Douglas MacArthur High School
    11/26/2000
Dowling Catholic High School
    5/4/1997
Dowling Catholic High School
    5/4/1997
Downers Grove Choral Society
    5/27/2022

Downers Grove Choral Society
    6/2/2018
Dr. Mary McLeod Bethune Legacy
    Children's Choir 6/27/2023
Dr. Nachef Concert Choir 5/26/2018
Drake University 6/9/2002
Drury Concert Choir 5/23/1999
Drury Singers 5/23/1999
Dudley High School 4/12/1998
Dudley High School 4/12/1998
Duke University 5/27/2017
Duluth High School 11/26/2000
Durango Choral Society 6/17/2018
Durango Choral Society 6/17/2018
E. D. White Catholic High School
    5/26/2018
East Bay Church of Religious Science
    11/25/2001
East Central College 3/19/2018
East Central University 4/9/2001
Eastern Connecticut State Alumni
    Chorus & Friends 11/13/2011
Eastern Connecticut State University
    Concert Chorale 11/13/2011
Eastern Kentucky University Choirs
    3/24/2002
Eastern Michigan University
    11/24/2006
Eastern Michigan University
    5/23/1999
Eastern New Mexico University
    3/28/2011
East High Varsity Concert Choir
    6/8/1997
East Lake HS/Suncoast Singers
    5/4/1997

East Lake HS/Suncoast Singers 5/28/2001

Edgewood College 3/21/2004

Edinburg North HS 4/28/2001

Edmond Santa Fe High School 3/25/2001

Edmonton Columbian Choirs 5/28/2018

Ed W. Clark High School 3/23/2008

El Camino Real Camerata 4/24/2011

El Dorado Adventist School 4/8/2001

El Dorado Chorale 3/2/2004

Elgin Master Chorale Children's Chorus 6/27/1999

Elmhurst Choral Union/Elmhurst College 4/16/2000

Emmanuel Episcopal Church 5/27/2001

Emmanuel United Methodist Church 11/24/2006

Emmaus High School 5/28/2019

Emporia High School Chorale 5/28/2000

Emporia High School Chorale 5/28/2000

Emporia State University 6/14/1998

Encino Park Elementary - Soaring Eagles 1/18/1999

English Lutheran Church Senior Choir of Wisconsin 5/30/1988

Enterprise High School 3/27/2017

Ephpheta Choir 5/23/1999

Epworth United Methodist Church Choir 5/27/2019

Erie High School 4/1/2018

Eufala First Baptist Church 5/26/1996

Eugene Concert Choir 5/28/2000

Eugene Concert Choir 6/20/2022

Eugene Concert Choir 5/28/2000

Evangel College 5/14/2000

Evangel College 5/14/2000

Evangel College 5/12/1996

Evanston Township High School 4/8/2001

Evansville Children's Choir 5/26/2012

Evansville Philharmonic Chorus 5/28/2011

Everett Chorale 5/29/2023

Everett Chorale 5/29/2023

Everett Chorale 5/28/2018

Evergreen Children's Chorale 5/29/2011

Evergreen Philharmonic Orch 5/28/2011

Evergreen Women's Chorale 5/26/2002

Fairfield High Preparatory 5/13/2023

Faith Lutheran Church 5/21/2001

Faith United Methodist Church 4/16/2002

Falcon Singers 3/15/1998

Fallbrook Union HS Choir 4/8/2001

Fallbrook Union HS Choir 6/22/1997

Falls City High School 5/28/2022

Falls City High School 5/26/2012

Fargo-Moorhead Youth Choir 6/1/2019

Fargo-Moorhead Youth Choir 6/3/2023

Farmingdale High School 4/16/2002

Fayetteville State University 4/9/2023

Festival Chorale Oregon 3/24/2002

Festival Chorus 4/28/2019

Festival Chorus of Westfield 3/25/2001

First Baptist Church 3/31/2019

First Baptist Church of Smyrna 2/18/2018

First Baptist Church of South Carolina Sanctuary Choir 5/30/1988

First Baptist Dothan 5/26/1996

First Congregational Church Crystal Lake 5/28/2018

First Lutheran Church in Fullerton 5/19/2001

First Presbyterian Church 11/20/2001

First Presbyterian Church 4/28/2001

First Presbyterian Church 5/29/2023

First Presbyterian Church 5/31/2019

First Presbyterian Church 5/28/2018

First Presbyterian Church, Bonita Springs 6/23/2023

First Presbyterian Church, Bonita Springs 6/7/2019

First Presbyterian Church 2/18/2001

First Presbyterian Church 2/18/2001

First Presbyterian Church in North Palm Beach 3/19/2018

First Presbyterian Church of Birmingham 4/1/2001

First Presbyterian Church of Honolulu 5/29/2000

First Presbyterian Church of Norfolk 5/26/2023

First Presbyterian Church of Turlock 11/27/2011

First UMC-Boerne 5/27/2001

First Unitarian Society of Madison Choirs 6/5/2021

First United Methodist Church 4/16/2002

First United Methodist Church of Arlington 5/30/2011

First United Methodist Church of Houma 5/26/2018

First United Methodist Church of Pittsburgh 5/26/2018

First United Methodist Church of San Diego 6/2/2002

First United Methodist Church of San Diego 5/9/1999

First United Methodist Church of San Diego 6/1/2018

First United Methodist Church of Webster Groves 6/26/2000

Fisk University 3/19/2022

Flagler Palm Coast High School Choir 3/26/2000

Flint Hills Masterworks Chorale 6/26/2000

Flint Symphony Chorus 5/30/1988

Flint Youth Symphony Orchestra 4/3/2000

Florida College 5/28/2018

Florida Youth Orchestra 4/7/2002

Florida Youth Orchestra 3/23/2008

FMC Missouri City 5/11/2019

Fordham University 4/16/2002

Fordham University 4/15/2001

Fort Collins HS Band 4/4/1988

Fort Lewis College 3/25/2001

Fort Worth First United Methodist Church 6/14/1998

Founder's Church of Religious Science 6/3/2001

Fountain Street Choir 5/30/1988

Francis Joseph Reitz High School
4/23/2000

Franklin, Hickory, And Cranberry
High School Choirs 5/28/2022

Franklin Central High School
11/25/2001

Franklin Elementary School 5/26/2023

Franklin Middle School 11/25/2001

Franklin Middle School 3/31/2002

Franklin Pierce High School
5/14/2000

Frank Phillips College 6/29/1997

Freeman High School Mixed Chorus
6/1/2019

Freeport High School 5/28/2011

Freeport High School Select Chorale
11/30/1997

Freeport High School Select Chorale
4/15/2001

Friends of First Fulshear FMC
5/11/2019

Friends of the Composer - M. Glasgow
6/20/2022

Friends of the Composer - M. Glasgow
6/11/2017

Friends of the Composer - M. Glasgow
6/14/2019

Fuquay Varina Choral Society
7/8/2023

Gadsden City High School Choir
11/23/2012

Gainesville Master Chorale
12/19/2023

Garden State Philharmonic Symphony
Soc. 6/9/2002

Gaylord Symphony Band 6/9/1996

Gay Men's Chorus of South Florida
5/26/2018

George Mason University Chorale And
Friends 5/28/2019

Georgetown Day School 5/27/2022

George Washington High School Band
5/8/1988

Georgia Southern University Chorus
4/1/2001

Germantown Concert Chorus
3/11/2023

Gig Harbor High School 4/6/2017

Girls Preparatory School 3/11/2002

Glenpool High School Warrior Singers
5/27/2019

Goddard-Eisenhower/First
Presbyterian Church 5/29/2018

Goddard - Eisenhower High School
Choirs 5/29/2018

Golden High School 6/6/1999

Goldenwest College 5/30/1999

Good Shepherd Catholic Community
Parish Choir 6/16/2019

Good Shepherd Lutheran Church
Sanctuary Choir 5/30/2022

Goshen College 3/28/1999

Goucher College 3/19/2018

Gould Academy 4/8/2012

Grace Choral Society of Brooklyn
4/16/2002

Grace Lutheran Church 11/30/1997

Grace Lutheran Church 11/30/1997

Grace Presbyterian Church Sanctuary
Choir 5/27/2001

Grace Presbyterian Church Sanctuary Choir 5/27/2019

Grambling State University Concert Choir 4/6/2017

Grambling State University Concert Choir 3/19/2022

Granbury High School 6/17/2001

Grand Canyon University 4/23/2018

Grand View University 5/21/2001

Great Bridge United Methodist Church 4/23/2018

Greater Atlanta Christian School Concert Choir 3/23/2019

Greater Atlanta Christian School Concert Choir 3/23/2019

Greater Newburyport Children's Chorus 6/25/2000

Great Falls College Community Choir 6/1/2018

Great Falls Young Peoples Choir 6/27/1999

Greenfield Community Choir 1/18/2004

Greensburg/Salem High School Choirs 6/18/2023

Greenville High School Chorus (Clark) 6/10/2000

Greenwood Singers 6/6/1999

Grossmont College 11/13/2011

Grossmont College 11/13/2011

Guelph Vocational CI 6/18/2023

Guest Conductor / OKBU And SNU Alumni Choir 4/28/2018

Guilford High School 4/1/2001

Gunma Junior Orchestra 4/3/2000

Guthrie High School 6/3/2001

Gwen Wyatt Chorale 1/18/1999

Gwen Wyatt Chorale 6/3/2001

Gwinnett Choral Guild 3/19/2000

Gwinnett School of MST 5/16/2023

H. B. Beal Secondary School / The London Singers 6/2/2018

Halifax Choral Society 4/24/2011

Hampton - Dumont High School 3/14/2011

Hannibal La Grange College 11/26/2000

Harding Academy Chorus 3/24/2002

Harding Academy Chorus 4/12/1998

Harding Academy Chorus 4/12/1998

Harding Academy Chorus 3/21/2004

Harding Academy Chorus 3/19/2000

Harding Academy Chorus 4/1/2018

Hardin-Simmons University 5/31/2019

HARDIN VALLEY ACADEMY 6/25/2023

Harmonia Choir of Ottawa 5/30/2011

Harmony Magnet Academy Symphony Orchestra 6/18/2017

Harper College 6/2/2002

Harpeth Hall HS 3/19/2022

Harriet Tubman Middle School 5/30/1999

Harrisburg High School 3/21/2004

Harrison High School 4/23/2000

Harrison High School 4/12/1998

Harrison High School 4/12/1998

Hartford Chorale 1/18/1998

Hartnell Community Choir 6/5/2017

Harvard-Westlake High School

4/4/2004

Harvey Browne Memorial Presbyterian Church 5/30/1988

Hastings High School 3/11/2002

Haverford School Celebrantes 4/8/2001

Hayes Barton Baptist Church 6/26/2022

Heard County High School 6/18/2023

Hempfield Area High School 6/18/2023

Henderson High School Choir 6/10/2019

Henderson Presbyterian Church 5/29/2023

Henry Clay High School 1/19/2004

Henry Moss Middle School 6/27/1999

Heritage Choir of Milwaukee 4/12/1998

Heritage Choir of Milwaukee 4/12/1998

Heritage Chorale of Milwaukee 4/12/1998

Heritage Festival Ensemble 4/3/1988

Heritage Signature Chorale 3/19/2018

Highland Community College 6/2/1997

Highland Community College 6/14/1998

Highland High School/Antelope Valley College 5/29/2023

High Point University 3/28/2011

Hightstown High School 6/18/2023

Hill Country Choir 5/11/2019

Hill Country Chorale 3/11/2002

Hillcrest High Ensemble 3/23/2019

Hillsboro Mennonite Brethren Church 2/17/2019

Hilton Head Island High School 4/24/2011

Hinsdale Central High School 5/29/2000

Hinsdale Central High School 5/11/1998

Hinsdale Covenant Church Chancel Choir 6/2/2018

Hochstein Youth Symphony Orchestra 4/14/2002

Hofstra University Concert Choir 1/14/2001

Holland Chorale/First Park Congregational 3/28/2011

Holland Hall High School 11/23/2012

Hollywood Master Chorale 6/16/2019

Holt High School 6/6/1999

Holy Guardian Angels School 11/23/2012

Holy Innocents' Episcopal School 6/4/2022

Holy Trinity Catholic 5/26/2002

Homer High School 4/16/2002

Homestead High School 2/18/2018

Hoover High School 5/28/2012

Hot Springs County High School 4/23/2000

Houston Academy 4/8/2001

Houston Baptist University 5/31/2019

Houston Cecilia Chamber Choir 4/15/2012

Houston Christian High School 3/14/2011

Houston Masterworks Chorus
   6/10/2019
Hudson High School 4/4/1988
Hudson High School/The River City
   Chorale 5/7/2000
Huntington Brass 5/29/1999
Huntington High School 3/19/2022
Huntsville Children's Choir 4/23/2018
Huntsville High School 4/15/2001
Huston-Tillotson University 4/9/2023
Hutchinson Community College
   5/30/1999
Hutchinson Community College
   4/9/2001
Hutchinson Community College
   5/29/1999
Idaho Falls Symphony Chorale
   3/2/2004
Immanuel Baptist 5/26/1996
Impressions Chorale 4/3/2000
Independence Messiah Choir
   11/24/2000
Indianapolis Children's Choir
   5/27/2017
Indiana Purdue University 5/27/2017
Indiana State University 4/4/2004
Indiana State University 4/4/2004
Indiana University of Pennsylvania
   12/1/1996
Indian River Charter High School
   3/31/2019
Indian River Choral Union 3/31/2019
Inner Light Ministries 2/19/2012
Interdenominational Theological
   Center 11/25/2001
Irvine Valley College 5/30/1999

Ishpeming Public Schools Concert
   Choir 5/30/2022
Isidore Newman School 4/23/2023
Island Chamber Singers 6/7/2019
ISO Symphonic Band 3/5/2001
ISO Symphony Orchestra 3/23/1997
Ithaca College Alumni 5/26/2018
Ithaca High School 11/24/2006
J.P. Stevens High School 5/9/1999
J.P. Stevens High School 5/9/1999
Jackson High School Honors Wind
   Ensemble 5/26/2012
Jackson High School Honors Wind
   Ensemble 5/29/2021
Jacksonville Children's Chorus
   6/25/2000
Jasper First United Methodist Church
   6/22/1997
Jefferson Choral Society 4/28/2001
Jenks High School 4/28/2001
Joanna Medawar Nachef Singers
   4/16/2000
Joanna Medawar Nachef Singers
   5/26/2018
John Wesley United Methodist Church
   Chancel Choir 5/27/2001
Jubilate Alumni Group 6/4/2022
Jubilate Warwick Youth Choir
   11/27/2011
Kalamazoo Singers 5/12/2002
Kansas City Kansas Community
   College 6/3/2022
Katy High School Band 6/10/2000
Katy High School Orchestra
   6/10/2000
Kearney High School 2/17/2002

Keene Chorale 3/11/2023
Kenai Peninsula Singers 4/16/2002
Kennett High School 3/21/2004
Kentridge High School 5/14/2000
Kentucky Baptist Convention Choirs
    5/29/1988
Kentucky Christian University Inc
    3/31/1997
Kentucky Wesleyan College/
    Owensboro Sym 5/28/2011
Killian Hill Christian School
    6/17/2018
Kingman High School 4/4/1999
Kingman High School 4/4/1999
King of Glory Choir 5/28/2012
Kingsmen Singers of Christian
    Heritage School 6/10/2019
Kingwood High School 4/28/2001
Kinkaid HS Choir 4/15/2001
Kjelson Singers 3/19/2000
Klein Oak High School 4/28/2001
Knox College Nova Singers 3/25/2001
Kofa High School 6/2/1997
Kutztown University of Pennsylvania
    6/30/2022
L.A. Vocal Core 6/3/2001
L.D. Bell High School Sym Orchestra
    6/18/2017
La Casa de Cristo Lutheran Church
    5/28/2018
Laguna Beach Chorale 5/29/2000
Laguna Beach Chorale 5/28/2012
Laguna Beach Chorale 6/1/2018
Lahser Knightsingers of Michigan
    5/30/1999
La Jolla Symphony & Chorus

5/27/2012
Lake County High School Choir
    4/16/2000
Lakeland Alumni Chorale 5/26/2012
Lakeland Alumni Chorale 5/30/2011
Lakeland Chorale 3/19/2000
Lakeland Chorale 1/13/2008
Lakeland Chorale 3/24/2002
Lakeland Chorale 5/19/2001
Lakeland Chorale 5/30/2011
Lakeland Chorale 6/29/1997
Lakeland Chorale 2/17/2002
Lake Orian Baptist School 6/17/2018
Lake Oswego HS 3/25/2001
Lake Oswego HS 2/18/2008
Lakeridge High School 3/19/2000
Lakeside Presbyterian Church
    6/8/2018
Lake Washington High School
    4/8/2001
Lancaster Mennonite School
    5/27/2023
Lanier Christian Academy 4/23/2018
Lansing Community College
    5/30/1999
LaPorte High School 11/25/2001
Laramie High School 5/1/1999
Larkin High School 11/25/2001
Lathrop High School 3/25/2001
Lathrop High School 3/21/2004
Lathrop High School Advanced Choir
    6/1/2019
Lawton Chiles High School 2/17/2019
Lebanon Community Chorus
    4/16/2000

Ledyard High School 4/1/2001

Lee's Summit High School 4/17/2022

Lee's Summit North High School 5/27/2001

Lee's Summit North High School 5/27/2001

Lee's Summit North High School 5/27/2001

Lee College Chorale/Baytown Community Chorus 5/21/2001

Lee College Singers of Tennessee 5/29/1988

Lee County High School 3/19/2022

Lehigh Valley Chorale 6/18/2023

Lehigh Valley High School For the Performing Arts 5/28/2018

Letourneau Singers 6/10/2022

Letourneau Singers 6/18/2023

Letourneau Singers 6/10/2019

Lewis & Clark Community College 5/30/2011

Lewisville High School 5/4/1997

Lexington Choral Society 1/20/1997

Lexington High School Choir 4/23/2023

Liberty-Eylau High School 4/28/2018

Liberty HS - Alumni 3/31/2019

Liberty Middle School 3/21/2004

Life Road Singers 6/1/2019

Lima Senior High School 5/26/1997

Lima Senior High School 5/26/1997

Limestone College 3/26/2000

Limon Junior/Senior High School 5/13/2023

Lincoln Choral Artists / Nebraska Wesleyan University 5/26/2012

Lincoln Choral Artists / Nebraska Wesleyan University 5/26/2018

Lincoln HS Choir 4/16/2000

Lincoln HS Choir 4/16/2000

Lincoln Southeast High School 2/21/2000

Lincoln Southeast High School 6/2/1997

Lincoln Trail College 2/21/2000

Lincoln University 11/20/2001

Lindsay Thurber Comprehensive High School 2/16/1998

Lindsay Thurber Comprehensive High School 4/9/2001

Lindsey Wilson College 6/2/2002

Lindsey Wilson College 4/23/2018

Livingston Parish Children's Choirs 5/30/2022

Living Word Worship Choir 5/27/2019

Long Beach High School 1/20/1997

Long Beach High School 1/20/1997

Long Island Choral Society 1/18/1998

Long Island Choral Society 6/27/1999

Long Island Masterworks Chorus 1/18/1998

Long Island Youth Orchestra 3/31/2002

Longview Civic Chorus 6/10/2019

Longwood University 5/13/2023

Longwood University 5/26/1996

Lord of Life Lutheran Church 5/26/2002

Lorraine Ann Davis 5/27/2019

Los Altos UMC/Chancel Choir 5/26/2002

Los Angeles Harbor College/Grant
 AME Church 6/27/2023
Los Gatos High School 2/16/1998
Loudon High School 6/2/2002
Louisiana Tech University 1/14/2001
Lourdes Singers 3/19/2000
Lowell High School Symphonic Band
 3/5/2001
Loyola Marymount University - Los
 Angeles 6/29/1997
Loyola Marymount University - Los
 Angeles 6/3/2022
Lubbock Children's Choir 6/27/1999
Mabel Barron Elementary School
 6/1/2019
Madrigals And Minstrels 11/27/2011
Magnolia High School 4/15/2001
Mamaroneck High School Swing Choir
 11/25/2001
Manchester United Methodist Church
 1/18/2000
Manchester United Methodist Church
 11/13/2011
Manchester University 5/28/2001
Manchester University 5/28/2001
Manchester University 5/30/2022
Mannes College/Westchester Choral
 Society 6/2/2002
Mansfield High School 5/23/1999
Maranatha Academy Senior High
 4/1/2018
Marble Collegiate Church 1/14/2001
Maria Carrillo High School/Take Note
 4/1/2002
Mariemont High School Choir
 5/25/2019

Marinette High School Chamber
 Choir 3/26/2000
Marist College 5/28/2011
Marlborough Chamber Choir
 4/17/2022
Marlborough Chamber Choir
 2/17/2019
Maroon Bel Canto Children's Chorus
 2/18/2008
Marquette Senior High School Chorale
 11/26/2000
Marshall School 4/6/2017
Mars Hill Faculty/Staff/Alumni
 Chorus 5/27/2017
Mars Hill University Choral Union
 6/29/1997
Mars Hill University Choral Union
 4/30/1986
Mars Hill University Choral Union
 5/27/2017
Martin Luther King High School
 4/4/2004
Massillon-Washington High School
 Chorus 4/12/1997
Master Chorale of South Florida
 6/16/2019
Mastersingers 5/13/2018
Master Works Adult Chorale
 6/10/2000
Masterworks Chorus of the Palm
 Beaches 5/21/2001
Mattanawcook Academy 1/20/1997
Matthews United Methodist Church
 1/18/2004
McCallie School Men's Glee Club
 3/11/2002

McCallie School Men's Glee Club
3/26/2000
McCallie School Men's Glee Club
3/28/2011
McCallum High School Band 6/2/1996
McCallum High School Band
2/19/2012
McCallum High School Band
6/21/2021
McDaniel College 5/27/2022
McFarlin Memorial United Methodist
Church 1/13/2008
McHenry High School Vocal Warriors
3/27/2017
McKinney High School Choir
4/28/2001
McMurry University 5/9/1999
McNair Academic High School Choir
5/28/2011
McNeil High School 5/14/2000
McPherson College 3/19/2022
Meeker High School 6/5/2017
Memorial Drive Christian Church
4/16/2002
Memphis Choral Arts 5/27/2022
Memphis State University 4/30/1986
Mena High School 11/25/2001
Mendelssohn Choir of Connecticut
4/4/1999
Menomonee Falls 4/15/2001
Meridian Community College
5/30/1999
Mesquite Civic Chorus of Texas
5/30/1988
Messalonskee High School Chamber
Singers 6/17/2001

Messalonskee High School Chamber
Singers 4/8/2012
Metropolitan Chorale 6/6/1999
Metropolitan Detroit Chorale
2/18/2001
Metropolitan Youth Orchestra of NY
6/2/2002
Metropolitan Youth Symphony
Orchestras of Atlanta 4/14/2002
Miami Dade Community College
Choral Department 4/7/2002
Michigan State University 6/7/2019
Michigan State University Children's
Choirs 4/6/2017
Mid-Columbia Mastersingers
5/26/2023
Midwest Center For Creative Arts
6/18/2023
Milton High School 6/6/1999
Milwaukee Childrens Choir 1/18/1999
Milwaukee Choristers 3/21/2004
Ministry of Youth Sports and Cultural
Affairs 5/27/2022
Ministry of Youth Sports and Cultural
Affairs 5/27/2022
Mission Valley Chorus 6/10/2019
Mississippi College 1/13/2008
Mississippi College Singers 2/17/2002
Mississippi Girlchoir 1/13/2008
Mississippi School of the Arts Chorale
1/13/2008
Mississippi State University Chorale
4/8/2012
Mississippi State University Chorale
3/19/2022

Mississippi State University Chorale
4/8/2012
Mississippi State University Chorale
4/21/2019
Mississippi University For Women
4/12/1997
Mississippi University For Women
4/12/1997
Missouri Baptist University 6/25/2023
Missouri Southern Concert Chorale
6/10/2019
Missouri State University 6/25/2023
Mitchell High School 2/18/2008
Moanalua High School 3/22/1998
Moberly High School 11/26/2000
Modesto Junior College 1/19/2004
Mohr South Haven High School
4/24/2011
Moline HS Choir & Trinity
Episcopalian Choir 3/23/2011
Monadnock Chorus / Keene State
College 4/26/1998
Monmouth Civic Chorus 3/24/2002
Monroe Symphony Chorus 6/5/2017
Montclair Kimberley Academy
5/26/1996
Montclair State University 4/15/2012
Montclair State University 6/25/2000
Montclair State University 6/17/2001
Monterey Peninsula Voices 4/17/2022
Montgomery Bell Academy 3/19/2022
Montgomery County Youth Orchestra
6/2/2002
Montgomery High School 4/1/2002
Montrose High school 2/18/2008
Moore High School 4/28/2018

Moorhead High School 3/26/2000
Moreau Catholic High School
4/23/2023
Morehead State University 4/30/1986
Morehouse College Glee Club
6/3/2022
Morris Hills High School 5/9/1999
Morris Hills High School 5/4/1997
Morris Hills High School 4/15/2001
Morris Knolls High School 5/28/2019
Mosinee HS Concert Choir /Wausau
Lyric Choir 3/27/2017
Mosinee HS Concert Choir /Wausau
Lyric Choir 3/23/2019
Most Precious Blood Catholic Church
5/28/2000
Most Precious Blood Catholic Church
5/28/2000
Mother AME Zion Church 4/16/2002
Mountain Empire Children's Choral
Academy 6/11/2017
Mountain View High School
6/18/2023
Mount Carmel Academy Chorale
2/17/2002
Mount St. Mary Academy Women's
Chorus 1/18/1999
Mount Vernon Academy Choir
4/23/2000
Mulberry Street U. Meth. Choir
6/4/2022
Music Makers Ensemble 5/28/2001
Music Moves Kids 5/28/2018
Muskegon Chamber Choir 5/30/1988
Mustard Seed School 4/8/2001

N. Stuart Baptist Church 6/1/2018
Naches Valley High School 5/14/2000
Napa Christian Academy 5/28/2011
Naperville Men's Glee Club 5/27/2022
Nashville Children's Choir 3/26/2000
Nathan Hale Concert Choir 5/30/2011
Nathan Hale High School 2/21/2000
National Collegiate Wind Ensemble
    5/27/2000
National Collegiate Wind Ensemble
    5/25/2002
National Collegiate Wind Ensemble
    5/26/2001
National Festival Orchestra 1/18/2004
National Festival Orchestra 1/20/2002
National Festival Orchestra 1/18/2004
National Festival Orchestra 1/18/1999
NATIONAL YOUTH ORCHESTRA
    1/19/1997
Naval Air Training Command Choir
    Alumni 12/19/2023
Near North Voices 3/19/2018
Nettleton High School 3/19/2000
New Braunfels High School 6/10/2000
New Covenant United Methodist
    Church 5/31/2019
New Dominion Choraliers 5/13/2023
New Hope Community Church
    12/1/1996
New Jersey Children's Choir 2/18/2001
New Jersey Children's Choir 1/18/1999
New Mexico Junior College 3/25/2001
New Orange County Children's Choir
    6/30/2022
New Orleans Children's Chorus/youth
    chr 5/27/2017
New Orleans Children's Chorus/youth
    chr 5/31/2019
New Orleans Children's Chorus/youth
    chr 5/30/2022
New Orleans Youth Chorale 4/8/2001
Newton High School 1/13/2008
New Trier High School 4/1/2018
New World Singers of Columbus
    Children's Choir 6/27/2023
New York Festival Singers 1/14/2001
New York University 4/8/2001
Nimitz High School 4/28/2001
Nixa High School Concert Choir
    6/9/2002
Noel Choir 5/28/2022
Nolan Wind Symphony 3/31/1997
Normal West High School 6/26/2000
North American Children's Chorale
    6/27/1999
North American Children's Chorale
    6/28/1998
North American Children's Chorale
    6/29/1997
North Carolina Central University
    4/9/2023
North Central Texas College
    5/26/1996
North Central University 5/19/2001
North Coast Singers 5/27/2012
Northeast Alabama Community
    College 5/30/1999
Northeast Alabama Community
    College 5/28/2001
Northeast Arkansas Community Choir
    1/13/2008

Northeastern State University Chorus
6/28/2021
Northern Kentucky University
6/4/2022
Northern Voices 3/21/2004
Northfield Nighthawk Choir 6/1/2019
North Florida Women's Chorale
5/30/2022
North Forsyth High School Choir
11/23/2012
North Hollywood High School
6/3/2001
North Kitsap High School 4/3/2000
North Shore Choral Society 5/28/2000
North Shore Choral Society 5/28/2000
Northside Christian School 6/17/2018
North United Methodist 5/26/2018
Northwestern Michigan College
6/25/2023
Northwestern State University
4/8/2001
Northwestern State University
3/23/1997
Northwestern University 5/28/2000
Northwestern University 5/28/2000
Northwest Presbyterian Church
6/30/2022
Nova Borealis 5/19/2018
Nutley High School Concert Choir
4/4/2004
Nutley High School Concert Choir
4/4/2004
Nutley High School Concert Choir
11/25/2001
Nutley High School Concert Choir
3/31/2002

Nyack College 3/14/2011
Nyack College 6/11/2000
Nyack College 11/20/2001
O'Fallon First United Methodist
Church 4/16/2002
Oak Knoll School of the Holy Child
5/26/2023
Oakland City University 5/12/2002
Oak Park High School Chamber Choir
2/16/1998
Oak Park High School Chamber Choir
3/27/2017
Oak Park High School Chamber Choir
3/31/2019
Oakridge Secondary School 5/19/2018
Oakridge Secondary School Concert
Choir 5/19/2018
Ohio State University 5/30/1988
Okarche Community Chorale
4/28/2001
Okemos High School 2/18/2001
Ola High School 6/20/2022
Ola High School 6/20/2022
Olathe North High School 1/18/2004
Old Dominion University 3/24/2002
Old Dominion University 3/27/2017
Old Lyme High School 6/6/1999
Olivet College 4/28/2001
Olympia Choral Society/Timberline
High School 5/30/1999
Omaha Cantata Choir/Soli Deo Gloria
Cant 6/26/2000
Omaha Symphonic Chorus 6/21/2019
ORANGE COUNTY FRIENDS OF
MUSIC 5/27/2017

Orange County School of the Arts 5/26/1996

Orange High School 5/27/2017

Orange Lutheran High School 4/15/2012

Oregon Repertory Singers Youth Choirs 5/26/2012

Original Scorpion Hollering Band 4/16/2000

Orlando Deanery Boychoir And Girls Choir 5/27/2001

Ottawa Kansas Chamber Choir 6/16/2019

Our Lady of Lourdes Academy Singers 3/21/2004

Our Lady of Prompt Succor Choir 5/29/2000

Owensboro Symphony Chorus 5/28/2011

Ozarks Select Choir 3/19/2000

Pacific Grove High School Breaker Choir 4/17/2022

Paducah-Tilghman High School 4/4/2004

Palisade High School 5/19/2018

Palmer Trinity School Wind Ensemble 4/8/2001

Palmetto Voices/Salem College 6/25/2022

Palmetto Voices/Salem College 6/23/2023

Palmetto Voices/Salem College 6/11/2017

Palm Middle/High School Choirs 4/3/2000

Palm Springs High School 4/6/2017

Park Hill United Methodist Church 5/29/1988

Parkway Middle School 6/27/1999

Pasadena Master Chorale 3/11/2002

Paschal High School 11/25/2001

Payson Civic Chorale 5/28/2019

Peachtree Baptist Church 1/18/1999

Peachtree Road United Methodist Church 5/30/1988

Pellissippi State Variations Choir 5/30/2022

Penfield High School Orchestra 5/25/1996

Peninsula High School 4/6/2017

Peninsula Musical Arts Association 6/23/2023

Penn High School 11/25/2001

Pennsylvania Youth Chorale 1/18/1999

Penn Yan Community Chorus 11/27/2011

Penn Yan Community Chorus 3/19/2012

Pfeiffer University 5/26/1996

Pfeiffer University 5/30/1988

Philharmonic Choir of the Newfoundland Symphony Orchestra 5/25/2019

Phoenix College Chamber Singers 3/5/2001

Pineville High School Band 3/23/1997

Piscataway High School 3/21/2004

Pius XI High School 11/26/2000

Plainfield High School 5/12/2002

Pleasantville High School 5/26/1996

Plymouth-Canton Educational Park 11/24/2006

Plymouth-Canton Educational Park 5/23/1999

Plymouth Church 6/17/2001

Plymouth Church Boys and Girls Choir 4/28/2001

Point Loma Nazarene University 5/27/2023

Pompton Lakes High School 5/26/2023

Pompton Lakes High School 6/1/2019

Pontiac Central High School 6/6/1999

Port Angeles High School Symphony Orchestra 4/1/2001

Port Angeles High School Symphony Orchestra 4/6/2017

Portland Chorale 12/1/1996

Portland Christian High School 3/2/2004

Portland Christian High School 6/17/2001

Portland Phoenix Chamber Choir 6/5/2022

Portland Symphonic Choir 6/17/2001

Portsmouth Choral Union 5/29/2000

Poteau High School Choir 5/26/1996

Poteau High School Choir 5/28/2000

Poteau High School Choir 5/28/2000

Poteau High School Choir 5/28/2012

Poteau High School Choir 5/30/2022

Prairie du Chien High School 4/9/2001

Prairie High School 4/8/2001

Presbyterian Church of Montclair 5/27/2001

Presentation High School 4/1/2002

Proclamation Chorale 6/5/2021

Project JOY Senior Serenaders 4/3/2000

Providence School of Jacksonville 5/29/2023

Pueblo South High School 3/19/2012

Purdy Concert Choir 6/10/2019

Pusch Ridge Christian Academy Advanced Ensemble 4/28/2019

Putnam City Schools 1/13/2008

Pyeongtaek City Women's Choir 6/1/2019

Queensborough Community College 1/18/1998

Queens University Chamber Singers 6/5/2022

Que the Music Academy 6/25/2023

Quitman High School 3/30/1997

Raceland Worthington High School 3/28/2011

Raleigh Boychoir 12/1/1996

Ramsay IB High School 5/13/2023

Randolph College 4/8/2012

Randolph High School 3/27/2017

Randy Pagel Choristers 3/31/2002

Raytown High School 11/26/2000

Redlands High School 5/26/1997

Redmond High School Studio Jazz Orchestra 4/21/2019

Red River Children's Choir/South Highland 4/16/2000

Reedley College 4/17/2022

Renaissance Singers/Meistersingers/ College of Bahamas 11/27/2011

Renton High School 11/26/2000

Renton High School 5/14/2000

Republic High School 5/26/1996
Reuter Center Singers 4/15/2012
Rhodes Singers 5/29/2017
Rhodes Singers 7/11/2018
Ribault High School 4/12/1998
Ribault High School 4/12/1998
Ribault High School 4/12/1998
Richland Two District Orchestra
    6/15/1997
Richland Two District Orchestra
    6/3/2001
Richmond Symphony Orchestra
    Chorus 6/7/2019
Rick Charles Choral Ensemble
    4/12/1998
Ridge Choral Society 6/29/1997
Ridgefield High School 5/28/2011
Ridge High School A Cappella Choir
    1/13/2008
Ridgevue High School 5/30/2022
Ridgewood Symphony Orchestra
    11/22/1998
Rincon University High School
    Concert Choir 4/8/2012
Rincon University High School
    Concert Choir 7/11/2018
Rio Hondo College 6/3/2001
Ritenour High School Concert Choir
    6/9/2002
River City Chorale 5/26/2018
River City Singers 5/29/2017
River City Singers 5/27/2019
Riverside Choral Society 6/10/2001
Rivertree Singers & Bob Jones
    University 6/25/2023

Roane State Comm. College 2/17/2002
Roane State Comm. College 3/26/2000
Roane State Community College
    3/2/2004
Robert Edgerton Alumni Singers
    6/25/2022
Robinson High School 6/26/2022
Rocketaires Chamber Singers
    6/6/1999
Rock Valley Community College
    12/30/1999
Rocky Hill High School Concert Choir
    11/26/2000
Rocky Mountain Chamber Singers
    3/5/2001
Rocky Mountain High School
    3/28/1988
Rogue Valley Chorale 3/26/2000
Rogue Valley Chorale 3/26/2000
Rolla High School Choir 4/12/1997
Rolling Hills Covenant Church
    6/14/1998
Rose State College 5/28/2018
Rossview Middle/High School Choirs
    6/25/2023
Rowan University / Greater South
    Jersey Chorus 11/25/2001
Rowan University / Greater South
    Jersey Chorus 4/8/2001
Rowan University / Greater South
    Jersey Chorus 5/7/2000
Roxbury Latin School 3/19/2000
Russian Chamber Chorus 6/11/2000
Rutgers Prep 11/26/2000
Sacramento City College Alums
    5/27/2012

Sacred Heart Church 6/9/2002
Sage Sound Singers 6/27/2023
Saint Agnes Academy and Strake Jesuit
    11/26/2000
Saint Dominic Academy 4/8/2001
Saint Dominic Academy 3/21/2004
Saint Dominic Academy 5/26/2012
Saint Dominic Academy 5/26/2023
Saint Francis Cabrini Choir of
    Littletown 6/29/1997
Saint George Greek Orthodox Church
    6/8/2018
Saint John's Evangelical Lutheran
    Church 6/6/1999
Saint Louis Symphony Chorus
    1/20/1998
Saint Luke's Presbyterian Church
    Choir 6/16/2019
Saint Mary's College 11/25/2001
Saint Paul's Singers 1/20/1997
Salem College Choirs 6/11/2017
Salem College Choirs 7/11/2018
Salpointe Catholic High School Choir
    4/28/2019
Samford University 5/28/2011
Samford University 5/28/2011
San Angelo Symphony Chorale
    6/29/1997
San Angelo Symphony Chorale
    5/29/1988
Sanctuary Choir of Flower Mound
    UMC And Friends 5/27/2019
Sandhills Community College Choir
    5/28/2022
San Diego Festival Chorus 6/3/2023
San Francisco Boys Choir 3/22/1998

San Jacinto College Choir 5/28/2011
San Joaquin Delta College Choir
    6/1/2019
San Jose State University 2/21/2000
San Jose Symphonic Choir 6/26/2000
San Jose Symphonic Choir 6/14/1998
San Marcos High School 3/11/2002
San Marin High School 4/9/2001
San Marin High School 2/16/1998
San Marin High School 4/9/2001
Santa Clarita Master Chorale
    5/16/2023
Santa Clarita Master Chorale
    5/26/2018
Santa Fe High School 6/3/2023
Santa Fe Symphony Chorus 6/18/2017
Santaluces High School 4/24/2011
Santa Maria de La Paz Choir
    6/18/2017
Santa Monica High School 3/31/2002
Santa Paula High School 6/25/2022
Santa Rosa Junior College 4/17/2022
Santo Niño Regional Catholic School
    Children's Choir 6/18/2017
Sao Paolo Ensemble 6/1/2018
Sarah Lawrence College, Yonkers
    5/7/2000
Sarasota High School 6/2/2018
Saugus High School 3/24/2002
Savannah Arts Academy 5/27/2012
Savannah Arts Academy 5/28/2012
Scarsdale High School 5/12/2002
Schola Cantorum of Arlington
    4/12/1997
Schola Cantorum of New Orleans
    2/17/2002

Schola Cantorum of Silicon Valley
    4/23/2023
Science Hill High School 4/12/1997
Scottsboro First Baptist Church
    5/26/1996
Scottsdale 3/19/2018
Second Presbyterian Church Sanctuary
    Choir 7/11/2018
Sedgwick Middle School 6/27/1999
Sedona Academy of Chamber Singers
    6/27/2023
Selinsgrove Area High School Honors
    Choir 4/8/2012
Selma First Baptist Church 5/26/1996
Seton Hill University 6/18/2023
Severn School 3/11/2023
Seycove Secondary 2/20/2011
Seymour High School 11/26/2000
Seymour High School 6/2/2002
Shattuck-St. Mary's School 5/13/2018
Shattuck- St Mary's School 6/2/1997
Shawnee High School 5/27/2019
Shawnee Mission East High School
    6/14/1998
Shawnee Mission East High School
    6/14/1998
Shenandoah Valley Children's Choir
    5/26/2012
Shenango Valley Chorale 5/28/2022
Shepaug Valley High School 6/3/2001
Shepherd of the Valley Lutheran
    Church 5/19/2001
Sheridan High School 5/12/2002
Sheridan High School 5/9/1999
Sheridan High School 5/4/1997
Sheridan High School 5/9/1999

Sheridan High School 4/15/2012
Shiloh Baptist Church 4/16/2002
Shoreline Commmunity College
    3/25/2001
Shorewood High School 6/17/2001
Shorewood High School 4/24/2011
Shorewood High School 4/23/2018
Shorewood High School Orch
    2/18/2018
Shorewood High School Orch
    4/9/2023
Shreveport Chorale 3/19/2022
Sierra Nevada Chorale 6/9/1996
Silver Sands Middle School 5/27/2001
Sine Nomine 6/1/2019
Sine Nomine Choral Society of Central
    Oklahoma 5/29/2017
Singers From Pacific Univ&Pacific
    Youth Choirs 6/2/2018
Singers From Pacific University &
    Pacific Youth Choirs 6/2/2018
Singers Marin 5/9/1999
Singers Marin 5/9/1999
Singers Marin/Wings of Song
    11/27/2011
Singers Marin/Wings of Song
    4/28/2018
Sioux Center High School 4/23/2000
Sioux City East High School
    6/10/2000
Skagit Valley College Chorale
    6/21/2019
Skagit Valley College Chorale
    5/30/2011
Smithtown Gospel Tabernacle
    5/19/2001

Snider High School Choir 1/18/2004

Snowflake High School 4/16/2000

Somers High School 5/21/2001

Sonoma State - Alumni 4/17/2022

Sonoma State University 4/17/2022

Sotoku High School Boys Choir
3/29/1998

Soulsville Charter School Chorale
2/18/2018

Sound Company 6/11/2017

South Brunswick High School
5/26/2012

South Brunswick High School
6/16/2019

Southeastern Chorale 5/29/2000

Southern California Master Chorale
5/30/2011

Southern Kentucky Choral Society
6/10/2019

Southern Nazarene University Chorale
1/13/2008

Southern Symphonic Chorus
6/10/2019

Southern Utah University 1/19/2004

Southfield Lathrup High School
5/26/1996

South Hadley Chorale 5/9/1999

South Hadley Chorale 5/9/1999

South Jones High School Choir
3/25/2001

South Laurel High Madrigal Singers
3/24/2002

South Pointe Middle School Band
5/23/1999

South Pointe Middle School Band
5/25/2002

South Suburban Christian Church
5/28/2012

Southwest Civic Chorus 5/29/2000

Southwestern College 3/19/2000

Southwestern College 2/20/2011

Southwestern College 6/1/2018

Southwestern Illinois College
5/29/2000

Southwest Miami Community Chorale
5/26/1997

Southwest Miami Silent Singers
5/26/1997

Southwest Mississippi Community
College 6/2/2002

Southwest Mississippi Community
College 5/28/2012

Southwest Texas University 5/14/2000

Southwood Lutheran Church
5/26/2002

Sparta High School 5/28/2011

Sparta High School 5/26/1997

Sparta High School 6/6/1999

Sparta High School 4/1/2002

Sparta High School 5/26/1996

Sparta High School Select Choir
5/19/2001

Sparta High School Select Choir
5/4/1997

Sparta High School Select Choir
1/13/2008

Sparta High School Select Choir
5/26/2012

Sparta High School Select Choir
5/12/2002

Spartanburg High School 3/26/2000

Special Delivery Vocal Ensemble
6/2/1997
Spence School 4/8/2001
Spokane Falls Community College
5/12/2002
Spokane Falls Community College
5/29/2000
Spokane Falls Community College
4/15/2012
Spokane Symphony Chorale 4/3/2000
Springfield Mid-America Singers
6/6/1999
Spring Hill High School 6/2/2002
Spring Valley High School 4/23/2018
St. Andrew's Episcopal Church
5/30/2022
St. Andrew's Episcopal School
1/18/2004
St. Andrew's Episcopal School
4/8/2012
St. Andrew's Episcopal School
3/27/2017
St. Andrew's Episcopal School
3/23/2019
St. Andrew's Presbyterian Church
5/30/2011
St. Andrews Episcopal School
1/13/2008
St. Andrew U.M.C. Charles Wesley Ch
4/3/2000
St. Charles High School Choir
4/12/1998
St. Charles High School Choir
4/12/1998
St. Charles High School Choir
3/24/2002

St. James United Methodist Church
5/28/2001
St. John Church - Grand Prairie
6/27/2023
St. Laurence Chamber Singers
5/29/2011
St. Laurence Chamber Singers
6/17/2018
St. Louis Community Chorus
1/20/1998
St. Louis Community Gospel Choir
6/25/2023
St. Margaret's Episcopal Church
5/30/1999
St. Mark's Evangelical Lutheran
Church 5/29/2000
St. Mark's Lutheran Church Choir
4/3/2000
St. Martin's Evangelical Lutheran
Church 11/30/1997
St. Mary's High School 5/26/1996
St. Mary's High School 4/9/2001
St. Mary's Inter Sch 4/1/2001
St. Mary's Inter Sch 3/26/2000
St. Mary's Inter Sch 3/26/2000
St. Michael's Episcopal Church
5/30/1999
St. Michael And All Angels Episcopal
Church 6/2/2018
St. Michael High School 6/3/2023
St. Norbert College 12/1/1996
St. Norbert College 3/19/2012
St. Norbert College Choirs 12/1/1996
St. Norbert College Choirs 3/19/2012
St. Norbert College Choirs 5/27/2019
St. Olaf Catholic Church 5/19/2001

St. Paul's United Methodist 5/9/1999
St. Paul Academy Chorale 2/18/2017
St. Paul Academy Community Chorale
    2/18/2017
St. Paul United Church of Christ
    11/13/2011
St. Philip's College 2/21/2000
St. Philip the Deacon Sanctuary Choir
    5/28/2018
St. Robert Catholic Church 5/30/1999
St. Stephen's Episcopal Church
    6/17/2001
St. Stephen's Episcopal School
    11/26/2000
St. Timothy's Episcopal Church
    11/23/2012
St. Ursula Academy 6/6/1999
Stambaugh Chorus 5/28/2022
Starkville High School Choir
    4/21/2019
State Fair Community College
    5/28/2011
State University of New York At
    Oswego 6/1/2018
Steilacoom High School 4/6/2017
Stephen F. Austin High School
    4/28/2001
St Michael's Episcopal Cathedral
    11/20/2001
St Paul's Episcopal Church 2/18/2001
St Paul's Episcopal Church 2/18/2001
Sullivan County Community Chorus
    5/28/2019
Summit Choral Society 6/1/2019
Summit Christian Academy Concert
    Chorale 4/1/2018

Summit County Community Choir
    6/6/1999
Sumter Civic Chorale & Morris
    College Chorale 6/25/2022
Sumter High School 6/29/1997
Sumter High School 4/4/2004
Sumter High School 6/29/1997
Sumter High School 4/4/2004
Sumter High School 6/29/1997
Sunset Symphony Youth Orchestra
    4/3/1988
Sun Valley Chapel Singers 5/31/2021
SUNY At Buffalo 6/10/2001
SUNY - at New Paltz 5/26/2002
Sweetwater High School 5/9/1999
Sylvan Hills High School 4/1/2018
Sylvania United Church of Christ
    5/28/2012
Synchroni Ekfrasi 7/7/2022
Tacoma Civic Chorus/Puget Sound
    5/28/2000
Tacoma Youth Symphony 5/7/2000
Takoma Camerata/Siglo church
    12/1/1996
Tallahassee First Baptist Church
    5/26/1997
Tallwood High School 4/23/2018
Tates Creek High School 1/19/2004
Tecumseh High School 4/23/2000
Tennessee Technological University
    5/13/2018
Tennessee Wind Symphony 6/18/2017
Texarkana Regional Chorale
    3/19/2022
Texarkana Regional Chorale
    4/28/2018

Texas A & M Commerce 4/26/1998
Texas A&M University 4/12/1998
Texas A&M University 4/26/1998
The Amy Murphy Studio 5/28/2011
The Amy Murphy Studio 6/1/2018
The Appalachian Children's Chorus
5/26/2002
The Appalachian Children's Chorus
5/25/2002
The Arcadian Chorale 2/17/2002
The Arcadian Chorale 6/10/2001
The Arcadian Chorale 6/18/2023
The Archdiocesan Choir of Galveston-
Houston 5/29/2011
The Archdiocesan Choir of Galveston-
Houston 5/29/2011
The Australian Waratah Girls Choir
And Alumni Chorus 4/9/2023
The Brearley School 4/8/2001
The Choirs of Indiana University
South Bend 4/28/2019
The Choral Society of West Georgia
5/30/2022
The Choristers of All Saints 2/18/2017
The Concordia Chorales 5/27/2019
The David Thye Singers 5/11/2019
The Detroit School of Arts Orchestra
5/27/2000
The Dunham School 2/17/2002
The Elm City Girls' Choir and The
United Girls' Choir 6/27/2023
The Elm City Girls' Choir and The
United Girls' Choir 5/30/2022
The Entertainers At Enterprise-Ozark
Community College 3/27/2017
The Festival Singers 6/2/2002

The Gay Men's Chorus of Tampa Bay
5/26/2002
The Gold Orchestra 5/26/2001
The Gregory School 4/28/2019
The Harmony Chorus 6/28/2021
The Harmony Singers of Pittsburgh
11/13/2011
The HBU Choral Union 11/25/2001
The Houston Choral Society
6/17/2018
The Independent School 4/4/1988
The Liberty Choirs 3/31/2019
The Lovett School 11/24/2006
The Maria A. Ellis Festival Ensemble
6/25/2023
The Master's University Alumni Choir
And University Singers 5/13/2018
The Master's University Chorale &
University Singers 5/13/2018
The Master Chorale of Tampa Bay
6/16/2019
The Multnomah Athletic Club
Balladeers 6/2/2018
The Oakridge School 4/15/2012
The Oakridge School 4/12/1997
The Oakridge School 4/28/2001
The Oasis United Church of Christ
Choir 5/30/2022
Theodore High School 3/26/2000
Theodore Roosevelt High School
6/3/2022
The Peninsula Singers 4/1/2001
The Princeton Festival 1/19/2004
The Ridgewood Singers 6/9/2002
The Seven Hills School Choir
5/25/2019

The Sheldon City of Music All-Star
    Chorus 6/25/2023
The Sound of the Northwest 2/19/2012
The Southern Union Sound 5/28/2001
The Southern Union Sound 5/26/1997
The Southern Union Sound 5/26/1997
The Southern Union Sound 5/30/1999
The Southern Union Sound 5/29/2023
The Southern Union Sound 5/30/2011
The Southern Union Sound 5/29/2017
The Southern Union Sound 5/27/2019
The Stockton Chorale 5/29/1988
The Stockton Chorale 6/1/2019
The Taghkanic Chorale 1/18/1998
The Tahoe Choir 5/23/1999
The Tahoe Choir 5/28/2012
The Towne Singers 1/18/2004
The Trey Clegg Singers, Inc. 6/3/2022
The University of Alabama 6/4/2022
The Village Voices/Westlake United
    Metho 6/17/2001
The West Shore Chorale 6/14/1998
The Women's Chorus of Dallas
    5/26/2002
The Women's Chorus of Dallas
    5/25/2019
The Women's Chorus of Dallas Alumni
    Singers 5/25/2019
Thomas Doherty High School
    6/5/2017
Thomas Jefferson High School
    For Science And Technology
    5/26/2002
Thompson Valley High School
    2/17/2002

Thrasher Memorial United Methodist
    Church Choir 4/23/2018
Thrasher Memorial United Methodist
    Church Choir 6/30/2022
Three Rivers Singers 6/4/2022
Thurman White Middle School
    6/26/2000
Thurman White Middle School
    3/31/2002
Tiffin University 6/3/2022
Tillamook Community Chorus
    4/1/2018
Toccoa Falls College Choir 5/31/2021
Toppenish High School 6/3/2023
Toronto Youth Wind Orchestra
    5/30/2011
Torrance West High School 6/3/2001
Transylvania Choral Society 4/23/2018
Treasure Valley Community College
    5/30/1988
Tremper High School Choir 5/26/1997
Tremper High School Choir 5/26/1997
Tri-Cities Christian School 6/11/2017
Trinity Baptist Church 12/1/1996
Trinity Lutheran Church 6/6/1999
Trinity Lutheran Church 5/26/2002
Trinity United Meth. Church Choir
    4/1/2001
Trinity United Methodist Church
    3/26/2000
Trinity Valley School 4/24/2011
Trinity Valley School 5/30/2022
Trinity Western University 5/27/2023
Tri-State Millenium Honors Orchestra
    12/30/1999
Troy University 5/29/2000

Truman High School 5/29/2017
Trumbull High School 6/2/2002
Trumbull High School 11/24/2006
Trumbull High School 6/26/2000
Tulsa Children's Chorus 11/23/2012
Tulsa Chorale 11/23/2012
Tulsa Memorial High School 6/2/2002
Turtle Creek Chorale 5/26/2002
UCLA Campus Choir 5/26/1996
UMass Dartmouth 6/5/2017
United High School 3/11/2002
United High School 5/14/2000
United Voices of Detroit 2/19/2012
Unity Harmony Rock Choir 2/19/2012
Université du Québec en Outaouais
  5/24/1997
University Glee Club 6/17/2001
University High School 3/19/2000
University High School 6/18/2023
University High Singers 2/17/2002
University of Arizona Symphonic
  Choir And Arizona Choir
  4/28/2019
University of Arizona Symphonic
  Choir And Arizona Choir
  5/30/2022
University of Arkansas 4/9/2000
University of Arkansas/Monticello
  3/26/2000
University of Arkansas at Little Rock
  6/26/2022
University of Arkansas Ft. Smith
  2/21/2000
University of California, Davis
  6/3/2001

University of California, San Diego
  11/13/2011
University of California - Santa Cruz
  5/26/2001
University of Central Arkansas Band
  4/23/2018
University of Central Florida
  5/28/2011
University of Chicago 4/3/2000
University of Cincinnati-Knox
  Presbyterian Church 6/8/2018
University of Colorado-Boulder
  3/5/2001
University of Colorado-Boulder
  4/1/2018
University of Connecticut 6/22/1997
University of Denver 2/17/2002
University of Evansville 4/23/2000
University of Evansville 5/28/2011
University of Florida 12/19/2023
University of Hartford 6/14/1998
University of Houston / Memorial
  Drive Presbyterian Church
  5/29/2011
University of Illinois- Chicago
  5/28/2000
University of Illinois- Chicago
  2/18/2008
University of Illinois- Chicago
  5/28/2000
University of Kansas University Singers
  6/26/2000
University of Louisiana Monroe And
  Community Singers 6/5/2017
University of Louisiana Monroe And
  Community Singers 7/11/2018

University of Maine 6/2/2002
University of Maine 6/5/2017
University of Minnesota-Duluth
    5/7/2000
University of Minnesota-Duluth
    5/30/1988
University of Minnesota-Duluth
    5/7/2000
University of Mississippi 4/27/1997
University of Missouri, Columbia
    6/14/2019
University of Missouri St. Louis
    4/16/2002
University of Nebraska - Kearney
    3/30/1997
University of Nebraska-Lincoln
    1/14/2001
University of Nebraska-Lincoln
    6/2/1997
University of Nebraska Omaha
    5/28/2011
University of Nevada, Reno And Faith
    Lutheran Church 7/10/2019
University of North Alabama
    2/17/2002
University of North Carolina, Asheville
    4/15/2012
University of Northern Colorado
    5/13/2023
University of Pittsburgh at Johnstown
    6/3/2023
University of Rochester 6/2/1996
University of South Carolina
    3/26/2000
University of Southern Indiana
    5/28/2011

University of South Florida / Timber
    Tones Community Chorus
    5/29/1988
University of Tennessee, Chattanooga
    4/30/1986
University of Tennessee - Southern
    6/18/2023
University of Texas at Arlington
    4/12/1997
University of Texas of the Permian
    Basin 5/19/2018
University of the Incarnate Word
    11/26/2000
University of the Ozarks 1/18/2004
University of the Ozarks 5/29/2017
University of Washington 5/14/2000
University of Washington 5/28/2022
University of Washington 3/31/2019
University of Western Australia Choral
    Society 5/30/2011
University of Wisconsin Milwaukee
    6/16/1996
University of Wisconsin Milwaukee
    6/16/1996
University of Wisconsin-Milwaukee
    5/23/1999
University of Wisconsin Parkside
    4/12/1998
University of Wisconsin Parkside
    4/12/1998
University of Wisconsin-Parkside
    4/12/1998
University of Wisconsin- Parkside
    Master Singers 3/21/2004
University of Wisconsin- Parkside
    Master Singers 4/12/1998

University Park United Methodist Church, Dallas 5/27/2019
University School of Jackson 2/18/2017
Upland High School 4/7/1996
Upper Columbia Academy Choraliers 6/16/2019
Urbana High School 4/16/2002
Usc Thornton School of Music 6/3/2023
Utah Valley Youth Symphony 4/24/1988
Uzee Brown Society of Choraliers 6/3/2022
Valdosta State University 3/19/2022
Valdosta State University 3/19/2022
Valencia High School 3/24/2002
Valhalla High School 3/19/2000
Valhalla High School 3/19/2000
Valley Christian High School Chorale 5/29/2017
Valley High School 5/21/2001
Valley View High School 1/13/2008
Vallivue High School 5/14/2000
Valparaiso University Chorus 5/27/2001
Vancouver Bach Choir 5/25/2019
Vancouver High School 2/16/1998
Vanguard University 5/21/2001
Vashon Island Chorale 5/28/2022
Vassar College 5/30/2011
Venice High School Chorus 6/17/2001
Venice High School Chorus 5/28/2011
Ventura High School Concert Choir 6/25/2022
Vermilion High School 4/23/2000

Vermilion High School 5/12/2002
Vero Beach Choral Society 4/28/2001
Versailles High School 6/9/2002
Vesper Chorale 5/11/2019
Vienna Choral Society 6/23/2023
Virginia Wesleyan University 4/23/2018
Virginia Wesleyan University 3/11/2023
Visual and Performing Arts Academy at Salem High School 3/11/2023
Viva La Musica 6/23/2023
Viva La Musica 6/16/2019
Viva La Musica 6/23/2023
Vocali 4/24/2011
Vocapella and Vox Polish 2/16/1998
VOICES Chorale 4/4/1999
Voices Chorale/Ctr for Music & Young Chi 4/8/2001
Voices Chorale/Ctr for Music & Young Chi 11/20/2001
Voices in Harmony / McHenry County College 11/23/2012
Voices Northwest 4/16/2000
Voices of Harambee 1/20/1997
Voorhees University 4/9/2023
W.E. Greiner Academy Choir 1/18/1999
Wagner College Choir 11/26/2000
Wagner College Choir 5/27/2023
Wagner College Choir 3/19/2022
Wake Christian School 6/17/2018
Wando High School 4/24/2011
Wando High School 4/24/2011
Warrensburg High School 12/1/1996
Warwick Chorale 6/8/2018

Warwick Valley Chorale 1/18/1998
Warwick Valley Chorale 1/19/2004
Warwick Valley Chorale 6/6/1999
Warwick Valley Chorale 5/21/2001
Warwick Valley Chorale 6/10/2019
Wasatch Chorale 5/27/2001
Washburn University 5/27/2001
Washburn University 5/27/2001
Wasilla HS/St. John Lutheran
    5/21/2001
Waterloo East High School 6/2/1997
Waterloo East High School 2/21/2000
Wausau Conservatory Choralation
    4/4/2004
Wayzata High School Orchestra
    5/27/2000
Webster Groves Presbyterian Church
    1/20/1997
Wellington High School 2/17/2019
Wellshire Presbyterian Church
    3/5/2001
Wendell P. Whalum Community
    Chorus 6/3/2022
West Allis Central 2/18/2001
Westchester Oratorio Society
    6/10/2001
Western Colorado Chorale 2/18/2008
Western Colorado Chorale 6/5/2017
Western Kentucky University
    4/30/1986
Western Kentucky University
    1/14/2001
Western Michigan University 6/6/1999
Western Nebraska CC Collegiate
    Chorale 5/26/2012
Western Oregon University 3/24/2002

Western Oregon University 5/30/1999
Western Oregon University 5/27/2022
West Essex High School Choir
    4/1/2001
Westfield Oratorio Singers 4/16/2002
Westfield State College 5/9/1999
Westfield State College 5/9/1999
Westfield State College Chorale
    3/25/2001
West Jessamine High School 4/9/2023
Westlake United Methodist Church
    4/28/2001
West Milford High School 6/16/2019
Westminster Christian School Orch
    4/7/2002
Westminster College 5/19/2018
Westminster College Choirs 3/31/2002
Westminster College Choirs 5/19/2018
Westminster Presbyterian Church
    5/27/2017
West Morris Mendham High School
    5/12/2002
West Ottawa High School - North
    4/8/2001
West Ridge Middle School 5/27/2001
West Springfield High School
    5/28/2001
West Tennessee Youth Chorus
    5/30/2022
West Valley Chorale/Shepherd of the
    Hills UMC 5/30/2011
West Virginia University 3/19/2000
Wetaskiwin Composite 2/16/1998
Wheat Ridge HS Band 3/28/1988
Whetstone High School 6/17/2001

Whippany Park High School
5/28/2011
Whippany Park High School
5/28/2012
Whippany Park High School
1/13/2008
Whitefish Bay High School Orchestra
6/15/1997
White Knoll High School Varsity
Choir 4/28/2019
White Oak High School 6/17/2001
White Plains High School 5/28/2011
Wichita East High School 5/26/1996
Wichita First Presbyterian Church
5/26/1996
Wichita State University 5/30/2011
Wichita State University Choirs
6/5/2021
Wichita State University Orchestra
5/30/2011
Wichita Symphony Orchestra
11/25/2001
Wicke Lourdes Singers 4/7/2002
Wilburton High School 5/29/2000
Wildwood Park For the Arts "Una
Voce" 6/26/2022
Wilkes Central High School Chamber
Singers 3/19/2022
Willamette Girlchoir 6/25/2000
Willcox United Methodist Church
5/28/2001
William Fremd High School 4/1/2001
William J. Palmer High School
5/19/2018
Willow Creek Children's Chorus
6/27/1999

Willow Springs High School 7/8/2023
Wilmington Girls' Choir 5/28/2018
Winders Ensemble 7/8/2023
Windham High School 4/12/1998
Windham High School 4/12/1998
Windham High School 4/12/1998
Windsong Southland Chorale
6/10/2001
Windsong Southland Chorale
6/10/2001
Windsong Southland Chorale
6/27/1999
Windsor Classic Chorale 5/19/2018
Windsor Symphony Orchestra Chorus
5/19/2018
Winnetka Bible Church 3/2/2004
Winnetka Bible Church 5/28/2001
Winnetonka HS Band 4/24/2011
Winona Secondary School 4/24/2011
Winsor School Chorus 3/19/2000
Winston-Salem Children's Chorus
2/18/2001
Winthrop University Choirs
5/28/2019
Wofford College 4/12/1997
Woodland Hills Community Church
4/28/2018
Worcester Children's Chorus
11/23/2012
Yakima Covenant Church 5/29/2000
Yavapai College Master Chorale
3/11/2023
Yellow Rose Singers 7/7/2022
Ygnacio Valley High School Wind
Ensemble 5/19/2001

Yongin-City Happy Women's Choir
6/1/2019
York High School 6/2/2002
York University 5/25/2019
Young People's Chorus of New York
City 6/25/2000
Young People's Chorus of New York
City 5/27/2001
Young People's Chorus of New York
City 5/30/1999
Young People's Chorus of New York
City 5/21/2001
Young People's Chorus of New York
City 4/8/2001
Young People's Chorus of New York
City 11/20/2001
Young People's Chorus of New York
City 4/16/2000
Young People's Symphony Orchestra
6/25/2000
Young Professionals Choral Collective
5/25/2019
Young Professionals Choral Collective
5/25/2019
Young Singers Festival 6/27/1999
Young Singers of Pennsylvania
11/24/1996
Youngstown Cantorum 5/28/2022
Young Voices of the Carolinaso
6/11/2017

Young Women's Chorus of Kentucky
6/17/2001
Youth Chorus of Wisconsin 4/3/1988
Youth Orchestra of San Antonio
6/26/2022
Zillah High School 5/14/2000

XIII. YOUTH INSTRUMENTAL ENSEMBLES WHICH HAVE PERFORMED IN CARNEGIE HALL SINCE 1984

Akron Symphony
Albuquerque Youth Symphony
Amity High School
Apple Valley High School Wind
Ensemble
Arapahoe High School
Atash And St. Stephen's Global
Ensemble
Atlanta Youth Wind Symphony
Atlantic Wind Symphony
Augustana College
Ballard High School
Barren County High School
Barron Collier High School Orchestra
Bayfield Troller Concert Band
Bergen Youth Orchestra
Boardman High School Symphonic
Band
Brookwood High School Orchestra
Bucknell University
California Institute of Technology
Carleton College
Carolina Youth Symphony

Central Bucks High School East
Central Conservatory of Music
Central Valley Youth Symphony
Century High School Patriot Wind
    Ensemble
Charlotte Symphony Youth Orchestra
Cheyenne Mountain High School Band
Chief Sealth High School
Colorado Springs Youth Symphony
Colorado State University
Connecticut Symphonic Winds
Coral Reef High School Orchestra
Coronado High School Band
Coronado High School Orchestra
Dayton Philharmonic Youth Orchestra
Desert Vista High Schools Bands
Desoto High School
Detroit High School
Diamond Bar High School
Dobson High School Orchestra
Eagle Valley High School
Eastern High School
Eastern Michigan University
Ed W. Clark High School
El Paso Youth Symphony Orchestra
Emporia State University Wind
    Ensemble
Etowah Youth Orchestra
Evanston Township High School
Everett Philharmonic Orchestra
Evergreen Philharmonic Orchestra
Farmingdale High School
Flint Youth Symphony Orchestra
Florida A & M University Wind
    Symphony
Florida Youth Orchestra

Foothill Band
Fort Collins High School Band
Francis Joseph Reitz High School
Gaylord Symphony Band
George Washington High School Band
Grand View University
Great Miami Youth Symphony
Greater New Orleans Youth Orchestra
Green Valley High School
Gulliver Preparatory Orchestra &
    Concert Band
Harmony Magnet Academy Symphony
    Orchestra
Hastings College Band
Henry Clay High School
Hochstein Youth Symphony Orchestra
Homestead High School
Huntington Brass
Indiana State University
ISO Symphonic Band
ISO Symphony Orchestra
Jackson High School Honors Wind
    Ensemble
James Logan High School Wind
    Symphony
Kansas City Symphony
Kansas State University
Katy High School Band
Katy High School Orchestra
Kingwood High School
L.D. Bell High School Symphony
    Orchestra
Lake Gibson High School
Lee's Summit North High School
Lewisville High School
Lincoln Preparatory Academy Band

Long Island Youth Orchestra

Maitland Symphony Orchestra

Mansfield High School

Marquette High Wind Ensemble

Maui-Vegas Strings

McCallum High School Band

Metropolitan Youth Orchestra of New York

Metropolitan Youth Symphony Orchestras of Atlanta

Mira Costa High School Orchestra-Manhattan Beach

Moanalua High School

National Collegiate Wind Ensemble

National Festival Orchestra

Natrona County High School Jazz Orchestra

New Trier High School

Nolan Wind Symphony

Norcross High School

Nordhoff High School Band

Normal West High School Band

Oakridge Secondary School

Olathe East High School Orchestra

Orange County School of the Arts

Ozarks Philharmonic Youth Orchestra

Palmer Trinity School Wind Ensemble

Pike's Peak Wind Symphony

Pineville High School Band

Plymouth-Canton Educational Park

Prairie du Chien High School

Reagan High School Orchestra

Redmond High School Studio Jazz Orchestra

Richland Two District Orchestra

Riddle High School Concert Band

Rochester Philharmonic Youth Orchestra

Rocky Mountain High School

Santa Monica High School Band

Sarasota Orchestra

Second National Wind Ensemble

Shepherd University Wind Ensemble

Shorewood High School, Washington

Shorewood High School, Wisconsin

South Miami Senior High School

South Pointe Middle School Band

Springfield Youth Symphony

St. Charles East High School

St. Charles North High School

Stephen F. Austin High School

Stockdale Christian School

Suzanne Middle School

Tacoma Youth Symphony

Tampa Metropolitan Youth Orchestra

Tennessee Wind Symphony

Texas A&M University

The Detroit School of Arts Orchestra

The Gold Orchestra

The Oakridge School

Toronto Youth Wind Orchestra

Torrance West High School

Tri-State Millenium Honors Orchestra

University of Arkansas

University of California - Santa Cruz

University of Central Arkansas Band

University of Central Missouri

University of Connecticut

University of Hartford

University of Nebraska Omaha

University of Nebraska-Lincoln

University of Rochester

University of Wisconsin Milwaukee
University of Wisconsin Parkside
Utah Valley Youth Symphony
Vassar College
Wayzata High School Orchestra
Western Michigan University
Westfield Middle School Band
Westfield State College
Westminster Christian School
    Orchestra
Whitefish Bay High School
Wichita State University
Wichita State University Orchestra
Wichita Symphony Orchestra
Winnetonka High School Band
Ygnacio Valley High School Wind
    Ensemble
Young People's Symphony Orchestra

XIV. Artists who have performed on MidAmerica Productions Chamber Music Series in Weill Recital Hall at Carengie Hall since 1987

Concert Date & Performer:
3/21/1987 Dinos Constantinides
3/21/1987 Louisiana State University
    New Music Ensemble
3/21/1987 Evelyn Petros
3/21/1987 Susan Faust Straley
10/24/1987 Stephen Brown
10/24/1987 Harry Sargous

10/24/1987 Dinos Constantinides
10/24/1987 Karen Hunt
05/29/1988 Paul Brandvik
05/29/1988 Bemidji Choir
06/20/1988 Jocelyn K. Jensen
06/20/1988 Robin C. Planer
06/20/1988 Boulder High School
    Chamber Choir
06/20/1988 Eldorado High School
    Mixed Choir
11/17/1988 Brian Suits
11/17/1988 David Fox
10/07/1989 Manhattan Philharmonic
    Chamber Players
10/21/1989 Gene Young
10/21/1989 Peabody Camerata
10/21/1989 Rheda Becker
10/21/1989 Elaine Bonazzi
11/11/1989 Michel Bettez
11/11/1989 Gilles Plante
11/11/1989 Guy Pelletier
11/11/1989 Francis Ouellet
11/11/1989 Normand Forget
11/11/1989 Alain Trudel
11/11/1989 Le Nouvel Ensemble
    Moderne
11/11/1989 Claude Lamothe
11/11/1989 Jacques Drouin
11/11/1989 Lorraine Vaillancourt
11/11/1989 Andre Moisan
11/11/1989 Rene Gosselin
11/11/1989 Julien Gregoire
11/11/1989 Vincent Dhavernas
11/11/1989 Lise Bouchard
11/11/1989 Brian Bacon
11/11/1989 Alain Giguère

11/11/1989 Claude Hamel
12/09/1989 Nita Karpf
12/09/1989 Douglas Keith
12/09/1989 John Connolly
12/09/1989 Glenda Goss
12/09/1989 Alan Thomas
12/09/1989 Jennifer Patti
12/09/1989 Idele Hitchcock
12/09/1989 Wayne Jones
12/09/1989 University of Georgia
    Contemporary Chamber Ensemble
12/09/1989 Ritchard Maynard
12/09/1989 Lewis Nielson
12/09/1989 Kenneth Broadway
12/09/1989 Joseph Lozier
12/09/1989 Lane Donaldson
01/27/1997 Lutz Rath
01/27/1997 Elysium String Quartet
01/27/1997 Lisa Ralia Heffter
01/27/1997 Jennifer Tiboris
01/27/1997 Leonid Levin
05/20/1997 Brass Mosaic
05/20/1997 Ken Soper
05/20/1997 Nathaniel Dickey
05/20/1997 Brendan Kierman
05/20/1997 David Workman
05/20/1997 Paul Erion
06/09/1997 Lutz Rath
06/09/1997 Elysium String Quartet
06/09/1997 Lisa Ralia Heffter
06/09/1997 Jennifer Tiboris
06/09/1997 Robert Chausow
06/11/1997 Matthew Morris
06/11/1997 Albemarle Ensemble
06/11/1997 Nancy Garlick
06/11/1997 Margaret Newcomb

06/11/1997 Dwight Purvis
06/11/1997 Kristen Hadden
06/11/1997 Content Sablinsky
06/18/1997 Eleonor Bindman
10/20/1997 Lutz Rath
10/20/1997 Elysium String Quartet
10/20/1997 Veronica Salas
10/20/1997 Jennifer Tiboris
10/20/1997 Robert Chausow
01/26/1998 Lutz Rath
01/26/1998 Elysium String Quartet
01/26/1998 Veronica Salas
01/26/1998 Jennifer Tiboris
01/26/1998 Robert Chausow
02/23/1998 Lutz Rath
02/23/1998 Eleonor Bindman
02/23/1998 Robert Chausow
02/23/1998 Maria Zouves
02/23/1998 Peter Weitzner
02/23/1998 Laura Conwesser
02/23/1998 Elysium String Quartet
02/23/1998 Veronica Salas
02/23/1998 Jennifer Tiboris
02/23/1998 Lukas Foss
03/17/1998 John Owings
03/17/1998 Fritz Gearhart
05/02/1998 Eleonor Bindman
05/27/1998 Stephen Brown
05/27/1998 Dinos Constantinides
05/27/1998 Andrea Gullickson
05/27/1998 Marianne Chaudoir
05/27/1998 Stephen Brown
06/10/1998 John Robinson
06/10/1998 Earl Williams
06/10/1998 Alan Givens
06/10/1998 Mark Marino

06/10/1998 Valerie Capers Jazz
    Quartet
06/10/1998 Valerie Capers
06/10/1998 Alan Givens
06/10/1998 Valerie Capers
11/04/1998 Lutz Rath
11/04/1998 Elysium String Quartet
11/04/1998 Veronica Salas
11/04/1998 Gary Levinson
11/04/1998 Jennifer Tiboris
11/24/1998 Roger Keyes
11/24/1998 Lynda Keith McKnight
11/24/1998 Helen Ann Shanley
11/30/1998 Lorne Munroe
11/30/1998 Martin Canin
11/30/1998 Gino Sambuco
11/30/1998 Irene Breslaw
11/30/1998 Filarmonia Quartet
02/14/1999 L. William Kuyper
02/14/1999 Robert Miller
02/14/1999 Oscar Ravina
02/22/1999 Jan Bastiaan Neven
02/22/1999 Miles Goldberg
02/22/1999 Huntington Piano Trio
02/22/1999 Blanka Bednarz
03/08/1999 Frederick Zlotkin
03/08/1999 Gerald Robbins
03/08/1999 Lyric Piano Quartet
03/08/1999 Karen Dreyfus
03/08/1999 Glenn Dicterow
03/22/1999 Lutz Rath
03/22/1999 L. William Kuyper
03/22/1999 R. Allen Spanjer
03/22/1999 Elysium String Quartet
03/22/1999 Veronica Salas
03/22/1999 Gary Levinson

03/22/1999 Jennifer Tiboris
03/22/1999 Naomi Drucker
03/22/1999 Stanley Drucker
03/22/1999 Timothy Cobb
03/22/1999 Joseph Robinson
04/04/1999 Naomi Drucker
04/04/1999 Blanche Abram
04/04/1999 Eriko Sato
04/04/1999 Deirdre Kingsbury
04/04/1999 Chris Finckel
04/04/1999 American Chamber
    Ensemble
04/04/1999 Lois Martin
04/04/1999 Deborah Wong
04/04/1999 Marilyn Sherman Lehman
05/11/1999 Dinos Constantinides
05/11/1999 Jan Grimes
05/11/1999 Patricia Martin
05/11/1999 Ivan Lalev
05/11/1999 Maria Traykova
05/11/1999 Kelly Smith Toney
05/11/1999 Lauren Davis
05/11/1999 Sarah Beth Hanson
05/11/1999 Patricia Martin
05/11/1999 Lisa McCullough
06/07/1999 Lutz Rath
06/07/1999 Elysium String Quartet
06/07/1999 Veronica Salas
06/07/1999 Gary Levinson
06/07/1999 Jennifer Tiboris
06/07/1999 Matej Oresic
06/07/1999 Rena Gendelman
06/07/1999 Elena Papandreou
06/16/1999 Cristina Valdes
06/16/1999 Vasil Kolkhidashvili
06/16/1999 Zurab Ninua

06/16/1999 Iris Derke
06/21/1999 Ivan Lalev
06/21/1999 Lisa McCullough
06/21/1999 Lori Bade
06/21/1999 Jan Grimes
06/21/1999 Sarah Beth Hanson
06/21/1999 Rosemary Caviglia
06/21/1999 Esther Lamneck
11/27/1999 Nicholas Denysenko
11/27/1999 Andre Papkov
11/29/1999 Leonard Hindell
11/29/1999 Mark Nuccio
11/29/1999 Marie Herseth Kenote
11/29/1999 L. William Kuyper
11/29/1999 R. Allen Spanjer
11/29/1999 Robert Botti
11/29/1999 Robert Miller
12/05/1999 Duo Nuova
12/05/1999 Kevin Class
12/05/1999 Timothy McAllister
12/10/1999 Idith Meshulam
12/10/1999 Andre Emelianoff
12/10/1999 Jorja Fleezanis
12/10/1999 Haleh Abghari
12/20/1999 Eugene Levinson
12/20/1999 Gina Levinson
12/21/1999 Daniel Druckman
12/21/1999 Jonathan Feldman
12/21/1999 Toby Appel
12/22/1999 Alan Stepansky
12/22/1999 Michael Gilbert
12/22/1999 Jennifer Gilbert
12/22/1999 Yoko Takebe
12/22/1999 Gerald Appleman
12/22/1999 Alan Gilbert
12/22/1999 David Kim

12/22/1999 Scott Yoo
12/22/1999 Alan Stepansky
02/01/2000 Marcantonio Barone
02/01/2000 Barbara Govatos
02/08/2000 Eleonor Auer
02/09/2000 Adam Unsworth
02/09/2000 Sheri Segal-Melcher
02/09/2000 Richard Amoroso
02/20/2000 Eileen Moon
02/20/2000 Naomi Drucker
02/20/2000 Stanley Drucker
02/20/2000 Elysium String Quartet
02/20/2000 Dorian Rence
02/20/2000 Jennifer Tiboris
02/20/2000 Lisa Eunhee Kim
02/20/2000 Lukas Foss
02/21/2000 Irene Breslaw
02/21/2000 Gino Sambuco
02/21/2000 Qiang Tu
02/21/2000 Martin Canin
02/21/2000 Filarmonia Quartet
03/01/2000 Barry Snyder
03/01/2000 Sylvia Rosenberg
03/01/2000 James Dunham
03/26/2000 Robert Miller
03/27/2000 Naomi Drucker
03/27/2000 Stanley Drucker
03/27/2000 Kazuko Hayami
04/17/2000 Sara Male
04/17/2000 Xun Pan
04/17/2000 Newstead Trio
04/17/2000 Michael Jamanis
04/21/2000 Anton Nel
04/21/2000 Sylvia Rosenberg
05/11/2000 Benjamin Schmid
05/16/2000 Robert deMaine

05/16/2000 Randall Hodgkinson	11/25/2000 Rebecca Stanton
05/16/2000 Helen Armstrong	11/25/2000 Alexandra Tregubov
05/16/2000 Gerard Reuter	11/25/2000 Mikhail Zeiger
05/16/2000 Louise Schulman	11/25/2000 Nicolas Mokhoff
05/22/2000 Benjamin Schmid	11/25/2000 Nikolai Kachanov
05/24/2000 Benjamin Schmid	01/08/2001 Quattro Mani
06/14/2000 Elizabeth Hainen	01/08/2001 Alice Rybak
06/14/2000 John Koen	01/08/2001 Susan Grace
06/14/2000 Anna Marie Ahn Petersen	01/11/2001 Mark Crayton
06/14/2000 Hirono Oka	01/11/2001 James Janssen
06/14/2000 Yayoi Numazawa	01/12/2001 Eleonor Bindman
09/30/2000 Qiang Tu	01/13/2001 Allen Krantz
09/30/2000 Hélène D. Jeanney	01/13/2001 Nancy Bean
10/09/2000 Jeffrey Khaner	01/13/2001 Duo Paganini
10/09/2000 Elizabeth Hainen	01/16/2001 Christos Tsitsaro
10/09/2000 Syrinx Trio	02/04/2001 Adam Unsworth
10/09/2000 Roberto Diaz	02/04/2001 Sheri Segal-Melcher
10/28/2000 Chris Finckel	02/04/2001 Amoroso Trio
10/28/2000 Naomi Drucker	02/04/2001 Richard Amoroso
10/28/2000 Lois Martin	02/12/2001 Linda Mark
10/28/2000 Deborah Wong	02/12/2001 Charles Rex Jr.
10/28/2000 Eriko Sato	02/12/2001 Christopher Rex
10/28/2000 Blanche Abram	02/12/2001 Linda Hohenfeld
10/28/2000 Marilyn Sherman Lehman	02/12/2001 Peter Kenote
11/08/2000 Dorel Fodoreanu	02/12/2001 Lisa Eunhee Kim
11/08/2000 Deniz Arman Gelenbe	02/12/2001 Leonard Hindell
11/08/2000 Arman Trio	02/12/2001 Elizabeth Dyson
11/08/2000 Constantin Bogdanas	02/12/2001 Mark Nuccio
11/18/2000 Huntington Brass Quintet	02/12/2001 Harriet Wingreen
11/18/2000 Alberto G. Suarez	02/12/2001 Jungsun You
11/18/2000 Bron Wright	02/16/2001 Chara Lacovidou
11/18/2000 Mark Emery	02/18/2001 Qiang Tu
11/18/2000 Tom Cupples	02/18/2001 Martin Canin
11/18/2000 Joseph R. Wilson	02/18/2001 Gino Sambuco
11/25/2000 Anatoly Panchoshnyy	02/18/2001 Filarmonia Quartet
11/25/2000 Mukund Marathe	02/19/2001 Elsa Ludewig-Verdehr

02/19/2001 Silvia Roederer
02/19/2001 Verdehr Trio
02/19/2001 Walter Verdehr
03/03/2001 Mark Nuccio
03/03/2001 Jonathan Feldman
03/03/2001 Sheryl Staples
03/11/2001 Barry Snyder
03/11/2001 Sylvia Rosenberg
03/19/2001 Qiang Tu
03/19/2001 Elysium Chamber
    Ensemble
03/19/2001 Hélène D. Jeanney
03/19/2001 Chin Kim
03/19/2001 L. William Kuyper
03/24/2001 Robert deMaine
03/24/2001 Helen Armstrong
03/24/2001 Emily Mitchell
04/02/2001 Richmond Harp Ensemble
04/02/2001 Lynnelle Ediger-Kordzaia
04/16/2001 Dorothy Lawson
04/16/2001 L. William Kuyper
04/16/2001 Irene Breslaw
04/16/2001 Hanna Lachert
04/16/2001 Yuval Waldman
04/16/2001 Waterville Ensembles
05/10/2001 Paul Green
05/10/2001 Kazuko Hayami
05/10/2001 Helen Armstrong
05/10/2001 Wolfram Koessel
10/08/2001 Alea III Chamber
    Ensemble
10/08/2001 Nelli Semitekolo
10/08/2001 Konstantinos Papadakis
10/08/2001 Joseph Foley
10/08/2001 Dimitris Dessylas
10/08/2001 Maria Karagevreki La Vita

10/08/2001 Gregoris Semitekolo
10/22/2001 Qiang Tu
10/22/2001 Hélène D. Jeanney
11/11/2001 Marie Herseth Kenote
11/11/2001 Robert Botti
11/11/2001 Paul Liljestrand
11/11/2001 Kenote Trio
11/11/2001 Neal S. Harnly
11/11/2001 Peter Kenote
11/18/2001 Dorothy Lawson
11/18/2001 David Witten
11/18/2001 Waterville Trio
11/18/2001 Hanna Lachert
11/25/2001 Qiang Tu
11/25/2001 Hélène D. Jeanney
11/25/2001 Eriko Sato
11/25/2001 L. William Kuyper
11/25/2001 Elysium Chamber
    Ensemble
11/25/2001 Veronica Salas
11/25/2001 Jennifer Tiboris
12/17/2001 Nicolas Mokhoff
12/17/2001 Anatoly Panchoshnyy
12/17/2001 Russian Chamber Chorus
    of New York
12/17/2001 Peter Nathan Foltz
12/18/2001 Bob Kaye
12/18/2001 Helen Schneide
12/20/2001 Alan Stepansky
12/20/2001 Alan Gilbert
12/20/2001 Michael Gilbert
12/20/2001 Jennifer Gilbert
12/20/2001 Yoko Takebe
12/20/2001 Reiko Uchida
12/20/2001 Kajsa William-Olsson
12/21/2001 Bob Kaye

12/21/2001 Helen Schneider
01/14/2002 Eleonor Bindman
01/15/2002 John Owings
01/15/2002 Fritz Gearhart
01/20/2002 L. William Kuyper
01/20/2002 Robert Miller
01/20/2002 Michael Slattery
01/20/2002 Oscar Ravina
01/21/2002 Alan Stepansky
01/21/2002 Montclair Chamber
     Ensemble
01/21/2002 Oscar Ravina
01/22/2002 Mansoon Han Kim
01/22/2002 Mihai Craioveanu
01/27/2002 Barry Snyder
01/27/2002 Sylvia Rosenberg
01/27/2002 Veronica Salas
01/27/2002 Lutz Rath
02/05/2002 Stanley Drucker
02/05/2002 Leonid Hambro
02/05/2002 Carter Brey
02/05/2002 Gerald Robbins
02/11/2002 Carter Brey
02/11/2002 Christopher O'Riley
02/16/2003 Wolfgang Laufer
02/16/2003 Fine Arts Quartet
02/16/2003 Yuri Gandelsman
02/16/2003 Efim Boico
02/16/2003 Ralph Evans
02/16/2003 Robert Thompson
02/17/2002 Dorel Fodoreanu
02/17/2002 Deniz Arman Gelenbe
02/17/2002 Arman Trio
02/17/2002 Constantin Bogdanas
03/24/2002 Qiang Tu

03/24/2002 Elysium Chamber
     Ensemble
03/24/2002 David Oei
03/24/2002 Veronica Salas
03/24/2002 Eriko Sato
03/24/2002 Jennifer Tiboris
03/24/2002 Cheryl Gobbetti Hoffman
03/24/2002 Paul Tardif
03/28/2002 Andrea Arese-Elias
03/28/2002 Carlos Elias
03/30/2002 John Hendrickson
03/30/2002 Rodica Oancea-Gonzalez
04/01/2002 Levon Ambartsumian
04/01/2002 ARCO Chamber
     Orchestra
04/01/2002 Levon Ambartsumian
04/07/2002 Elena Papandreou
04/21/2002 Jenia Manoussaki
05/05/2002 Jonathan Feldman
05/05/2002 Sheryl Staples
05/18/2002 Allen Krantz
05/18/2002 Nancy Bean
05/18/2002 Lloyd Smith
06/02/2002 Qiang Tu
06/02/2002 ElysiumChamber
     Ensemble
06/02/2002 L. William Kuyper
06/02/2002 Veronica Salas
06/02/2002 Eriko Sato
06/02/2002 Jennifer Tiboris
06/02/2002 Hélène D. Jeanney
06/03/2002 Gerard Reuter
06/03/2002 Gerald Robbins
06/03/2002 Helen Armstrong
06/03/2002 James Kreger
06/05/2002 Quattro Mani

06/05/2002 Alice Rybak
06/05/2002 Susan Grace
06/05/2002 Quattro Mani
06/05/2002 David Colson
06/05/2002 John Kinzie
06/11/2002 Apostolos Paraskévas
06/11/2002 Erika Tordeus Paraskevas
06/11/2002 Anthony P. De Ritis
06/11/2002 Del Lewis
06/12/2002 Lenuta Ciulei
06/17/2002 Kirsten Agresta
06/17/2002 Carolyn Filak Royan
09/29/2002 Adam Unsworth
09/29/2002 Sheri Segal-Melcher
10/06/2002 Cheryl Gobbetti Hoffman
10/06/2002 Susan Fancher
10/06/2002 Anthony Miranda
10/21/2002 William Ransom
10/21/2002 William Preucil
10/21/2002 Martin Chalifour
10/21/2002 Cecylia Arzewski
10/27/2002 John Novacek
10/27/2002 David Chan
10/27/2002 Rafael Figueroa
11/01/2002 Todd Palmer
11/01/2002 Kazuko Hayami
11/01/2002 Helen Armstrong
11/01/2002 Robert deMaine
11/10/2002 Pamela Pecha
11/10/2002 Laura Silverman
11/10/2002 Doris Lederer
11/10/2002 C. Thomas Shaw
11/10/2002 Akemi Takayama
11/17/2002 Leonard Hindell
11/17/2002 Pascual Martinez Forteza
11/17/2002 Renée Siebert

11/17/2002 L. William Kuyper
11/17/2002 Robert Miller
11/17/2002 Robert Botti
11/17/2002 L. William Kuyper
11/24/2002 Elizabeth Hainen
11/24/2002 David DePeters
11/26/2002 Levon Ambartsumian
11/26/2002 Carmelo de los Santos
11/26/2002 ARCO Chamber
    Orchestra
12/01/2002 Qiang Tu
12/01/2002 Elysium Chamber
    Ensemble
12/01/2002 L. William Kuyper
12/01/2002 Veronica Salas
12/01/2002 Eriko Sato
12/01/2002 Jennifer Tiboris
12/01/2002 David Oei
01/12/2003 Michael Parloff
01/12/2003 Ken Noda
01/12/2003 Mariko Anraku
01/12/2003 Cynthia Phelps
01/12/2003 Juliette Kang
01/12/2003 Nicholas Eanet
01/16/2003 Robert McDonald
01/16/2003 Sylvia Rosenberg
01/16/2003 David Geber
01/22/2003 Dorel Fodoreanu
01/22/2003 Deniz Arman Gelenbe
01/22/2003 Arman Trio
01/22/2003 Constantin Bogdanas
01/27/2003 Eleonor Bindman
02/02/2003 Qiang Tu
02/02/2003 Elysium Chamber
    Ensemble
02/02/2003 Hélène D. Jeanney

02/02/2003 Veronica Salas
02/02/2003 Eriko Sato
02/02/2003 Jennifer Tiboris
02/02/2003 Naomi Drucker
02/02/2003 Carter Brey
02/09/2003 Torleif Thedéen
02/09/2003 Anders Kilström
02/23/2003 Anatoly Sheludyakov
02/23/2003 Levon Ambartsumian
03/01/2003 Wolfgang Laufer
03/01/2003 Fine Arts Quartet
03/01/2003 Yuri Gandelsman
03/01/2003 Efim Boico
03/01/2003 Ralph Evans
03/09/2003 Robert Botti
03/09/2003 Dena Levine
03/09/2003 Stephanie Taylor
03/09/2003 Eric Bartlett
03/09/2003 Lionel Party
03/23/2003 Irina Kats
03/23/2003 Mihai Craioveanu
04/12/2003 Melvin Chen
04/13/2003 Stanley Drucker
04/13/2003 Kazuko Hayami
04/13/2003 Chris Finckel
04/13/2003 Veronica Salas
04/13/2003 Jennifer Tiboris
04/13/2003 Eriko Sato
04/27/2003 Carter Brey
04/27/2003 Benjamin Pasternack
05/04/2003 Elizabeth Dyson
05/04/2003 Joseph Robinson
05/04/2003 Robert Rinehart
05/04/2003 Carmit Zori
05/04/2003 Timothy Cobb
05/04/2003 Mary Kay Robinson

05/10/2003 Chris Finckel
05/10/2003 American Chamber
    Ensemble
05/10/2003 Naomi Drucker
05/10/2003 Marilyn Sherman Lehman
05/10/2003 Lois Martin
05/10/2003 Deborah Wong
05/10/2003 Eriko Sato
05/11/2003 Qiang Tu
05/11/2003 Elysium Chamber
    Ensemble
05/11/2003 L. William Kuyper
05/11/2003 Veronica Salas
05/11/2003 Eriko Sato
05/11/2003 Jennifer Tiboris
05/11/2003 David Oei
05/11/2003 Hélène D. Jeanney
05/29/2003 Eric Nestler
05/29/2003 Kathryn Fouse
05/29/2003 Eugene Osadchy
05/29/2003 Julia Bushkova
05/29/2003 Leonard Candelaria
06/04/2003 Mark Shuman
06/04/2003 Helen Armstrong,
06/04/2003 Gerald Robbins
06/04/2003 Louise Schulman
06/08/2003 Charles Koslowske
06/08/2003 Kara Guggenmos
06/10/2003 Jeffrey Butler
06/10/2003 John Hendrickson
06/10/2003 Tre Voci Piano Trio
06/10/2003 Rodica Oancea-Gonzalez
06/17/2003 Margaret Lucia
06/17/2003 Jon Robert Cart
10/01/2003 Orrett Rhoden

10/01/2003 Virginia-Gene
    Rittenhouse
10/07/2003 Adam Neiman
10/07/2003 Philippe Quint
10/07/2003 Andrey Tchekmazov
10/24/2003 Gerald Robbins
10/24/2003 Helen Armstrong
10/24/2003 Nathaniel Rosen
10/24/2003 Jesse Levine
10/26/2003 The Owings-Gearhart Duo
10/26/2003 John Owings
10/26/2003 Fritz Gearhart
11/09/2003 Anton Nel
11/09/2003 Sylvia Rosenberg
12/04/2003 Quattro Mani
12/04/2003 Alice Rybak
12/04/2003 Susan Grace
12/04/2003 David Colson
12/07/2003 Julie Nishimura
12/07/2003 David Bilger
12/07/2003 Barbara Govatos
12/07/2003 Ricardo Morales
12/07/2003 Efe Baltacigil
12/07/2003 Daniel Matsukawa
12/13/2003 Christina Jennings
12/13/2003 Marcantonio Barone
12/13/2003 Orchestra 2001 Chamber
    Ensemble
12/13/2003 James Freeman
12/13/2003 Angela Nelson
12/13/2003 David Nelson
12/13/2003 Kenneth Miller
12/13/2003 William Kerrigan
12/13/2003 Marcantonio Barone
12/13/2003 Ann Crumb
01/11/2004 John Novacek

01/11/2004 David Chan
01/11/2004 Deborah Hoffman
01/11/2004 Edward Arron
02/01/2004 Katz-Shteinberg Duo
02/01/2004 Dmitri Shteinberg
02/01/2004 Shmuel Katz
02/08/2004 Renée Siebert
02/08/2004 Daniel Avshalomov
02/08/2004 Peter Winograd
02/08/2004 Margo Tatgenhorst
    Drakos
02/08/2004 American String Quartet
02/08/2004 Laurie Carney
02/22/2004 Anatoly Sheludyakov
02/22/2004 Levon Ambartsumian
03/14/2004 Melvin Chen
03/20/2004 Chris Finckel
03/20/2004 American Chamber
    Ensemble
03/20/2004 Naomi Drucker
03/20/2004 Lois Martin
03/20/2004 Deborah Wong
03/20/2004 Eriko Sato
03/20/2004 Marilyn Sherman Lehman
04/24/2004 Heasook Rhee
04/24/2004 Ilya Grubert
04/25/2004 Richard Amoroso
04/25/2004 Sheri Segal-Melcher
04/26/2004 Sonia Wieder-Atherton
04/26/2004 David Oei
05/02/2004 Irina Kats
05/02/2004 Mihai Craioveanu
05/22/2004 Jonathan Golove
05/22/2004 Cheryl Gobbetti Hoffman
05/22/2004 Tony Arnold
05/23/2004 Clancy Newman

05/23/2004 Natalie Zhu
05/23/2004 Christina Castelli
10/20/2004 Mika Stoltzman
10/20/2004 Russell Hartenberger
10/20/2004 Bill Douglas
10/20/2004 Garry Kvistad
10/20/2004 Joseph Gramley
10/27/2004 Rohan De Silva
10/27/2004 Helen Armstrong
10/27/2004 Joseph Anderer
11/01/2004 Peter Steffens
11/01/2004 David Korevaar
11/01/2004 Clavier Trio
11/01/2004 Arkady Fomin
11/23/2004 Levon Ambartsumian
11/23/2004 ARCO Chamber
   Orchestra
01/23/2005 Evgeny Rivkin
01/25/2005 Barry Snyder
01/25/2005 Sylvia Rosenberg
01/25/2005 James Dunham
01/29/2005 Marie Herseth Kenote
01/29/2005 Neal S. Harnly
01/29/2005 Barbara Allen
01/29/2005 Peter Kenote
01/29/2005 Kenote Trio
01/29/2005 Philip Smith
01/30/2005 Pascual Martinez Forteza
01/30/2005 Robert Miller
01/30/2005 L. William Kuyper
01/30/2005 Leonard Hindell
01/30/2005 Renée Siebert
02/03/2005 Eleonor Bindman
02/03/2005 Wanda Glowacka
02/06/2005 Wolfgang Laufer
02/06/2005 Fine Arts Quartet

02/06/2005 Yuri Gandelsman
02/06/2005 Efim Boico
02/06/2005 Ralph Evans
02/12/2005 Hélène D. Jeanney
02/12/2005 Vladimir Tsypin
02/12/2005 Anatoly Trofimov
02/12/2005 Tamara Volskaya
02/12/2005 Vladimir Tsypin
02/13/2005 Arash Amini
02/13/2005 John Haines-Eitzen
02/13/2005 Vandermark Ensemble
02/13/2005 Robert Kesselman
02/13/2005 Julie Nishimura
02/13/2005 Burchard Tang
02/13/2005 Che-Hung Chen
02/13/2005 Kimberly Fisher
02/13/2005 Zachary DePue
03/06/2005 Stephen Carlson
03/12/2005 Naomi Drucker
03/12/2005 Blanche Abram
03/12/2005 Eriko Sato
03/12/2005 Chris Finckel
03/12/2005 Marilyn Sherman Lehman
03/12/2005 Deborah Wong
03/12/2005 The Clarinet Band
03/12/2005 Amy Shapiro
03/12/2005 Claude Weinberg
03/12/2005 Jess Gross
03/12/2005 Lawrence Sobol
03/12/2005 Mindy Dragovich
03/12/2005 Peter Weinberg
03/12/2005 Robert Yamins
03/12/2005 Stanley Drucker
03/12/2005 Robert Wagner
03/12/2005 Eva Conti
03/12/2005 Lois Martin

03/12/2005 Joseph Bongiorno
03/13/2005 Anatoly Sheludyakov
03/13/2005 Levon Ambartsumiar
03/29/2005 Lynn Kompass
03/29/2005 Marcia Porter
04/03/2005 Sara Sant'Ambrogio
04/03/2005 Laura Ardan
04/03/2005 William Ransom
04/03/2005 Vega String Quartet
04/03/2005 Yinzi Kong
04/03/2005 Christine Sohn
04/03/2005 Jessica Shuang Wu
04/03/2005 Brice Andrus
04/03/2005 Jun-Ching Lin
04/03/2005 Emory Chamber Music
   Society of Atlanta
04/09/2005 Peter Steffens
04/09/2005 David Korevaar
04/09/2005 Arkady Fomin
04/10/2005 Hélène D. Jeanney
04/10/2005 Matitiahu Braun
04/23/2005 Carolyn Ellman
04/23/2005 Serafin String Quartet
04/23/2005 Ruth Frazier
04/23/2005 Kate Ransom
04/23/2005 Luigi Mazzocchi
05/01/2005 Jerry Grossman
05/01/2005 Michael Parloff
05/01/2005 Warren Jones
05/01/2005 Gregory Zuber
05/01/2005 Timothy Cobb
05/01/2005 Lawrence Dutton
05/07/2005 Carol Wincenc
05/07/2005 Gerard Reuter
05/07/2005 Gerald Robbins
05/07/2005 Louise Schulman

05/07/2005 Helen Armstrong
05/07/2005 Wolfram Koessel
05/08/2005 Hélène D. Jeanney
05/08/2005 Hanna Lachert
05/08/2005 Qiang Tu
05/08/2005 Waterville Trio
05/15/2005 Margaret Lucia
05/15/2005 Jon Robert Cart
06/05/2005 Gregory Beaver
06/05/2005 Chiara String Quartet
06/05/2005 Jonah Sirota
06/05/2005 Julie Yoon
06/05/2005 Rebecca Fischer
06/05/2005 Simone Dinnerstein
06/07/2005 Gregory Zuber
06/07/2005 Linda Hall
06/07/2005 Gregory Zuber
06/07/2005 Patricia Zuber
06/07/2005 Scott Kuney
06/07/2005 Lino Gomez
06/12/2005 Jeffrey Butler
06/12/2005 Fidelis String Quartet
06/12/2005 Wei Jiang
06/12/2005 Mihaela Oancea-Frusina
06/12/2005 Rodica Oancea-Gonzalez
06/12/2005 Ilgin Aka
06/12/2005 Cristian Macelaru
10/26/2005 Andrew Armstrong
10/26/2005 Helen Armstrong
10/26/2005 Edward Arron
10/30/2005 Peter Steffens
10/30/2005 David Korevaar
10/30/2005 Clavier Trio
10/30/2005 Arkady Fomin
11/12/2005 Cheryl Gobbetti Hoffman
11/12/2005 Cheryl Priebe Bishkoff

11/12/2005 Jacob Greenberg
01/21/2006 Dennis Joseph
01/21/2006 Eleonor Bindman
02/04/2006 Leonard Hindell
02/04/2006 Pascual Martinez Forteza
02/04/2006 L. William Kuyper
02/04/2006 Robert Botti
02/04/2006 Robert Miller
02/04/2006 Qiang Tu
02/04/2006 Fiona Simon
02/04/2006 Irene Breslaw
02/05/2006 Christopher Smith
02/11/2006 Ensemble "Russian
    Carnival"
02/11/2006 Nataliya Vsevolodskaya
02/11/2006 Tamara Volskaya
02/11/2006 Mayya Kalikhman
02/11/2006 Anatoly Trofimov
02/11/2006 Leonid Bruk
02/22/2006 Quattro Mani
02/22/2006 Alice Rybak
02/22/2006 Susan Grace
03/01/2006 Barry Snyder
03/01/2006 Sylvia Rosenberg
03/04/2006 Chris Finckel
03/04/2006 American Chamber
    Ensemble
03/04/2006 Naomi Drucker
03/04/2006 Deborah Wong
03/04/2006 Lois Martin
03/04/2006 Blanche Abram
03/04/2006 Patricia Spencer
03/05/2006 Darima Alexandru
03/05/2006 Alberto J. Rodriguez-Ortiz
03/07/2006 Aglaia Koras
04/06/2006 H. Robert Reynolds

04/06/2006 Detroit Chamber Winds
    and Strings
04/09/2006 Clancy Newman
04/09/2006 Jose Franch-Ballester
04/09/2006 Jasmine Choi
04/09/2006 Bridget Kibbey
04/09/2006 Teng Li
04/09/2006 Ayano Ninomiya
04/09/2006 Korbinian Altenberger
04/09/2006 Karen Slack
04/09/2006 Simone Dinnerstein
04/13/2006 Robert Miller
04/13/2006 Eilana Lappalainen
04/17/2006 Antonio Di Cristofano
04/23/2006 Qiang Tu
04/23/2006 Elysium Chamber
    Ensemble
04/23/2006 L. William Kuyper
04/23/2006 Veronica Salas
04/23/2006 Eriko Sato
04/23/2006 David Oei
04/23/2006 Hélène D. Jeanney
04/24/2006 Kenneth Christensen
04/24/2006 Liza Hella
05/07/2006 Lawrence Stomberg
05/07/2006 Serafin String Quartet
05/07/2006 Ruth Frazier
05/07/2006 Kate Ransom
05/07/2006 Timothy Schwarz
05/14/2006 Renée Siebert
05/14/2006 Barbara Allen
05/14/2006 Daniel Avshalomov
05/22/2006 Nicolas Kavakos
05/22/2006 Anny Totsiou
05/22/2006 Artis Piano Trio
05/22/2006 Yannos Margaziotis

05/24/2006 Rafael Figueroa
05/24/2006 David Chan
05/24/2006 Shai Wosner
05/30/2006 Jenia Manoussaki
05/30/2006 Peter Clemente
05/30/2006 Jiri Barta
05/30/2006 Olympic Trio
05/31/2006 David Oei
05/31/2006 Hélène D. Jeanney
06/04/2006 America's Dream
    Chamber Artists
06/04/2006 Eveline Kuhn
06/04/2006 Bridget Kibbey
06/04/2006 Dov Scheindlin
06/04/2006 Cyrus Beroukhim
06/04/2006 Tim Fain
06/04/2006 Arash Amini
06/04/2006 Alan R. Kay
06/04/2006 Stephen Sas
06/04/2006 Alexandra Knoll
06/04/2006 Michi Wiancko
06/04/2006 Rieko Aizawa
06/04/2006 Maurycy Banaszek
06/12/2006 Hélène D. Jeanney
06/12/2006 Lilia Donkova
06/19/2006 Hakan Sensoy
06/25/2006 Hélène D. Jeanney
06/25/2006 Emil-Silviu Ciobota
10/01/2006 Jesus Castro-Balbi
10/01/2006 David Korevaar
10/01/2006 Clavier Trio
10/01/2006 Arkady Fomin
10/07/2006 Warren Jones
10/07/2006 Laura Hamilton
10/23/2006 Leonel Morales

10/28/2006 Chamber Orchestra
    Kremlin
10/28/2006 Misha Rachlevsky
10/29/2006 Evgeny Rivkin
10/31/2006 Heasook Rhee
10/31/2006 Amaury Coeytaux
11/05/2006 Katz-Shteinberg Duo
11/05/2006 Dmitri Shteinberg
11/05/2006 Shmuel Katz
11/19/2006 James Gardner
11/19/2006 Mary Jane Johnson
11/20/2006 Chamber Orchestra
    Kremlin
11/20/2006 Misha Rachlevsky
11/27/2006 Gianfranco Pappalardo
    Fiumara
11/29/2006 Aglaia Koras
1/20/2007 Qiang Tu
1/20/2007 Hélène D. Jeanney
1/20/2007 Waterville Trio
1/20/2007 Hanna Lachert
1/21/2007 David Calhoun
1/21/2007 Johannes Somary
1/21/2007 Kinor String Quartet
1/21/2007 Kathleen Foster
1/21/2007 Robin Zeh
1/21/2007 Yuval Waldman
1/21/2007 Susanne Peck
1/30/2007 Barry Snyder
1/30/2007 Sylvia Rosenberg
02/11/2007 Michael Parloff
02/11/2007 John Novacek
02/11/2007 Barbara Barrie
02/11/2007 Rafael Figueroa
02/11/2007 Deborah Hoffman
02/11/2007 Hsin-Yun Huang

02/11/2007 David Chan
02/24/2007 Guang Wang
02/24/2007 Moffett Morris
02/24/2007 Lorenzo Sanford
02/24/2007 William Ransom
02/24/2007 Gary Motley Jazz Quartet
02/24/2007 Gary Motley
02/24/2007 Dwight Andrews
02/24/2007 Jessica Shuang Wu
02/24/2007 Yinzi Kong
02/24/2007 Wei Wei Le
02/25/2007 Judy Huang
03/03/2007 Chris Finckel
03/03/2007 American Chamber
    Ensemble
03/03/2007 Naomi Drucker
03/03/2007 Lois Martin
03/03/2007 Eriko Sato
03/03/2007 Blanche Abram
03/03/2007 Marilyn Sherman Lehman
03/04/2007 Joy Puckett Schreier
03/04/2007 Danielle Talamantes
03/11/2007 Andrey Ponochevny
03/11/2007 Emanuel Borok
04/22/2007 Aglaia Koras
04/23/2007 Ariane Lallemand
04/23/2007 Hélène D. Jeanney
04/23/2007 L'Aurore Trio
04/23/2007 Yuval Waldman
05/06/2007 Gerald Appleman
05/06/2007 Hélène D. Jeanney
05/06/2007 Matitiahu Braun
06/10/2007 Jeremy McCoy
06/10/2007 Stephanie Mortimore
06/10/2007 Mary Hammann
06/10/2007 David Heiss

06/10/2007 Rebecca Pechefsky
06/10/2007 Elizaveta Kopelman
06/22/2007 American Youth Harp
    Ensemble
06/22/2007 Lynnelle Ediger-Kordzaia
09/23/2007 Evgeny Rivkin
09/23/2007 Levon Ambartsumian
09/23/2007 Shakhida Ambartsumian
09/30/2007 Lawrence Stomberg
09/30/2007 Serafin String Quartet
09/30/2007 Ana Tsinadze
09/30/2007 Kate Ransom
09/30/2007 Timothy Schwarz
10/01/2007 Elizaveta Kopelman,
10/01/2007 Anastasia Khitruk
10/01/2007 Andrey Tchekmazov
10/07/2007 Jesus Castro-Balbi
10/07/2007 David Korevaar
10/07/2007 Clavier Trio
10/07/2007 Arkady Fomin
11/04/2007 Aglaia Koras
12/08/2007 Evangeline Benedetti
12/08/2007 Kiyoshi Tamagawa
12/08/2007 Serena Benedetti
12/08/2007 Stanley Drucker
12/09/2007 Ieva Jokubaviciute
12/09/2007 Yulia Ziskel
12/10/2007 Gil Sullivan
02/10/2008 Jesus Castro-Balbi
02/10/2008 David Korevaar
02/10/2008 Clavier Trio
02/10/2008 Arkady Fomin
03/22/2008 American Chamber
    Ensemble
03/22/2008 Naomi Drucker
03/22/2008 Marilyn Sherman Lehman

03/22/2008 Deborah Wong
03/22/2008 Jess Gross
03/22/2008 Mindy Dragovich
03/22/2008 Stanley Drucker
03/22/2008 Karen Lehman
03/22/2008 Eriko Sato
03/22/2008 Lois Martin
03/22/2008 Chris Finckel
03/22/2008 Blanche Abram
03/24/2008 The Bridge Duo
03/24/2008 Michael Hampton
03/24/2008 Matthew Jones
03/30/2008 Narciso Solero
03/30/2008 Jon Robert Cart
03/30/2008 Csilla Lakatos
03/30/2008 Rowan University String
    Quartet
03/30/2008 Jon Robert Cart
03/30/2008 Ferenc Lakatos
03/30/2008 Set Rodrigues
03/30/2008 Christopher Atanasiu
04/13/2008 Aglaia Koras
04/19/2008 Mirna Ogrizovic
04/19/2008 Alexander Ambartsumian
04/19/2008 Levon Ambartsumian
04/19/2008 Josip Petrac
04/19/2008 Anatoly Shelucyakov
04/19/2008 Shakhida Azimkhodjaeva
04/19/2008 ARCO Chamber
    Orchestra
04/20/2008 Margaret Cornils Luke
04/20/2008 Maho Nabeshima
04/21/2008 Christiane Klonz
04/26/2008 Li-Pi Hsieh
04/26/2008 Edita Orlinyte

04/27/2008 Qiang Tu
04/27/2008 Hélène D. Jeanney
04/27/2008 Elysium Chamber
    Ensemble
04/27/2008 L. William Kuyper
04/27/2008 Veronica Salas
04/27/2008 Eriko Sato
04/27/2008 David Oei
06/01/2008 Irina Mozyleva
06/01/2008 Vladimir Tsypin
06/01/2008 Artistic Club Luba
    Chamber Ensemble
06/01/2008 Susan Walters
06/05/2008 Mikhail Zeiger
06/05/2008 Adrian Daurov
06/05/2008 Hanna Golodinskii
06/05/2008 Alexander Kisselev
06/15/2008 Ilonka Rus
06/15/2008 Mihaela Oancea-Frusina
06/15/2008 Rodica Oancea-Gonzalez
09/21/2008 Clipper Erickson
09/21/2008 Lenuta Ciulei
10/05/2008 Jesus Castro-Balbi
10/05/2008 David Korevaar
10/05/2008 Clavier Trio
10/05/2008 Arkady Fomin
11/16/2008 Aglaia Koras
01/19/2009 Pascal Archer
01/19/2009 Barry Snyder
01/19/2009 Sylvia Rosenberg
02/15/2009 Texas Harmony Chorus
02/15/2009 Darlene Rogers
02/22/2009 David Oei
02/22/2009 Hélène D. Jeanney
03/28/2009 Lynnen Yakes
03/28/2009 Eleonor Bindman

04/05/2009 Jesus Castro-Balbi	10/29/2010 Levon Ambartsumian
04/05/2009 David Korevaar	10/29/2010 Shakhida Ambartsumian
04/05/2009 Clavier Trio	10/29/2010 Alexander Ambartsumian
04/05/2009 Arkady Fomin	10/29/2010 Anna Seda Ambartsumian
04/26/2009 Aglaia Koras	11/30/2010 Yeo Jung Kim
06/05/2009 Dionisio Camacho	11/30/2010 Hyo Jung Kim
06/18/2009 Tali Tadmor	12/01/2010 Seunghee Lee
06/18/2009 Courtney Huffman	12/15/2010 Hiroko Izumi
10/11/2009 Jesus Castro-Balbi	12/15/2010 Yoko Maria
10/11/2009 David Korevaar	01/15/2011 Maimy Fong
10/11/2009 Clavier Trio	01/15/2011 Indra Thomas
10/11/2009 Arkady Fomin	02/12/2011 Dieter Flury
10/25/2009 Rira Lim	02/12/2011 Maria Prinz
11/05/2009 Aglaia Koras	03/04/2011 Motoki Hirai
11/19/2009 Sergei Babayan	03/11/2011 Margaret Cornils Luke
11/19/2009 Anastasia Khitruk	03/11/2011 Sharon Jensen
02/11/2010 Denitsa Laffchieva	03/11/2011 Rebekah Demaree
02/11/2010 Maria Prinz	03/11/2011 Barry Ellis
02/11/2010 Ofer Canetti	03/11/2011 John Marco
03/01/2010 Aglaia Koras	03/11/2011 Laura Medisky
03/26/2010 Margaret Cornils Luke	03/25/2011 Roger Admiral
03/26/2010 Sharon Jensen	03/25/2011 Guillaume Tardif
06/06/2010 Joseph Mayes	03/26/2011 Tanya Prochazka
06/06/2010 Kathleen Mayes	03/26/2011 Sylvia Shadick-Taylor
06/06/2010 Jon Robert Cart	03/26/2011 Talia Pura
06/06/2010 Kaleb Magnussen	04/02/2011 Judy Huang
06/06/2010 Jamie Mann	04/09/2011 Brad Ritchie
10/10/2010 Jesus Castro-Balbi	04/09/2011 Atlanta Chamber Players
10/10/2010 David Korevaar	04/09/2011 Laura Ardan
10/10/2010 Clavier Trio	04/09/2011 Christina Smith
10/10/2010 Arkady Fomin	04/09/2011 Paula Peace
10/16/2010 Benjamin C. Myers	04/09/2011 Justin Bruns
10/16/2010 Hsiu-Hui Wang	04/09/2011 Elizabeth Koch
10/16/2010 Gemini Piano Trio	04/09/2011 Catherine Lynn
10/16/2010 Sheng-Tsung Wang	05/03/2011 Jeffrey Butler
10/25/2010 Aglaia Koras	05/03/2011 Danny A. Granados

05/03/2011 Fidelis String Quartet
05/03/2011 Joan DerHovsepian
05/03/2011 Mihaela Oancea-Frusina
05/03/2011 Rodica Oancea-Gonzalez
05/03/2011 Judy Dines
05/09/2011 Aglaia Koras
05/17/2011 Jon Robert Cart
05/17/2011 Regina DiMedio-Marrazza
05/17/2011 Adeline Tomasone
05/17/2011 Alison Mersiowski
05/17/2011 Amanda Heckman
05/17/2011 Christina Raczka
05/17/2011 Elaine Petrosino-Roehm
05/17/2011 Melissa Stives
05/17/2011 Owen Cunningham
05/17/2011 Samantha McCloud
05/17/2011 Thomas Meany
05/17/2011 Vincent DuBeau
05/17/2011 Rowan Flute Ensemble
05/23/2011 Ottawa Bach Choir
05/23/2011 Lisette Canton
05/23/2011 Andrew Day
05/23/2011 Agnes Zsigovics
05/23/2011 Kathleen Radke
05/23/2011 Jean-Sebastien Kennedy
05/23/2011 Jeff Boyd
05/23/2011 Heather Lynn Smith
10/16/2011 Bryan Cheng
10/16/2011 ChengÇ Duo
10/16/2011 Silvie Cheng
11/14/2011 Anastasia Khitruk
11/14/2011 Mike Block
11/14/2011 Elena Baksht
11/29/2011 Aglaia Koras
12/18/2011 Ang Li
01/08/2012 Gulimina Mahamuti

01/08/2012 Selim Giray
01/11/2012 Montclair State University
    Flute Studio
01/11/2012 Jon Robert Cart
01/11/2012 Marissa Silverman
01/11/2012 Susan Palma Nidel
01/11/2012 Tanya Dusevic Witek
01/11/2012 Dmitri Korneev
01/11/2012 Gary Schocker
01/21/2012 Erin Chung
01/21/2012 Quinton Morris
02/05/2012 Mario Prisuelos
02/17/2012 Ensemble MidtVest,
02/17/2012 Alexander Kasper
02/17/2012 Tommaso Lonquich
02/17/2012 Charlotte Norholt
02/17/2012 Neil Page
02/17/2012 Peter Kirstein
02/17/2012 Sanna Ripatti
02/17/2012 Ana Feitosa
02/17/2012 Karolina Weltrowska
02/17/2012 Matthew Jones
02/17/2012 Jonathan Slaatto
02/17/2012 Martin Qvist Hansen
03/04/2012 American Youth Harp
    Ensemble
03/04/2012 Lynnelle Ediger-Kordzaia
03/04/2012 Alexander Kordzaia
03/05/2012 Dieter Flury
03/05/2012 Flury-Prinz Duo
03/05/2012 Maria Prinz
03/07/2012 Judy Huang
03/12/2012 Martina Frezzotti
03/22/2012 Douglas Harvey
03/22/2012 Artisan Quartet
03/22/2012 Bruce Williams

03/22/2012 Paula Bird
03/22/2012 Richard Kilmer
03/25/2012 Jesus Castro-Balbi
03/25/2012 Lin/Castro-Balbi Duo
03/25/2012 Gloria Lin
04/01/2012 Evelina Puzaite
04/09/2012 Qiang Tu
04/09/2012 Giampiero Sobrino
04/09/2012 Elysium String Quartet
04/09/2012 Veronica Salas
04/09/2012 Eriko Sato
04/09/2012 Mayuki Fukuhara
04/26/2012 Noreen Cassidy-Polera
04/26/2012 Jung-Mi Kim
05/18/2012 Margaret Cornils Luke
05/18/2012 Sharon Jensen
10/06/2012 Ronda Metszies
10/06/2012 Kent Sangster's Obsessions
    Octet
10/06/2012 Jeff Johnson
10/06/2012 Jamie Cooper
10/06/2012 Jamie Cooper
10/06/2012 Chris Andrew
10/06/2012 Kent Sangster
10/06/2012 Rhonda Henshaw
10/06/2012 Joanna Ciapka-Sangster
10/06/2012 Neda Yamach
10/07/2012 Jesus Castro-Balbi
10/07/2012 David Korevaar
10/07/2012 Clavier Trio
10/07/2012 Arkady Fomin
12/02/2012 Judy Huang
12/03/2012 James Vaughan
12/03/2012 Ivan Zenaty
01/22/2013 Patrick Howle
01/22/2013 Reena Berger Natenberg

01/28/2013 Elena Baksht
01/28/2013 Anastasia Khitruk
02/03/2013 Jiaxin Tian
02/11/2013 Duo Concertante
02/11/2013 Timothy Steeves
02/11/2013 Nancy Dahn
02/22/2013 Irrera Brothers
02/22/2013 Joseph Irrera
02/22/2013 John Irrera
03/04/2013 Patrick Gallois
03/04/2013 Maria Prinz
03/06/2013 Montclair State University
    Chamber Orchestra
03/06/2013 Heather Flemming
03/06/2013 Nicholas Tzavaras
03/06/2013 The Shanghai Quartet
03/06/2013 Honggang Li
03/06/2013 Weigang Li
03/06/2013 Yiwen Jiang
03/06/2013 Cali Camerata
04/04/2013 Erling R. Eriksen
04/04/2013 Camilla Ediassen
04/21/2013 Bryan Cheng
04/21/2013 ChengÇ Duo
04/21/2013 Silvie Cheng
05/28/2013 Margaret Cornils Luke
05/28/2013 Sharon Jensen
05/28/2013 Genevieve Gourley
05/28/2013 Hannah Schatz
10/06/2013 Jesus Castro-Balbi
10/06/2013 David Korevaar
10/06/2013 Clavier Trio
10/06/2013 Arkady Fomin
10/06/2013 Guillermo Figueroa
10/13/2013 Ambartsumian Violins
10/13/2013 Shakhida Ambartsumian

10/13/2013 Levon Ambartsumian
10/13/2013 Alexander Ambartsumian
10/13/2013 Anna Seda Ambartsumian
11/23/2013 Aleyson Scopel
12/08/2013 Judy Huang
12/11/2013 Celimene Daudet
12/16/2013 Gil Sullivan
01/11/2014 Alastair Edmonstone
01/11/2014 Quinton Morris
01/11/2014 David Jolley
01/11/2014 Jessie Wright Martin
01/11/2014 John B. O'Brien
01/11/2014 Selim Giray
02/05/2014 Motoki Hirai
03/06/2014 Patrick Gallois
03/06/2014 Maria Prinz
03/08/2014 Montclair State University
    Vocal Accord
03/08/2014 Heather J. Buchanan
03/08/2014 Frances Rowell
03/08/2014 KerriAnn Dubari
03/08/2014 Soyeon Kim
03/08/2014 Lori McCann
03/08/2014 Steven W. Ryan
03/08/2014 Julianne Froehlich
04/06/2014 Jonathan Slaatto
04/06/2014 Ensemble MidtVest
04/06/2014 Martin Qvist Hansen
04/06/2014 Karolina Weltrowska
04/06/2014 Yavor Petkov
04/06/2014 Tommaso Lonquich
04/06/2014 Neil Page
04/06/2014 Charlotte Norholt
04/06/2014 Peter Kirstein
04/06/2014 David Samuel
04/06/2014 Matthew Jones

05/13/2014 Sean Botkin
05/13/2014 Margaret Cornils Luke

XV. International Choirs which have performed since 2005 at the Festival of the Aegean on the island of Syros, Greece

Canada
Canadian University College Choral
    Union, Alberta, 2012
Kamloops Choristers, British
    Columbia, 2010
Etobicoke Youth Choir, Ontario, 2011
France
Choeur d'Enfants d'Ile-de-France,
    Paris, 2010, 2012, 2014, 2016, 2018
Italy
The Rome Philharmonic Orchestra
    Soloists, 2005
Poland
The Choir of the Podlasie Opera and
    Philharmonic,
Bialystok, 2008
United States
Birmingham Concert Chorale, AL,
    2010
Sun Valley Community Church
    Traditional Choir, Tempe, AZ,
    2017
Rincon/University High School
    Concert Choir, Tucson, AZ, 2018
Kairos Youth Choir, Berkeley, CA,
    2011, 2017

Southwestern College Concert Choir, Chula Vista, CA, 2009, 2013

Towne Singers, La Canada, CA, 2012

Nova Voce, Los Angeles, CA, 2011

Vocal Ensemble of Mira Costa High School, Manhattan Beach, CA, 2010

Contra Costa Youth Choir, Walnut Creek, CA, 2011

Durango Choral Society, CO, 2011

Connecticut Master Chorale, Danbury, CT, 2011

Brevard Community Chorus, Cocoa, FL, 2011

Indian River Charter High School Choir, Vero Beach, FL, 2012

The Michael O'Neal Singers, GA, 2010

Wesleyan Concert Chorus, Macon, GA, 2011

Camerata Singers, Pocatello, ID, 2017

Second Presbyterian Church Sanctuary Choir, Indianapolis, IN, 2018

Bethel College Voices of Triumph, Mishawaka, IN, 2018

Johnson County Chorus, Overland Park, KS, 2012

Northeast Louisiana Chorus, Monroe, LA, 2018

Columbia Collegiate Chorale of Maryland, MD, 2008

The Barstow School Chamber Singers, Kansas City, MO, 2014

Lincoln Choral Artists, Lincoln, NE, 2015

Nebraska Wesleyan University Choir, Lincoln, NE, 2015

St. Paul United Methodist Church Chancel Choir, Lincoln, NE, 2015

Western Nebraska Community College Collegiate Chorale, Scottsbluff, NE, 2015

Children's Chorus of Sussex County, NJ, 2015

The Arcadian Chorale of New Jersey, Matawan, NJ and Richmond Choral Society, NY, 2011

The Continuo Arts Symphonic Chorus, Summit, NJ, 2019

Warwick Valley Chorale, NY, 2011

The Taghkanic Chorale, Yorktown Heights, NY, 2011

Asheville Choral Society Collective, Asheville, NC, 2019

Sardis Presbyterian Church Sanctuary Choir, Charlotte, NC, 2011

Salem College Choir, Winston-Salem, NC, 2013, 2018

Winston-Salem Youth Chorus and Palmetto Voices, Winston-Salem, NC, 2018

University of Nevada of Reno, NV, 2019

Knox Choir of Presbyterian Church, Cincinnati, OH, 2011

Edmond Community Chorale, OK, 2013

Tulsa Oratorio Chorus, OK, 2011

Heart of the Valley Children's Choir, Corvallis, OR, 2014

Cantemus Women's Choir, Kingsport, TN, 2019

Highlands Youth Enseble, Bristol, TN, 2014

King College Symphonic Choir, TN, 2010, 2014

Gethsemane Lutheran Church, Austin, TX, 2011

Proclamation Chorale, Fort Worth, TX

Yellow Rose Singers, San Antonio, TX, 2012, 2017

Fort Worth Academy Choir, TX, 2011

Randolph College Chorale, Lynchburg, VA, 2013

XVI. Greek Choirs which performed since 2005 at the Festival of the Aegean on the island of Syros, Greece.

Ambitus Choir, Athens

Athens Choir Ensemble, 2013

Athens Singers, 2015

Members of the University of Athens Chorus, 2015

Byzantine Traditional Choir, 2015

City of Athens Choir, 2013

Choir of the National Conservatory of Athens (Ethnikon Odeio), 2009- 2013

Choir of Emporiki Bank, Athens, 2012

Choir "Synchroni Ekfrasi", Athens, 2013

Athens Singers and Nakas Conservatory, Athens, 2006, 2009

Choir of the Employees' Union of the Bank of Greece, Athens, 2011, 2012

Choir of University of Athens, 2011- 2013

"Manolis Kalomoiris"Children's Choir, 2011- 2013

Camerata Vocalis, Corfu, 2010

Corfu Municipal Choir "San Giacomo," Corfu, 2016

Ionian University Department of Musical Studies, Corfu, 2009

Ionian Harmony Men's Choir of Corfu, 2013

Corfu Island Children's Choir and Mixed Choir, 2012

Choir of Lykeion Ellinidwn Ioanninon, Ioannia, 2013-2014

Kallitexnimata of Keratsini, Greece, 2019

Members of Solartissimo of Larissa Conservatory, Larissa, Greece, 2017, 2018

The Choir of Eptanisii of Patras, 2011

Polyphonic Choir of Patras, 2012, 2013

Choir of Filarmoniki Conservatory of Patras, 2012-2014

University of Patras Choir, 2012, 2013

Scientists' Choir of Philothei, 2011, 2012

Youth & Children's Choir Armonia Preveza, 2011, 2014

Municipal Choir of Rhodes, 2014

St. Nicholas Greek Orthodox Church of Syros Men's Chorus, Syros, 2010

Chorus of Syros Musical Club, 2013, 2019

Syros Opera Chorus, Syros, 2006

Choir Coro Antico of Conservatory K. Matsigos, Thessaloniki, Greece

XVII. International Artists who appeared, since 2005, at the Festival of Aegean on the island of Syros, Greece

Acte II: Olanna Goudeau & Ashley Renee Watkins, Sopranos, 2015

Ray Adams, Choral Director, 2012

Agapios Agapiadis, Dancer, 2013

Luise Breyer Aiton, Soprano/GOS, 2017

Marina Alexander, Choral Director, 2011

Dimitris Alexandridis, Tenor, GOS, 2016

Voula Amiradaki, Soprano, 2017

Giada Amparan, Mezzo-soprano, 2006

Mariza Anastasiades, Soprano, 2019

Scott Anderson, Choral Director, 2017

Seija Anderson, Choral Director/GOS, 2013

Konstantin Andreiev, Tenor, 2015

Chris Andrew, Piano, Obsessions Octet, 2014

Dena Marie Andrews, Soprano, 2019

Spyros Anemis, Bassist, 2013

Adrian Angelico, Mezzo-soprano, 2019

Katarina Angelopoulou, Sets/Costumes, 2013

Stefano Anselmi, Baritone, 2006

Andreou Antonios, Trombonist, 2013

Tassos Apostolou, Bass-baritone, 2009, 2010

Graciela Araya, Mezzo-soprano, 2012

Ioannis Argyriou, Conductor, 2019

Jennifer Arnold, Mezzo-soprano, 2017

Luk Artois, Timpanist, Percussionist, 2013

Leandra Ashton, Actor, 2009

Amalia Askordalaki, Mezzo-soprano, 2019

Richard Aslanian, Artistic Staff, 2002

Fotini Athanasaki, Mezzo-soprano, 2012, 2013, 2015

Katherine Austin, Pianist, 2012

Mariella Baier, Soprano, 2017

Antonis Batsakis, Tenor, 2019

Mareena Boosamra Ball, Guest Conductor and Choral Director, 2018

Daniel Borowski, Bass, 2018

Francis Bardot, Guest Conductor and Choral Director, 2010, 2012, 2014, 2016, 2018

Brenda Belohoubek, Soprano, 2019

Stavros Beris, Choral Director, 2012, 2013

Esteban Berlanga, Dancer, 2010

Yiannis Benetos, Dancer, 2013

Simona Bertini, Soprano, 2006

Linda Mack Berven, Choral Director, 2011

Vangelis Bikos, Dancer, 2012, 2013

Maria Bildea, Harpist, 2008

James Bingham, Choral Director, 2008

Lucy Black, Actor, 2009

Richard Block, Bass-baritone, GOS Young Artist, 2011, 2013

Wiktor Bockman, Conductor, 2012

Dirk Boiy, Conductor, 2013, 2015, 2016

Alessio Borraggine, Tenor, 2017
Jonathan Boudevin, Baritone, 2015
Vicky Bourcha, Dancer, 2013
Jerome Boutillier, Baritone, 2018
Jessica Boyd, Soprano 2015
Joseph Brent, Tenor, 2011
Margaret Brown, Choral Director, 2010
Frederick Burchinal, Baritone, 2011
Florient Cador, Dancer, 2018
Io Calochristos, Asst. to Mr. Zanella, 2011-2013
Joseph Calzada, Baritone, 2019
Nicholas Canellakis, Cellist, 2016, 2017
Deanna Carter, Movement, Dancer, 2013
Carol Castel, Staging Director, 2000, 2001, 2007
Jorge Parada Castellano; Guitars, Mandolin, and Mandola; 2019
Rosario Castro, Dancer, 2010
Ricardo Castro, Dancer, 2010
Anais Chalendard, Dancer, 2010
Deborah Chandler, Choral Director, 2018
Lena Chatzigrigoriou, Production Manager, 2010-2013
Elena Chavdarova-Isa, Mezzo-soprano, 2013
Vera Cheknova, Soprano, 2014
Stanislav Chernenkov, Bass, 2016
Vinicio Chieli, Lighting Designer, 2010, 2011
Evita Chioti, Soprano, 2015
Won Whi Choi, Tenor, GOS Resident Artist, 2014

Joanna Ciapka-Sangster, Violinist, Obsessions Octet, 2014
Zhani Ciko, Conductor, 2012
Pablo Gonzalez Cobo, Irish Bouzouki and Lavta, 2019
Liliana Del Conde, Soprano, 2012
Ivan Conrad, Baritone, GOS Young Artist, 2016
Philip Copeland, Choral Director, 2010
Raffaele Costantini, Bass-baritone, 2005
Graham Cox, Pianist, 2013-2015, 2019
Stanley Curtis, Choral Director, 2011
Anita Cyrier, Choral Director, 2012
Brent Davis, Baritone, 2011
Damian Davis, Actor, 2009
Eleni Davou, Mezzo-sopano, 2014
Benjamin Dawkins, Bass, 2011
Kenneth DeBoer, Choral Director, 2011
Sharon DeBoer, Accompanist, 2011
Brian Delate, Actor, 2012
Josephine Delledera, Soprano, 2011
Patricia Denmark, Choral Director and Conductor, 2019
Luc De Meulenaere, Actor, 2013
Chris De Moor, Actor, 2013
Mimi Denissi, Actress, 2011
Shannon DeVine, Baritone, 2009
Christos Diakoumis, Drums, 2013
Dangelo Fernando Diaz, GOS Young Artist, 2014
Bruce Dickerson, Choral Director, 2014
Raymond Dils, Clarinetist, 2013

Athena Dimitrakopoulou, Soprano, 2015

Elton Dimrotchi, Dancer, 2013

Carla Dirlikov, Mezzo-soprano, 2010

Nicolas Di Virgilio, Master Teacher, Coach, 2000

Liri Doll, Soprano, 2019

Juan Cabello Donayre, Violin and Lyra, 2019

Miguel Drake-McLaughlin, Cinematographer, 2012

Naomi Drucker, Clarinetist, 2010

Stanley Drucker, Clarinetist, 2010

Olympia Dukakis, Actress, 2011, 2015

Norman Dunfee, Pianist, 2007

Reda El Wakil, Bass-baritone, 2010

Olga Esina, Dancer, 2010

Nikos Euthymiadis, Choral Director, 2017

Constantine Th. Evangelatos, Choral Director, 2011

Kostas Evangelatos, Choral Director, 2012

Yiorgos Fakanas, Bassist, 2013

Maria Farantouri, Folk Singer, 2010

Massimiliano Fichera, Baritone, 2016

Jakub Fiebig, Orchestra Executive Manager,
2009-2011, 2015-2019

Giannis Filias, Tenor, 2010

W. Patrick Flannagan, Choral Director, 2010, 2014

Athanasios Foskolos, Choral Director, 2013

Stephen Fox, Conductor, 2011

Maria Fragkogiani, Mezzo-soprano, 2015

Anna Fragou, Dancer, 2013

Jeshua Franklin, Choral Director, 2018

Carroll Freeman, Teacher GOS, 2002, 2011

Niki Rosa Frei, Mezzo-soprano, GOS Young Artist, 2014

Louise Fribo, Hoher Soprano, 2019

Abbie Furmansky, Voice Teacher GOS, 2011-2017, 2019

Janet Galvan, Guest Conductor, 2011

Melodie Galloway, Choral Director and Conductor, 2019

Augusto Garcia, Bass, 2013

Amilia Gaspari, Dancer, 2012, 2013

Theo Gavaliatsis, Tenor, 2012

Todd Geer, Tenor, 2007

Filli Georgiadou, Soprano, 2010

Lina Geronikou, Choral Director, 2012, 2013,, 2015

Christina Giannapoulou, Teacher, 2011

Piero Giuliacci, Tenor, 2016

Julian Gjojdeshi, Tenor, 2012

Anooshah Golesorki, Baritone, 2012, 2014

Benito Gonzales, Piano, Dimitri Vassilakis Quartet, 2014

Teresa-Marie Gotanco, Soprano, 2019

Tabea Graser, Soprano/GOS, 2017

Alexandra Gravilescu, Dancer, 2018

Tamara Gura, Mezzo-soprano, 2018

Danielle Halbwachs, Soprano, 2013

Lara Hall, Violinist, 2012

Michael Hayden, Choral Director, 2010

Tina Johns Heidrich, Choral Director, 2011

Robby Hellyn, Bassist, 2013

Christin-Marie Hill, Mezzo-soprano, 2013

Daniel Holstro, GOS Composer, 2014

Takako Horaguchi, Mezzo-soprano, 2005

Jens Huebner, Lighting, Set Design, 2012, 2013, 2015-2019

Raymond Hughes, Conductor, Pianist, 2007, 2009

Fortino Ibarra, Conductor/Pianist/ GOS, 2017

Keith Ikaia-Purdy, Tenor, Voice Teacher, 2012-2014

Antonino Interisano, Tenor, 2009

Evrydiki Issaakidou, Dancer, 2012, 2013

Antoniy Ivanov, Choral Director, 2011, 2016

Walker J. Jackson, Tenor/GOS, 2017

Louise Jardine, Choral Director, 2011

Terre Johnson, Guest Conductor, 2010

Matthew Jones, Violin, Ensemble MidtVest, 2014

Shayna Jones, Soprano, GOS Young Artist, 2014

Mark Jurgenson, Tenor/GOS, 2017

Stavroula Kaburakis, Dancer, 2012

Klodjan Kacani, Tenor, 2012

Michael Kalentzis, Choral Director, 2014

Christina Kalliaridou, Choral Director, 2012

Stella Kaltsou, Lighting Designer, 2012, 2013, 2015, 2016

Nikolaos Karagiaouris, Bass, GOS Student, 2012-2014, 2016, 2017

Kimon Karoutzos, Bass, Stratos Vougas Quartet, 2014

Eleni Karaindrou, Composer, 2013

Mania Karavassili, Dancer, 2013

Dimitrios Karavelis, Choral Director, 2013

Lefki Karpodinis, Pianist, 2018

Edvin Kastrati, Bass, 2012

Afroditi Kasouta, Soprano, 2015

Ioannis Kavouras, Tenor, 2016

Dimitri Kavrakos, Bass, 2012, 2013

Marios Kazas, Pianist/GOS, 2017, 2019

Theodoros Kerkezos, Saxophone, 2015

Viktoria Horoshunova, Soprano, GOS Young Artist, 2016

Richard Kidd, Actor, 2009

Melody Kielisch, Soprano, 2006, 2007

Sergej Kiselev, Tenor, 2006

Jeffrey Kitson, Choral Director, 2015

Spyros Klapsis, Choral Director, 2010, 2011, 2013

Konstantinos Klironomos, Tenor, 2009

Marta Kluczynska, Conducting Associate, 2017, 2018

Wolfgang Kluge, Pianist/Assistant Conductor/GOS, 2017, 2019

Taryn Knerr, Soprano, 2013

Beatrice Knop, Dancer, 2010

Giorgos Kolios, Set Design Concept; Technical Director, 2010, 2019

George Kontrafouris, Piano, Stratos Vougas Quartet, 2014

Dimitris Kontizas, Sound & Light, 2014

Nikos Kontzias, Sound & Light, 2012, 2014

Asiya Korepanova, Pianist, 2016

Stefanos Koroneos, Baritone, 2019

Anton Koruti, Dancer, 2012, 2013

Vassilis Kostopoulos, Bass, 2013-2015, 2017

Vanessa Kourkoulou, Dancer, 2013

Kirill Kourlaev, Dancer, 2009

Adonis Kourutis, Dancer, 2013

Maria Koussouni, Dancer, 2010- 2013

Zafris Koutelieris, Bass, 2010, 2013

Rainer Krenstetter, Dancer, 2010

Sydney Kucine, Soprano, 2019

Alex Drakos Ktistakis, Drummer, 2013

Edyta Kulczak, Mezzo-soprano, 2008

Asteris Kutulas, Filmmaker, 2011

Dimitris Kyriazis, Electric Bass, Spyros Anemis, 2013

Chen Laks, Soprano, 2012

Akis Lalousis, Baritone, 2009

Iris Lamanna, Guest Conductor, 2011

Robert E. Lamb, Conductor, 2011

David Lander, Lighting Design, 2011

Eilana Lappalainen, Soprano, Artistic Director, GOS, 2005-2019

Jennifer Larmore, Mezzo-soprano, 2007

Juana Rodriguez Larreta; Dancer and Percussionist: Egyptian Darbuka, Bendir, Cajon Flamenco; 2019

Kostantinos Latsos, Tenor, 2017

Gerard Lavalle, Actor, 2013

James Lavender, Actor, 2009

Anastasios Lazarou, Baritone, GOS Young Artist, 2013

Michael Wade Lee, Tenor, 2014, 2019

Mikaela Leivadaara, 2015

Joseph Lim, Baritone, 2016

Dimitris Livadiotis, Drums, Stratos Vougas Quartet, 2014

Tommaso Longquich, Clarinet, Ensemble MidtVest, 2014

Michelle L. Louer, Guest Conductor and Choral Director, 2018

Manos Loutas, Bass, Dimitri Vassilakis Quartet, 2014

Thomas Louziotis, Choral Director, 2011-2013

Israel Lozano, Tenor, 2011

Alessandro Luciano, Tenor, 2018

David Lynch with Human Touch, 2007

Nina Lyristakis, Mezzo-soprano, 2019

Gary L. Mabry, Choral Director, 2012, 2017

Petros Magoulas, Bass, 2019

Lianne Maitland, Viola, Obsessions Octet, 2014

Christina Makridou, Dancer, 2013

Eustathios Makris, Choral Director, 2013

Miranda Makrynioti, Mezzo-soprano, 2017, 2018

Nikos Maliaras, Choral Director, 2011-2013, 2015

David Malis, Baritone, Director, 2013, 2018

Jenia Manoussaki, Pianist, 2006, 2013, 2015, 2016, 2017

Myrsini Margariti, Soprano, 2010, 2011

Nikos Masourakis, Baritone, 2019

Thomas Massey, Tenor, 2013

Pietro Masi, Baritone, 2005

Maria Francesca Mazzara, Soprano, 2005

Nancy Meckler, Director, 2011

Peter Meineck, Artistic Director Aquila, 2009, 2012

Sofia Meineck, Actor, 2012

Manu Melaerts, Trumpet, 2013

Maria Emma Meligopoulou, Choral Director, 2011

Deborah A. Mello, Choral Director, 2015

Natalia Melnik, Mezzo-soprano, 2015

Raul Melo, Tenor, 2010

Eltion Merja, Dancer, 2018

Irene Messoloras, Conductor, 2011

Ronda Metszies, Cello, Obsessions Octet, 2014

Lissa Meyvis, Soprano, 2015, 2016

Georgios Michalakis, Actor/Narrator, 2015, 2016

Maria Michalopoulou, Choral Director, 2019

Gilmond Miftari, Tenor, 2012

Giorgio Aristo Mikroutsikos, Tenor, 2006, 2007

Gary Miller, Choral Director, 2012

Kailey Miller, Mezzo-soprano, GOS Apprentice, 2014

Sherrill Milnes, Artistic Director, 2000

Igor Milos, Dancer, 2010

Ricardo Mirabelli, Tenor, 2013

Ann Moeller, Conductor, 2011

Carmine Monaco, Bass, 2005

Paco Montalvo, Violinist, 2013

Armando Mora, Baritone, 2006

Theodore Moraitis, Bass, 2011

Amedeo Moretti, Tenor, 2005

Jane DeLoach Morison, Choral Direcctor, 2014

Erica Muller, Soprano, 2012, 2014

Wendolin Pazitka Munroe, Choral Director, 2012

Katrien Nauwelaerts, Soprano, 2013

Carol Nelson, Choral Director, 2014

Karl Nelson, Choral Director, 2013

Karl Nelwelsen, Sprano, GOS Apprentice, 2014

Mary-Ellen Nesi, Mezzo-soprano, 2013

Alexander Neskov, Dancer, 2012, 2013

Lisa Newill-Smith, Soprano, 2015

Russi Nikoff, Bass, 2010

Lloyd Notice, Actor, 2009

Jiri Novak, Assistant Stage Director, 2010, 2011

Cian O'Mahony, Bassoonist, 2013

Michael O'Neal, Choral Director, 2010

Camille Ortiz-Lafont, Soprano, GOS Resident Artist, 2014, 2017

George Pachos, Stage Director, GOS, 2013

Pier Paolo Pacini, Director, GOS, 2011

Giovanni Pacor, Conductor, 2016-2019

Grigor Palikarov, Conductor, 2013, 2014

Giovanni Battista Palmieri, Tenor, 2008

Eleni Panagiotopoulou, Soprano, 2012

Tania Panayanopoulou, Pianist, 2005

Sergio Panajia, Tenor, 2005

Emmanuel Papadopoulos, Baritone, 2015

Manos Papadopoulos, Bass, 2014

Marios Papadopoulos, Pianist, 2019

Christos Papageorgiou, Pianist, 2012, 2013, 2015, 2016, 2017

Elia Papaioannou, Pianist, 2013

Marissia Papalexiou, Mezzo-soprano, 2010, 2011

Stratos Papanoussis, Dancer, 2013

Manolis Papasifakis, Coach, Accompanist, 2000, 2011-2013, 2015, 2016, 2017, 2019

Dimitris Papatheodorou, Choral Director, 2013

Michalis Pappas, Dancer, 2013

Maya Pardo, Mezzo-soprano, 2019

Gian Luca Pasolini, Tenor, 2018

Alessandra Pasquali, Assistant Choreographer, 2011

Takis Paterelis, Saxophonist, 2013

Jonathan Peacock, Choral Director, 2017

Eno Peci, Dancer, 2009, 2010, 2011

Galen Dean Peiskee, Accompanist, 2011

Carry Persson, Bass-baritone, 2018

Sofia Pintzou, Dancer, 2011, 2018

Benoit Pitre, Bass-baritone/GOS, 2017

Mina Polychronou, Soprano, 2013

Pantelis Polychronidis, Pianist, 2015, 2016, 2019

George Polyhronakos, Drums, Dimitri Vassilakis Quartet, 2014

Andreas Post, Baritone, 2015, 2016

Rosa Poulimenou, Soprano and Choral Director, 2008, 2010

Christina Poupalou, Soprano, 2015, 2016

William Powers, Bass-baritone, 2007

Maria Prinz, Pianist, 2014

Ta'u Pupu'a, Tenor, 2019

Rafail Pylarinos, Conductor, 2016

Quartetto L'Anima, String Quartet, 2017

Ellen Rabiner, Contralto, 2008

Nikoleta Rallis, Soprano/GOS Young Artist, 2013

Kostas Rassidakis, Baritone, 2010

Maria Ratkova, Mezzo-soprano, 2012

Marina Rechkalova, Choral Director, 2012-2014

Caitlin Redding, Mezzo-soprano, 2018, 2019

Liat Lidor Reich, Soprano/GOS, 2017

Marlynn Rey, Choral Director, 2017

Beth Richey, Choral Director, 2012

Rogelio Riojas-Nolasco, Assistant Conductor, 2011-2013

Renato Ripo, Cellist, 2014

Virginia-Gene Rittenhouse, Conductor, 2008

Earl Rivers, Guest Conductor, 2011

Juan Antonio Rodriguez; Clarinet, Kaval, Irish Flute, Bagpipes, and Whistle; 2019

Mitchell Roe, Tenor, 2013

Gianni Romangiolli, Director, 2005, 2006

Katerina Roussou, Mezzo-soprano, 2016, 2018

Veoniki Roussou, Pianist, 2013

Yiorgos Roussos, Master of Ceremonies, 2013

Viktor Rud, Baritone, 2019

Terry Russell, Choral Director, 2009, 2013

John Rutter, Composer, Conductor, 2012, 2014

Klaus Salge, Filmmaker, 2011

Alessandra Salmieri, Movement, Dance, 2013

David Samuel, Viola, Ensemble MidtVest, 2014

Desiree Sanchez, Director & Production Designer, 2009, 2012

Kent Sangster, Jazz Director, 2014

Craig Sanphy, Tenor, 2015, 2019

Manos Saridakis, Pianist, 2013

Karina Sarkissova, Dancer, 2009

Alicia Saunders, Flutist, 2008

Dirk Schattner, Stage Director, 2012-2016

Katherin Schwessinger, Soprano, GOS Young Artist, 2016

Michael Seibel, Sprechrolle/Stage Director, 2019

Sonja Sepulveda, Choral Director, 2013, 2018

Alexandra Sesenton, Soprano, GOS, 2016

Anastasia Serdsev, Apprentice conductor, 2015

Arkady Serper, Accompanist, 2011, 2017

Laura Kakis Serper, Choral Director/ Guest Conductor, 2011, 2017

Dimitris Sgouros, Pianist, 2012

Vaishnavi Sharma, Actor, 2009

Tim Sharp, Principal Guest Conductor, 2011

Martin Sherman, Playwright, 2011

Igor Siatzko, Dancer, 2013

Angeliki Sigourou, Choreographer GOS, 2011-2013, 2015

Selena Siri, Soprano, GOS Young Apprentice, 2016

Karina Skreszewska-Trapezanidou, Soprano, 2009

Jan Snmets, Trombonist, 2013

Detlef Soelter, Stage Director, 2016-2019

Daisuke Sogawa, Assistant Stage Director, Japanese Consultant, 2017

Stavros Solomos, Choral Director, 2012, 2013

Thanassis Solomos, Dancer, 2013

Femke Sonnen, Violinist, 2013

Mikhail Sosnovsky, Dancer, 2009

Spyros Souladkis, Pianist, 2015-2018

Lena Sourmeli, Conductor, 2011

Tamara Alves Dornelas Souza, Dancer, 2018

Randall Speer, Choral Director, 2013

Pavel Sporcl, Violinist, 2016

Mark Stamper, Choral Director, 2011

Elizabeth Stanworth, Soprano, GOS YoungArtist, 2016, 2017

Valentin Stefanov, Choral Director, 2011, 2013-2014

Aneliya Stefanova, Choral Director, 2014

Alina Stergianou, Dancer, 2013

Chen Stern, Mezzo-soprano, 2013

Rita Stinner, Choral Director, 2015

Valentin Stoica, Dancer, 2018

Antonio Stragapede, Bass, 2006, 2008

Dina Strani, Stage Director, 2019

Marilena Striftobola, Soprano, 2014-2018

Daniel Sutton, Pianist, GOS, 2011-2017, 2019

Peter Svensson, Tenor, 2012

Aliya Tanikpaev, Dancer, 2009

Iuliia Tarasova, Soprano, GOS, 2016

Taximi, 2007, 2008

John Taylor, Bassist, Obsessions Octet, 2014

Foskolos Tchanos, Bass, 2012

James Tennant, Cellist, 2012

Mikis Theodorakis, Composer, 2011, 2018

Charalambos Theotokatos, Choral Director, 2015

David R. Thye, Chorus Master, 2018

Peter Tiboris, Festival Founder and Conductor, 2005-2019

Roger Tilley, Choral Director, 2015

Paul Torkelson, Choral Director, 2019

Bradley Trammel, Tenor, 2011

Sotiris Triantis, Baritone, GOS, 2014

Marilena Trikoglou, Mezzo-soprano, 2015

Trio 92: Maciej Skarbek, Pianist; Nadja Kalmyova, Violinist; Loukia Loulaki, Cellist, 2015

Dimitra Trypi, Soprano, 2019

Christian Tschelebiew, Bass, 2019

Lisa Tsikoudis, Movement, Dance/GOS, 2013, 2015

Irini Tsirakidis, Soprano, 2007, 2013

Costas Tsourakis, Bass, 2018

Christina Gourgoura Tsourounaki, Mezzo-soprano, GOS, 2015, 2016

Randal Turner, Baritone, 2013

Natalia Ushakova, Soprano, 2011

Danielle Vaillancourt, Mezzo-soprano, GOS Young Artist, 2014, 2016

Veronika Vakondiou, Pianist/GOS, 2013, 2015

Nicky Vanoppen, Dancer, 2011

Katerina Vasilikou, Choral Director, 2012, 2013

Miguel Angel Vasquez, Baritone/GOS, 2017

Dimitri Vassilakis, Saxophonist, Composer, 2014

Argiris Vassileiou, Bass, 2014

Maria Vassilopoulos, GOS Italian Coach, 2011, 2013-2017, 2019

Augusto Garcia Vazquez, Bass, 2012

Carlos Vazquez, Pianist, GOS, 2012, 2013

Katrien Verbeke, Pianist, 2013

Dimitris Vezyroglou, Pianist, GOS, 2013, 2016

Diego Alvaez Vilches, Baitone, GOS Young Artist, 2014

Stefano Viti, Baritone, 2005, 2006

Stratos Vougas , Tenor Saxophone, Stratos Vougas Quartet, 2007, 2014, 2018

Elizabeth Wakehouse, Actor, 2012

Michael Brownlee Walker, Pianist, GOS Faculty, 2013-2015

Franziska Wallner-Hollinek, Dancer, 2011

Heather Watson, Soprano, GOS Young Apprentice, 2016

Johannes Weigand, Stage Director, 2017

Karolina Weltrowska, Violinist, Ensemble MidtVest, 2014

Brent Werzner, Actor, 2012

Nadine Whitney, Choral Director, 2011

Candace Wicke, Choral Director and Conductor, 2019

Kathryn Wieckhorst, Soprano/Stage Manager, 2013, 2015, 2016, 2019

Richard Sheridan Willis, Actor, 2012

Alexander Winn, Baritone, GOS Young Artist, 2014

David Wishart, Pianist, 2015

William Wyman, Conductor, 2015

Yannis Xylas, Pianist, Cembalist, 2005, 2006, 2011

Maria Yakovleva, Dancer, 2009

Neda Yamach, Violinist, Obsessions Octet, 2014

Lifan Yang, Tenor, 2015, 2019

Stella Yiaglou, Pianist, 2013

Yasmin Yitzhak-van der Hall, Mezzo-soprano, 2014

Paul Zachariades, Male mezzo-soprano, 2011

Damir Zakirov, Tenor, 2018

Renato Zanella, Festival Dance Director, Choreographer, Director, 2009-2013, 2017, 2018

Vasko Zdravkov, Baritone, GOS Young Artist, 2014, 2017

Danilo Zeka, Dancer, 2011-2013

Zoe Zeniodi, Conductor, 2014, 2015, 2016, 2017

Lydia Zervanos, Soprano, 2015, 2016, 2017

Konstantinos Zervos, Baritone, 2013

Michalis Zouloufos, Actor, 2013

Maria Zouves, Artist-in-Residence, 2000

ZZ Trio: Myrsini Margariti, Soprano; Natalia Gerakis, Flutist; Zoe Zeniodi, Pianist, 2015

XVIII. INTERNATIONAL DANCE ENSEMBLES AND ORCHESTRAS THAT HAVE APPEARED, SINCE 2005, AT THE FESTIVAL OF THE AEGEAN, SYROS, GREECE

Dance Ensembles:

Akropoditi Dance Theater of Syros, Greece

Greek National Opera Ballet

Ballet of the National Opera of
Bucharest, Romania
Orchestras:
Bohuslav Martinů Philharmonic,
Czech Republic, 2007
New England Symphonic Ensemble,
2006
Pan-European Philharmonia, Poland,
2009-2011, 2015-2019

Pazardzhik Symphony Orchestra,
2013, 2014
Rome Philharmonic, 2005
Soloists of the National Opera House
of Brussels, 2013
Symphony Orchestra of the National
Theatre of Opera and Ballet,
Tirana, Albania, 2012

XIX. GREEK LANGUAGE TRANSLATIONS

ΠΡΟΛΟΓΟΣ ΤΟΥ JOHN RUTTER

Αν είχα ένα βιβλιοπωλείο θα δυσκολευόμουν πολύ να αποφασίσω πού ακριβώς να τοποθετήσω το βιβλίο «Peter Tiboris: a Musical Odyssey». Ανήκει άραγε στις βιογραφίες, στην κοινωνική ιστορία, στη μουσική, στις επιχειρηματικές σπουδές, στα ταξίδια ή μήπως είναι ένα βιβλίο αυτοβοήθειας; Περιλαμβάνει όλες αυτές τις κατηγορίες και ακόμη περισσότερες, με την απόλυτα συναρπαστική ιστορία ενός Αμερικανού μουσικού από μια μικρή πόλη του Ουισκόνσιν, εγγονού Ελλήνων μεταναστών, με μεγάλα όνειρα για τον τομέα της μουσικής που έχει επιλέξει, και τα οποία πραγματοποιεί. Η οδύσσειά του τον οδηγεί στη Νέα Υόρκη ως ιδρυτή και επικεφαλής μιας εταιρείας που φέρνει χιλιάδες μουσικούς από όλη την Αμερική για να εμφανιστούν στο Carnegie Hall και παίρνει χιλιάδες άλλους για να εμφανιστούν στις μεγάλες μουσικές πόλεις της Ευρώπης και όχι μόνο. Μαθαίνουμε για την ελληνική του κληρονομιά, για τη φτώχεια που οδήγησε τους παππούδες του να αναζητήσουν μια νέα ζωή στην Αμερική, για την Ελληνορθόδοξη Πίστη και Παράδοση που η οικογένειά του διατήρησε σταθερά σε μια νέα χώρα και που τον στηρίζει μέχρι σήμερα. Βλέπουμε τους οικογενειακούς δεσμούς που στηρίζουν τόσο έντονα την ελληνοαμερικανική ζωή, το ήθος και την εργασιακή ηθική που του εμφύσησε με ευγένεια ο ευγενικός πατέρας του.

Είμαι Βρετανός· για αιώνες οι πρόγονοί μου ασκούσαν τα βιοτεχνικά τους επαγγέλματα στα γεμάτα υγρασία νησιά μας, μέχρι που οι ευρύτερες εκπαιδευτικές ευκαιρίες του εικοστού αιώνα μας ανέδειξαν σε υψηλότερες επαγγελματικές τάξεις - κάτι που δεν αποτελεί υλικό για μια συναρπαστική αφήγηση. Μου προκαλεί δέος να σκέφτομαι ότι σχεδόν πίσω από κάθε Αμερικανό κρύβεται μια δραματική οικογενειακή ιστορία, συχνά φτώχειας και διώξεων ... ο πόνος της εγκατάλειψης μιας αγαπημένης πατρίδας, οι ελπίδες και οι φόβοι που βίωσαν οι μετανάστες καθώς άρχιζαν ξανά τη ζωή τους σε μια νέα χώρα, η αφομοίωση σε μια νέα κουλτούρα, οι ιστορίες επιτυχίας που απολαμβάνουν ορισμένοι, η αναζήτηση των προγονικών ριζών που μπορεί να έρθει με μια μεταγενέστερη γενιά. Στην περίπτωση του Peter Tiboris τα έχουμε όλα αυτά· παρενθετικά, θυμάται ότι δεν θα ζούσε στην Αμερική αν δεν είχε προηγηθεί η φυλλοξήρα που έπληξε τη γαλλική σοδειά σταφυλιών τη δεκαετία του 1880. (Μπορείτε να μάθετε το γιατί στο κεφάλαιο X).

Ο Αλέξανδρος Κιτροέφ καταγράφει αυτό το κομμάτι της εκπληκτικής ιστορίας της Αμερικής, μέσα από την ιστορία ενός νεαρού άνδρα που βρίσκει το δρόμο του στον κόσμο της μουσικής - σίγουρα μια περίπτωση της παλιάς ρήσης που λέει ότι δεν επιλέγεις τη μουσική ως τρόπο ζωής, αλλά αυτή σε επιλέγει. Γνωρίζουμε τους μέντορες του Peter και μαθαίνουμε τις πρώτες επιρροές που τον επηρέασαν, αλλά στη συνέχεια τα γεγονότα παίρνουν μια απρόβλεπτη τροπή καθώς παρασύρεται στο παράλληλο σύμπαν της επιχειρηματικότητας - όχι από επιθυμία για πλούτη ή καταξίωση, αλλά για να κυνηγήσει το όραμά του να ανεβάσει ερασιτέχνες και σπουδαστές μουσικούς στον κόσμο της υψηλού επιπέδου επαγγελματικής εκτέλεσης, προσφέροντάς τους το ... Carnegie Hall.

Εδώ είναι που μπαίνω εγώ στην ιστορία. Ξεκινώντας το 1988, μετά από πρόσκληση του Peter, έχω διευθύνει ως προσκεκλημένος μαέστρος πάνω από 130 συναυλίες, οι περισσότερες από αυτές στο Carnegie Hall, και η εμπειρία αυτή με ολοκλήρωσε τόσο όσο ελπίζω και τους ερμηνευτές. Το να βλέπεις 200 έφηβους (ή και ενήλικες) τραγουδιστές να μεταμορφώνονται μέσα σε σαράντα οκτώ ώρες από το «δείξε μου αν μπορείς να το κάνεις αυτό» σε μία ομάδα γεμάτη γνήσια χαρά καθώς προετοιμάζουν, ας πούμε, το Ρέκβιεμ του Μότσαρτ ή του Μπραμς είναι η εμπειρία που θέλει να έχει κάθε δάσκαλος μουσικής, και πιστεύω ότι αυτό είναι που οδηγεί και τον Peter. Ένα από τα πιο όμορφα και ανταποδοτικά πράγματα που μπορούμε να κάνουμε στη ζωή μας είναι να μεταδίδουμε αυτό που γνωρίζουμε και αγαπάμε σε μια νεότερη γενιά ή σε συνομηλίκους μας. Καθώς διαβάζουμε αυτό το χρονικό της ζωής του Peter γίνεται φανερό ότι μπορεί να χαρακτηριστεί ως "μουσικός", "μαέστρος" και "επιχειρηματίας", αλλά νομίζω ότι έχει επίσης χαραγμένο στην ψυχή του το "δάσκαλος".

Δεν μπορώ, φυσικά, να είμαι αμερόληπτος, αλλά προσπαθώ να είμαι αντικειμενικός για τις παραστάσεις στις οποίες συμμετέχω, και θα έλεγα ότι το πλαίσιο που έχουν δημιουργήσει ο Peter και οι συνάδελφοί του της MidAmerica για τις παραστάσεις που δίνουμε είναι όσο το δυνατόν ιδανικότερο, με σχολαστικά σχεδιασμένα προγράμματα, έντονες και λεπτομερείς πρόβες και μια αίσθηση αυξανόμενου ενθουσιασμού καθώς ετοιμαζόμαστε να ανέβουμε στη σκηνή. Τα καταφέρνουμε πάντα όταν φτάνουμε εκεί; Η εκτίμησή μου είναι συντριπτικά θετική: από τις 130 και πλέον παραστάσεις που έχω διευθύνει, ίσως μισή ντουζίνα ήταν θαυματουργές (όταν συμβαίνει κάτι ανεξήγητο και εκπληκτικό), οι περισσότερες από τις υπόλοιπες ήταν συν ή πλην του "πράγματι πολύ ευπαρουσίαστες" - και αναπόφευκτα υπήρξαν μερικές όπου ήμουν τρομερά ευτυχής που δεν είχαμε κριτικό των New York Times στην πρώτη σειρά.

Ο Peter είναι ένας πολύπλευρος μουσικός, και η διεύθυνση ορχήστρας είναι ένα σημαντικό νήμα που διατρέχει ολόκληρη τη ζωή του. Καθώς διαβάζετε αυτό το βιβλίο, θα πάρετε μια αίσθηση του τι ωθεί έναν μαέστρο να ρισκάρει τα πάντα βρισκόμενος μπροστά σε εκατοντάδες ερμηνευτές και με το κοινό ως άγριο ζώο στην πλάτη του.

Ομολογώ ότι δεν είμαι ακόμα σίγουρος ότι γνωρίζω ο ίδιος την απάντηση σε αυτό, αλλά μου άρεσε που πλησίασα λίγο, διαβάζοντας τις σκέψεις του πάνω σε αυτή την πιο ορατή αλλά και άυλη μορφή μουσικής δραστηριότητας.

Είναι ταιριαστό το γεγονός ότι η αφήγηση του Αλέξανδρου Κιτροέφ για την οδύσσεια του Peter τελειώνει με την επιστροφή του στην πατρογονική του πατρίδα, την Ελλάδα. Αν δεν έχετε επισκεφθεί ποτέ το ειδυλλιακό νησί της Σύρου, όπου διοργανώνεται κάθε χρόνο το Φεστιβάλ Αιγαίου, θα πρέπει να το κάνετε. Το φεστιβάλ βρίσκεται πλέον στα ικανά χέρια της καταπληκτικής γυναίκας του Peter, της τραγουδίστριας της όπερας Eilana, και αν επισκεφθείτε το νησί την εποχή του φεστιβάλ, αυτή και η ομάδα της θα σας εγγυηθούν μια εμπειρία που θα θυμάστε για πολλά χρόνια.

Θα μπορούσε κανείς να επιτύχει αυτό που πέτυχε ο Peter; Λοιπόν, αν είναι αλήθεια ότι ο καθένας μπορεί να γίνει πρόεδρος των Ηνωμένων Πολιτειών, τότε ναι· αν είμαστε πιο ρεαλιστές, τότε όχι. Ο συνδυασμός της μουσικής διορατικότητας, του οράματος, της ενέργειας, της δέσμευσης και της αποφασιστικότητας του Peter να αξιοποιήσει στο έπακρο τις όποιες ευκαιρίες του προσφέρει η ζωή είναι τουλάχιστον ασυνήθιστος. Είναι αρκετά σεμνός για να ισχυριστεί ότι "όλα γίνονται για τη μουσική", και φυσικά είναι, αλλά πιστεύω ότι διαβάζοντας αυτό το βιβλίο θα μείνετε με τη σκέψη "ναι, αλλά υπάρχουν πολλά περισσότερα από αυτό". Εγώ πάντως εμπνεύστηκα διαβάζοντας για όλα αυτά, σε αυτό το συναρπαστικό χρονικό μίας αξιόλογης ζωής.

ΚΕΦΑΛΑΙΟ 1: ΤΟ ΕΚΚΛΗΣΙΑΣΤΙΚΟ ΟΡΓΑΝΟ ΣΤΟ SHEBOYGAN

Για χιλιάδες Αμερικανούς, εκ των οποίων πολλοί είναι μέλη ερασιτεχνικών και ημιεπαγγελματικών μουσικών συνόλων, χορωδιών, μπάντας και ορχηστρών, η απάντηση στην ερώτηση «Πώς φτάνεις στο Carnegie Hall» είναι μέσω του Παναγιώτη Τιμπόρη, τον πανεπιστημιακό καθηγητή μουσική που έγινε μαέστρος ορχήστρας και επιχειρηματίας κάνοντας κάτι τελείως επαναστατικό. Η εταιρεία που δημιούργησε στις αρχές της δεκαετίας του 1980 ξεκίνησε ένα πρόγραμμα που επέτρεψε σε χορωδίες από όλη τη χώρα να εμφανιστούν στο περίφημο Carnegie Hall, τη μέγιστη συναυλιακή σκηνή, σε μια ευκαιρία που για όλους σχεδόν ήταν μοναδική στη ζωή τους. Εμφανίζονταν με δικά τους οικονομικά μέσα, αλλά η MidAmerica εξασφάλιζε μια ομαλή λειτουργία που εγγυόταν ότι θα παρουσιάζονται στον πιο διάσημο μουσικό χώρο στον κόσμο, μια εμπειρία που τους άφηνε πλημμυρισμένους από υπερηφάνεια και συγκίνηση. Αυτό που ήταν επαναστατικό στο όραμα του Τιμπόρη και στον τρόπο με τον οποίο το υλοποίησε δεν ήταν μόνο το ότι ήταν μια τόσο καινοτόμος ιδέα, αλλά επίσης αντιπροσώπευε έναν εκδημοκρατισμό του κόσμου της κλασικής μουσικής της Νέας Υόρκης, καθιστώντας την εμπειρία του Carnegie διαθέσιμη σε όλους.

Συνδυάζοντας την παραγωγή συναυλιών με τον πυρήνα του σκοπού της, να φέρνει μουσικούς οργανισμούς στη Νέα Υόρκη, η MidAmerica έγινε μία από τις σημαντικότερες εταιρείες παραγωγής που σχετίζονται με το Carnegie Hall. Είναι ο πιο γόνιμος παρουσιαστής χορωδιακών συναυλιών στην ιστορία του Carnegie Hall που χρονολογείται από τις 5 Μαΐου 1891, στα εγκαίνια της αίθουσας, όταν ο Τσαϊκόφσκι διηύθυνε την πρώτη συναυλία. Επιπλέον, η MidAmerica έφτασε στην επιτυχία της με λίγο προσωπικό και πενιχρούς πόρους, αλλά τα κατάφερε επειδή ο Τιμπόρης αποδείχθηκε εξαίρετος ηγέτης. Όπως το έθεσε ένας από τους στενότερους συνεργάτες του, ο Παναγιώτης Τιμπόρης ήταν και είναι μια ασταμάτητη δύναμη και ένα αμετακίνητο αντικείμενο, ένας συνδυασμός που εξασφάλισε την επιτυχία του οράματός του. Και η επιτυχία της MidAmerica αναγνωρίστηκε παγκοσμίως, ίσως απρόθυμα από μερικούς υψηλά ιστάμενους μουσικοκριτικούς, αλλά πάντα από κορυφαίους μουσικούς που έπαιζαν ή διηύθυναν ή συνδέονταν με άλλο τρόπο με τα προγράμματά της. Και πάνω στα φτερά αυτού του καλλιτεχνικού και επιχειρηματικού εγχειρήματος ο Τιμπόρης μπόρεσε να χτίσει μια εξίσου επιτυχημένη καριέρα ως διεθνώς αναγνωρισμένος μαέστρος συμφωνικής ορχήστρας. Η δημιουργία ενός καταξιωμένου καλοκαιρινού φεστιβάλ στο νησί του Αιγαίου, τη Σύρο, αποτέλεσε το επιστέγασμα της καριέρας του.

Πολλοί από τους συνεργάτες του Τιμπόρη κατά τη διάρκεια των ετών αναγνωρίζουν τα πολλαπλά ταλέντα του και το κύρος του ως μαέστρου, αλλά κυρίως του αποδίδουν την επιτυχία του να βοηθήσει εκατοντάδες χορωδίες και χιλιάδες μουσικούς καλλιτέχνες να εμφανιστούν στο Carnegie Hall. Ο Tim Sharp, επί μακράν εκτελεστικός διευθυντής της Αμερικανικής Ένωσης Διευθυντών Χορωδιών που εργάστηκε για τη MidAmerica, θεωρεί ότι η μοναδική, τεράστια συμβολή του Τιμπόρη είναι ότι ανύψωσε τη χορωδιακή μουσική και την ανέβασε στην κορυφαία συναυλιακή σκηνή του κόσμου. Και το έκανε μόνος του, με την έννοια ότι ήταν ο πρώτος που το σκέφτηκε, που το δοκίμασε και τελικά το πέτυχε κάνοντας το υψηλή τέχνη, ξανά και ξανά επί σαράντα χρόνια. Επιπλέον, ξεπέρασε μια σειρά από εμπόδια λόγω της σαφούς κατανόησής του τι έκανε και μέσω της αδιάλλακτης επιμονής του. Ο Sharp ουσιαστικά εννοεί ότι ο Τιμπόρης προώθησε τη χορωδιακή μουσική με ένα μοναδικό όραμα και επιτυχία με τον τρόπο που ο Brian Epstein προώθησε τους Beatles και τους έκανε επιτυχημένους.

Η προέλευση του Παναγιώτη Τιμπόρη και η ζωή στη γενέτειρά του, παρέχουν μερικές ενδείξεις ότι επρόκειτο να γίνει μαέστρος κλασικής μουσικής και παραγωγός μουσικών συναυλιών. Μία από αυτές ήταν ότι σε ηλικία εννέα ετών άρχισε να παίζει όργανο στην Ελληνική Ορθόδοξη εκκλησία του Άγιου Σπυρίδωνα. Εγγονός Ελλήνων μεταναστών, μεγάλωσε ως Αμερικανός. Αυτό υποδηλώνει, τουλάχιστον θεωρητικά, ότι θα μπορούσε να έχει επιλέξει όποιο επάγγελμα ήθελε. Αλλά ακόμη και οι Αμερικανοί διαμορφώνονται από την οικογενειακή τους ιστορία και την πολιτιστική τους κληρονομιά. Πράγματι, υπήρχε ένα μοναδικό σύνολο επιλογών που έκανε ο Παναγιώτης πέραν των επιρροών του οικογενειακού του υπόβαθρου. Ο Παναγιώτης είναι Ελληνοαμερικανός τρίτης γενιάς, με άλλα λόγια ήταν οι παππούδες του που μετανάστευσαν από την Ελλάδα και εγκαταστάθηκαν στις Ηνωμένες Πολιτείες. Όπως συνέβαινε με τόσες άλλες ευρωπαϊκές εθνοτικές ομάδες που έφτασαν στην Αμερική στις αρχές του εικοστού αιώνα, το πρότυπο που ακολουθούσε η οικογένεια ήταν ότι η πρώτη γενιά συνήθως ασχολείτο με κάποιο είδος χειρωνακτικής εργασίας ή άνοιγε μια μικρή επιχείρηση, και χάρη στη σκληρή δουλειά τους τα παιδιά τους, ειδικά τα αγόρια, ήταν σε θέση να συνεχίσουν τις σπουδές τους και να ακολουθήσουν μια καριέρα ως υπάλληλοι ή στελέχη. Και αυτό ίσχυε ακόμη περισσότερο για τα παιδιά τους, όπως ο Παναγιώτης και ο μικρότερος αδελφός του Γκας. Ο πατέρας τους κατάφερε να σπουδάσει και να γίνει οδοντίατρος- και ο Γκας έκανε το ίδιο. Αντίθετα, ο Παναγιώτης ακολούθησε έναν διαφορετικό δρόμο, σπούδασε μουσική, έγινε καθηγητής μουσικής και στη συνέχεια έγινε διεθνώς αναγνωρισμένος αρχιμουσικός και παραγωγός συναυλιών. Ειδικά στην περίπτωση των ελληνοαμερικανικών οικογενειών, αυτή ήταν μια ιδιαίτερη πορεία καριέρας. Σε αντίθεση με άλλες εθνοτικές ομάδες ευρωπαϊκής καταγωγής, όπως οι Εβραίοι ή οι Ιταλοί, οι Ελληνοαμερικανοί δεν είχαν πλούσια παράδοση συνθετών και εκτελεστών κλασικής μουσικής στην Ευρώπη ή στον Νέο Κόσμο.

Όταν ο Παναγιώτης γεννήθηκε το 1947, υπήρχαν πολύ λίγα ελληνικά ονόματα στον κόσμο της αμερικανικής κλασικής μουσικής, αν και μεγάλα. Ο Δημήτρης Μητρόπουλος ήταν ο αρχιμουσικός της Συμφωνικής Ορχήστρας της Μινεάπολης, μια θέση στην οποία υπηρετούσε από το 1937. Ωστόσο, ο Μητρόπουλος θεωρείτο πάντα ένας Ευρωπαίος που είχε εισέλθει στον κόσμο της κλασικής μουσικής της Αμερικής. Το ακόμη μεγαλύτερο όνομα, η Μαρία Κάλλας, ήταν ελάχιστα γνωστή όταν γεννήθηκε ο Παναγιώτης. Ένα χρόνο νωρίτερα είχε κάνει το ντεμπούτο της στο εξωτερικό, στην Ιταλία το 1946, και το ντεμπούτο της στη Metropolitan Opera θα ερχόταν το 1956. Και παρόλο που ήταν κόρη Ελλήνων μεταναστών και γεννήθηκε στη Νέα Υόρκη, κανείς δεν τη θεωρούσε ποτέ Ελληνοαμερικανίδα. Η Κάλλας ήταν μια διεθνής ντίβα της όπερας. Αυτό σήμαινε ότι δεν υπήρχαν σχεδόν καθόλου πρότυπα για τον Παναγιώτη όσον αφορά την καταγωγή του. Λιγότερο γνωστός στο ευρύ κοινό ήταν ο Νίκος Μοσχονάς, ένας μπάσος της όπερας που γεννήθηκε στην Ελλάδα και εκανε το ντεμπούτο του στη Νέα Υόρκη στη Metropolitan Opera το 1937 και τραγούδησε εκεί μέχρι το 1971, συνολικά και εντυπωσιακά 719 παραστάσεις. Μετά τη συνταξιοδότησή του, ο Μοσχονάς δίδαξε στην Academy of

Vocal Arts στη Φιλαδέλφεια, την πόλη στην οποία πέθανε το 1975 λίγο πριν από τα εξηκοστά όγδοα γενέθλιά του. Το 1940 ο Μοσχονάς είχε εμφανιστεί στη Νέα Υόρκη για να συγκεντρώσει χρήματα για να βοηθήσει την Ελλάδα στην προσπάθειά της για τον Β' Παγκόσμιο Πόλεμο και ο πιανίστας ήταν ένας Έλληνας γεννημένος στην Αμερική, ο Κωνσταντίνος Καλλίνικος. Γεννημένος στη Νέα Υόρκη το 1913, ο Καλλίνικος θα αποτελούσε την εξαίρεση στον κανόνα που ήθελε τα περισσότερα παιδιά Ελλήνων μεταναστών να κάνουν καριέρα στις επιχειρήσεις ή να γίνονται γιατροί ή δικηγόροι. Ο Καλλίνικος δεν ήταν μόνο πιανίστας αλλά και μαέστρος - το ντεμπούτο του ως μαέστρος στη New York City Opera έγινε το 1958 - και έγινε γνωστός ως ο επί μακράν συνοδός του διάσημου Ιταλοαμερικανού βαρύτονου Mario Lanza. Υπήρχαν επίσης μερικοί άλλοι Ελληνοαμερικανοί στον κόσμο της κλασικής μουσικής των Ηνωμένων Πολιτειών που ήταν σύγχρονοι του Τίμπορη, και τους περισσότερους από αυτούς θα τους συναντήσουμε αργότερα σε αυτό το βιβλίο.

Ωστόσο, υπήρχε ένα είδος μουσικής με το οποίο ήταν εξοικειωμένοι οι Έλληνες μετανάστες και το οποίο έφεραν μαζί τους στην Αμερική στις αρχές του εικοστού αιώνα. Ήταν η μουσική της Λειτουργίας, του Βυζαντίου και της θρησκείας τους, της Ελληνικής Ορθοδοξίας, η οποία είχε επιβιώσει μέσα στους αιώνες, αν και είχε υποστεί αλλαγές. Η Ελληνική Ορθοδοξία είναι η εκδοχή του Χριστιανισμού που επικράτησε στην Ανατολική Μεσόγειο και την Ανατολική Ευρώπη, και της οποίας ο τίτλος "Ορθοδοξία" σημαίνει το αληθινό δόγμα χωρίς να υποδηλώνει μια συντηρητική εκδοχή του χριστιανισμού, όπως κάνει ο ορθόδοξος ιουδαϊσμός για την αντίστοιχη πίστη. Μια δημοφιλής εκδοχή αυτής της βυζαντινής μουσικής είχε αναπτυχθεί στην Ελλάδα από τον Ιωάννη Σακελλαρίδη (1853-1938), έναν Έλληνα μουσικό και ψάλτη, ο οποίος πρότεινε μια απλουστευμένη εκδοχή του διαδεδομένου ρεπερτορίου της βυζαντινής ψαλτικής που ισχυριζόταν ότι είχε καθαρίσει από τις ανατολίτικες επιρροές.

Η άνοδος των δυτικών μουσικών στυλ στις εκκλησίες της Αθήνας συνέπεσε με την άνοδο της ελληνικής μετανάστευσης στις Ηνωμένες Πολιτείες. Οι μετανάστες έφεραν στον Νέο Κόσμο τόσο την παραδοσιακή βυζαντινή ψαλμωδία όσο και τη νέα αθηναϊκή θρησκευτική μουσική, αλλά διαπίστωσαν ότι το νέο πολιτισμικό τους περιβάλλον ήταν πιο φιλόξενο για τη δεύτερη. Έργα ρωσικού τύπου δεν ήταν άγνωστα στην Αμερική, αλλά ήταν η μουσική του Σακελλαρίδη που σύντομα έγινε αποδεκτή ως "παραδοσιακή" στις ελληνορθόδοξες εκκλησίες της. Αυτό προφανώς οφειλόταν εν μέρει στην απλότητά της, στην εύκολη διαθεσιμότητα των συχνά ανατυπωμένων μουσικών εκδόσεων και στη στενή μελωδική ομοιότητα μεγάλου μέρους της με πιο παραδοσιακές μορφές ψαλτικής. Σημαντική ήταν επίσης η ενεργή καλλιέργειά της από επιφανείς μουσικούς και κληρικούς. Αρκετοί μαθητές του Σακελλαρίδη μετανάστευσαν στις Ηνωμένες

Πολιτείες και ανέλαβαν και άλλες μουσικές θέσεις: Γεώργιος Αναστασίου (Washington, DC και αργότερα Tarpon Springs, Florida), Άγγελος Δέσφης (Los Angeles) και Χρήστος Βρυωνίδης (1894-1961), ο πρώτος καθηγητής βυζαντινής ψαλμωδίας στην Ελληνική Ορθόδοξη Θεολογική Σχολή του Τιμίου Σταυρού, την αρχιεπισκοπική σχολή που βρίσκεται σήμερα στο Brookline της Μασαχουσέτης. Η συνέχεια της μουσικής ανάπτυξης σύμφωνα με τις δυτικές κατευθύνσεις εξασφαλίστηκε από την υποστήριξη των Αρχιεπισκόπων Αθηναγόρα (1931-49), Μιχαήλ (1949-59) και Ιακώβου (1959-96), οι οποίοι προώθησαν μικτές χορωδίες με όργανα. Ο πατέρας του Παναγιώτη, Αναστάσιος, ήταν ένας από τους πολλούς Έλληνες μετανάστες που ασπάστηκαν αυτή τη θρησκευτική μουσική και εξέφρασε την αγάπη του γι' αυτήν με το να γίνει ψάλτης και αργότερα διευθυντής χορωδίας στην εκκλησία που η οικογένεια επισκεπτόταν τακτικά, τον Άγιο Σπυρίδωνα, στο Sheboygan του Wisconsin. Όπως θα δούμε, η ενασχόληση του πατέρα του με την εκκλησιαστική μουσική επηρέασε βαθιά τον Παναγιώτη και μπορεί να ειπωθεί ότι αποτέλεσε το σημείο εισόδου του στον ευρύτερο κόσμο της μουσικής.

ΑΠΟ ΤΗΝ ΠΕΛΟΠΟΝΝΗΣΟ ΣΤΟ SHEBOYGAN, WISCONSIN

Οι παππούδες και οι γιαγιάδες του Παναγιώτη Τιμπόρη ήταν μεταξύ των χιλιάδων Ελλήνων που μετανάστευσαν στις Ηνωμένες Πολιτείες στις αρχές του εικοστού αιώνα. Το όνομα της οικογένειας ήταν Τσιμπούρης εκείνη την εποχή και ο παππούς του Παναγιώτης Αναστάσιος ήταν ένας από τους χιλιάδες Έλληνες που αναζήτησαν ένα καλύτερο μέλλον στις Ηνωμένες Πολιτείες στις αρχές του αιώνα. Το χωριό στο οποίο γεννήθηκε ο Παναγιώτης το 1871 και το οποίο άφησε πίσω του ήταν το Δεδέμπεη. Βρισκόταν στο νοτιοδυτικό τμήμα της Αρκαδίας, της κεντρικής περιοχής της Πελοποννήσου. Το Δεδέμπεη ήταν πολύ μικρό για να αξίζει να αναφερθεί στις πολυάριθμες ιστορικές ή ταξιδιωτικές καταγραφές της Πελοποννήσου του 19ου αιώνα. Μεταξύ των πολύ λίγων είναι και μία που παρουσιάζει τον Θεόδωρο Κολοκοτρώνη, τον στρατιωτικό οπλαρχηγό που ηγήθηκε της ελληνικής επανάστασης κατά των Οθωμανών το 1821, να φτάνει εκεί το συγκεκριμένο έτος και να σταματάει για να σκεφτεί την επόμενη κίνησή του σε μία από τις πρώτες μάχες της εκστρατείας. Το Δεδέμπεη εμφανίζεται επίσης σε ένα βιβλίο του Βρετανού αρχαιοδίφη τοπογράφου William Martin Leake με τίτλο Peloponnesiaca που εκδόθηκε το 1848. Το 1927 μια ελληνική κυβερνητική επιτροπή που ανέλαβε να μετονομάσει τα τούρκικα ονόματα χωριών σε ελληνικά μετονόμασε το Δεδέμπεη σε Τριπόταμο που σημαίνει τρία ποτάμια. Ήταν μια απόφαση που βασίστηκε στη θέση του χωριού κοντά στον Αλφειό ποταμό και σε δύο από τους παραποτάμους του. Ο ποταμός Αλφειός που έρεε κοντά στο χωριό ήταν, κατά τη μυθολογία, ένας από τους ποταμούς που ανακατεύθυνε ο Ηρακλής στον πέμπτο του μόχθο προκειμένου να καθαρίσει τη κοπριά των στάβλων του Αυγεία.

Όπως συνηθιζόταν τότε, ο Παναγιώτης Τσιμπούρης παντρεύτηκε μια γυναίκα από το χωριό του. Η Καλλιόπη Φωτοπούλου γεννήθηκε στο Δεδέμπεη το 1880 και παντρεύτηκαν το 1897, όταν εκείνος ήταν 26 ετών και εκείνη 16. Η Καλλιόπη ήταν ένα από τα δέκα παιδιά, εννέα κορίτσια και ένα αγόρι. Ο μεγάλος αριθμός των αδελφών της δεν ήταν σπάνιος, οι αγροτικές οικογένειες είχαν την τάση να κάνουν πολλά παιδιά, επειδή τα ποσοστά θνησιμότητας ήταν υψηλά, αν και σε καθοδική πορεία στην Πελοπόννησο τις δύο τελευταίες δεκαετίες του 19ου αιώνα. Τα παιδιά βοηθούσαν επίσης τις αγροτικές οικογένειες με τις εργασίες στα χωράφια. Η Καλλιόπη γέννησε έναν γιο, τον Κωνσταντίνο, το 1898 και μια κόρη, την Ασημώ, λίγα χρόνια αργότερα.

Το Δεδέμπεη και η υπόλοιπη Πελοπόννησος είχαν γνωρίσει μια σύντομη περίοδο ευημερίας τη δεκαετία του 1880, όταν τα σταφύλια της αντικατέστησαν τα γαλλικά σταφύλια στις διεθνείς αγορές, επειδή οι αμπελώνες της Γαλλίας είχαν πληγεί από μια ασθένεια. Οι αγρότες της Πελοποννήσου και των γειτονικών νησιών του Ιονίου στράφηκαν στην καλλιέργεια σταφυλιών. Οι περισσότεροι από αυτούς διέθεταν μικρά οικόπεδα, συνήθως όχι μεγαλύτερα από τέσσερα στρέμματα, αλλά αυτό δεν τους εμπόδισε να ανταποκριθούν στην άνοδο της τιμής της σταφίδας. Οι σταφίδες ήταν σταφύλια χωρίς κουκούτσια που αποξηραίνονταν και εξάγονταν και είχαν μεγάλη ζήτηση στην Ευρώπη και ιδιαίτερα στη Βρετανία. Οι σταφίδες χρησιμοποιούνταν στις διάφορες αγγλικές πουτίγκες που αποτελούσαν βασικό συστατικό της κουζίνας της χώρας αυτής. Η Ελλάδα κατόρθωσε ακόμη και να εξάγει τις σταφίδες της στις Ηνωμένες Πολιτείες, παρά την αντίσταση των καλλιεργητών μιας παρόμοιας σταφίδας στην Καλιφόρνια. Όταν το 1896 οι σταφιδοπαραγωγοί κατάφεραν να πείσουν την κυβέρνηση να επιβάλει δασμό στην εισερχόμενη σταφίδα, οι New York Times σχολίασαν ότι το μέτρο δεν είχε "βοηθήσει πολύ τον καταναλωτή. Αργότερα, η ζήτηση για την ελληνική σταφίδα θα δημιουργηθεί λόγω της τεράστιας διαφοράς στη γεύση, τον χωρίς σπόρους καρπό της και την ποιότητά της". Δυστυχώς για την Ελλάδα, όμως, η Γαλλία ξεπέρασε την επιδημία και η ζήτηση για ελληνική σταφίδα έκανε ξαφνική βουτιά και δεν ανέκαμψε ποτέ. Ο μικροκαλλιεργητής που είχε γίνει μικροεπιχειρηματίας έπρεπε τώρα να γίνει μετανάστης προκειμένου να πληρώσει τα χρέη της οικογένειας και να τη βοηθήσει να διατηρήσει ένα από τα κύρια καθήκοντά της στην αγροτική Ελλάδα, να εξασφαλίσει μια αξιοσέβαστη προίκα για να παντρευτούν οι κόρες της.

Τότε ξεκίνησε η υπερατλαντική μετανάστευση. Οι περισσότεροι Έλληνες μετανάστες από την Αρκαδία κατευθύνθηκαν προς τις μεσοδυτικές πολιτείες, ανταποκρινόμενοι στις ευκαιρίες εργασίας που υπήρχαν εκείνη την εποχή. Αν και η συντριπτική πλειοψηφία των Ελλήνων προέρχονταν από αγροτικές περιοχές και είχαν ασχοληθεί με τη γεωργία, επέλεξαν να αναλάβουν κάθε είδους εργασία που μπορούσε να αναλάβει ένας ανειδίκευτος εργάτης ή που απαιτούσε σχετικά γρήγορη εκπαίδευση στη δουλειά. Η ιδέα ήταν ότι θα κέρδιζαν αρκετά χρήματα και θα επέστρεφαν στην Ελλάδα μετά από μερικά χρόνια. Τελικά, λιγότεροι από ένας στους τέσσερις από αυτούς κατάφεραν να το κάνουν αυτό: οι υπόλοιποι εγκαταστάθηκαν μόνιμα στις Ηνωμένες Πολιτείες, όπως και ο Παναγιώτης Τσιμπούρης. Οι πρώτοι μετανάστες από τις Πελοποννησιακές περιοχές της Αρκαδίας, της Λακωνίας και της Μεσσηνίας εγκαταστάθηκαν στο Σικάγο, τόσοι πολλοί μάλιστα που οι Έλληνες το ονόμασαν "Σικαγούπολη". Άλλοι κατευθύνθηκαν προς το St Louis που ήταν η πύλη προς τη Δύση και τις δουλειές στα ορυχεία και στον σιδηρόδρομο. Άλλοι, μεταξύ των οποίων και ο Τσιμπούρης, κατευθύνθηκαν βόρεια στο Wisconsin και ήταν μεταξύ εκείνων που εγκαταστάθηκαν στο Sheboygan. Η απόφασή τους να εγκατασταθούν εκεί, σε ένα κλίμα που ήταν τόσο βάναυσα ψυχρότερο από αυτό της Ελλάδας, ήταν μια απόδειξη της αποφασιστικότητάς τους να βρουν δουλειά και να αξιοποιήσουν στο έπακρο την απόφασή τους να έρθουν στην Αμερική.

Όταν επισκέφθηκα το Τριπόταμο με τον Τιμπόρη τον Μάρτιο του 2023, το χωριό ήταν εγκαταλελειμμένο. Τα περισσότερα μικρά αγροτικά χωριά στην Ελλάδα είναι άδεια, αλλά υπήρχε ένας επιπλέον λόγος για το Τριπόταμο. Χρησιμοποιώντας το δικαίωμα της απαλλοτρίωσης, η ελληνική εταιρεία ηλεκτρισμού (ΔΕΗ) επρόκειτο να επεκτείνει την κοντινή εξόρυξη λιγνίτη και να απαλλοτριώσει το χωριό. Το χωριό βρίσκεται σε διαδικασία μεταφοράς σε άλλη τοποθεσία εκεί κοντά και το καλοκαίρι του 2022 πραγματοποιήθηκε μια τελευταία Λειτουργία στην τοπική εκκλησία, στην οποία ένας από τους πολυελαίους ήταν δωρεά της οικογένειας Τσιμπούρη. Η εκκλησία βρισκόταν σε διαδικασία μεταφοράς, αλλά ο ιερέας, π. Βασίλειος Δάρρας είχε τα κλειδιά της μισοάδειας εκκλησίας και μας έδειξε την χάραξη του ονόματος Τσιμπούρης στον πολυέλαιο, ο οποίος πρόκειται να αποσυναρμολογηθεί και να κρεμαστεί στη νέα εκκλησία. Καθώς περπατούσαμε στο χωριό πέσαμε πάνω σε έναν κάτοικο της περιοχής, ο οποίος είχε έρθει εκείνη την ημέρα για να απομακρύνει κάποια φυτά από τον κήπο του σπιτιού του πριν τα παρασύρουν οι μπουλντόζες της ΔΕΗ. Ήξερε τα ονόματα πολλών κατοίκων του Τριπόταμου που είχαν πάει στην Αμερική. Ο Παναγιώτης Τιμπόρης δεν τους είχε ακουστά, και δεν είχαν εγκατασταθεί πουθενά κοντά στο Sheboygan του Wisconsin, όπου θα μπορούσαν να διατηρήσουν δεσμούς με τον παππού του. Μόνο όταν πολύ μεγάλος αριθμός μεταναστών από τον ίδιο τόπο μετανάστευε στην Αμερική ήταν σε θέση να σχηματίσει κάποιου είδους κοινωνία, συνήθως γνωστή ως αδελφότητα. Το Τριπόταμο δεν είχε τους αριθμούς για μια τέτοια πολυτέλεια.

Ο Παναγιώτης Τσιμπούρης έφτασε στη Βοστώνη τον Μάρτιο του 1903 με πλοίο της εταιρείας Dominion Line μετά από ένα ταξίδι που διήρκεσε σχεδόν τέσσερις εβδομάδες. Η Καλλιόπη έμεινε πίσω, αλλά ο Παναγιώτης έφερε μαζί του τον Κωνσταντίνο και την Ασημώ, τα δύο τους παιδιά, ώστε να ξεκινήσουν τις σπουδές τους και ως ένδειξη ότι αναμενόταν να μείνει στις Ηνωμένες Πολιτείες μακροπρόθεσμα. Αυτό δεν συνέβαινε με τους περισσότερους Έλληνες μετανάστες που ήλπιζαν ότι θα έβγαζαν αρκετά χρήματα και θα επέστρεφαν μετά από λίγα χρόνια. Εκείνη τη χρονιά σημειώθηκε ρεκόρ αφίξεων από την Ελλάδα, πάνω από 14.000. Οι αριθμοί κορυφώθηκαν σε περίπου 45.000 αναχωρήσεις ετησίως μέχρι το 1907. Όταν οι Ηνωμένες Πολιτείες περιόρισαν δραστικά τη μετανάστευση από τη Νοτιοανατολική Ευρώπη στις αρχές της δεκαετίας του 1920, υπήρχαν περίπου 350.000 Έλληνες στη χώρα. Η αυξανόμενη ξενοφοβία που προκάλεσε την επιβολή περιορισμών στον αριθμό των εισερχόμενων Ευρωπαίων οδήγησε επίσης στην αύξηση του αριθμού των Ελλήνων που απέκτησαν την αμερικανική υπηκοότητα. Ο Παναγιώτης ήταν πολύ μπροστά από την εποχή του. Έγινε Αμερικανός πολίτης το 1908 και άλλαξε το μικρό του όνομα σε Peter, το οποίο οι Έλληνες θεωρούσαν αποδεκτό αγγλισμό του Παναγιώτη. Πολλοί Έλληνες μετανάστες αγγλοποιούσαν το μικρό τους όνομα και πολύ συχνά το επώνυμό τους εκείνη την εποχή για να ακούγονται λιγότερο ξένοι. Η οικογένεια Τσιμπούρη ήταν μπροστά από την εποχή της κρίνοντας και από το γεγονός ότι η Καλλιόπη συνάντησε τον σύζυγό της στην Αμερική μετά από σχεδόν δώδεκα χρόνια, το 1914. Πολύ λίγες γυναίκες, ακόμη και παντρεμένες, εγκατέλειπαν την Ελλάδα για να εγκατασταθούν στις Ηνωμένες Πολιτείες τόσο νωρίς. Μόνο όταν επρόκειτο να εφαρμοστούν οι μεταναστευτικοί περιορισμοί από το Κογκρέσο, πολλοί Έλληνες μετανάστες είτε έστειλαν για τις συζύγους τους είτε προσκάλεσαν «νύφες» να τους ακολουθήσουν στην Αμερική γύρω στο 1920.

Η Καλλιόπη θα περιγράψει το ταξίδι της στον εγγονό της Παναγιώτη πολλά χρόνια αργότερα. Έφυγε από το Τριπόταμο και πήγε στο λιμάνι του Πειραιά και ταξίδεψε στη Χάβρη της Γαλλίας, όπου επιβιβάστηκε σε ένα πλοίο με περίπου 800 Έλληνες μετανάστες που θα τους μετέφερε στην άλλη πλευρά του Ατλαντικού. Εκείνη την εποχή το ταξίδι που χρειαζόταν για να διασχίσει τον Ατλαντικό ήταν μεταξύ οκτώ και δώδεκα ημερών. Όσοι επέβαιναν στην τρίτη θέση, όπως η Καλλιόπη, έπρεπε να φέρουν τα δικά τους κλινοσκεπάσματα. Η διαδικασία υποδοχής των μεταναστών στη Βοστώνη ήταν λιγότερο οργανωμένη συγκριτικά με εκείνη στο Ellis Island, αλλά η Καλλιόπη έφτασε στον Νότιο Σταθμό της Βοστώνης και ταξίδεψε με τρένο για το Σικάγο, ένα ταξίδι που εκείνη την εποχή διαρκούσε πάνω από 24 ώρες. Στο Σικάγο επιβιβάστηκε σε ένα άλλο τρένο για το τελευταίο σκέλος ενός μεγάλου ταξιδιού προς το Sheboygan. Σύμφωνα με όσα θυμόταν, το εισιτήριο για το ταξίδι με το πλοίο κόστισε 8 δολάρια και ολόκληρο το ταξίδι διήρκεσε τρεις μήνες.

Θυμήθηκε τις κακουχίες που υπέστη ενώ ταξίδευε στην τρίτη θέση ενώ κοιμόταν κάτω από το κατάστρωμα με τα κλινοσκεπάσματα που έφερε μαζί της. Άκουσε επίσης ότι ένας στους τέσσερις από τους περίπου 800 επιβάτες του πλοίου πέθανε κατά τη διάρκεια του ταξιδιού στον Ατλαντικό. Ο αριθμός αυτός είναι σίγουρα υπερβολικός, αλλά ενδεικτικός των φόβων που δημιουργούνταν σε όλους όσοι έκαναν το δύσκολο πέρασμα. Έφτασε στο Sheboygan τον Μάιο του 1914 βρίσκοντας τα δύο παιδιά της πλέον ενήλικα.

Η επιλογή του Παναγιώτη να κατευθυνθεί στη μικρή βιοτεχνική πόλη του Sheboygan ήταν ασυνήθιστη, παρόλο που οι Έλληνες που εγκαταστάθηκαν εκεί έβρισκαν εύκολα δουλειά. Εκείνη την εποχή το Sheboygan ήταν μια πολυσύχναστη μεταποιητική πόλη της οποίας το μέγεθος αυξήθηκε από 26.000 κατοίκους το 1910 σε 31.000 το 1920. Οι αρχικοί έποικοι ήταν κυρίως Γερμανοί μετανάστες. Τον Απρίλιο του 1916 η εφημερίδα Sheboygan Press εκθείαζε τις αρετές της πόλης του Wisconsin σε ένα πρωτοσέλιδο άρθρο με τίτλο "Το Sheboygan και η υπόσχεση για το μέλλον". Διακηρύσσοντας ότι η σταθερότητα μιας πόλης, η ανάπτυξή της και το μέλλον της εξαρτώνται από τις βιομηχανίες της, το άρθρο δήλωνε ότι "καμία πόλη παρόμοιου μεγέθους δεν έχει πιο ελπιδοφόρο μέλλον από το Sheboygan". Επιπλέον, "η ικανοποίηση κυριαρχεί. Είναι μια πόλη που δεν καυχιέται, αλλά φιλοξενεί μέσα της ποιοτικά ιδρύματα με ποιοτικά αγαθά όσον αφορά τον χώρο των πωλήσεων. Είναι αναμφισβήτητα το μεγαλύτερο κέντρο επίπλων στη βόρεια Δύση και απολαμβάνει την υπερήφανη διάκριση να διαθέτει τρία από τα μεγαλύτερα εργοστάσια εμαγιέ στον κόσμο".

Το μεγαλύτερο από αυτά τα εργοστάσια εμαγιέ που ανέφερε η εφημερίδα ανήκε στην Kohler Co. όπου βρήκε δουλειά ο Τσιμπούρης. Η εταιρεία ιδρύθηκε από έναν Αυστριακό μετανάστη, τον J. M. Kohler, το 1887 στο Riverside, ένα τμήμα του Sheboygan, το οποίο μετονομάστηκε σε Kohler και έγινε πόλη της εταιρείας. Μετά από μια τυχαία συνάντηση με έναν Έλληνα μετανάστη από την Αρκαδία, ο οποίος τον εντυπωσίασε με το εργασιακό του ήθος, ο Kohler του ζήτησε να φέρει όσους συμπατριώτες του ήταν πρόθυμοι να μετακομίσουν στο Wisconsin. Όταν λοιπόν ο Παναγιώτης Τσιμπούρης σχεδίαζε να μεταναστεύσει, υπήρχαν ήδη Έλληνες που εργάζονταν για την Kohler και άλλοι έβρισκαν δουλειά στα εργοστάσια επίπλων, στα βυρσοδεψεία και στους σιδηροδρόμους της πόλης, οπότε για τον ίδιο το Sheboygan ήταν προφανής προορισμός. Αφού εργάστηκε στην Kohler, ο Παναγιώτης άνοιξε μια αίθουσα μπιλιάρδου και αργότερα εργάστηκε για την Northern Furniture Company με έδρα το Sheboygan.

Η ΖΩΗ ΤΩΝ ΜΕΤΑΝΑΣΤΩΝ ΣΤΟ SHEBOYGAN

Οι Έλληνες εγκαταστάθηκαν στη νότια πλευρά του Sheboygan γύρω από την Indiana Avenue, σχηματίζοντας μια μικρή ελληνική πόλη. Ανάμεσά τους ήταν ίσως και 250 οικογένειες από την περιοχή της Αρκαδίας. Σύμφωνα με μια εκτίμηση, τρεις στους τέσσερις Έλληνες του Sheboygan ζούσαν στη Λεωφόρο Indiana ή γύρω από αυτήν, μεταξύ της 7ης και της 14ης οδού. Σχεδόν όλοι αυτοί οι Έλληνες μετανάστες ήταν νέοι, ανύπαντροι άνδρες που ζούσαν σε "συνεταιριστικά νοικοκυριά" ή πανσιόν. Τα αρχεία της πόλης αναφέρουν μια πανσιόν που ανήκε στους Nicholas και Barbara Leider στην Indiana Avenue, επιβεβαιώνοντας ότι οι ενοικιαστές της ήταν κατά κύριο λόγο Έλληνες μέχρι το 1915, όταν ο γιος του Leider την πούλησε σε έναν Έλληνα, τον Γιώργο Βελώνη. Το ακίνητο τελικά μετατράπηκε σε διαμερίσματα και για μικρά διαστήματα λειτούργησε εκεί και ταβέρνα αφού μεταπωλήθηκε σε άλλους Έλληνες. Η ελληνική κατοχή του κτιρίου έληξε το 2002. Το όνομα του Τσιμπούρη δεν εμφανίζεται στον κατάλογο των οικοτρόφων, αν και έζησε αρχικά στη Λεωφόρο Ιντιάνα πριν αποκτήσει το δικό του σπίτι στην ίδια λεωφόρο στο νούμερο 1126.

Στη Λεωφόρο Ιντιάνα ή γύρω από αυτήν μπορούσε κανείς να βρει ελληνικά καταστήματα, κουρεία, σαλούν, ράφτες και, κυρίως, καφενεία. Στο καφενείο οι Έλληνες άνδρες συναναστρέφονταν, αντάλλασσαν νέα από την πατρίδα τους και χαλάρωναν παίζοντας χαρτιά. Πολύ συχνά ένα πίσω δωμάτιο ήταν το μέρος όπου οι πελάτες έπαιζαν χαρτιά για χρήματα. Ο τζόγος ήταν για πολλούς Έλληνες μια μορφή ψυχαγωγίας και σε αντίθεση με τον εργασιακό χώρο μπορούσαν να επιδείξουν παραδοσιακά ανδρικά χαρακτηριστικά, όπως η παλικαριά και η ανάληψη ρίσκου. Ο μη αδειοδοτημένος τζόγος αυτού του είδους ήταν φυσικά παράνομος. Η πρώτη είδηση που αναφέρει ότι Έλληνες συνελήφθησαν και τους επιβλήθηκε πρόστιμο επειδή έπαιζαν χαρτιά σε ένα καφενείο στη Λεωφόρο Indiana εμφανίστηκε στον Sheboygan Press τον Νοέμβριο του 1909. Αλλά οι ειδήσεις για τους Έλληνες της περιοχής δεν ήταν πάντα αρνητικές: η ίδια εφημερίδα είχε αναφέρει ότι η ελληνική κοινότητα παρουσίασε ένα θεατρικό έργο τον Ιανουάριο του 1908. Το Sheboygan ήταν επίσης τόπος διεξαγωγής αγώνων από Έλληνες μετανάστες που είχαν γίνει επαγγελματίες παλαιστές που περιόδευαν. Η παλαιότερη τέτοια περίπτωση ήταν εκείνη που ο Demetral, ο "Τρομερός Έλληνας" που περιόδευε στη χώρα σταμάτησε στο Sheboygan για έναν αγώνα πάλης. Το πραγματικό του όνομα ήταν Βασίλειος Δημητρέλης και καταγόταν από την Αρκαδία της Πελοποννήσου. Η εφημερίδα Sheboygan Press ανέφερε ότι "η ελληνική παροικία στο Sheboygan έχει μαζέψει συνολικά 500 δολάρια για να ποντάρει στον συμπατριώτη της και είναι πολύ ενθουσιασμένη". Επειδή ο αγώνας επρόκειτο να διεξαχθεί Κυριακή, διακόπηκε από την αστυνομία και η εφημερίδα ανέφερε ότι παρευρέθηκαν 300 Έλληνες, συμπεριλαμβανομένων και γυναικών, οι οποίοι αναγκάστηκαν να επιστρέψουν στον "οικισμό" τους, γεγονός που υποδηλώνει την ύπαρξη μιας μικρής ελληνικής πόλης κοντά στην Indiana Avenue. Ο αγώνας έγινε την επόμενη μέρα μπροστά σε 400 θεατές και ο Demetral κέρδισε, προς μεγάλη χαρά των Ελλήνων του Sheboygan.

Πανηγυρικές στιγμές όπως αυτές που ακολούθησαν τη νίκη των περιοδευόντων Ελλήνων παλαιστών ήταν ελάχιστες σε μια εποχή που γνώρισε την άνοδο της ξενοφοβίας στις Ηνωμένες Πολιτείες και στο Ουισκόνσιν. Όταν οι Έλληνες άρχισαν να εγκαθίστανται στην Indiana Avenue, κάποιοι την αποκαλούσαν "λεωφόρο του σκόρδου", μια άστοχη υποτιμητική φράση, επειδή το σκόρδο δεν κατέχει τόσο εξέχουσα θέση στην ελληνική κουζίνα όσο για παράδειγμα στις ιταλικές συνταγές. Ωστόσο, στο Sheboygan η ξενοφοβία ήταν σχετικά υποτονική, επειδή το κατεστημένο της πόλης γνώριζε πολύ καλά ότι τα εργοστάσια παραγωγής εμαγιέ, επίπλων και άλλων ειδών βασίζονταν στην εργασία των Αυστριακών, Ελλήνων, Εβραίων, Λιθουανών, Ρώσων και Σλάβων μεταναστών. Η εκτίμηση για τους μετανάστες αυξήθηκε και τα αρνητικά δημοσιεύματα στις εφημερίδες έγιναν πιο σπάνια. Ένα άρθρο του 1910 προσέφερε στους μετανάστες ένα προσβλητικό «κομπλιμέντο» όταν ανέφερε ότι το Sheboygan ήταν μια "καλή ηθική πόλη" με σχετικά χαμηλή εγκληματικότητα, παρόλο που είχε ανάμεσά της αρκετές ομάδες μεταναστών που θεωρούνταν ότι είχαν "ενοχλητικές τάσεις". Και καθώς οι μετανάστες αφομοιώνονταν σταθερά στους αμερικανικούς τρόπους, ακούγονταν συγκρατημένοι έπαινοι.

Ο Παναγιώτης Τσιμπούρης πιθανόν να σύχναζε σε μία ή περισσότερες από τις καφετέριες και ίσως να είχε παρακολουθήσει και κάποιον από τους Έλληνες πλανόδιους παλαιστές, αλλά εκεί που αφιέρωνε μεγάλο μέρος του ελεύθερου χρόνου του ήταν στην Ελληνική Ορθόδοξη εκκλησία του Αγίου Σπυρίδωνα. Η θρησκεία έπαιζε μεγάλο ρόλο στη ζωή των Ελλήνων μεταναστών, ιδίως εκείνων που όπως ο Παναγιώτης είχαν μεγαλώσει σε αγροτικές περιοχές της χώρας, όπου οι παραδόσεις ήταν βαθιές και η εκκλησία ήταν εξίσου σημαντική με το σχολείο. Στις Ηνωμένες Πολιτείες η εκκλησία και οι λειτουργίες της θύμιζαν στους μετανάστες τη ζωή στην πατρίδα, τους συνέδεαν μεταξύ τους και ήταν ο δίδυμος πυλώνας της ταυτότητάς τους μαζί με τη χρήση της ελληνικής γλώσσας. Η εκκλησία ήταν το πρώτο πράγμα που οι Έλληνες εγκαθιστούσαν όπου και αν εγκαταστάθηκαν, αφού πρώτα είχαν ιδρύσει μια "κοινότητα", μια κοινοτική οργάνωση. Το κοινοτικό συμβούλιο, μαζί με έναν ιερέα που εγκαταστάθηκε στο Sheboygan το 1905, τον Αιδεσιμότατο Νικόλαο Βελώνη, αγόρασαν γη στην οδό 1425 S. 10th Street για τον σκοπό αυτό. Ήταν καλή κίνηση, καθώς βρισκόταν αρκετά κοντά στο κέντρο της ελληνικής γειτονιάς, αλλά και αρκετά μακριά από τα εργοστάσια και τις επιχειρήσεις της Indiana Avenue. Το κτίριο της εκκλησίας, εξαιρουμένου του σημερινού καμπαναριού, ολοκληρώθηκε το 1906 και είναι μία από τις παλαιότερες Ορθόδοξες εκκλησίες που βρίσκονται στην Αμερική. Το καμπαναριό προστέθηκε το 1916. Η ολοκλήρωση της εκκλησίας γιορτάστηκε την ημέρα των Χριστουγέννων του 1906 και δύο χρόνια αργότερα ο ναός εγκαινιάστηκε επίσημα. Το 1910 αναγνωρίστηκε επίσημα και σε μια συνεδρίαση που πραγματοποιήθηκε το καλοκαίρι και εκλέχθηκαν οι αξιωματούχοι της εκκλησίας. Επίτιμος πρόεδρος ήταν ένας νέος ιερέας, ο αιδεσιμότατος James Raggos, πρόεδρος ο Peter Jumes και αντιπρόεδρος ο Παναγιώτης Τσιμπούρης. Το επώνυμό του γράφτηκε ελαφρώς διαφορετικά, αλλά όσον αφορά το μικρό του όνομα, ήδη χρησιμοποιούσε το όνομα Peter, την αγγλική μορφή του Παναγιώτη. Ο Παναγιώτης θα παρέμενε ενεργός στην εκκλησία του για όλη του τη ζωή. Το 1911 η εκκλησία ξεκίνησε ένα ελληνικό σχολείο - ο δάσκαλος, Χριστόφορος Κρούστος είχε τέσσερις τάξεις που συναντιόντουσαν τα βράδια, μεταξύ 7 και 10μμ. Εκείνη την εποχή υπήρχαν περίπου 700 Έλληνες στο Sheboygan και η ζήτηση για τη σχολική εκπαίδευση των παιδιών στην ελληνική γλώσσα αυξανόταν. Μπορεί οι Έλληνες να αγγλοποιούσαν τα ονόματά τους και να έκαναν ό,τι μπορούσαν για να προσαρμοστούν στο νέο περιβάλλον, αλλά η διδασκαλία της μητρικής γλώσσας στα παιδιά τους θεωρούνταν εξίσου σημαντική με τη διατήρηση της ελληνορθόδοξης πίστης τους.

ΟΙ ΓΟΝΕΙΣ ΤΟΥ ΠΑΝΑΓΙΩΤΗ, ERNEST ΚΑΙ STELLA

Το 1916 η Καλλιόπη, σε ηλικία 36 ετών τότε, έφερε στον κόσμο το τρίτο τους παιδί, ένα αγόρι, το οποίο βάφτισαν Αναστάσιο, δίνοντάς του το όνομα του παππού του από τον πατέρα του, όπως συνηθίζεται στην Ελλάδα. Ήταν μια εποχή που οι Έλληνες πάλευαν να γίνουν αποδεκτοί στην αμερικανική κοινωνία και συχνά άλλαζαν το μικρό τους όνομα σε μια αγγλική εκδοχή. Ο Αναστάσιος έγινε Έρνεστ. Όταν ο Έρνεστ ήταν ενός έτους, η Καλλιόπη αποφάσισε ότι δεν της άρεσε να ζει στο Sheboygan, περίπου 5.300 μίλια μακριά από το Δεδέμπεη και αρκετά πιο κρύο. Μετακόμισε πίσω στην Ελλάδα το 1917 παίρνοντας μαζί της τον Έρνεστ, σε μια επίσκεψη που αποδείχθηκε σύντομη: επέστρεψαν και οι δύο το 1919. Όταν μπήκαν στην Ελλάδα, η Καλλιόπη έδωσε ως τόπο γέννησης του γιου της την Ελλάδα και όχι τις Ηνωμένες Πολιτείες, πιθανώς επειδή ντρεπόταν να πει ότι είχε γεννηθεί στην Αμερική, πράγμα σπάνιο για τους Έλληνες εκείνα τα πρώτα χρόνια του εικοστού αιώνα. Αυτό δημιούργησε ένα απροσδόκητο πρόβλημα για τον Έρνεστ, διότι τον καθιστούσε αυτομάτως Έλληνα πολίτη και κατά συνέπεια επιλέξιμο για την εκπλήρωση της εθνικής θητείας στο στρατό, η οποία ήταν υποχρεωτική για όλους τους Έλληνες. Φοβόταν επίσης ότι τα ιατρικά του προσόντα θα τον καθιστούσαν υπόχρεο να υπηρετήσει για κάποιο χρονικό διάστημα ακόμη και σε μεταγενέστερο στάδιο της ζωής του. Έτσι, περίμενε να κλείσει τα εβδομήντα του χρόνια, γεγονός που τον απάλλασσε οριστικά από κάθε τέτοια υποχρέωση, προκειμένου να επιστρέψει στην Ελλάδα χωρίς να εμπλακεί στη θρυλική γραφειοκρατία της πατρίδας του.

Το πηγαινέλα της Καλλιόπης, αν και σπάνιο στην περίπτωση των γυναικών, δεν ήταν ασυνήθιστο εκείνη την εποχή. Παρά τις τεράστιες αποστάσεις και τις δύσκολες συνθήκες ταξιδιού υπήρχαν πολλοί Έλληνες που επέστρεφαν στην πατρίδα για σύντομη παραμονή, αλλά οι περισσότεροι δεν την έβρισκαν πολύ φιλόξενη. Πέρα από τις τεράστιες διαφορές στο βιοτικό επίπεδο και τις καθημερινές ανέσεις, η χώρα ήταν πολιτικά πολωμένη για το αν η Ελλάδα έπρεπε να συμμετάσχει στον Α΄ Παγκόσμιο Πόλεμο. Πράγματι, η υπερατλαντική μετανάστευση από την Πελοπόννησο και άλλες περιοχές της χώρας συνεχίστηκε με αμείωτη ένταση. Η Καλλιόπη γύρισε πίσω στο Sheboygan και αυτή τη φορά θα έμενε εκεί μόνιμα.

Μεγαλώνοντας στο Sheboygan, ο Ερνεστ ακολούθησε την πορεία πολλών άλλων παιδιών Ελλήνων μεταναστών, ωστόσο έδειξε επίσης μια ιδιαίτερη αγάπη για τις θεατρικές παραστάσεις και τη μουσική, την οποία, αργότερα, θα κληροδοτούσε στον γιο του Παναγιώτη. Από τη μία πλευρά έκανε μαθήματα ελληνικής γλώσσας και παρακολουθούσε υπάκουα τις λειτουργίες στην εκκλησία του Αγίου Σπυρίδωνα, κατέβαλε προσπάθεια στο σχολείο και έγινε δίγλωσσος και από την άλλη άρχισε να εμφανίζεται σε σχολικές θεατρικές παραστάσεις. Ο Άγιος Σπυρίδων έγινε τόσο μεγάλο μέρος της ζωής του όσο ήταν και του πατέρα του και θα γινόταν ένας από τους ψάλτες της εκκλησίας. Φοίτησε στο δημοτικό σχολείο Longfellow, λίγα τετράγωνα μακριά από το σπίτι του στην Indiana Avenue. Το αρχικό κτίριο του σχολείου, που δεν υπάρχει πια, φαινόταν εντυπωσιακό, σε όμορφο ρομανικό στυλ, αν και ήταν ταπεινό, αποτελούμενο από δύο τούβλινους ορόφους και ένα ψηλό πέτρινο υπόγειο. Διέθετε οκτώ μεγάλες αίθουσες με ευρύχωρους κεντρικούς χώρους. Μια προσθήκη χτίστηκε το 1918. Περίπου την ίδια εποχή, ο Αμερικανικός Ερυθρός Σταυρός χρηματοδοτούσε ένα πρόγραμμα σχολικού γάλακτος. Το γάλα παρέχονταν δωρεάν σε όσους δεν μπορούσαν να πληρώσουν το κόστος. Οι μαθητές που μπορούσαν να το αντέξουν οικονομικά χρεώνονταν δύο λεπτά για το γάλα τους. Η υποκριτική του Ernest στην τοπική εφημερίδα αναφέρθηκε για πρώτη φορά το 1926, όταν ήταν στην τετάρτη τάξη και συμμετείχε σε ένα έργο με τίτλο "Μια τρελή Χριστουγεννιάτικη τάξη". Το όνομά του εμφανίζεται ξανά όταν συμμετείχε σε ένα θεατρικό έργο στην έκτη τάξη, δύο χρόνια αργότερα. Το 1929 ο νεαρός Ernest εμφανίστηκε σε μία παράσταση που ανέβασε το Ελληνικό Σχολείο προς τιμήν της Ημέρας της Ελληνικής Ανεξαρτησίας. Ήταν επίσης δημοφιλής και καλός μαθητής. Το 1932 ο Ernest αποφοίτησε από το Γυμνάσιο ως αντιπρόεδρος της τάξης του. Αποφοίτησε από το Λύκειο το 1935 και συνέχισε στο Πανεπιστήμιο Marquette, ένα καθολικό πανεπιστήμιο στο Ουισκόνσιν, από το οποίο αποφοίτησε το 1941 με πτυχίο οδοντιατρικής. Η απόφασή του σχετικά με το τι ειδικότητα θα ακολουθούσε ήταν σχεδόν βέβαιο ότι οφειλόταν στην αιτία του θανάτου του πατέρα του τον Ιούνιο του 1932, σε ηλικία 60 ετών. Ο Παναγιώτης πέθανε στο νοσοκομείο St. Nicholas στο Sheboygan μετά από ασθένεια αρκετών εβδομάδων. Είχε μια σοβαρή μόλυνση στα δόντια του, η οποία δεν μπορούσε να αντιμετωπιστεί αποτελεσματικά - τα αντιβιοτικά δεν ήταν ακόμη διαθέσιμα - και εξαπλώθηκε στην καρδιά και τους πνεύμονές του προκαλώντας το θάνατό του.

Ένα χρόνο μετά το θάνατο του Παναγιώτη πέθανε ο μεγαλύτερος γιος του Κωνσταντίνος. Ήταν ιδιοκτήτης αίθουσας μπιλιάρδου, παντρεμένος με έναν γιο και μια κόρη και ζούσε στο Antigo, μια πόλη κοντά στο Sheboygan. Είχε αλλάξει το όνομά του σε Gustav όταν απέκτησε την αμερικανική υπηκοότητα. Η αλλαγή από ελληνικό σε γερμανικό όνομα ήταν προφανής επιλογή αν ήθελε κανείς να ενσωματωθεί σε μια πόλη στην οποία οι παλαιότερες καθιερωμένες ελίτ ήταν κυρίως γερμανικής καταγωγής. Και εκατοντάδες "Κωνσταντίνοι" σε όλη την Αμερική έγιναν επίσημα ή ανεπίσημα "Γκας" για τον ίδιο λόγο. Υπήρξαν τουλάχιστον δύο βουλευτές των ΗΠΑ με αυτό το όνομα, ο Γκας Μπιλιράκης από τη Φλόριντα και ο Γκας Γιάτρον από την Πενσυλβάνια.

Ο Ernest κατατάχθηκε στο στρατό μετά την είσοδο των Ηνωμένων Πολιτειών στον Β' Παγκόσμιο Πόλεμο, όπως και εκατοντάδες άλλοι Ελληνοαμερικανοί. Κατατάχθηκε στο οδοντιατρικό σώμα και με το βαθμό του λοχαγού τοποθετήθηκε στο εξωτερικό, στις Αλεούτιες Νήσους, τον Ιούνιο του 1943, ενώ οι αμερικανικές και καναδικές δυνάμεις ολοκλήρωναν την εκστρατεία για την εκδίωξη των ιαπωνικών δυνάμεων που είχαν αποβιβαστεί εκεί το 1942. Η είδηση σχετικά με την αποστολή του που δημοσιεύθηκε στην εφημερίδα The Sheboygan Press στις 13 Δεκεμβρίου 1943, περιείχε τη φωτογραφία του με στολή, αλλά η λεζάντα έγραφε λανθασμένα το όνομά του ως Τριμπούρης. Αυτός ή κάποιος άλλος λόγος τον έκανε να αποφασίσει να αλλάξει το επώνυμό του σε Τιμπόρης, το οποίο ήταν πιο εύκολο στην ορθογραφία. Αυτό έγινε το 1946, τη χρονιά που παντρεύτηκε τον Νοέμβριο τη Στέλλα Μηνά στην εκκλησία του Αγίου Σπυρίδωνα. Ακολούθησε δείπνο και δεξίωση στην οποία συμμετείχαν 300 καλεσμένοι. Ο Ernest είχε ήδη ξεκινήσει ένα οδοντιατρείο στο Sheboygan, ένα επάγγελμα που συνέχισε να ασκεί με μεγάλη αφοσίωση και αγάπη μέχρι τα ογδόντα του χρόνια.

Η μέχρι τότε ιστορία της ζωής της Στέλλας ήταν από πολλές απόψεις αντιπροσωπευτική της ζωής των Ελληνοαμερικανίδων στο πρώτο μισό του εικοστού αιώνα. Γεννήθηκε στο Waukegan του Ιλινόις, ένα βιομηχανικό προάστιο του Σικάγο, όπου ο ελληνικής καταγωγής πατέρας της Μιχάλης, γνωστός και ως Mike, ήταν ιδιοκτήτης του "Royal Restaurant" στην Washington Street και η οικογένεια ζούσε στο ίδιο κτίριο. Ο Μηνάς αγόρασε το εστιατόριο το 1914 το οποίο είχε πολύ καλή φήμη. Μια τοπική εφημερίδα το περιέγραφε ως καθαρό και τακτικό με πολύ καλά γεύματα και σέρβις και με σνακ να σερβίρονται όλες τις ώρες. Η επιχείρηση εστιατορίου ήταν το πιο συνηθισμένο επάγγελμα των Ελληνοαμερικανών όχι μόνο τότε αλλά και καθ' όλη τη διάρκεια του εικοστού αιώνα. Στη δεκαετία του 1920 ο Menas έγινε ιδιοκτήτης μιας αίθουσας μπιλιάρδου. Και οι δύο επιχειρήσεις είχαν τις προκλήσεις τους, με τους πελάτες να προσπαθούν με διάφορους τρόπους να αποφύγουν την πληρωμή ή απλά να γίνονται θορυβώδεις και να παίζουν τυχερά παιχνίδια στο χώρο. Ο Μιχάλης και η σύζυγός του Δήμητρα απέκτησαν οκτώ παιδιά, τρεις κόρες και πέντε γιους, η Στέλλα ήταν η τρίτη κόρη και γεννήθηκε τον Απρίλιο του 1923. Η οικογένεια Menas αποφάσισε να απομακρυνθεί από την περιοχή του Σικάγο και να μετακομίσει στο Sheboygan κάποια στιγμή στη δεκαετία του 1930. Το όνομα της Στέλλας εμφανίζεται σε μια λίστα παιδιών σε ένα χριστουγεννιάτικο θεατρικό έργο στο δημοτικό σχολείο Longfellow το 1934 και τέσσερα χρόνια αργότερα ως παίκτρια σε ένα τουρνουά βόλεϊ του Γυμνασίου.

Το 1941 η Στέλλα εργαζόταν εθελοντικά για την Ελληνική Ένωση Αρωγής Πολέμου (GWRA). Ήταν μια εθνική οργάνωση που ιδρύθηκε από κορυφαίους Ελληνοαμερικανούς αμέσως μετά την είσοδο της Ελλάδας στον Β' Παγκόσμιο Πόλεμο τον Οκτώβριο του 1940. Αυτό έγινε με την έναρξη του πολέμου που η φασιστική Ιταλία προσπάθησε ανεπιτυχώς να εισβάλει και να κατακτήσει την Ελλάδα. Παρά τις αντιξοότητες ο ελληνικός στρατός κατάφερε να απωθήσει τις ανώτερες ιταλικές δυνάμεις πίσω από τα ελληνοαλβανικά σύνορα. Ενώ ο δημοκρατικός κόσμος χαιρέτιζε τον ηρωισμό των Ελλήνων, τα παραρτήματα της GWRA σε όλες τις Ηνωμένες Πολιτείες κινητοποιήθηκαν προκειμένου να συγκεντρώσουν χρήματα και υλικά για να τα στείλουν στην Ελλάδα για να βοηθήσουν την προσπάθεια. Θα συνέχιζε το έργο της και μετά την τελική κατοχή της Ελλάδας από τις γερμανικές και ιταλικές δυνάμεις από το 1941 μέχρι την απελευθέρωσή της το 1944. Όπως συνέβη σε πολλές τέτοιες περιπτώσεις εθελοντικής εργασίας για την ενίσχυση της πατρίδας, οι Ελληνοαμερικανίδες, συμπεριλαμβανομένων των νεαρών γυναικών, έπαιξαν καθοριστικό ρόλο, παρόλο που η ηγεσία της ελληνοαμερικανικής κοινότητας ήταν αποκλειστικά ανδρική και οι ελληνοαμερικανικές οικογένειες διατηρούσαν μια παραδοσιακή πατριαρχική δομή που κρατούσε τις νεαρές γυναίκες προστατευμένες στο σπίτι. Η Στέλλα εντάχθηκε επίσης σε μια ομάδα πλεξίματος του Ερυθρού Σταυρού μαζί με πολλές άλλες νεαρές Ελληνοαμερικανίδες στο Sheboygan.

Οι δραστηριότητες αυτές συνεχίστηκαν καθ' όλη τη δεκαετία του 1940, επειδή η GWRA ασχολήθηκε επίσης με την ενίσχυση της ελληνικής μεταπολεμικής ανοικοδόμησης. Στις δεκαετίες που ακολούθησαν η Στέλλα δραστηριοποιήθηκε στη Φιλόπτωχο των Κυριών του Αγίου Σπυρίδωνα, κάτι που έγινε ευκολότερο μετά τον γάμο της, επειδή ο σύζυγός της Ernest συμμετείχε στη ζωή της εκκλησίας. Η Φιλόπτωχος ήταν υπεύθυνη για την οργάνωση και τη λειτουργία των φιλανθρωπικών πρωτοβουλιών και των κοινωνικών εκδηλώσεων της εκκλησίας.

Ο Ernest θα παρέμενε ψάλτης στην εκκλησία του για εξήντα χρόνια με ένα διάλειμμα όταν έλειπε στο κολέγιο και στο ιατρικό σώμα κατά τη διάρκεια του Β' Παγκοσμίου Πολέμου. Υπηρέτησε για πολλά χρόνια στο διοικητικό συμβούλιο της εκκλησίας του Αγίου Σπυρίδωνα, μεταξύ των οποίων αρκετά ως πρόεδρος και ως διευθυντής της χορωδίας. Ήταν ενεργός στα δρώμενα της ελληνικής κοινότητας, όπως οι εκδηλώσεις μνήμης για την επέτειο της ελληνικής επανάστασης του 1821. Έπαιζε επίσης κλαρινέτο, αν και ποτέ δημοσίως. Έκανε εξάσκηση και έπαιζε μόνο στο σπίτι, για τη δική του ευχαρίστηση, όπως έλεγε στους γιους του. Είχε μεγάλη συλλογή δίσκων και έπαιζε κλασική μουσική και όπερα τόσο στο σπίτι όσο και στο οδοντιατρείο του. Ο Ernest, τον οποίο και οι δύο γιοι του περιγράφουν ως έναν αξιοπρεπή και σεμνό άνθρωπο του οποίου η ζωή ήταν επικεντρωμένη στην οικογένειά του, την εκκλησία του και το επάγγελμά του, θα είχε βαθιά επιρροή και στους δύο γιους του. Και μετέδωσε την αγάπη του για τη μουσική και στους δύο.

Η Στέλλα γέννησε δύο αγόρια αμέσως μετά τον γάμο της με τον Έρνεστ. Ο Παναγιώτης ήταν ο μεγαλύτερος και γεννήθηκε στις 31 Οκτωβρίου 1947. Όπως ήταν το ελληνορθόδοξο έθιμο, ο Παναγιώτης βαπτίστηκε έξι μήνες μετά τη γέννησή του, τον Μάρτιο του 1948. Ο αδελφός του Gus, που πήρε το όνομά του από τον εκλιπόντα θείο του Gustav (Κωνσταντίνος) γεννήθηκε τον επόμενο χρόνο, τον Δεκέμβριο. Ένα τρίτο αγόρι, ο Μιχαήλ, γεννήθηκε το 1951, αλλά πέθανε όταν ήταν μόλις τεσσάρων ετών, επειδή είχε υδροκεφαλία. Δύο χρόνια αργότερα η Στέλλα γέννησε ένα τέταρτο αγόρι, το οποίο όμως γεννήθηκε νεκρό.

ΟΙΚΟΓΕΝΕΙΑΚΕΣ ΥΠΟΘΕΣΕΙΣ

Θα ήταν δύσκολο να υπερεκτιμήσει κανείς τη σημασία της οικογένειας στη ζωή των Ελλήνων μεταναστών στην Αμερική. Η οικογένεια και οι ισχυροί δεσμοί που την κρατούν ενωμένη ήταν ένα πολιτισμικό χαρακτηριστικό που εξασφάλιζε την επιβίωση στην αγροτική Ελλάδα σε ένα περιβάλλον στο οποίο οι κυβερνητικές και κοινωνικές υπηρεσίες και άλλοι θεσμοί ήταν σχεδόν ανύπαρκτοι, οι πόροι ήταν λιγοστοί και όσοι βρίσκονταν εκτός των άμεσων κοινωνικών δικτύων της οικογένειας και του χωριού θεωρούνταν δυνητική απειλή. Οι μετανάστες στην Αμερική διατήρησαν ισχυρούς οικογενειακούς δεσμούς ως μέσο επιβίωσης στο νέο, ξένο και ενίοτε εχθρικό περιβάλλον. Η οικογένεια, σε συμμαχία με την εκκλησία, διατήρησε τις αξίες και τις παραδόσεις του Παλαιού Κόσμου και την ελληνική ταυτότητα, η οποία εκφράστηκε μέσω της γλώσσας, της θρησκείας και της υπερηφάνειας για τις παρακαταθήκες της Αρχαίας Ελλάδας. Η ελληνική οικογένεια των μεταναστών στην Αμερική ήταν επίσης μια πατριαρχική οικογένεια. Ο πατέρας ήταν ο βιοπαλαιστής και το πρότυπο της σκληρής εργασιακής ηθικής που αναμενόταν να ενστερνιστεί ολόκληρη η οικογένεια και ήταν ο αδιαμφισβήτητος επικεφαλής της. Οι μητέρες μπορούσαν να ασκούν επιρροή, αρκεί να παρέμεναν εντός του ρόλου που τους είχε ανατεθεί. Οι γιοι είχαν πολύ μεγαλύτερη ελευθερία σε σύγκριση με τις κόρες, των οποίων η "τιμή" έπρεπε να προστατεύεται με κάθε κόστος. Όμως η ελευθερία και τα προνόμια που απολάμβαναν οι γιοι εξαρτιόνταν από την πίστη που επιδείκνυαν προς τους δύο γονείς.

Η οικογένεια Τιμπόρη δεν αποτελούσε εξαίρεση σε αυτή τη γενικευμένη εικόνα, αλλά προς τιμήν του, ο Ernest κέρδισε πραγματικά τον σεβασμό των γιων του δίνοντας το παράδειγμα της αφοσίωσης στη δουλειά του και στην οικογένειά του. Ο Παναγιώτης και ο αδελφός του θυμούνται ότι ο πατέρας τους έδινε μεγάλη σημασία στην εκπαίδευσή τους, κάτι που ήταν άλλο ένα χαρακτηριστικό των Ελλήνων μεταναστών. Η οικογένεια του Ernest έκανε πολύ λίγες διακοπές, επειδή προτιμούσε να ξοδεύει τα χρήματα που κέρδιζε ως οδοντίατρος στην εκπαίδευση των γιων του παρά να πηγαίνουν διακοπές ή σε άλλες μορφές διασκέδασης. Δούλευε σκληρά όλη μέρα από Δευτέρα έως Σάββατο και αφιέρωνε τον λιγοστό ελεύθερο χρόνο του στο να παίζει κλαρινέτο και να κάνει εργασίες για την εκκλησία του Αγίου Σπυρίδωνα. Σε ελάχιστες περιπτώσεις πήγαινε στο Milwaukee για να παρακολουθήσει αγώνες μπέιζμπολ των Brewers και φυσικά το πρωί της Κυριακής ήταν αφιερωμένο στην εβδομαδιαία λειτουργία στην εκκλησία. Η Στέλλα ακολουθούσε αυτόν τον τρόπο λειτουργίας, συμμετείχε ενεργά στις δραστηριότητες της εκκλησίας και υποστήριζε τους γιους της καθώς ανέπτυσσαν τις φιλοδοξίες και τα οράματα τους για το μέλλον.

Η γιαγιά Καλλιόπη (ή γαγιά, όπως την αποκαλούσαν οι εγγονοί της) ήταν επίσης μεγάλο μέρος της δεμένης οικογενειακής μονάδας του Τιμπόρη, και ήταν ιδιαίτερα στοργική και προστατευτική με τον Παναγιώτη, τον μεγαλύτερο εγγονό της. Ζούσε στον πρώτο όροφο του οικογενειακού σπιτιού στη λεωφόρο Indiana 1126 και ο Παναγιώτης συνήθιζε να κοιμάται εκεί, ενώ ο Gus μαζί με τους γονείς τους βρίσκονταν στον δεύτερο όροφο. Ο Παναγιώτης περνούσε περισσότερο χρόνο με τη γαγιά του στον κάτω όροφο παρά με τους γονείς του και αυτό δεν άρεσε πάντα στη μητέρα του και υπήρχαν κάποιες στιγμές οικογενειακής έντασης. Στη συνέχεια, το 1960, ολόκληρη η οικογένεια μετακόμισε σε ένα νέο μονώροφο σπίτι κοντά στο South High School του Sheboygan και τα προβλήματα χωροταξίας λύθηκαν.

Αυτό που παρέμεινε σταθερό και για τα δύο αδέλφια ήταν η ήσυχη, αποφασιστική παρουσία του πατέρα τους στη ζωή τους. Δεν είναι περίεργο που ο Gus επέλεξε να ακολουθήσει το επάγγελμα του πατέρα του και να γίνει οδοντίατρος. Ο Παναγιώτης αντίθετα, επέλεξε να ακολουθήσει την αγάπη του πατέρα του για τη μουσική και το χορωδιακό τραγούδι και να το ασκήσει επαγγελματικά. Και οι δύο γιοι προσπάθησαν να ανταποκριθούν στα υψηλά πρότυπα που είχε θέσει ο πατέρας τους, ο Παναγιώτης ίσως περισσότερο λόγω της επιλογής που έκανε να κάνει καριέρα στη μουσική, η οποία ερχόταν στη ζωή του πατέρα του αμέσως μετά την οδοντιατρική. Αυτό το κίνητρο που μετέφερε στον Παναγιώτη θα τον συνόδευε σε όλη του τη ζωή.

Gus

Το 1964, όταν ο Gus ήταν μόλις δεκαέξι ετών, μαζί με τον Michael Sweeney, έναν συμμαθητή του, κέρδισαν ένα βραβείο σε μια έκθεση σε όλη την κομητεία για μια εργασία σχετικά με τις εσωτερικές αλλαγές των δοντιών λόγω εξωτερικών ερεθισμάτων. Σπούδασε οδοντιατρική στο Πανεπιστήμιο Marquette, όπως ακριβώς είχε κάνει και ο πατέρας του Ernest. Ο Gus άνοιξε το δικό του ιατρείο στο Sheboygan το 1973, τη χρονιά που πήρε το πτυχίο του.

Τώρα πλέον συνταξιοδοτημένος, ο Gus διατηρεί την ήπια συμπεριφορά που πρέπει να υπήρξε πολύ ανακουφιστική για τους ασθενείς του. Η βαθιά αγάπη που τρέφουν τα αδέλφια μεταξύ τους είναι εμφανής. Ο Gus χαμογελούσε, όπως κάνει συχνά, όταν μιλήσαμε για την επιλογή καριέρας του Παναγιώτη. Ο Παναγιώτης είναι όλο παραστάσεις, είπε ο Gus, είτε βρίσκεται στη σκηνή, είτε εκτός σκηνής. Ο Gus είχε επίσης μουσικές κλίσεις ως νεαρό αγόρι. Οι πρώτες παραστάσεις που θυμάται ο Gus ήταν μια μπάντα που αποτελείτο από τον ίδιο, τον Παναγιώτη και έναν ξάδελφό τους. Η μπάντα έπαιζε ελληνική μουσική στις εγκαταστάσεις της εκκλησίας του Αγίου Σπυρίδωνα. Ήταν δέκα χρονών, ο Gus έπαιζε ντραμς, ο Peter έπαιζε ακορντεόν και ο George Brett, ο ξάδελφός τους, κλαρινέτο το οποίο και έπαιζε πολύ καλά. Ο Gus, ο Παναγιώτης και ο George έπαιξαν επίσης πιάνο σε ένα σχολικό ρεσιτάλ που πραγματοποιήθηκε στην Ευαγγελική Εκκλησία του Ebenezer τον Οκτώβριο του 1957. Και ο Παναγιώτης, μαζί με τον Γιώργο και τον Γιάννη Ρεζεβούλη έπαιξαν επίσης "αρκετά βυζαντινά έργα". Ο Παναγιώτης, στα δέκα του χρόνια, ήταν ήδη οργανίστας στην εκκλησία του Αγίου Σπυρίδωνα.

Ο Gus παντρεύτηκε τη Linda Lukovsky το 1978 και η τελετή έγινε στην εκκλησία του Αγίου Σπυρίδωνα. Κατά τη διάρκεια της επόμενης δεκαετίας ο Gus ακολούθησε τα βήματα του πατέρα του όχι μόνο ως οδοντίατρος στο Sheboygan αλλά και ως πολύ ενεργός στην εκκλησιαστική ζωή. Έγινε ένας από τους διοργανωτές του ετήσιου πανηγυριού ελληνικών τροφίμων που συγκέντρωνε χρήματα για την εκκλησία και έγινε επίσης μέλος του διοικητικου συμβουλίου της. Η σύζυγος του Γκας, η Λίντα, συμμετείχε επίσης έντονα. Ο Παναγιώτης ήταν φυσικά παρών στον γάμο του αδελφού του και η ανακοίνωση της εφημερίδας τον περιέγραφε ως "Παναγιώτης Τίμπορης της Ουρμπάνα". Αυτό συνέβαινε επειδή τότε φοιτούσε στο Πανεπιστήμιο του Ιλινόις στην Urbana Champaign παρακολουθώντας διδακτορικές σπουδές χορωδιακής μουσικής εκπαίδευσης. Για τον ίδιο ήταν μια φυσική εξέλιξη από το παίξιμο του οργάνου στον Άγιο Σπυρίδωνα, το οποίο έκανε μέχρι την αποφοίτησή του από το λύκειο το 1966.

Ο Παναγιώτης έτρεφε έναν θερμό, στοργικό σεβασμό για τον αδελφό του Gus που τους συνόδευε σε όλη τους τη ζωή. Ο σεβασμός του προς τον μεγαλύτερο αδελφό οφειλόταν στην αφοσίωση του Gus στην οδοντιατρική και στο γεγονός ότι δούλευε στενά με τον πατέρα τους Ernest, φροντίζοντάς τον και στρώνοντας το δρόμο προς τη συνταξιοδότησή του από την οδοντιατρική. Παρόλο που ο Παναγιώτης είχε μετακομίσει μακριά, φρόντιζε να επισκέπτεται συχνά τον αδελφό του στο Sheboygan ή να οργανώνει ταξίδια με τις συζύγους τους. Ένα σημαντικό μέρος των επισκέψεων στο Sheboygan ήταν να παίζουν γκολφ μαζί με τον πατέρα τους στο γήπεδο γκολφ Riverdale, νότια του Sheboygan. Αυτό συνέβαινε συχνά και πολλές φορές το παιχνίδι ξεκινούσε το βράδυ, αφού ο Έρνεστ έκλεινε το οδοντιατρείο του στις 6 το απόγευμα.

PETER TIBORIS, ΟΡΓΑΝΙΣΤΑΣ ΣΤΟΝ ΑΓΙΟ ΣΠΥΡΙΔΩΝΑ

Οι ελληνορθόδοξες εκκλησίες έχουν σχεδιαστεί για να δημιουργούν μια αίσθηση δέους και σεβασμού. Οι λιτές μορφές που είναι ζωγραφισμένες σε εικόνες κοιτούν από ψηλά, και υπάρχει έντονη μυρωδιά θυμιάματος και αναμμένων κεριών. Οι Ορθόδοξοι σχετίζονται με τον Θεό αρχικά μέσω των αισθήσεων και όχι προσπαθώντας να κατανοήσουν τον γραπτό λόγο. Μέσα σε αυτό το ατμοσφαιρικό περιβάλλον ο Παναγιώτης είχε αναλάβει τα καθήκοντα του οργανίστα της εκκλησίας σε πολύ νεαρή ηλικία - λίγο πριν από τα δέκατα γενέθλιά του το 1957. Η ανακοίνωση στην τοπική εφημερίδα έγραφε: "μαθητής της τετάρτης τάξης του σχολείου Longfellow, ο νεαρός οργανίστας έχει αποκτήσει ικανοποιητική γνώση της βυζαντινής μουσικής υπό την καθοδήγηση του Πατέρα Πέτρου Μούρτου????. Από τεσσάρων ετών συμμετέχει ενεργά στα εκκλησιαστικά πράγματα ως παπαδοπαίδι και του αρέσει πάντα να παίρνει μέρος στις εκκλησιαστικές δραστηριότητες. Τα τελευταία δύο χρόνια είναι μαθητής πιάνου της κ. Ευγενίας Μάγιερ".

Ο Παναγιώτης θυμάται έντονα την αίσθηση της κοινότητας που παρείχε η ενορία του Αγίου Σπυρίδωνα και τους εορτασμούς των θρησκευτικών και ελληνικών εθνικών εορτών, καθώς και τις τακτικές δραστηριότητές της: το σχολείο ελληνικής γλώσσας, το Κατηχητικό, τα παζάρια με τα γλυκά, τον ετήσιο έρανο, το φεστιβάλ χορού το καλοκαίρι και φυσικά τη χορωδία. Θυμάται ότι χρειάστηκε να επιμεληθεί ποιήματα για τον εορτασμό της Ημέρας της Ελληνικής Ανεξαρτησίας, στις 25 Μαρτίου, συμπεριλαμβανομένων στίχων για τον Έλληνα επαναστάτη ήρωα Θεόδωρο Κολοκοτρώνη. Υπήρχαν μαθήματα παραδοσιακών ελληνικών χορών για αγόρια και κορίτσια, όπου έμαθε δύο από τους πιο γνωστούς χορούς, το συρτό και το τσάμικο οι οποίοι χορεύονταν στις πολλές εκδηλώσεις που διοργάνωνε η εκκλησία.

Ο Παναγιώτης κράτησε σταθερά την ταυτότητα που του εμφύσησαν οι γονείς του και η εκκλησία. Είχε πάντα συνείδηση των ελληνικών του ριζών και μου είπε ότι "από τη στιγμή της γέννησής μου μέχρι και σήμερα έχω πάντα πλήρη επίγνωση των ελληνικών μου ριζών που φυτεύτηκαν από τη στιγμή που άκουσα για πρώτη φορά και στη συνέχεια άρχισα να μαθαίνω ελληνικά". Η ζωή του στην εκκλησία και ιδιαίτερα η ενασχόλησή του ως οργανοπαίχτη και οι τυπικά ελληνικοί ισχυροί οικογενειακοί δεσμοί μαζί με τις εθνικές και θρησκευτικές εκδηλώσεις μνήμης ενίσχυσαν την εθνική του ταυτότητα. Ο Παναγιώτης θυμάται όλα αυτά ως μια συνεχή και μακρόχρονη διαδικασία που τελικά απέδωσε καρπούς. Το απολάμβανε και το αγαπούσε, και όλο αυτό τον έκανε να αισθάνεται ότι είναι ιδιαίτερος ως Ελληνοαμερικανός, επειδή αυτή η ταυτότητα συνεπαγόταν και την επίκληση της συνέχειας του ελληνικού πολιτισμού από την αρχαιότητα μέχρι σήμερα. Έγινε μανιώδης αναγνώστης κλασικών ελληνικών κειμένων, ιδίως θεατρικών έργων και των γραπτών αρχαίων φιλοσόφων όπως ο Αριστοτέλης, ο Πλάτωνας και ο Σωκράτης.

Το παίξιμο του εκκλησιαστικού οργάνου στην εκκλησία ήταν το κατώφλι του Παναγιώτη στον κόσμο της μουσικής. Παραδοσιακά, η Ορθόδοξη Εκκλησία δεν χρησιμοποιεί μουσικά όργανα κατά τη διάρκεια της Λειτουργίας. Δεν είναι βέβαιο γιατί εισήχθησαν τα όργανα στις Ορθόδοξες εκκλησίες της Αμερικής, αλλά ίσως να αποτελεί μια προσπάθεια "δυτικοποίησης". Από τα μέσα του εικοστού αιώνα αρκετές Ελληνικές Ορθόδοξες εκκλησίες εγκατέστησαν εκκλησιαστικό όργανο. Ο Αρχιεπίσκοπος Αθηναγόρας που ανέλαβε την Ελληνική Αρχιεπισκοπή το 1931 ήταν μεγάλος υποστηρικτής του οργάνου και ενθάρρυνε τη χρήση του στην Αμερική. Αν και ο ίδιος το ενθάρρυνε, είναι πιθανό ότι ήταν ήδη σχετικά διαδεδομένο και νωρίτερα. Στις αρχές του 20ού αιώνα, ιερείς και άλλοι στην Αμερική είχαν αρχίσει να συνθέτουν νέα Ορθόδοξη εκκλησιαστική μουσική που εγκατέλειπε τους παραδοσιακούς βυζαντινούς τρόπους και τη μονοφωνική γραμμή. Η νέα μουσική με ευρωπαϊκές κλίμακες παρουσιάστηκε συχνά σε δυτικοποιημένο ύφος μέσω χορωδιών που συνοδεύονταν από όργανα. Μεταξύ αυτών που συνδέθηκαν με το προοδευτικό στυλ ήταν ο Γιώργος Αναστασίου, ο οποίος έφτασε στις ΗΠΑ από την Κύπρο το 1920. Εγκαταστάθηκε στο Τάρπον Σπρινγκς το 1924, όπου έγινε διευθυντής του Ελληνικού Ενοριακού Σχολείου, οργάνωσε τη Βυζαντινή Χορωδία και υπηρέτησε ως κορυφαίος ψάλτης στην Ελληνική Ορθόδοξη Εκκλησία του Αγίου Νικολάου από το 1931 έως το 1941.

Επί του παρόντος, το Εθνικό Συμβούλιο Μουσικών της Ελληνικής Ορθόδοξης Εκκλησίας, στη θέση του σχετικά με τη χρήση των οργάνων στην εκκλησία, αναφέρει ότι ο κύριος σκοπός του οργάνου είναι να βοηθά τη χορωδία και το εκκλησίασμα στη "διατήρηση του ακριβούς τονισμού", καθώς πολλοί ενορίτες και εθελοντές μέλη της χορωδίας μπορεί να μην έχουν ιδιαίτερες μουσικές κλίσεις ή μουσικό υπόβαθρο.

Πατερας Πητερ Μουρτος

Η σημαντικότητα του εκκλησιαστικού οργάνου για τον Παναγιώτη ήταν τεράστια. Το γεγονός ότι ο Παναγιώτης έγινε οργανίστας της εκκλησίας ενώ ο πατέρας του ήταν υπεύθυνος της χορωδίας επιβεβαίωσε τη στενή σχέση των δύο και τη μουσική επιρροή του Ernest στο γιο του. Καθώς όμως μεγάλωνε, υπήρχαν και άλλοι μέντορες έτοιμοι να τον καθοδηγήσουν. Ο Παναγιώτης έμαθε να παίζει όργανο στον Άγιο Σπυρίδωνα υπό την καθοδήγηση του ιερέα, Πατέρα Πήτερ Μούρτου. Γεννημένος στην Αμαλιάδα της Πελοποννήσου το 1922 ο Μούρτος ακολούθησε μια ασυνήθιστη πορεία προς την ιεροσύνη. Πολέμησε στην πλευρά της ΕΑΜικής αντίστασης κατά τη διάρκεια του Β' Παγκοσμίου Πολέμου και στη συνέχεια άλλαξε στρατόπεδο και πολέμησε στον ελληνικό στρατό κατά τη διάρκεια του ελληνικού εμφυλίου πολέμου κατά των κομμουνιστών μεταξύ 1946 και 1949. Υπηρέτησε επίσης ως μέλος της αστυνομικής δύναμης της Αθήνας κατά τη διάρκεια της οποίας εγγράφηκε στο Πανεπιστήμιο Αθηνών ως φοιτητής της Θεολογίας. Αργότερα μετακόμισε στις Ηνωμένες Πολιτείες και αποφοίτησε από το Union Theological Seminary της Νέας Υόρκης και έλαβε επίσης το μεταπτυχιακό του στη Θεολογία και Ιστορία Θρησκειών. Ο Άγιος Σπυρίδων ήταν η πρώτη του ενορία στις Ηνωμένες Πολιτείες, έφτασε εκεί το 1954. Μιλούσε άπταιστα αγγλικά και μπορούσε να τραγουδάει και να συνθέτει, έγινε γρήγορα ένας ισχυρός και ενεργός ηγέτης της ενορίας και της κοινότητας, ο οποίος τάχθηκε ευθέως κατά των φυλετικών διακρίσεων. Όπως συμβαίνει συνήθως με τους ισχυρογνώμονες ιερείς, ο Μούρτος αποξένωσε ορισμένους από τους ενορίτες του και υπήρξαν εντάσεις και διαφωνίες μεταξύ ορισμένων μελών της εκκλησίας. Ο Μούρτος και ο Ernest Τιμπόρης που είχαν την ίδια ηλικία έγιναν στενοί φίλοι και περνούσαν πολύ χρόνο μαζί - ο Ernest ήταν ο ψάλτης στην εκκλησία και διευθυντής της χορωδίας και αυτό εδραίωσε τη φιλία τους. Ο Παναγιώτης θυμάται τον Μούρτο ως έναν αυστηρό και πειθαρχημένο μουσικό που τον δίδαξε όχι μόνο πώς να παίζει το όργανο αλλά και πώς να τραγουδάει με βάση την ελληνορθόδοξη νευματική σημειογραφία, μια μορφή μουσικής σημειογραφίας που προϋπήρχε της εφεύρεσης της πεντάγραμμης σημειογραφίας. Ο Μούρτος την είχε μάθει στο ιεροδιδασκαλείο που είχε παρακολουθήσει στην Ελλάδα. Ο Παναγιώτης πιστεύει ότι μπορεί και να ήταν ο μόνος άνθρωπος στη χώρα που μπορούσε να διαβάζει νευματική σημειογραφία και να τραγουδάει ταυτόχρονα.

Ο Παναγιώτης δεν εξασκούνταν και έπαιζε όργανο μόνο στην εκκλησία. Μπορούσε να εξασκείται στο τεράστιο εκκλησιαστικό όργανο του θεάτρου Sheboygan, επειδή ο επιστάτης, ο Χρήστος Σπανομίχος, ένας Έλληνας μετανάστης από την Καλαμάτα, του επέτρεπε να παίζει ενώ εκείνος σκούπιζε τα πατώματα. Το μεγάλο όργανο με τους τεράστιους σωλήνες τριών χειροκίνητων κλαβιέμ τύπου «βαριετέ» ήταν ένα απομεινάρι από την εποχή του βωβού κινηματογράφου, όταν χιλιάδες κινηματογραφικές αίθουσες εξαρτιόνταν από τη ζωντανή μουσική συνοδεία για τις προβολές των ταινιών αυτών. Ήταν πολύ πιο προσιτό να έχεις ένα "Mighty Wurlitzer" με μερικούς οργανοπαίχτες σε τέτοιες αίθουσες από το να πληρώνεις για μια πλήρη ορχήστρα ή ακόμη και μια μέτρια μπάντα που θα έπαιζε καθημερινά στην τάφρο της ορχήστρας. Η εμφάνιση του λόγου στον κινηματογράφο μείωσε σταδιακά τη χρήση αυτών των οργάνων στον κόσμο της ψυχαγωγίας, αλλά αρκετά επιβίωσαν σε αίθουσες όπως αυτή του Sheboygan. Το θέατρο είναι σήμερα γνωστό ως Stefanie H. Weill Center for the Performing Arts.

Ο Παναγιώτης μαζί με τον πατέρα του παρακολούθησαν το πρώτο Ελληνικό Ορθόδοξο Συνέδριο Χορωδιών στο Σικάγο το 1958 όπου ο Παναγιώτης ήταν ο οργανίστας. Το 1964 ανακυρήχθηκαν και οι δύο αντιπρόσωποι του Sheboygan στο δεύτερο Ελληνικό Ορθόδοξο Συνέδριο Χορωδιών που έγινε στο Σάιντ Λούις τον Οκτώβριο του 1964. Ο Παναγιώτης έπαιζε όργανο όχι μόνο κατά τη διάρκεια της Λειτουργίας αλλά και σε πολλά ακόμη εκκλησιαστικά, κοινοτικά και σχολικά δρώμενα, συμπεριλαμβανομένων γάμων και συναυλιών. Βασικά, στα περισσότερα από αυτά έπαιζε ο Παναγιώτης, αν και όχι σε όλα. Επίσης εμφανίστηκε ως μέλος μιας ελληνικής μπάντας με το όνομα «Σολ Δίεση» η οποία αποτελείτο από παιδιά κάτω των 12 ετών. Ο Παναγιώτης έπαιζε ακκορντεόν, ο αδερφός του Γκας τα μπόγκος και ο ξάδερφός τους ο George Brett, ο οποίος τελικά έγινε ποδίατρος, κλαρινέτο. Το ρεπερτόριο τους συμπεριλάμβανε μία γκάμα ελληνικών χορών. Οι παραστάσεις του Παναγιώτη συχνά αναφέρονται στην τοπική εφημερίδα. Το 1961, στο ετήσιο επίσημο μεσημεριανό γεύμα των βοηθών ιατρών στο Sheboygan αναφέρθηκε ότι «ο Παναγιώτης Τιμπόρης, ο γιος του ιατρού και της κυρίας ιατρού Ερνεστ Τιμπόρη ενθουσίασε το κοινό παίζοντας έργα στο ηλεκτρικό όργανο». Υπήρξε τελικά πολύ κοινό που θα απολάμβανε τον Παναγιώτη στο μέλλον.

Κεφαλαιο 60 Το Φεστιβαλ Του Αιγαιου

Η σύγχρονη Ελλάδα έχει μακρά παράδοση σε μουσικές και θεατρικές παραστάσεις, αρχής γενομένης με την δημιουργία του Φεστιβάλ Αθηνών από την Ελληνική Κυβέρνηση το 1955 με στόχο να προωθήσει την καλλιτεχνική και θεατρική δημιουργία και έμμεσα να προωθήσει τον τουρισμό. Τον πρώτο χρόνο του φεστιβάλ εμφανίστηκε η φιλαρμονική της Νέας Υόρκης με διευθυντή τον Δημήτρη Μητρόπουλο. Από τότε τα καλοκαιρινά φεστιβάλ πολλαπλασιάστηκαν σε όλη την Ελλάδα και μάλιστα ένα τρίτο από αυτά τα φεστιβάλ έχουν ως έδρα τους κάποιο νησί. Τα περισσότερα από αυτά επικεντρώνονται στην κλασική μουσική - η οποία αναφέρεται και ως δυτικοευρωπαϊκή μουσική από κάποιους. Παρόλη την οικονομική κρίση στην Ελλάδα από το 2009 και μεταγενέστερα ο αριθμός των φεστιβάλ αυξήθηκε.

Μουσικοκριτικός κατά τη διάρκεια της κρίσης έγραφε τα ακόλουθα: «Η αύξηση του αριθμού των φεστιβάλ δυτικοευρωπαϊκής μουσικής στην σύγχρονη Ελλάδα, όπως επίσης και η επιμονή τους να πετύχουν κάτω από δυσμενείς συνθήκες, χωρίς άλλο μπορούμε να πούμε ότι σχετίζεται με τη λειτουργία και τους σκοπούς που εξυπηρετεί κάθε φεστιβάλ. Πραγματικά, σε μία χώρα όπου η οικειότητα στους κατοίκους της δυτικοευρωπαϊκής μουσικής ως άκουσμα είναι αρκετά χαμηλότερη από τον μέσο Ευρωπαϊκό όρο, η άνθηση όλων αυτών των φεστιβάλ δεν αποδίδεται τόσο πολύ στην ικανοποίηση μίας ήδη υπάρχουσας μεγάλης «ζήτησης» για αυτή τη μουσική αλλά περισσότερο έχει σκοπό να αυξήσει την «προσφορά» ώστε να εξυπηρετήσει τους στόχους των Φεστιβάλ, δηλαδή τη μουσική εκπαίδευση, τις συνεργασίες και δικτύωση των καλλιτεχνών και έμμεσως τον τουρισμό.»

Και τους τρεις αυτούς σκοπούς τους υπηρέτησε το φεστιβάλ του Αιγαίου με αποτελεσματικότητα. Όσον αφορά την εκπαίδευση, το καλλιτεχνικό και επαγγελματικό μοντέλο του μαέστρου Τιμπέρη δίνει από τη φύση του έμφαση στην εκπαίδευση, δηλαδή δίνει τη δυνατότητα σε ερασιτεχνικές χορωδίες να εμφανιστούν και να ερμηνεύσουν έργα σε μεγάλες θεατρικές σκηνές, να συναντηθούν καλλιτεχνικά με καινούργιους μαέστρους αλλά και να δοκιμαστούν σε εναλλακτικές μορφές και τρόπους ερμηνείας. Ο Τιμπόρης έδωσε αυτή την ευκαιρία τόσο σε χορωδίες όσο και σε νεαρούς τραγουδιστές από την Ελλάδα και το εξωτερικό που είχαν τη δυνατότητα να τραγουδήσουν στις όπερες που παρουσίασε στη Σύρο. Και όπως θα δούμε, η σύζυγος και συνεργάτης του Τιμπόρη κ. Λαπαλάινεν δημιούργησε ένα στούντιο όπερας προσφέροντας εκπαίδευση και προγύμναση σε νέους τραγουδιστές

Η δικτύωση καλλιτεχνών που λαμβάνει χώρα στα φεστιβάλ μουσικής με τη μορφή δημοσίων σχέσεων είναι επωφελής για όλους όσους συμμετέχουν. Ο μαέστρος Τιμπόρης με τη σειρά του δέχτηκε προσκλήσεις να διευθύνει και σε άλλες πόλεις στην Ευρώπη, αλλά και επίσης όσοι είχε προσκαλέσει στο δικό του φεστιβάλ είχαν την ευκαιρία να διασυνδεθούν μεταξύ τους και με άλλους Έλληνες καλλιτέχνες.

Όσον αφορά τον τουρισμό: αν και δεν έχουμε ακριβή στοιχεία είναι ασφαλές να συμπεράνουμε ότι όταν σε μία χρονιά 400 χορωδοί έφτασαν στο νησί για να συμμετέχουν στο φεστιβάλ τα οφέλη για την τοπική τουριστική κοινωνία και το νησί συνολικά είναι προφανή.

Γνωρίζοντας καλά η δημοτική διοίκηση τη σημασία του φεστιβάλ δεν χρέωνε την χρήση των δημόσιων χώρων ή την επιπλέον εργασία του εργατικού δυναμικού της.

Σύμφωνα με μία έρευνα η Σύρος πραγματικά ζούσε από το φεστιβάλ του Αιγαίου κατά το μήνα Ιούλιο, ένα φεστιβάλ το οποίο προσείλκυε συμμετέχοντες από όλο τον κόσμο.

Επιπλέον, ένας από τους λόγους που το φεστιβάλ ήταν πιο δημοφιλές από το άλλο φεστιβάλ το οποίο προϋπήρχε στο νησί - το διεθνές μουσικό φεστιβάλ των Κυκλάδων - είναι ότι το φεστιβάλ του μαέστρου Τιμπόρη είχε επίκεντρο του την όπερα ενώ το άλλο την μουσική δωματίου.

Παρόλα αυτά, το να διοργανώσεις ένα φεστιβάλ κλασικής μουσικής σε ένα μικρό Αιγαιοπελαγίτικο νησί με έναν πληθυσμό 20 χιλιάδων το οποίο στο ζενίθ του το έτος 2019 είχε 200.000 τουριστικές αφίξεις κατά τη διάρκεια της περιόδου Ιουνίου - Σεπτεμβρίου ενέχει σημαντικούς κινδύνους όπως: τοπική διοικητική υποστήριξη και έκδοση αδειών σε μία χώρα με δαιδαλώδη γραφειοκρατία, τα υπέρ και τα κατά των τοπικών υποδομών και η στάση των ντόπιων σε αυτό το εγχείρημα σε μία χώρα όπου υπάρχει βαθιά ριζωμένη μία καχυποψία ως προς κάθε επιχειρηματική καινοτομία. Επιπλέον, για να περάσουμε στις λεπτομέρειες του φεστιβάλ, είναι πολύ σημαντικό να επιλέγεται να παρουσιαστεί μουσική η οποία θα έχει ανταπόκριση σε ένα ευρύ κοινό και θα είναι προσαρμοσμένη, κυριολεκτικά και μεταφορικά, στις ανάγκες ενός κοινού το οποίο απολαμβάνει καλοκαιρινές διακοπές στις παραλίες και είναι απίθανο να ρέπει προς πιο σοβαρές και απαιτητικές μορφές κλασσικής μουσικής.

Ο μαέστρος Τιμπόρης λοιπόν ήταν ο κατάλληλος άνθρωπος ικανός να ανταπεξέλθει σε όλες αυτές τις δυσκολίες του εγχειρήματος. ταν ο μόνος που, αναφερόμενος στο Αιγαιοπελαγίτικο νησί της Σύρου στο ζενίθ της τουριστικής περιόδου, πίστευε ότι: «Εγώ θα το φτιάξω και το κοινό θα έρθει» όπως λέει ένα Αμερικανικό ρητό. Γνωστός για το πείσμα του λοιπόν μπορούσε κάλλιστα να αναμετρηθεί με το τέρας τη Ελληνικής γραφειοκρατίας, καθώς η δυσφορία και αγανάκτηση που του προκαλούσε μετριαζόταν απο την αγάπη του για την Ελλάδα και την αποφασιστικότητά του να φέρει κλασσική μουσική στη γη των προγόνων του. Όσο για την επιλογή του ρεπερτορίου, γνώριζε ότι δεν μπορούσε να παρουσιάζει το ρεπερτόριο που συχνά παρουσίαζε στο Carnegie

Hall, δηλαδή κάποια πιο σπάνια έργα ή κάπως ξεχασμένους συνθέτες. Τα ονόματα των συνθετών που έργα τους θα παρουσιάζονταν στο Φεστιβάλ Αιγαίου θα ήταν όλα οικεία, όπως Μπετόβεν, Πουτσίνι, Ροσσίνι και Μότσαρτ.

ΜΙΑ ΜΕΡΑ ΕΝΑΣ ΜΠΗΚΕ ΜΕΣΑ Σ' ΕΝΑ ΘΕΑΤΡΟ.

« Όσο και αν ήταν φιλόδοξα – ως και αεροβασίες – τα σχέδια του μαέστρου όχι μόνο πραγματοποιήθηκαν αλλά στέφθηκαν και με επιτυχία. Το Φεστιβάλ αναδείχθηκε σε ένα ευρύτατα αναγνωρισμένο καλλιτεχνικό γεγονός και αποτέλεσε έναν πολιτιστικό μαγνήτη για τους φίλους της μουσικής τέχνης στο νησί μας». Αυτά ήταν τα λόγια του Γιάννη Δεκαβάλλα, που διατέλεσε για μακρύ χρονικό διάστημα δήμαρχος της Ερμούπολης στο όμορφο Κυκλαδίτικο νησί της Σύρου. Ο δήμαρχος ήταν ένα από τα λίγα πρόσωπα που ο Τιμπόρης είχε εκμυστηρευτεί τα φιλόδοξά του σχέδια. Από τους πρώτους που κατά την δεκαετία του 1980 έμαθαν για τα σχέδια του μαέστρου ήταν ο Gene Carr, εκτελεστικός διευθυντής της American Symphony Orchestra και ο Ελληνοαμερικανός συνθέτης Ντίνος Κωνσταντινίδης, καθηγητής στο Πανεπιστήμιο Louisiana State. Όλοι τους έγιναν μάρτυρες της εκπλήρωσής τους και εξεπλάγησαν.

Ο Δεκαβάλλας αναφέρθηκε στην πρώτη του συνάντηση με τον Μαέστρο Τιμπόρη το 1999 στο Δημαρχείο στην Ερμούπολη. Σε αυτή τη συγκεκριμένη περίοδο της καριέρας του Ο Πίτερ είχε διευθύνει σε αρκετές συναυλίες στην Ελλάδα όλα αυτά τα χρόνια και έψαχνε για κάποιο μέρος που θα μπορούσε να δημιουργήσει μία βάση και να οργανώνει μουσικές εκδηλώσεις εκεί κάθε καλοκαίρι . Αρχικά είχε προσπαθήσει να δημιουργήσει κάτι παρόμοιο στο νησί της Μυκόνου, το οποίο όμως δεν ευοδώθηκε. Η Μύκονος ήδη έχει ένα όνομα ως τουριστικός προορισμός υψηλού επιπέδου, γνωστή για τη νυχτερινή ζωή και την φιλικότητα προς την ΛΟΑΤΚΙ κοινότητα. Δεν υπάρχουν όμως οι απαραίτητες υποδομές ούτε η δυνατότητα από τις διοικήσεις των τοπικών κοινοτήτων να συνεισφέρουν εμπράκτως για να υποστηρίξουν το είδος του φεστιβάλ κλασικής μουσικής που ο μαέστρος Τιμπόρης είχε κατά νου. Με τη βοήθεια του γνωστού συλλέκτη και ξενοδόχου Δημήτρη Τσίτουρα γνώρισε ορισμένους γνωστούς του στη Μύκονο, ανάμεσα τους τον ξενοδόχο Σταύρο Γλαντζή, τον Τάσσο Σταμπόγλη και τους Δημήτρη και Αλεξάνδρα Ολούφ που του σύστησαν να εξετάσει τη περίπτωση της Σύρου. Ο Τσίτουρας παρέμεινε στενός φίλος του Τιμπόρη, έγινε ένα είδος ανεπίσημος έμπιστος σύμβουλος για την αντιμετώπιση της Ελληνικής πραγματικότητας και για θέματα αισθητικής.

Η Σύρος είναι ένα νησί το οποίο ανήκει στο ίδιο σύμπλεγμα Αιγαιοπελαγίτικων νησιών που χαρακτηρίζονται από τα λευκά τους σπίτια το οποίο ονομάζεται Κυκλάδες.

Η Σύρος όμως, παρόλο που είναι η πρωτεύουσα των Κυκλάδων, δεν μπορεί να ανταγωνιστεί τη Μύκονο ή τη Σαντορίνη ως διεθνής τουριστικός προορισμός αν και έχει τον δικό της κοσμοπολίτικο αλλά και πολύ προσωπικό χαρακτήρα, κυρίως λόγω της παρουσίας της καθολικής κοινότητας, υπόλειμμα της Βενετοκρατίας κατά την περίοδο του Μεσαίωνα. Επίσης κατά την διάρκεια του δέκατου ένατου αιώνα η Σύρος ήταν ένα από τα πλουσιότερα εμπορικά και ναυπηγοεπισκευαστικά λιμάνια στην Ανατολική Μεσόγειο με σπουδαίο ναυπηγείο.

Το Θεατρο Απολλων

Βλέποντας ο δήμαρχος τον ενθουσιασμό του μαέστρου Τιμπόρη κατάλαβε ότι υπάρχουν μεγάλες πιθανότητες να εδραιώσει μία μόνιμη παρουσία στη Σύρο και τον οδήγησε να δει από κοντά το θέατρο Απόλλων, το οποίο βρίσκεται δίπλα στην μεγαλεπήβολη πλατεία της Ερμούπολης και στο μεγαλοπρεπές νεοκλασικό δημαρχιακό μέγαρο. Ο Τιμπόρης είχε εντυπωσιαστεί όταν παλιότερα το είχε δει εξωτερικά αλλά έμεινε άναυδος τώρα που μπήκε μέσα για πρώτη φορά. Πάραυτα λοιπόν αποφάσισε ότι η Σύρος θα είναι το καλλιτεχνικό καλοκαιρινό του σπίτι στην Ελλάδα και το ανακοίνωσε ο ίδιος στον δήμαρχο Δεκαβάλλα όταν επέστρεψε για να επισκεφτεί το θέατρο άλλη μία φορά, προσθέτοντας ότι μία μέρα θα ξαναπαρουσιαστεί όπερα ξανά σε αυτή την αίθουσα όπως και παλιότερα.

Πολλά χρόνια αργότερα ο Τιμπόρης έγραψε στο πρόγραμμα του Φεστιβάλ του Αιγαίου του 2014 τα ακόλουθα: «Θυμάμαι όταν έφτασα στη Σύρο από τη Μύκονο αρκετά χρόνια πριν και αναρωτιόμουν αν ήταν πραγματικά δυνατόν να υπάρχει ένα μεγάλο θέατρο όπερας σε αυτό το μικρό αλλά σημαντικό Κυκλαδίτικο νησί. Από τη στιγμή όμως που ανέβηκα τα 11 σκαλοπάτια και πέρασα το κατώφλι του, ότι αμφιβολία και να είχα έκανε πέρα. Το συναίσθημα που ένιωσα, θα ήθελα να προσθέσω, ήταν το ίδιο όταν μπήκα στην αίθουσα του Carnegie Hall για πρώτη φορά στις 24 Νοεμβρίου του 1983. Σκεφτόμουν λοιπόν, πως είναι δυνατόν να υπάρχει ένα τέτοιο μεγαλοπρεπές θέατρο σε αυτό το Κυκλαδίτικο νησί; και θεωρούσα τον εαυτό μου πολύ τυχερό πού ανακάλυψα αυτό το θέατρο στην συγκεκριμένη αυτή στιγμή της ζωής μου.»

Ένα τέτοιο θέατρο αρμόζει σε ένα νησί το οποίο έζησε τόσο μεγάλη ευημερία και το αδιάκοπο πήγαινε-έλα Ελλήνων και ξένων εμπόρων. Γνωστό επίσης ως la piccola Scala κατασκευάστηκε μεταξύ 1862 και 1864 σε σχέδιο του Ιταλού αρχιτέκτονα Pietro Sampo. Παραμένει ως σήμερα το αρχιτεκτονικό στολίδι της Σύρου και ένα από τα παλαιότερα κλειστά θέατρα της εποχής μας. Λέγεται ότι ο η πηγή έμπνευσης για την κατασκευή του ήταν το περίφημο θέατρο όπερας La Scala του Μιλάνου, εντούτοις άλλες επιρροές είναι επίσης προφανείς. Η αίθουσα και η διπλή αψίδα του προσκηνίου με τους κίονες σε κορινθιακό ρυθμό έχουν εμπνευστεί από τη Σκάλα του Μιλάνου, το ανακαινισμένο θέατρο Σαν Κάρλο στη Νάπολη, το θέατρο στο Καστελφράνκο κοντά στην Βενετία και το Teatro de la Pergola στην Φλωρεντία. Ο θόλος με την αντιστήριξη του έλκουν από τις γαλλικές αρχιτεκτονικές παραδόσεις του 19ου αιώνα. Η εναρκτήρια παράσταση στο θέατρο Απόλλων φαίνεται ότι ήτανε η όπερα La Favorita (Η ευνοουμένη) του Γκαετάνο Ντονιτσέττι στις 3 Οκτωβρίου του 1864, αν και άλλες πηγές υποστηρίζουν ότι η εναρκτήρια παράσταση ήταν η όπερα Rigoletto του Τζουζέπε Βέρντι στις 20 Απριλίου 1864.

Οι οπερατικές και θεατρικές παραστάσεις αποτέλεσαν το κέντρο της καλλιτεχνικής ζωής στην Ερμούπολη. Αναφορές της εποχής από ξένους ταξιδιώτες μιλάνε γιά πλουσιότατα ανεβάσματα έργων όπερας και θεάτρου και για το καλοντυμένο και «σικ» κοινό που τα παρακολουθούσε. Το θέατρο Απόλλων φιλοξένησε πολυάριθμους θιάσους όπερας και θεάτρου, τόσο Ελληνικούς όσο και Ιταλικούς. Όταν όμως τα ατμόπλοια άρχισαν σιγά-σιγά να αντικαθιστούν τα ιστιοφόρα πλοία η οικονομία της Ερμούπολης άρχισε να φθίνει με αποτέλεσμα τν σταδιακή μείωση των παραστάσεων όπερας οι οποίες τελικά αντικαταστάθηκαν πλήρως από παραστάσεις θεάτρου από ελληνικούς θιάσους. Κατά τη διάρκεια του Δευτέρου Παγκοσμίου Πολέμου το θέατρο υπέστη ζημιές και την δεκαετία του 1950 το θέατρο κρίθηκε ακατάλληλο για παραστάσεις. Οι προσπάθειες για ανακαίνιση του καθυστέρησαν πολύ και τελικά οι εργασίες άρχισαν την δεκαετία του 1980 και το θέατρο ξανάνοιξε το 2000 μετά από μία μακρά περίοδο προσεκτικής αποκατάστασης και αναπαλαίωσης από μία ομάδα επικεφαλής της οποίας ήταν ο αρχιτέκτονας Πέτρος Πικιώνης, υπό από την αιγίδα του Υπουργείου Πολιτισμού και με την αρωγή του δήμου Ερμούπολης.

Το Φεστιβαλ Του Αιγαιου Γεννιεται

Παρά το γεγονός ότι η Ελλάδα είναι ένα μοντέρνο κράτος, το οποίο ανήκει στην Ευρωπαϊκή Ένωση, εν τούτοις δεν είναι γενικά ως χώρα ανοιχτή σε νέες ιδέες και πρωτοβουλίες. Μία γενική αδιαφορία, εφησυχασμός και ανοχή στον τρόπο που παραδοσιακά γίνονται οι δουλειές στην Ελλάδα αλλά και η απροθυμία να αναλάβουν ρίσκα είναι κάτι κοινότοπο στην Ελλάδα. Αντίθετα, οι Έλληνες της διασποράς είναι πιο ανοιχτοί σε προκλήσεις προσπαθώντας να δοκιμάσουν κάτι καινούργιο. Τον 5ο π.Χ. αιώνα στο βιβλίο του «Ιστορίαι» ο Ηρόδοτος γράφει ότι ο Περίανδρος, τύραννος της Κορίνθου, ζήτησε – μέσω ενός αγγελιαφόρου του - απο τον Θρασύβουλο, τύραννο της Μιλήτου, συμβουλές σχετικά με το πώς να κυβερνά. Ο Θρασύβουλος πήρε τον αγγελιοφόρο του Περίανδρου και τον πήγε σε έναν σιτοβολώνα, αντί να του απαντήσει ευθέως. Εκεί, έκοψε μπροστά του όλα τα καλύτερα και ψηλότερα στάχια. Αυτό λοιπόν μετέφερε στον Περίανδρο ο αγγελιοφόρος. Ο Περίανδρος το ερμήνευσε σωστά, ότι δηλαδή ο συνετός κυβερνήτης «απομακρύνοντας» άνδρες που είναι αρκετά ισχυροί για να τον αμφισβητήσουν προλαμβάνει τις διάφορες προκλήσεις στην εξουσία του. Αυτή η δημοφιλής στους σύγχρονους Έλληνες ιστορία μας δείχνει την σύγχρονη δυσαρέσκεια πρός καθετί που πάει αντίθετα με το κατεστημένο (απ' ότι δηλαδή θεωρείται κοινότυπο, παραδεκτό και συνηθισμένο).

Όπως λέει ο ίδιος ο Παναγιώτης Τιμπόρης, δεν αρέσκεται να υπεραναλύει και να κολλάει στα εμπόδια που ορθώθηκαν μπροστά του κατά την δημιουργία του Φεστιβάλ του Αιγαίου. Συμπληρώνει όμως ότι αν δεν ήταν Ελληνοαμερικανός, ελληνικής καταγωγής δηλαδή, θα είχε σταματήσει την προσπάθεια πολύ πριν το έργο του ολοκληρωθεί. Ο Γιάννης Ρώτας, οικονομολόγος στην Ερμούπολη ο οποίος έγινε στενός του φίλος, θυμάται ότι όταν ό Τιμπόρης μιλούσε για το θέατρο και για τα σχέδιά του ως μία «ευκαιρία» υπήρχαν πάρα πολλοί στο ακροατήριο πού δυσαρεστήθηκαν γιατί δεν μπορούσαν να σκεφτούν ότι το όραμα αυτό του Τιμπόρη θα είναι επωφελές και για όλο το νησί.

ΕΝΑ ΒΡΑΔΙ ΣΤΟ ΚΡΑΤΗΤΗΡΙΟ

Παρόλες τις δυσκολίες, τελικά η αποφασιστικότητα και το πείσμα του μαέστρου Τιμπόρη μαζί με την επιθυμία του να δημιουργήσει κάτι αξιόλογο στην πατρίδα των προγόνων του έφερε τελικά τα επιθυμητά αποτελέσματα και έκανε το όραμα του να πραγματοποιηθεί. Ο Τιμπόρης δεν τα έβαλε κάτω ακόμη όταν πέρασε σε ένα κελί στο τοπικό αστυνομικό τμήμα της Σύρου, εμπειρία που χαρακτήρισε μία καθόλου αστεία φαρσοκωμωδία. Αυτό συνέβη διότι μετά από έλεγχο της αστυνομίας βρέθηκε να οδηγεί μόνο με την αμερικανική άδεια οδήγησης στην κατοχή του, χωρίς διεθνή άδεια οδήγησης κάτι που είχε θεσπισθεί ως αναγκαιότητα προ εβδομάδων, αφού είχε ήδη αφιχθεί ο Τιμπόρης στην Ελλάδα. Είχε προηγηθεί μια ελαφρά σύγκρουση μοτοσυκλέτας με το αυτοκίνητο του Τιμπόρη που οδηγούσε στη πλατεία της Ερμούπολης καθ' οδόν σε μια δεξίωση μετά από μία μεγάλη συναυλία. Παρόλο πως το μόνο που έγινε ήταν μία μικρή ζημιά στη πόρτα του αυτοκινήτου του μαέστρου, οδηγήθηκε στο τμήμα λόγω του θέματος της άδειας παρά τις εξηγήσεις που παρείχε ο φίλος και συνάδελφος μαέστρος Χρήστος Παπαγεωργίου που ήταν μαζί στο αυτοκίνητο εκείνο το βράδυ. Στο τμήμα ο αστυνομικός υπηρεσίας τον πληροφόρησε πως η παράβαση ανήκε στη κατηγορία του αυτόφωρου και έπρεπε να παραμείνει στο τμήμα μέχρι να φθάσει ο εισαγγελέας το πρωί. Του επέτρεψε να μείνει στον χώρο της αναμονής – ήταν ήδη μετά τα μεσάνυχτα. Αλλά ο επόμενος αστυνομικός υπηρεσίας που ήρθε επέμενε πως ο Τιμπόρης έπρεπε να μείνει σε ένα κελί στο υπόγειο του αστυνομικού τμήματος (!). Όταν επιτέλους κατέφθασε το άλλο πρωί ο εισαγγελέας μπόρεσε να φύγει ο Τιμπόρης, κατάκοπος και ενοχλημένος. Όπως έφευγε, ο εν λόγω αστυνομικός του είπε φεύγοντας πως τον ευχαριστεί για όλα όσα είχε κάνει για το νησί, και πως αυτός και η οικογένεια του θα πήγαιναν στην αποψινή παράσταση. «Γύρισα τη πλάτη σε αυτόν το ανόητο» είπε ο Τιμπόρης, «και βγήκα από το τμήμα να πάω στη πρωινή πρόβα». Μετά από μερικές μήνες, χάρη στις ενέργειες του φίλου και δικηγόρου Μάνθου Μανθόπουλου, ο Τιμπόρης αθωώθηκε από το δικαστήριο της Ερμούπολης. Υπήρξε και μία χιουμοριστική νότα για τον Τιμπόρη σε όλη αυτή την υπόθεση. Μαζί με αυτόν και η Eilana, που τον πείραζε για το ό,τι είχε γίνει έλαβε κλήση διότι το αυτοκίνητο ήταν δικό της και έφερε ευθύνη διότι άφησε τον Παναγιώτη να οδηγήσει το αυτοκίνητο. Ο Μανθόπουλος διευθέτησε και αυτή τη περίπτωση. Για οποιονδήποτε άλλο ντόπιο Έλληνα του διαμετρήματός του θα ήτανε πιο διαλλακτικοί οι αστυνομικοί, για κάποιον ξενόφερτο όμως, όπως φαίνεται, ίσχυαν άλλοι κανόνες. Κανένα εμπόδιο όμως, είτε ανθρώπινο είτε τεχνικό δεν είναι ανυπέρβλητο για αυτόν και στο τέλος μπόρεσε να υλοποιήσει το όραμά του, να παρουσιάσει συναυλίες στο θέατρο Απόλλωνα στην υπέροχη εκκλησία της Αναστάσεως και στην κεντρική πλατεία.

Η μαέστρος Ζωή Ζηνιώδη θεωρεί ότι μαζί με τον μοναδικό συνδυασμό πείσματος και ισχυρογνωμοσύνης με αφοπλιστική γοητεία του μαέστρου Τιμπόρη άλλο ένα από τα χαρακτηριστικά του είναι η δυνατότητα που έχει να συγχωρεί και να βαδίζει μπροστά. Γράφει λοιπόν σε ένα email: «Συνέβη ένα περιστατικό κατά τη διάρκεια ενός φεστιβάλ και ο Παναγιώτης ήταν πολύ δίκαιος με τους εμπλεκόμενους, κάποιοι όμως δεν έδειχναν το ίδιο και σε αυτόν. Πάντα κρατούσε ίσες αποστάσεις και προσπαθούσε να κατανοήσει και τους υπόλοιπους, προσπαθώντας να βρει λύση σε οποιοδήποτε πρόβλημα και να συμβιβάσει τα πράγματα. Στο συγκεκριμένο περιστατικό, μία ημέρα μετά από το κονσέρτο μας στην εκκλησία, πήγα να τον βρω λίγο πριν την γενική πρόβα. Ήταν μόνος του και καθόταν με δάκρυα στα μάτια του. Κάθισα δίπλα του και τον ρώτησα αν χρειάζεται βοήθεια. Τότε με κοίταξε και χαμογέλασε και είπε: «όχι γιατί είμαι υπομονετικός και συγχωρώ...».[*]

Ο μαέστρος Τιμπόρης και ο δήμαρχος Δεκαβάλλας άρχισαν να δουλεύουν μαζί και κάθε καλοκαίρι, μετά την πρώτη του επίσκεψη του 1999, οργανώνονταν συναυλίες στην Σύρο. Αρκετοί κάτοικοι από το νησί διαπίστωσαν την σπουδαιότητα αυτών που προσπαθούσε να πραγματοποιήσει και πρόσφεραν την βοήθειά τους. Ένας σημαντικός σύμμαχος που έγινε στενός φίλος του Παναγιώτη ήταν και ο συριανός στην καταγωγή Μπάμπης Κουλούρας, συνθέτης, στιχουργός και εκτελεστής, γνωστός διεθνώς ως διευθυντής μουσικών και ποιητικών συνόλων με διεθνή παρουσία, δίνοντας μεγάλο βάρος στο ποιητικό έργο του Έλληνα Αλεξανδρινού ποιητή Κωνσταντίνου Καβάφη.

Πριν τη δημιουργία του Φεστιβάλ Αιγαίου ο μαέστρος Τιμπόρης ίδρυσε την «Όπερα Αιγαίου» κατά τη διάρκεια της οποίας 21 καλλιτέχνες από όλο τον κόσμο μαζί με καλλιτεχνικό και διοικητικό προσωπικό 15 ατόμων έφτασαν στην Ελλάδα τον Ιούλιο του 2000 για μία τουρνέ που περιλάμβανε πρόβες, συναυλίες, παρακολούθηση άλλων κοντσέρτων, τουριστικές επισκέψεις και συνάντηση με τον τενόρο Πλάσιντο Ντομίνγκο. Με επικεφαλής τον Παναγιώτη Τιμπόρη το καλλιτεχνικό προσωπικό συμπεριλάμβανε ως καλλιτεχνικό διευθυντή τον Sherrill Milnes, σκηνοθέτη την Carol Castel, τον Nicolas Di Virgilio στην διδασκαλία και προετοιμασία, τη Maria Zouves ως φιλοξενούμενη καλλιτέχνη, τον Jonathan Griffiths χοράρχη και τον Μανώλη Παπασηφάκη ως μουσικό προγυμναστή και συνοδό πιάνου. Συναυλίες δόθηκαν σε Αθήνα, Άνδρο, Πάρο καθώς και στην Πελοπόννησο.

Το Φεστιβαλ Του Αιγαιου Ξεκινα

Η έναρξη του φεστιβάλ Αιγαίου δόθηκε το 2005. Η πρώτη όπερα που παρουσιάστηκε στο θέατρο Απόλλων - μετά από 100 χρόνια «σιωπής» ήταν «Ο κουρέας της Σεβίλλης» του Ροσσίνι στις 14 Ιουλίου 2005, μία παραγωγή του φεστιβάλ Αιγαίου με τον Μαέστρο Τιμπόρη διευθυντή ορχήστρας. Ο Gianmaria Romagnoli ήταν ο σκηνοθέτης και η διανομή ήταν ως εξής: Figaro: Pietro Masi, βαρύτονος, Rosina: Maria Francesca Mazzara, σοπράνο, Almaviva: Amedeo Moretti, τενόρος, Dr. Bartolo: Carmine Monaco, μπάσσος, Don Basilio: Raffaele Costantini, μπάσσο-βαρύτονος, Fiorello: Stefano Vito, βαρύτονος, Berta: Takako Horaguchi, μεσόφωνος. Την ορχήστρα αποτελούσαν σολίστες απο την Φιλαρμονική Ορχήστρα της Ρώμης και οι πιανίστες Γιάννης Ξυλάς και Τάνια Παπαγιαννοπούλου. Ο Δήμαρχος Δεκαβάλλας έγραψε ότι «τα συναισθήματα του κοινού κατά τη διάρκεια της πρεμιέρας, ειδικότερα των κατοίκων του νησιού που παρακολουθούσαν την παράσταση ήταν απερίγραπτα».

Την επόμενη χρονιά, 2006, το φεστιβάλ διευρύνθηκε και διήρκεσε τέσσερις ημέρες, εορτάζοντας τα 250 χρόνια από την γέννηση του Μότσαρτ. Ο Τιμπόρης διήυθυνε την όπερα «Ντον Τζοβάννι» του Μότσαρτ με τον βαρύτονο Arnando Mora στον ομώνυμο ρόλο, την Eilana Lappalainen ως Ντόνα Άννα και τον Antonio Stragapede ως κυβερνήτη. Οι επόμενες δύο ημέρες είχαν μία συναυλία αποκλειστικά με έργα του

Μότσαρτ και μία συναυλία με επιλογές από μιούζικαλ του Μπρόντγουεϊ, όπως West Side Story, Oklahoma!, My Fair Lady, Candide, South Pacific, Carousel, The King and I, Porgy and Bess. Η συναυλία με έργα Μπρόντγουεϊ επαναλήφθηκε και στο γειτονικό νησί της Πάρου.

Με την υποστήριξη του δημάρχου Δεκαβάλλα και το επόμενο έτος 2007, είχαμε ένα πολύ επιτυχημένο φεστιβάλ. Στην εναρκτήρια συναυλία Γκαλά του φεστιβάλ ο μαέστρος Τιμπόρης διεύθυνε την φιλαρμονική ορχήστρα Bohuslav Martinů από την Τσεχία με σολίστα τη μεσόφωνο Ειρήνη Τσιρακίδη. Τις επόμενες τρεις βραδιές, πάλι με την συνοδεία της φιλαρμονικής ορχήστρας από την Τσεχία υπό τον Μαέστρο Τιμπόρη, παρουσιάστηκαν: η Ελληνική πρεμιέρα της σπάνιας μονόπρακτης όπερας «Ζανέτο» του Πιέτρο Μασκάνι (με την μεσόφωνο Jennifer Larmore στον ομώνυμο ρόλο και την σοπράνο Eilana Lappalainen ως Σύλβια) καθώς και συναυλία με αποσπάσματα από όπερες με τους σολίστες Eilana Lappalainen σοπράνο, Jennifer Larmore μεσόφωνο, Todd Geer τενόρο and William Powers μπάσο-βαρύτονο. Τέλος, κατά παρέκκλιση από τον χαρακτήρα της κλασσικής μουσικής του φεστιβάλ, είχαμε σε εμφανίσεις στην κεντρική πλατεία Μιαούλη της Ερμούπολης τον Έλληνα σαξοφωνίστα Στράτο Βουγά με το δικό του quintetto Jazz όπως επίσης και παραδοσιακή ελληνική ρεμπέτικη μουσική με το συγκρότημα Ταξίμι, το οποίο έχει ως έδρα του την Σουηδία.

Κάθε έτος το Φεστιβάλ συνέχιζε να μεγαλώνει με γοργούς ρυθμούς, τόσο σε μεγέθη όσο και σε διεθνή εμβέλεια. Το Φεστιβάλ του 2008 παρουσίασε μέλη της Manhattan Philharmonia της Νέας Υόρκης, τη χορωδία Columbia Collegiate Chorale από το Maryland και τη χορωδία και Φιλαρμονική ορχήστρα της όπερας Podlasie από το Bialystock της Πολωνίας.

Το 2009, το πέμπτο ετήσιο Φεστιβάλ παρουσίασε τους: Raymond Hughes ως προσκεκλημένο μαέστρο, Peter Meineck σκηνοθέτη του Aquila Theatre of New York, Renato Zanella χορογράφο και σκηνοθέτη όπως επίσης και την Pan-European Philharmonia Orchestra, τη χορωδία Southwestern College Concert Choir απο την Chula Vista της Καλιφόρνιας υπό τη διεύθυνση της Teresa Russell, μέλη της χορωδίας του Εθνικού Ωδείου Αθηνών με χοράρχη τον Σπύρο Κλάψη, το χορωδιακό σύνολο Athens Singers και μέλη του τμήματος μουσικών σπουδών του Ιόνιου Πανεπιστήμιου.

Ο χορογράφος και σκηνοθέτης Renato Zanella θα επέστρεφε στο φεστιβάλ για δύο ακόμα καλοκαίρια. Το 2011 διορίστηκε καλλιτεχνικός διευθυντής του μπαλέτου της Εθνικής Λυρικής Σκηνής στην Αθήνα και παρέμεινε σε αυτή τη θέση γιά τέσσερα χρόνια, παράλληλα συνέχισε όμως να λαμβάνει μέρος και στο φεστιβάλ του Αιγαίου. Γεννημένος στη Βερόνα ξεκίνησε την καριέρα του ως χορευτής και αργότερα συνέχισε ως χορογράφος σε παραστάσεις όπερας.

Το 6ο Φεστιβάλ Αιγαίου 2010

Το 6ο Φεστιβάλ Αιγαίου το 2010 άνοιξε με την όπερα «Κάρμεν» του Μπιζέ με τον μαέστρο Τιμπόρη διευθυντή ορχήστρας και τον Renato Zanella ως σκηνοθέτη. Η καταξιωμένη μεσόφωνος Carla Dirlikov Canales με καταγωγή Βούλγαρο-Μεξικανική τραγούδησε τον επώνυμο ρόλο. Η Carla κάνει διεθνή καριέρα και είναι αναγνωρισμένη ως υπέρμαχος των τεχνών και του Πολιτισμού. Ο Κουβανό-Αμερικανός τενόρος Raul Melo ερμήνευσε τον ρόλο του Don José. Σημαντικό επίσης ήταν το γεγονός ότι συμμετείχαν στη διανομή και πολλοί Έλληνες τραγουδιστές. Το εύρος του Φεστιβάλ ήταν εμφανές στον μακρύ κατάλογο των συμμετεχόντων και στην ποικιλία των μουσικών ειδών. Ενδεικτικά αναφέρουμε τα κονσέρτα που δίνονταν κατά την ώρα του ηλιοβασιλέματος στον Ιερό Ναό του Αγίου Νικολάου και το κονσέρτο με την θρυλική Μαρία Φαραντούρη, γνωστή διεθνώς από τη στενή και μακροχρόνια συνεργασία της με τον συνθέτη Μίκη Θεοδωράκη.

Οι χορωδίες που συμμετείχαν απο Ελλάδα, Η.Π.Α. και Καναδά ήταν: το Birmingham Alabama Concert Chorale υπό τη διεύθυνση του Philip Copeland, το Vocal Ensemble of Mira Costa High School από το Manhattan Beach της Καλιφόρνιας υπό τη διεύθυνση του Michael Hayden, οι Michael O'Neal Singers από τη Georgia υπό τη διεύθυνση του Michael O'Neal, το King College Symphonic Choir από το Tennessee υπό τη διεύθυνση του W. Patrick Flannagan, οι Kamloops Choristers από τη British Columbia του Καναδά υπό τη διεύθυνση της Margaret Brown καθώς και τρεις χορωδίες από την Ελλάδα: Η Camerata Vocalis από την Κέρκυρα υπό τη διεύθυνση της Ρόζας Πουλημένου, μέλη της χορωδίας του Εθνικού Ωδείου Αθηνών με χοράρχη τον Σπύρο Κλάψη και η Χορωδία Ανδρών του Ορθόδοξου Ιερού Ναού Αγίου Νικολάου της Σύρου.

Francis Bardot

Στο Φεστιβάλ Αιγαίου 2010 ξεχωρίζει μια σημαντική παιδική χορωδία απο το Παρίσι, η Coeur d'Enfants d'Ile-de-France υπό τη διεύθυνση του Francis Bardot. Ήταν η πρώτη τους εμφάνιση στο Φεστιβάλ και ακολούθως θα εμφανίζονταν στο Φεστιβάλ κάθε δύο χρόνια. Ο Bardot ήδη έφερνε τις παιδικές του χορωδίες στη Σύρο για αρκετά χρόνια, με την υποστήριξη της Καθολικής Εκκλησίας. Ο Bardot είναι ένας πολυπράγμων άνθρωπος.

με βαθιά αγάπη και σεβασμό για την αρχαία και την σύγχρονη Ελλάδα όπως επίσης και τους ανθρώπους της και την Ελληνική ορθοδοξία. Ως σολίστας τενόρος, με ειδίκευση στα ορατόρια, ήδη από την ηλικία των 18 ετών έδωσε 2000 κονσέρτα στην Γαλλία και στο εξωτερικό και έχει συμμετέχει σε 20 ηχογραφήσεις με γνωστές εταιρείες όπως RCA και Deutsche Grammophon.

Γαλουχημένος με βαθιά αγάπη για τις κλασικές σπουδές έγινε καθηγητής στο Institut Supérieur de Pédagogie (παιδαγωγικό ινστιτούτο) του Institut Catholique de Paris (Καθολικό ινστιτούτο του Παρισιού) σε ηλικία 24 ετών και ακολούθως δίδαξε λατινικά, αρχαία ελληνικά, κλασσική γαλλική λογοτεχνία και φιλοσοφία. Εκεί ίδρυσε την πρώτη σχολή χορωδίας για παιδιά. Κατόπιν αποφάσισε να αφιερώσει τη ζωή του αποκλειστικά στη μουσική διεύθυνση χορωδιών και ορχηστρών. Ίδρυσε πολλές τέτοιες χορωδίες στην Γαλλία και ως χοράρχης έκανε εμφανίσεις σε πολλές χώρες ανά την υφήλιο.

Ο Francis Bardot και ο Παναγιώτης Τιμπόρης γνωρίστηκαν για πρώτη φορά στη Σύρο το 2009 και όπως θυμάται ο Bardot η πρώτη συνάντηση ήταν πολύ έντονη παρομοιάζοντας την σαν ηλεκτρικό ρεύμα. Ο Bardot θεωρεί τον Τιμπόρη ως έναν αδερφό κάτι το οποίο δεν μπορεί να μας εκπλήσσει καθόλου μια που μοιράζονται πολλά κοινά, ξεκινώντας από την ηλικία τους. Ο Bardot γεννήθηκε το 1946, ένα έτος πριν από τον Τιμπόρη. Και οι δυο τους είναι βαθιά θρησκευόμενοι, ο Bardot καθολικός και ο Τιμπόρης ελληνορθόδοξος. Και οι δύο αφιέρωσαν τη ζωή τους στη μουσική. Ο Bardot εντυπωσιάστηκε από τον τρόπο που ο Τιμπόρης συνδυάζει το οργανωτικό ταλέντο, ειδικά επειδή προσλαμβάνει διοικητικό προσωπικό το οποίο έχει μουσικές γνώσεις. Αναγνωρίζει επίσης το εξαιρετικό του ταλέντο ως μαέστρος το οποίο για πρώτη φορά διαπίστωσε όταν ο Τιμπόρης διεύθυνε Μπετόβεν χωρίς τη βοήθεια παρτιτούρας.[87]

ΤΟ ΕΛΛΗΝΙΚΟ ΣΤΟΥΝΤΙΟ ΟΠΕΡΑΣ

Στα πλαίσια του Φεστιβάλ Αιγαίου του 2010 έκανε την πρώτη του εμφάνιση το Ελληνικό Στούντιο Όπερας με μία συναυλία Γκαλά. Η Eilana Lappalainen ίδρυσε το ελληνικό studio όπερας το 2010 σε συνεργασία με το φεστιβάλ. Πρόκειται για ένα καλοκαιρινό πρόγραμμα που, εστιάζοντας στη φόρμα του κλασικού τραγουδιού, συνδυάζει την μελέτη διαφόρων έργων με παραστάσεις μπροστά σε κοινό. Είναι προσαρμοσμένο για νεαρούς καλλιτέχνες που ξεκινούν την καριέρα τους στον κόσμο της όπερας. Το πρόγραμμα προσφέρει εντατική καθοδήγηση, εκμάθηση και ανάπτυξη δεξιοτήτων επί σκηνής για νεαρούς τραγουδιστές που ενδιαφέρονται να προετοιμαστούν για ακροάσεις όπερας σε τοπικό και διεθνές επίπεδο. Το στούντιο όπερας εμφανίστηκε πάλι το 2011 και το 2012 ως εναρκτήριες παραστάσεις στο Φεστιβάλ. Το ίδιο συνέβη και το 2013 ενώ το 2014 έκλεισε με τη συναυλία του, ως φινάλε, το Φεστιβάλ. Τότε πια είχε καθιερωθεί ως σταθερό/μόνιμο κομμάτι του φεστιβάλ.

Μουσικη σε Καιρους Κρισης

Δύο μήνες πριν την έναρξη του έκτου φεστιβάλ Αιγαίου στη Σύρο ξέσπασαν βίαιες διαδηλώσεις στην πρωτεύουσα Αθήνα που στοίχισαν τη ζωή σε τρία άτομα όταν διαδηλωτές έριξαν χειροβομβίδες μέσα σε μία τράπεζα. Η Ελλάδα είχε εισέλθει σε μία μακρά οικονομική κρίση σχεδόν μιας δεκαετίας από την οποία θα έβγαινε το 2018. Οι διαδηλώσεις το 2010 ήταν ενάντια σε μία σειρά μέτρων λιτότητας που επηρέασαν αρνητικά τους μισθούς τις συντάξεις των πολιτών που σε συνδυασμό με την αυξημένη φορολογία βύθισαν πολλά ελληνικά νοικοκυριά στην ανέχεια. Επόμενο ήταν αυτές οι οριζόντιες περικοπές σε κυβερνητικά προγράμματα να επηρεάσουν αρνητικά και τις τέχνες στην Ελλάδα οι οποίες κατά κύριο λόγο λαμβάνουν κυβερνητικές επιδοτήσεις παρά ιδιωτικές ενισχύσεις. Αυτές οι κυβερνητικές επιδοτήσεις σε κάποιους από τους μεγαλύτερους ελληνικούς πολιτιστικούς φορείς όπως το Μέγαρο Μουσικής Αθηνών μειώθηκαν ως και 75% σε σύγκριση με τις προ οικονομικής κρίσης εποχές.[88] Παρόλα αυτά, οι πολιτιστικοί φορείς που είχαν χρηματοδότηση από το εξωτερικό ή αυτοί που είχαν χαμηλό προϋπολογισμό κατάφεραν να επιζήσουν. Μπορούμε να πούμε ότι αυτή η κρίση πυροδότησε ένα αυξημένο ενδιαφέρον γιά τις τέχνες γενικά και ειδικά σε τοπικό επίπεδο. Αυτήν την εποχή που οι άνθρωποι ταξίδευαν λιγότερο η μείωση της τιμής των εισιτηρίων η οποία παρατηρήθηκε επίσης αποδίδεται σε αυτή την τάση.

Τα Αιγαιοπελαγίτικα νησιά, συμπεριλαμβανομένης και της Σύρου, ήταν φυσικό να επηρεαστούν και αυτά από την κρίση, όπως και όλη η υπόλοιπη χώρα. Η εισροή τουριστικού συναλλάγματος κατά τους καλοκαιρινούς μήνες βοήθησε να αμβλυνθούν λίγο οι συνέπειες απο τα μέτρα της οικονομικής λιτότητας. Βλέποντας το από αυτήν την οπτική γωνία η παρουσία του Φεστιβάλ Αιγαίου κάθε καλοκαίρι είχε οικονομικά μια μεγάλη ευεργετική επίδραση στο νησί. Επιπλέον, όπως πάντα η μουσική μπορεί να εμπνέει, να συνδέει και να ενώνει τους ανθρώπους και στη συγκεκριμένη περίπτωση να ανεβάσει το πεσμένο τους ηθικό.

Το 7ο Φεστιβαλ Αιγαιου το 2011

Ένα από τα επαναλαμβανόμενα μοτίβα - για να χρησιμοποιήσουμε και έναν μουσικό όρο - στην ζωή του Παναγιώτη Τιμπόρη είναι οι επέτειοι. Ασχολούμενος πολύ με το ζήτημα, πάντα προετοίμαζε κονσέρτα τα οποία τιμούν τις επετείους γέννησης ή θανάτου σημαντικών συνθετών. Επίσης, είναι πολύ σημαντικές γι' αυτόν οι επέτειοι που σχετίζονται με τη δική του επαγγελματική ζωή, όπως για παράδειγμα η ίδρυση της εταιρείας του με την ονομασία MidAmerica το 1983, ένα χρόνο πριν από το ντεμπούτο του στη Νέα Υόρκη. Οι περισσότερες από αυτές τις επετείους σηματοδοτούνται όταν πρόκειται για ένα στρογγυλό αριθμό ετών αλλά όχι πάντα. Για παράδειγμα, στο πρόγραμμα του φεστιβάλ Αιγαίου 2011 συμπεριέλαβε μία ανοιχτή επιστολή στους «φίλους του Φεστιβάλ» μιλώντας με πολύ συναισθηματισμό για το επερχόμενο 7ο φεστιβάλ και, όπως συνηθίζει πάντα, αναγνώρισε όλους του τους συνεργάτες και τους ευχαρίστησε γενναιόδωρα.

Συγκεκριμένα έγραφε: «ακόμα και εγώ δυσκολεύομαι να το πιστέψω ότι το φεστιβάλ Αιγαίου έχει φτάσει στον έβδομο χρόνο. Μου φαίνεται σαν να ήταν χθες πού ο δήμαρχος Δεκαβάλλας και εγώ υπογράψαμε ένα μνημόνιο συνεργασίας με μία δεκαετή προοπτική για το Φεστιβάλ. Οι στόχοι που θέσαμε ήταν βέβαια περιορισμένοι, παρόλα αυτά είχαν ουσία και περιεχόμενο. Κανένας δεν φανταζόταν ότι θα είχαμε ξεπεράσει αυτούς τους στόχους και τώρα ανοίγουμε καινούργιους δρόμους ώστε να γίνει το Φεστιβάλ κάτι το ξεχωριστό και ιδιαίτερο, όχι μόνο στην Ελλάδα αλλά και διεθνώς. Ήταν 14 Ιουλίου του 2005 όταν παρουσιάσαμε την πρώτη μας όπερα, τον Κουρέα της Σεβίλλης του Ροσσίνι, η οποία ήταν η πρώτη όπερα που παρουσιάστηκε στο θέατρο Απόλλων για περισσότερα από 105 χρόνια με σκηνικά, κοστούμια, διανομή και ορχήστρα εξ' ολοκλήρου απο την Ιταλία. Από τότε παρουσιάσαμε τις όπερες Cavalleria Rusticana, Zanetto, Don Giovanni, Carmen, Tosca και φέτος παρουσιάζουμε το αθάνατο αριστούργημα του Βέρντι La Traviata.

Παρουσιάσαμε μπαλέτα διεθνών προδιαγραφών με τον χορογράφο Renato Zanella, Shakespeare και Όμηρο με το θέατρο Aquila και τον σκηνοθέτη Peter Meineck, Συμφωνικά έργα, κονσέρτα, παραδοσιακή μουσική, Ελληνική μουσική, εκκλησιαστική μουσική στον Ορθόδοξο καθεδρικό του Αγίου Νικολάου, καθώς και την καινούρια συνιστώσα του Φεστιβάλ, το Ελληνικό στούντιο όπερας, που ίδρυσε η Eilana Lappalainen, Σολίστες διεθνούς διαμετρήματος και χορωδίες απο τις Η.Π.Α., Γαλλία, Καναδά και Ελλάδα (φέτος οι διευθυντές χορωδίας που θα εμφανιστούν είναι οι Tim Sharp, Earl Rivers και Janet Galvan).

Σπουδαία χορωδιακά έργα με εκατοντάδες τραγουδιστές να συμμετέχουν σε αλησμόνητες συναυλίες στην εκκλησία του Αγίου Νικολάου και φέτος για πρώτη φορά θα φέρουμε το φεστιβάλ στην πλατεία Μιαούλη για να παρουσιάσουμε το έργο Carmina Burana καθώς και έργα του Μίκη Θεοδωράκη. Και σαν να μην ήταν αρκετά όλα αυτά, θα έχουμε και την μεγάλη ηθοποιό του θεάτρου και κινηματογράφου Ολυμπία Δουκάκη να τιμήσει το μεγάλο νησί της Σύρου με την παρουσία της.

Είναι τόσο πολλοί οι συντελεστές που θα ήθελα να ευχαριστήσω και επειδή δεν θέλω να αφήσω κάποιον έξω που να μην τον αναφέρω θα ήθελα να εκφράσω από καρδιάς ένα μεγάλο ευχαριστώ σε όλους σας. Με την ενθουσιώδη υποστήριξή σας το φεστιβάλ έχει μεγαλώσει, έχει ωριμάσει και έχει ξεπεράσει τα όρια της Ελλάδας. Όλα αυτά λοιπόν μας οδηγούν στο εορταστικό έτος 2014, όταν το θέατρο Απόλλων θα εορτάσει την 150η του επέτειο. Στις 20 Απριλίου 1864 το θέατρο άνοιξε τις πόρτες του για πρώτη φορά με την όπερα του Βέρντι «Ριγκολέτο». Θα κάνουμε και εμείς το ίδιο το 2014 εορτάζοντας επίσης και τα 10 χρόνια του φεστιβάλ Αιγαίου. Εδώ αξίζει να αναφέρω ότι 20 Απριλίου 2014 πέφτει Κυριακή του Πάσχα! Δεν θα μπορούσα να κλείσω αυτήν την επιστολή χωρίς να αναφέρω όλους όσους έχουν υποστηρίξει το Φεστιβάλ καθώς και τους «φίλους του Φεστιβάλ», το δήμαρχο Δεκαβάλλα και το δημοτικό συμβούλιο, τους Ιωάννη Κεράνη και Ιωάννη Πιταούλη και – πολύ σημαντικό - τους χορηγούς από τις Ηνωμένες Πολιτείες Αμερικής που συνεισφέρουν 85% της χρηματοδότησης για το Φεστιβάλ. Ένα μεγάλο ευχαριστώ και για το προσωπικό της εταιρείας μου MidAmerica Productions στη Νέα Υόρκη που αυτή την χρόνια εορτάζει 29 έτη παρουσίας στο ιστορικό Carnegie Hall.»

CARMINA BURANA ΚΑΤΩ ΑΠΟ Τ' ΑΣΤΕΡΙΑ

Η Carmina Burana είναι μία καντάτα, αποτελούμενη από 24 κομμάτια, η οποία διαρκεί περίπου πενήντα πέντε λεπτά. Όταν μίλησε ο μαέστρος Τιμπόρης με τον δήμαρχο Δεκαβάλλα για το σχέδιό του να παρουσιάσει αυτήν την καντάτα σε ανοιχτό χώρο ο δήμαρχος ανησύχησε. Μία παράσταση σε έναν κλειστό χώρο όπου έρχονται θεατές που αγαπούν τη μουσική και γνωρίζουν τι θα παρακολουθήσουν είναι κάτι εντελώς διαφορετικό από μία παράσταση σε εξωτερικό χώρο, ανοιχτή για όλο το κοινό που έχει τη διάθεση να την παρακολουθήσει αλλά έχει ελάχιστες μουσικές γνώσεις και «υπόβαθρο». Ο χώρος που επιλέχθηκε ήταν η τεράστια πλατεία Μιαούλη στο κέντρο της Ερμούπολης μπροστά ακριβώς από το μεγαλοπρεπές δημαρχιακό Μέγαρο χτισμένο σε νεοκλασικό στυλ. Όπως ήταν φυσικό τίποτα δεν μπορούσε να σταματήσει τον μαέστρο και έτσι στις 17 Ιουλίου 2011 στις 22:00 το βράδυ έλαβε χώρα η συναυλία όπως είχε προγραμματιστεί στην πλατεία Μιαούλη. Συμμετείχαν οι σολίστες: Μυρσίνη Μαργαρίτη σοπράνο, Πώλ Ζαχαριάδης, άρρεν κοντράλτο και ο Αμερικανός βαρύτονος Frederick Burchinal. Τους συνόδευσε η φιλαρμονική ορχήστρα Pan European Philharmonia και 400 τραγουδιστές απο χορωδίες προερχόμενες απο τον Καναδά, τις Ηνωμένες Πολιτείες και την Ελλάδα. Οι χορωδοί συντάχθηκαν κλιμακωτά και κατά μήκος των σκαλοπατιών του δημαρχιακού Μεγάρου και η ορχήστρα τοποθετήθηκε ακριβώς μπροστά και από κάτω, σε μία μεγάλη υπερυψωμένη πλατφόρμα. Στο τέλος της συναυλίας το κοινό χειροκροτούσε όρθιο, μία που, όπως αναφέρει και ο δήμαρχος

Δεκαβάλλας: «το κοινό είχε την ευκαιρία να ζήσει μία μοναδική στην ζωή του εμπειρία, δικαιώνοντας έτσι το όραμα του μαέστρου Τιμπόρη.»

Η δημοσιογράφος Λίτσα Χαραλάμπους, η οποία έχει ως βάση της το νησί της Σύρου, θυμάται ότι ήρθαν άνθρωποι από όλη την πόλη της Ερμούπολης για να παρακολουθήσουν τη συναυλία και δεν υπήρχαν αρκετά καθίσματα για όλους, με αποτέλεσμα να γυρίσουν πίσω στα σπίτια τους και να φέρουν τις δικές τους καρέκλες ή σκαμνιά. Από την πρώτη της συνάντηση με τον μαέστρο στη Σύρο η δημοσιογράφος ένιωσε ένα ισχυρό δέσιμο μαζί του. Τον περιγράφει ως έναν γίγαντα με αγγελικό πρόσωπο, υγρά μάτια και πλατύ χαμόγελο. Έκτοτε παρέμεινε μία μεγάλη θαυμάστρια και υποστηρίκτρια των προσπαθειών του. Πιστεύει ότι ο μαέστρος βοήθησε την Σύρο να αναδειχθεί και προσέφερε πολλά στο νησί κρατώντας πάντα μία ήρεμη, σεμνή αλλά και χιουμοριστική διάθεση.

Ήταν πραγματικά πολύ φιλόδοξο το σχέδιο να παρουσιαστεί σε εξωτερικό χώρο το έργο Carmina Burana ειδικά αν λάβουμε υπόψη μας ότι εκείνη τη χρονιά το φεστιβάλ ήταν μεγαλύτερο από ποτέ και συμπεριλάμβανε πολλές άλλες μεγάλες και απαιτητικές συναυλίες. Την ίδια βραδιά, μετά το «Κάρμινα Μπουράνα» ακούστηκαν αποσπάσματα από την «Σουίτα από τον Ζορμπά» του Μίκη Θεοδωράκη: «Αστεράκι», «Χασάπικο», «Στρώσε το στρώμα σου» με την μεσόφωνο Μαρισία Παπαλεξίου. Στα πλαίσια του Φεστιβάλ υπήρχε επίσης μία συναυλία προς τιμήν της επετείου των εκατό ετών από τον θάνατο του Γκούσταβ Μάλερ το 1911 με τον Τιμπόρη να διευθύνει την ορχήστρα Pan-European Philharmonia με σολίστα την Eilana Lappalainen.

Επίσης είχαμε δύο παραστάσεις-αναγνώσεις του έργου «Rose» από την Ολυμπία Δουκάκη. Το έργο «Rose» γραμμένο από τον Martin Sherman είναι ένα θεατρικό με μία πρωταγωνίστρια επί σκηνής το οποίο μιλά για την ιστορία της εβραϊκής διασποράς μετά τον δεύτερο Παγκόσμιο Πόλεμο όπως τα διηγείται μία μετανάστρια η οποία ταξίδεψε από την Ουκρανία στο Miami Beach των Ηνωμένων Πολιτειών. Μέσα στο πένθος της, θρηνώντας και αναπολώντας για ένα αγαπημένο πρόσωπο, το οποίο παραμένει χωρίς όνομα ως τις τελευταίες στιγμές του έργου, η πρωταγωνίστρια μας μιλάει για την παιδική της ηλικία σε ενα ρωσικό χωριό, το γάμο της και τα όσα τρομερά έζησε σε ένα γκέτο της Βαρσοβίας, την «Έξοδο» της με προορισμό το Ισραήλ - ένα κράτος που εκείνη την εποχή ήταν εν τη γενέσει του - το δεύτερό της γάμο στο Atlantic City των Ηνωμένων Πολιτειών, την επαγγελματική της επιτυχία ως ξενοδόχος στο Μαϊάμι και στο τέλος την διάψευση των προσδοκιών της και την απογοήτευση της από την σύγχρονη Εβραϊκή κουλτούρα. Η Δουκάκη ερμήνευσε τον ρόλο τόσο στο Λονδίνο όσο και στο Broadway και έλαβε θερμότατες κριτικές.

Ο ΜΙΚΗΣ ΘΕΟΔΩΡΑΚΗΣ ΚΑΙ ΤΟ ΦΕΣΤΙΒΑΛ ΑΙΓΑΙΟΥ

Για τους κατοίκους της Σύρου η άφιξη του ίδιου του Μίκη Θεοδωράκη στο νησί κατά τη διάρκεια του φεστιβάλ Αιγαίου εκείνης της χρονιάς ήταν ένα εξαιρετικά συναρπαστικό γεγονός. Ήταν παρών στην προβολή των δύο ντοκιμαντέρ των Αστέρη Κούτουλα (κινηματογραφιστή και παραγωγό μουσικών και άλλων εκδηλώσεων, μεγαλωμένου στην Ρουμανία και Γερμανία) και Klaus Salge. Και τα δύο ντοκιμαντέρ Μίκης Θεοδωράκης ο συνθέτης και Μίκης Θεοδωράκης ήλιος και χρόνος ερευνούν τη ζωή και το έργο του μεγάλου σύνθετη. Πριν από τις προβολές ο δήμος της Ερμούπολης και η Σύρος τον ανακήρυξαν επίτιμο δημότη για τη συνεισφορά του την πολιτισμική αλλά και πολιτική στην Ελλάδα.

Τις επόμενες τρεις βραδιές μετά την παρουσίαση των ντοκιμαντέρ το φεστιβάλ του Αιγαίου παρουσίασε την παγκόσμια πρεμιέρα του μπαλέτου «Medea's Choice» (η επιλογή της Μήδειας) ένα έργο που είναι βασισμένο σε μουσική από την όπερα Μήδεια του Μίκη Θεοδωράκη. Πρόκειται για μία μονόπρακτη παρουσίαση σε χορογραφία Ρενάτο Τζανέλλα με πρωταγωνίστρια την Μαρία Κουσουνή από την Εθνική Λυρική Σκηνή στον ρόλο της Μήδειας, πλαισιωμένη απο τους Danilo Zeka, Franziska Hollinek, Eno Peci, Sofia Pintzou και Nicky Vanoppen στους υπόλοιπους ρόλους και με τη συμμετοχή του χοροθεάτρου «Ακροποδητί» της Σύρου. Οι παραστάσεις είχαν μεγάλο αντίκτυπο στο κοινό και ο ίδιος ο Θεοδωράκης ήταν φανερά συγκινημένος μετά το τέλος της παράστασης. Ο Αστέρης Κούτουλας έφτιαξε ένα φίλμ βασισμένο σε αυτήν την παράσταση το οποίο πρωτοπαρουσιάστηκε το 2013 με τον τίτλο «Ανακυκλώνοντας την Μήδεια». Το φιλμ αυτό κέρδισε το βραβείο Cinema for Peace Most Valuable Documentary Award στο Διεθνές κινηματογραφικό Φεστιβάλ του Βερολίνου το 2014.

ΦΕΣΤΙΒΑΛ ΤΗΣ ΧΡΟΝΙΑΣ !

Αναπόφευκτα ίσως, σίγουρα όμως δικαιολογημένα, το Φεστιβάλ Αιγαίου 2011 αναγνωρίστηκε για την ποιότητά του. Η Ελληνική Ένωση Κριτικών Θεάτρου και Παραστατικών Τεχνών απένειμε στο Φεστιβάλ το βραβείο «Festival of the Year Award in Greater Greece». Ο δήμαρχος Ιωάννης Δεκαβάλλας παρέλαβε το βραβείο σε τελετή που πραγματοποιήθηκε τον Δεκέμβριο του 2011 στην Αθήνα και το παρουσίασε στον Μαέστρο Τιμπόρη κατά την εναρκτήρια συναυλία του Φεστιβάλ Αιγαίου στο θέατρο Απόλλων της Σύρου το 2012. Σε αυτή την εναρκτήρια συναυλία ο μαέστρος

Τιμπόρης διευθύνε τη Συμφωνική Ορχήστρα του Εθνικού Θεάτρου όπερας και μπαλέτου της Αλβανίας. Παρουσιάστηκαν δύο έργα του Μπετόβεν: το πέμπτο κονσέρτο για πιάνο και ορχήστρα με σολίστα τον Δημήτρη Σγούρο στην πρώτη του εμφάνιση στο φεστιβάλ καθώς και η συμφωνία αριθμός 9 με σολίστες τη σοπράνο Maria Ratkova τον τενόρο Keith Ikaia-Purdy και τον μπάσο Δημήτρη Καβράκο και χορωδίες από τον Καναδά, τις Ηνωμένες Πολιτείες και την Ελλάδα. Κατά τη διάρκεια του φεστιβάλ 2012 παρουσιάστηκαν επίσης: Η όπερα «Σαλώμη» του Ρίχαρντ Στράους με την σοπράνο Eilana Lappalainen σε έναν από τους ρόλους που την καθιέρωσαν και ένα κονσέρτο στην πλατεία Μιαούλη με τον Μαέστρο και συνθέτη John Rutter να διευθύνει την ορχήστρα.

Ήδη μετά από τόσα χρόνια το Φεστιβάλ Αιγαίου είχε αρχίσει να γίνεται γνωστό σε όλη την Ελλάδα. Ανακοινώσεις του προγράμματος συναυλιών του άρχισαν να εμφανίζονται στο ίντερνετ. Το Critic's Point, ένα ελληνικό διαδικτυακό περιοδικό που ασχολείται με μουσική, θέατρο, χορό και γενικά τις τέχνες, έστειλε έναν ανταποκριτή για να καλύψει δύο εκδηλώσεις στα πλαίσια του φεστιβάλ. Στην κριτική του ο Κωνσταντίνος Καράμπελας Σγούρδας εγκωμίασε την αλβανική ορχήστρα, τον «ρυθμό και ευαισθησία» του John Rutter την μαεστρία του Τιμπόρη τις χορωδίες και τη χορογραφία του Zanella, όπως επίσης έγραψε πολύ κολακευτικά λόγια για τον πιανίστα Χρήστο Παπαγεωργίου.[89]

150 ΧΡΟΝΙΑ ΘΕΑΤΡΟ ΑΠΟΛΛΩΝ 1864 - 2014

Το 10ο φεστιβάλ Αιγαίου το καλοκαίρι του 2014 συνέπεσε με την επέτειο των 150 χρόνων του θεάτρου Απόλλων. Η ακριβής ημερομηνία της επετείου ήταν 20 Απριλίου και ο μαέστρος Τιμπόρης βρισκόταν στην Ερμούπολη εκείνο τον καιρό. Απογοητευμένος, τη στιγμή που τίποτα επισήμως δεν είχε προχωρήσει, εκείνο το βράδυ, το οποίο συνέπεσε να είναι επίσης Κυριακή του Πάσχα, προσκάλεσε τον Γιάννη Ρώτα και τη γυναίκα του να πιούν μαζί με την Eilana ένα μπουκάλι σαμπάνια στα σκαλιά μπροστά από το θέατρο. Ένας πιο επίσημος δημόσιος εορτασμός θα έπρεπε να περιμένει ως το καλοκαίρι. Στην ανοιχτή επιστολή που συμπεριέλαβε στο πρόγραμμα του φεστιβάλ ο Τιμπόρης έκανε μία αναδρομή στο φεστιβάλ και έγραφε: «Πάνω από 100 συναυλίες σε 10 χρόνια και με την υποστήριξη των φίλων του Φεστιβάλ έχουμε παρουσιάσει χιλιάδες διεθνώς καταξιωμένους καλλιτέχνες συμπεριλαμβανομένων: 55 χορωδιών, ορχηστρών, εκατοντάδων σολιστών, σκηνοθετών και τεχνικού προσωπικού, και μελών του Ελληνικού στούντιο όπερας σε 16 όπερες, κονσέρτα στην πλατεία Μιαούλη, συναυλίες θρησκευτικής μουσικής, κονσέρτα για παιδιά, μπαλέτο, θέατρο, ελαφρά μουσική, τζαζ, συμφωνίες και ορατόρια μπροστά σε ένα απόλυτα ικανοποιημένο κοινό. Το νησί της Σύρου και ειδικότερα η πόλη της Ερμούπολης έχουν αποκτήσει φήμη όχι μόνο σε όλη την Ελλάδα αλλά και πέρα από τα σύνορα της ως ένας καλοκαιρινός προορισμός για πολύ υψηλού επιπέδου καλλιτεχνικό προγραμματισμό».

Το Φεστιβάλ άνοιξε τον Ιούλιο με ένα κονσέρτο στην Πλατεία Μιαούλη με έργα Πουτσίνι, ως φόρος τιμής στον μεγάλη συνθέτη. 450 καλλιτέχνες από εννέα χώρες παρουσίασαν αποσπάσματα απο τις όπερες Tosca, La Bohème, Turandot και Madama Butterfly. Την συμφωνική ορχήστρα του Pazardzhik της Βουλγαρίας διηύθυναν ο μαέστρος Τιμπόρης και ο φιλοξενούμενος μαέστρος Grigor Palikarov. Συμμετείχαν χορωδίες από τη Γαλλία, Ελλάδα και τις Ηνωμένες Πολιτείες. Το Φεστιβάλ διήρκεσε δύο εβδομάδες και περιελάβανε παραστάσεις κλασσικής μουσικής για παιδιά και τρείς ημέρες με κονσέρτα Τζάζ.

2015: ΣΗΜΕΙΟ ΚΑΜΠΗΣ

Αυτό ήταν το τελευταίο Φεστιβάλ κατά τη διάρκεια της δημαρχίας του Ιωάννη Δεκαβάλλα, ο οποίος αποφάσισε να αποχωρήσει μετά από 24 έτη στη δημαρχία. Ευχαριστώντας τον έγραψε στο πρόγραμμα του φεστιβάλ ο Παναγιώτης Τιμπόρης: «ειδική μνεία πρέπει να κάνω στον φίλο μου τον δήμαρχο Ιωάννη Δεκαβάλλα. Γνωριστήκαμε πριν από 15 χρόνια κατά τη διάρκεια της πρώτης μου επίσκεψης στο νησί και από τότε έχουμε διατηρήσει μία διαρκή φιλική σχέση. Χωρίς αυτόν δεν θα υπήρχε το φεστιβάλ του Αιγαίου. Η υποστήριξη ήταν έμπρακτη, τόσο σε προσωπικό όσο και σε επαγγελματικό επίπεδο. Ήταν πάντα ευγενής, πάντα φιλικός, πάντα με σεβασμό και ειλικρίνεια».

Στο πρόγραμμα του φεστιβάλ της επόμενης χρονιάς συνεχάρη τον Γεώργιο Μαραγκό και την Θωμαή Μενδρινού για την εκλογή τους το 2015 ως δήμαρχος και αντιδήμαρχος πολιτισμού αντίστοιχα. Και συνέχισε να τους ευχαριστεί για την υποστήριξή τους κάθε χρόνο. Η δημοσιογράφος Λίτσα Χαραλάμπους από την Ερμούπολη, η οποία ήταν μία από τις πιο ένθερμες υποστηρίκτριες του φεστιβάλ στο νησί, πιστεύει ότι η καινούργια διοίκηση δεν έκανε αρκετά για να υποστηρίξει και να χρηματοδοτήσει το φεστιβάλ και θυμάται ότι αυτή η επιφυλακτικότητα οδήγησε στην ακύρωση μίας συναυλίας σε εξωτερικό χώρο το 2017.[90]

Το Φεστιβαλ Συνεχιζει

Στο πρόγραμμα του Φεστιβάλ Αιγαίου 2016 ο Τιμπόρης ανέφερε τα προβλήματα που δημιουργούνται απο την μείωση της χορηγίας, παράλληλα όμως δήλωσε οτι παραμένει αφοσιωμένος στο Φεστιβάλ και στο νησί για το 2016. Έγραφε: «Το να δημιουργείς και να αναπτύσσεις ένα Φεστιβάλ τέτοιου διαμετρήματος είναι ένα επιχείρημα περίτεχνο και πολύπλοκο, το οποίο γίνεται ακόμη δυσκολότερο όταν υπάρχει έλλειψη χορηγίας για πολιτιστικές εκδηλώσεις. Το ευχάριστο είναι ότι έχουμε μπορέσει, προς το παρόν τουλάχιστον, να ξεπεράσουμε αυτές τις δυσκολίες. Το Φεστιβάλ είναι μέρος της καλλιτεχνικής και οικονομικής ανάπτυξης της Σύρου. Θα κάνω ότι είναι δυνατόν ώστε να συνεχιστεί η καλλιτεχνική μας δραστηριότητα σε αυτό το μοναδικό και όμορφο νησί. Αυτή τη χρονιά η όπερα που παρουσιάζουμε είναι το γνωστό δράμα του Λεονκαβάλο «Οι παλιάτσοι». Θα παρουσιάσουμε κι άλλα αριστουργήματα όπως την έκτη συμφωνία του Τσαϊκόφσκι, τη «λειτουργία σε καιρό πολέμου» και το κοντσέρτο για βιολοντσέλο του Χάυντν, την τραγική εισαγωγή του Μπράμς, το κονσέρτο αριθμός 1 για πιάνο και ορχήστρα του Σοπέν και το κοντσέρτο για βιολί και ορχήστρα του Μπετόβεν. Επιπλέον, όπως πάντα, θα έχουμε και τις δραστηριότητες του Ελληνικού στούντιο όπερας. Η Σύρος είναι το σπίτι μας. Η Σύρος είναι το μέρος που διαλέξαμε να βρισκόμαστε. Η Σύρος είναι το μέρος που θα παραμείνουμε. Εκτιμούμε και ενθαρρύνουμε τη δική σας συνεχιζόμενη συμμετοχή και υποστήριξη στο σκοπό μας.»

Όποια και να ήταν τα εμπόδια που συναντούσε το φεστιβάλ ο Παναγιώτης Τιμπόρης ήταν ως συνήθως αισιόδοξος, για να μην πούμε και ενθουσιώδης, όπως βλέπουμε και από το πρόγραμμα του 2017: «Το γεγονός ότι τόσες πολιτιστικές εκδηλώσεις λαμβάνουν χώρα σε ένα από τα πιο απίθανα μέρη που μπορεί να φανταστεί κάποιος, στο νησί της Σύρου δηλαδή, είναι κάτι το σπουδαίο. Η Σύρος έχει καταφέρει να έχει μία παρουσία στον διεθνή καλλιτεχνικό χάρτη. Και γιατί όχι; Υπάρχει άλλο πιο όμορφο μέρος από τις Κυκλάδες για να βρίσκεται κανείς κατά τη διάρκεια του Ιουλίου χαλαρώνοντας και απολαμβάνοντας τις συναυλίες που παρουσιάζουν αριστουργήματα της δυτικοευρωπαϊκής μουσικής στο μέσον του Αιγαίου; Δεν νομίζω. Απο το 2005 έχουν πραγματοποιηθεί 250 εκδηλώσεις οι οποίες συμπεριλαμβάνουν 13 όπερες. Συνολικά είχαμε πάνω από 7.500 επισκέπτες καλλιτέχνες από 43 διαφορετικές χώρες.»

«Για να συνοψίσουμε: το νησί αλλάζει με έντονους ρυθμούς λόγω των πρωτοβουλιών και της ηγεσίας σε πολλούς τομείς αλλά ιδιαίτερα λόγω του δημάρχου Γιώργου Μαραγκού. Η Eilana κι εγώ τον συγχαίρουμε για το όραμα του και τις πρωτοβουλίες του. Τις αλλαγές που έχουν συντελεστεί στη Σύρο όχι μόνο της έχουν ακούσει αλλά και της έχουνε νιώσει στο παγκόσμιο μουσικό στερέωμα. Χωρίς αμφιβολία είναι πραγματικές και πάλλονται. Εδώ να αναφέρουμε ότι ο συντονισμός και η ανάπτυξη των καλλιτεχνικών δραστηριοτήτων οδηγούνται από την αντιδήμαρχο πολιτισμού Θωμαή Μενδρινού η οποία δουλεύει ακούραστα όχι μόνο για το Φεστιβάλ του Αιγαίου αλλά και για τις καλλιτεχνικές δραστηριότητες όλου του έτους, από τον Ιανουάριο ως το Δεκέμβριο.»

«Φέτος το φεστιβάλ είναι μεγαλύτερο από κάθε άλλη χρονιά και περιλαμβάνει όπερα, έργα συμφωνικής μουσικής, μπαλέτο, το ελληνικό στούντιο όπερας, μουσική δωματίου, παραδοσιακή μουσική και μουσικά εργαστήρια με συνεργάτες από 26 χώρες και περισσότερους από 350 φιλοξενούμενους καλλιτέχνες.

Την επιστολή μου αυτή την ξεκίνησα δηλώνοντας για το Φεστιβάλ ότι είναι το Σάλτσμπουργκ του Αιγαίου. Μήπως είναι υπερβολική κάποια τέτοια σύγκριση; Δεν νομίζω, και αυτό διότι περιγράφει ακριβώς τη φύση του φεστιβάλ. Ένα φεστιβάλ που έχει σημαντική πολιτιστική και οικονομική επίδραση στην Σύρο και σε όλες τις Κυκλάδες. Το φεστιβάλ της Σύρου έχει αλλάξει τις ζωές των ανθρώπων και είναι αυτό ακριβώς το οποίο καθοδηγεί τις παραγωγές μας στο Κάρνεγκι Χολ από το 1983: ότι δηλαδή ένα-ένα κονσέρτο αλλάζουμε τις ζωές των ανθρώπων.»

Όσο για τους καλλιτέχνες του φετινού φεστιβάλ, δικαίωσαν την αισιοδοξία του Τιμπόρη σχετικά με τα επιτεύγματα ως τωρα αλλά και το μέλλον του Φεστιβάλ. Κάτω από το όνομα Τιμπόρης ως ιδρυτής, γενικός διευθυντής και μουσικός διευθυντής του φεστιβάλ και το όνομα Lappalainen ως καλλιτεχνική διευθύντρια των παραγωγών όπερας του φεστιβάλ και γενική διευθύντρια του ελληνικού στούντιο όπερας και μάνατζερ του φεστιβάλ υπάρχει ένας εντυπωσιακός κατάλογος συμμετεχόντων που περιλαμβάνουν τους:

Ορχήστρα Pan-European Philharmonia από τη Βαρσοβία με τον εκτελεστικό διευθυντή της Jakub Friebig, 311 προσκεκλημένοι καλλιτέχνες και προσωπικό παραγωγής, Giovanni Pacor μαέστρος στην όπερα Madama Butterfly, Johanes Weigand, σκηνοθέτης της Madama Butterfly, Renato Zanella που χορογράφησε το Μπαλέτο της Εθνικής Όπερας του Ρουμανίας, Detlef Soelter σκηνοθέτης της όπερας Don Giovanni, Fortino Ibarra μαέστρος στην όπερα Don Giovanni, Jens Huebner Διευθυντής παραγωγής, σκηνογράφος και διευθυντης φωτισμού και Marta Kluzynska, βοηθός μαέστρου της Pan-European Philharmonia. Σημαντική είναι επίσης η παρουσία και ελλήνων καλλιτεχνών που τους φέραμε στο προσκήνιο: Χρήστος Παπαγεωργίου, πιανίστας, Νικόλαος Κανελλάκης, βιολοντσελίστας, Τζένια Μανουσάκη, πιανίστα και μαέστρος Ζωή Ζενιώδη ως ειδική μουσικός σύμβουλος του Τιμπόρη.

Το φεστιβάλ του 2016 ήταν το πρώτο από τα τέσσερα συνεχόμενα στα οποία ο Giovanni Pacor έλαβε μέρος στο φεστιβάλ ως φιλοξενούμενος διευθυντής ορχήστρας, κατά την διάρκεια των οποίων σφυρηλάτησε μία υπέροχη φιλία με τον Τιμπόρη, όπως θυμάται και ο ίδιος με συναισθηματισμό. Γεννήθηκε στην Τεργέστη της Ιταλίας το 1957 από Ιταλό πατέρα και Ελληνίδα μητέρα μελέτησε βιολί ως το 1980 και μετά ασχολήθηκε με την διεύθυνση ορχήστρας. Διετέλεσε καλλιτεχνικός διευθυντής της Εθνικής Λυρικής Σκηνής από το 2008 ως το 2010 και από τις παράγωγες της δικής του θητείας ξεχωρίζουν όπερες που παρουσιάστηκαν για πρώτη φορά στην Ελλάδα από συνθέτες όπως Rossini, Bellini, Zemlinsky, Dvořák, Donizetti, Piazzolla, Ξαρχάκος και Γιάννης Κωνσταντινίδης. Εκείνο τον καιρό γνώρισε και τον Παναγιώτη Τιμπόρη για πρώτη φορά, ενώ την σύζυγό του Eilana την είχε γνωρίσει μερικά χρόνια νωρίτερα όταν αυτή είχε τραγουδήσει το ρόλο της Σαλώμης στην όπερα της Τεργέστης. Δυστυχώς λόγω των περικοπών στον προϋπολογισμό της Εθνικής Λυρικής Σκηνής αλλά και λόγω του γενικότερου κλίματος κοινωνικής αστάθειας ο Pacor αποφάσισε ότι δεν θα μπορούσε να δουλεύει παραγωγικά στην Αθήνα.

Στο φεστιβάλ του 2016 ο Pacor ανέλαβε κάποια από τα καθήκοντά αρχιμουσικού του Τιμπόρη τα οποία δεν μπορούσε να διεκπεραιώσει λόγω προβλημάτων υγείας. Ο Pacor επέστρεψε το 2017 για να διευθύνει την όπερα Madama Butterfly του Puccini με την Eilana Lappalainen στον πρωταγωνιστικό ρόλο και τον Ιταλό τενόρο Alessio Boraggine ως υποπλοίαρχος Pinkerton. Το Φεστιβάλ άνοιξε ο ίδιος ο μαέστρος Τιμπόρης διευθύνοντας έργα των Μότσαρτ και Τσαϊκόφσκι ενώ το φινάλε του φεστιβάλ ήταν μια γκαλά παράσταση με τα αστέρια του μπαλέτου της Εθνικής όπερας της Ρουμανίας υπό τη διεύθυνση και χορογραφία του Renato Zanella.

ΠΡΟΒΛΗΜΑΤΑ ΥΓΕΙΑΣ

Τον καιρό που ο Pacor τον αντικατέστησε ο Τιμπόρης δεν είχε μόνο μία απλή αδιαθεσία. Τον Μάιο του 2015 οι ιατρικές εξετάσεις έδειξαν καρκινικά κύτταρα στο στομάχι του και η διάγνωση ήταν 1ο στάδιο καρκίνου του στομάχου. Τον Σεπτέμβριο του ίδιου έτους υπεβλήθη σε εγχείρηση, κατά τη διάρκεια της οποίας ολόκληρο το στομάχι του αφαιρέθηκε από τον δόκτορα Marc Reiner στο νοσοκομείο Mount Sinai της Νέας Υόρκης. Η εγχείρηση ήταν επιτυχής και ο ασθενής ξεπέρασε τον υπαρκτό κίνδυνο που ιατρικές επεμβάσεις σαν αυτή ενέχουν. Η επέμβαση επίσης ήταν η αιτία για μια δραματική μείωση του όγκου και του βάρους του. Για δεκαετίες προσπαθούσε ανεπιτυχώς να κάνει κάτι με το βάρος του με αποτέλεσμα να έχει ένα μεγάλο όγκο και να είναι πολλά κιλά υπέρβαρος. Τότε ήταν που τον γνώρισε η δημοσιογράφος Χαραλάμπους και μίλησε για αυτόν ότι είναι ένας γίγαντας με αγγελικό πρόσωπο. Μετά την εγχείρηση όμως αυτό ανήκει στο παρελθόν και επιπλέον έδωσε τη δυνατότητα στον Παναγιώτη να έχει πολύ περισσότερη ενεργητικότητα. Και πάντα ευχαριστεί τον Pacor που τον αντικατέστησε και βοήθησε στο Φεστιβάλ εκείνο το καλοκαίρι.⁹¹

Ο Τιμπόρης αντιμετώπισε άλλο ένα πρόβλημα υγείας το 2020 και το Σεπτέμβριο του ίδιου έτους ο Δρ. Steve Xydas αντιμετώπισε με επέμβαση το πρόβλημα σε δύο αρτηρίες στην καρδιά του. Μπροστά σε αυτό το σοβαρό πρόβλημα άλλαξε τις συνήθειες του ριζικά και άρχισε να ασκείται σε καθημερινή βάση, με αποτέλεσμα η ανάρρωση και βελτίωση της υγεία του να εκπλήξει και τους ίδιους τους γιατρούς του.

Η ΕΠΕΤΕΙΟΣ ΤΟΥ ΡΟΣΙΝΙ

Το φεστιβάλ Αιγαίου 2018 συνέπεσε με την επέτειο των 150 ετών από το θάνατο του Ιταλού συνθέτη Gioacchino Rossini, οπότε η εναρκτήρια συναυλία του φεστιβάλ ήτανε το Θρησκευτικό έργο «Στάμπατ Μάτερ» το οποίο βασίζεται στη χριστιανική υμνολογία σχετική με την οδύνη της παρθένου κατά τη διάρκεια της Σταυρώσεως. Ο μαέστρος Τιμπόρης διηύθυνε την Pan European Philharmonia με τους σολίστες Eilana Lappalainen σοπράνο, Κατερίνα Ρούσσου μεσόφωνος, Alessandro Luciano τενόρος και Daniel Borowsky μπάσος. Η σκηνή του θεάτρου Απόλλωνα ήταν κατάμεστη με χορωδίες που ήρθαν από τη Γαλλία και τις Ηνωμένες Πολιτείες. Στο δεύτερο μέρος του προγράμματος παρουσιάστηκε η Πέμπτη Συμφωνία του Τσαϊκόφσκι. Η δεύτερη βραδιά του φεστιβάλ ήταν και πάλι αφιερωμένη στο Ροσίνι. Παρουσιάστηκε η κωμική του όπερα La Cenerentola η οποία βασίζεται στο παραμύθι της σταχτοπούτας. Ο Ροσίνι συνέθεσε αυτήν την όπερα σε ηλικία 25 ετών η οποία και ακολούθησε την επιτυχία του κουρέα της Σεβίλλης. Μέσα σε τρεις εβδομάδες το 1816 είχε ολοκληρώσει την όπερα η οποία θεωρείται ότι περιέχει από τις καλύτερες στιγμές της γραφής του τόσο για σολιστικά κομμάτια (άριες) όσο και για φωνητικά σύνολα. Την όπερα διηύθυνε ο Giovanni Pacor, προσκεκλημένος μαέστρος του φεστιβάλ, σηματοδοτώντας την τρίτη συνεχόμενη χρονιά συμμετοχής του. Το φεστιβάλ του 2018 έκλεισε με μία χορευτική παράσταση της Όπερας του Μίκη Θεοδωράκη Ηλέκτρα η οποία χορογραφήθηκε από τον Renato Zanella, με τη συνεργασία του Αστέρη Κούτουλα. Οι χορευτές ήταν από Αλβανία , Βραζιλία, Γαλλία, Ελλάδα και Ρουμανία.

ΑΡΙΑΔΝΗ ΣΤΗ ΣΥΡΟ

Νοτιοανατολικά της νήσου Σύρου σε μια ευθεία απόσταση 30 μιλίων βρίσκεται το νησί της Νάξου. Είναι μέρος του συμπλέγματος των νησιών του Νοτίου Αιγαίου που ονομάζονται Κυκλάδες, στο οποίο σύμπλεγμα ανήκει και η Μύκονος και η Σαντορίνη. Όλοι γνωρίζουμε ότι εδώ και δεκαετίες η Σαντορίνη και η Μύκονος είναι παγκοσμίως διάσημοι τουριστικοί προορισμοί. Από τα υπόλοιπα κυκλαδίτικα νησιά όμως η Νάξος ήταν η πρώτη της οποίας το όνομα έγινε γνωστό παγκοσμίως, Όχι λόγω της φυσικής ομορφιάς της αλλά εξαιτίας της όπερας «Αριάδνη στη Νάξο» (Ariadne auf Naxos) του Ρίχαρντ Στράους. Πρόκειται για μία όπερα στην οποία παρουσιάζεται άλλη μία όπερα εμπνευσμένη από την ελληνική μυθολογία ως μέρος της πλοκής. Ο Θησέας έφυγε από την Αθήνα με προορισμό την Κρήτη για να σκοτώσει το Μινώταυρο, ένα πλάσμα μισός άνθρωπος και μισός ταύρος, το οποίο βρισκόταν κρυμμένο μέσα σε έναν λαβύρινθο. Η Αριάδνη, κόρη του βασιλιά της Κρήτης, ερωτεύτηκε τον Θησέα και του έδωσε τον γνωστό μίτο ο οποίος του έδωσε τη δυνατότητα να βγει από το λαβύρινθο αφού είχε σκοτώσει τον Μινώταυρο. Όταν έφυγε ο Θησέας από την Κρήτη πήρε μαζί του και την Αριάδνη ως νύφη του. Κατά τη διάρκεια του ταξιδιού τους σταμάτησαν στο νησί της Νάξου. Κάποια στιγμή στα κρυφά, και ενώ η Αριάδνη κοιμόταν, ο Θησέας έφυγε συνεχίζοντας το ταξίδι του για την Αθήνα χωρίς αυτήν. Η όπερα «Αριάδνη στη Νάξο» ξεκινάει ακριβώς σε αυτό το σημείο.

Η όπερα παρουσιάστηκε για πρώτη φορά στην Ελλάδα από τη Λυρική Σκηνή το 1974. Η πιο πρόσφατη παραγωγή της ήταν το 2009 με μαέστρο τον Giovanni Pacor. Με το φεστιβάλ Αιγαίου 2019 ο μαέστρος Τιμπόρης έφερε την όπερα Αριάδνη στη Νάξο όσο πιο κοντά γίνεται στο νησί της Νάξου, μία που η όπερα δεν έχει παρουσιαστεί ποτέ στο νησί όπου διαδραματίζεται. Η Eilana Lappalainen τραγούδησε τον πρωταγωνιστικό ρόλο και στους υπόλοιπους κύριους ρόλους είχαμε τη μεσόφωνο Adrian Angelico, την σοπράνο Louise Fribo, τον τενόρο Ta'u Pupu'a και τον βαρύτονο Στέφανο Κορωναίο. Το πλούσιο πρόγραμμα του φεστιβάλ περιελάμβανε την πρώτη εμφάνιση του Ελληνοκύπριου πιανίστα και μαέστρου Μάριου Παπαδόπουλου, ιδρυτή και μουσικού διευθυντή της Oxford Philharmonic, της ορχήστρας δηλαδή του πανεπιστημίου της Οξφόρδης.

Χωρίς να γνωρίζει ότι δεν θα υπάρξουν φεστιβάλ κατά τα επόμενα δύο χρόνια εξαιτίας της πανδημίας Κόβιντ-19, ο μαέστρος Τιμπόρης εξέφρασε τις σκέψεις του, με μία στοχαστική διάθεση, στο πρόγραμμα του φεστιβάλ για το 2019. Εκφράζοντας τις ευχαριστίες τις δικές του και της Eilana, αναφέρθηκε στην προσφορά του Φεστιβάλ στο νησί της Σύρου και για πρώτη φορά ανέφερε τις δικές του ελληνικές ρίζες: «Αυτό που συνέβη τα τελευταία 15 χρόνια είναι εξαιρετικό από κάθε άποψη. Εκατοντάδες παραστάσεις με χιλιάδες καλλιτέχνες που επισκέφθηκαν τη Σύρο, προερχόμενοι από πάνω από 50 χώρες από όλο τον κόσμο οι οποίοι μοιράστηκαν το μουσικά ταλέντα τους μπροστά σε πολυάριθμο κοινό μουσικόφιλων. Επιπλέον, ο οικονομικός αντίκτυπος στο νησί της Σύρου ήταν σημαντικότατες και τώρα το νησί χαίρει διεθνούς αναγνώρισης. Φτάνοντας λοιπόν στην 15η επέτειο και στο φετινό φεστιβάλ είναι σημαντικό και αναγκαίο το ότι η Eilana και εγώ κάνουμε μία ανασκόπηση και ευχαριστούμε όλους για την γενναιόδωρη υποστήριξη και ενθάρρυνση που μας έδωσαν για τη δημιουργία και ανάπτυξη ενός τόσο μεγάλου και σημαντικού φεστιβάλ σε ένα μέρος που δεν το φανταζόταν κανένας, όντας μακριά από μία μητροπολιτική περιοχή και στο μέσον του Νοτίου Αιγαίου το οποίο βεβαίως είναι γεμάτο ιστορία και ομορφιά. Δεν είναι τυχαίο το γεγονός και δεν πρέπει να προξενεί έκπληξη το ότι νιώθω μιά έλξη γι' αυτό τον ιστορικό χώρο. Ως Ελληνοαμερικάνος έλκω την καταγωγή μου από τη Μεγαλόπολη της Αρκαδίας, απ' όπου μετανάστευσε η οικογένειά μου στις αρχές του 20ου αιώνα. Καθ' όλη τη διάρκεια της ζωής μου έχω διατηρήσει στενές επαφές με την ιστορία, τον πολιτισμό της Ελλάδας και τους Έλληνες».

Μία εβδομάδα πριν από την έναρξη του Φεστιβάλ του 2019 στις εθνικές εκλογές που πραγματοποιήθηκαν το κόμμα της Νέας Δημοκρατίας κέρδισε και επέστρεψε στην εξουσία μετά από 4 ½ χρόνια. Αυτό συνέπεσε και με το τέλος της οικονομικής, κρίσης καθώς η χώρα βγήκε από την οικονομική επιτήρηση τον Αύγουστο του 2018. Υπήρχε μία γενικότερη αίσθηση ότι τα χειρότερα είχαν περάσει και ανακουφισμένος ο κόσμος και όλη η χώρα επιστρέφουν σιγά-σιγά στην κανονικότητα. Υπό αυτές τις συνθήκες το φεστιβάλ Αιγαίου, το οποίο άντεξε κατά την διάρκεια της κρίσεως, μπορούσε αισιόδοξα να ατενίζει το μέλλον με ακόμα μεγαλύτερη σιγουριά. Η επένδυση αλλά και η δέσμευση η οποία εκφράστηκε με το πρόγραμμα του 2019 ήταν αυθεντική και γνήσια από την πρώτη στιγμή πού ο μαέστρος Τιμπόρης έφτασε στο νησί της Σύρου το 1999.

Το 2016, ένα χρόνο μετά το πρώτο φεστιβάλ Αιγαίου που πραγματοποιήθηκε στο νησί, ο Παναγιώτης και η Eilana αγόρασαν ένα πολύ όμορφο κάτασπρο εξοχικό στο Δανί στην δυτική ακτή του νησιού από όπου μπορεί κανείς να δει τον ήλιο να βυθίζεται στο Αιγαίο πέλαγος κατά το ηλιοβασίλεμα. Μιλώντας με τον στενό φίλο τού Παναγιώτη, τον συριανό μηχανικό Ιωάννη Ρώτα, μας περιέγραψε πόσο πολύ δουλειά ήταν απαραίτητο να γίνει στη σπίτι για να ενδυναμωθούν τα θεμέλια, διότι το σπίτι είχε οικοδομηθεί και στηριζόταν σε μία πλαγιά απέναντι από τη θάλασσα. Αυτό το γεγονός, όπως και κάθε τι άλλο σχετικό με την ζωή του Παναγιώτη Τιμπόρη, ήταν συμβολικό της υπομονής και επιμονής για να «χτιστεί» κάτι σε πείσμα όλων των αντίξοων καταστάσεων. Η Eilana, της οποίας η οικογένεια ασχολούνταν με τον κατασκευαστικό τομέα, επιτήρησε την κατασκευή του σπιτιού σε πολυεπίπεδο σχήμα δημιουργώντας ένα παραδοσιακό νησιώτικο σπίτι μαζί με μία πισίνα που αντικρύζει το πέλαγος. Υπήρχαν πολλά ακόμη να γίνουν στη Σύρο ξεκινώντας το 2020. Δυστυχώς όμως η πανδημία έβαλε μία «παύση» σε όλα τα σχέδια, αλλά όπως αποδείχτηκε, αυτή η «παύση» δεν διήρκεσε πολύ.

Επιλογος

Ο Παναγιώτης Τιμπόρης χαρακτηρίζει το τρόπο που διευθύνει έναν που αφήνει την ορχήστρα να παίξει ελεύθερα. Πιστεύει πως ένας αρχιμουσικός δεν πρέπει να διευθύνει υπερβολικά και πρέπει να βρει τρόπους να κάνει τους μουσικούς να παίξουν για αυτόν και να τους κάνει να δείξουν τον καλύτερο εαυτό τους. Αυτό μπορεί μεν να είναι αλήθεια αλλά είναι μονάχα η κορυφή του παγόβουνου που αναδεικνύει τον προσηνή και χαρισματικό του χαρακτήρα. Αλλά μέχρι να φτάσει σε αυτό το σημείο που βρίσκεται επικεφαλής της ορχήστρας η των επιχειρηματικών δραστηριοτήτων του και έχει τη δυνατότητα να νοιώθει άνετα έχει δουλέψει εξαιρετικά σκληρά. Αυτά που κρύβονται κάτω από την επιφάνεια του νερού και είναι ο Παναγιώτης Τιμπόρης προσπαθεί αυτή η βιογραφία να αποκαλύψει. Η πλούσια διαδρομή της ζωής του μέχρι σήμερα έχει εξεταστεί με τη βοήθεια αμέτρητων συζητήσεων που είχαμε και μηνυμάτων που ανταλλάξαμε οι δυο μας, συνεντεύξεις που μου παραχώρησαν ευγενικά μέλη της οικογένειάς του μαζί και η Εϊλάνα Λαπαλάινεν, οι πιο στενοί τους συνεργάτες στην Ελλάδα και στις Ηνωμένες Πολιτείες, άρθρα εφημερίδων και τα εκτενή στοιχεία που βρίσκονται στην ιστοσελίδα της MidAmerica Productions.

Τη φράση «τον άντρα τον πολυμήχανο» που βρίσκουμε στην αρχή της Οδύσσειας του Ομήρου την έχουν μεταφράσει στα Αγγλικά μεταφραστές με διαφορετικές λέξεις. Για παράδειγμα ο Robert Fitzgerald το αποδίδει ως άνδρα εξασκημένο να αντιμετωπίζει καταστάσεις με πολλούς τρόπους. Ο Robert Fagles τον αποκαλεί άνδρα που ελίσσεται ενώ μία μετάφραση που χρησιμοποιεί μία πιο καθημερινή γλώσσα από τις άλλες δημοσιεύτηκε πρόσφατα από την Emily Wilson και χαρακτηρίζει τον Οδυσσέα περίπλοκο άνδρα. Όλοι αυτοί οι χαρακτηρισμοί αρμόζουν τη περίπτωση του Παναγιώτη Τιμπόρη. Όπως έκανε ο Οδυσσέας πήγε σε ένα ταξίδι, μεταφορικά και κυριολεκτικά. Αυτό που έκανε με τη μεταφορική έννοια ήταν μία αναζήτηση επιτυχίας και αναγνώρισης ως παρουσιαστή συναυλιών κλασσικής μουσικής και ως αρχιμουσικός. Το δεύτερο ήταν ένα ταξίδι από το Sheboygan, Wisconsin στη Νέα Υόρκη και από εκεί στην Ευρώπη και πέρα από αυτήν, μέχρι να αποκτήσει ένα δεύτερο σπίτι στην Ελλάδα, τη γη των προγόνων του.

Για να πετύχει σε αυτά τα δύο του ταξίδια ο Τιμπόρης κινητοποίησε όλες τις αρετές που του παρείχαν η προσωπικότητά του, η ανατροφή του, η εκπαίδευσή του και οι εμπειρίες ζωής του. Η προσωπικότητά του φαίνεται πως αποτελείται από ένα αξιοσημείωτο μίγμα της χαρισματικής και επηρεασμένης από την θρησκεία μετριοφροσύνης του πάτερα του Αναστάσιου και τη γεμάτο αυτοπεποίθηση ντομπροσύνη του καθηγητή Charles Leonhard, καθώς και τη θέληση να πετύχουν στη ζωή και να διαδώσουν τη γνώση για τη μουσική που ωθούσε τους δύο αυτούς άνδρες. Ο Αναστάσιος Τιμπόρης ενστάλαξε την αγάπη για τη μουσική στο γιό του μαζί με ένα σεβασμό για τη γη των προγόνων του. Παράλληλα, παραμέρισε και υποστήριξε την επιλογή καριέρας του γιου του. Ο Leonhard καθήλωσε τον Παναγιώτη με τη παρουσία του και τις βαθιές του γνώσεις, τον ενέπνευσε και τον ενεργοποίησε. Μπορούμε να πούμε πως ο Παναγιώτης δεν επέτρεψε ποτέ στον εαυτό του να απομακρυνθεί από τις αγαθές σκιές του πατέρα του και του καθηγητή του. Κατά κάποιο τρόπο παρέμεινε ο πιστός γιός και ο επιμελής μαθητής, κάτι που απαιτούσε συνεχή προσπάθεια να κάνει όλα πιο πολλά για να ανταποκριθεί στα ψηλά πρότυπα που είχαν καθιερώσει. Πολύ κάτω από την επιφάνεια διατηρούσε μια ανασφάλεια για τον εαυτό του, την φυσική του κατάσταση και για τον ψυχισμό του, τις διανοητικές του δυνάμεις και το ταλέντο του. Ο Τιμπόρης αντέδρασε με μία ακατάπαυστη και πεισμωμένη προσπάθεια να δημιουργήσει μουσική και να τη μοιραστεί με όσο πιο πολύ κόσμο μπορούσε να έρθει σε επαφή. Η άσβεστη φλόγα που τον προωθούσε καίει ακόμη λαμπρά τη στιγμή αυτή που συμπληρώνει το 75ο έτος της ηλικίας του. Αυτή την ορμή που βγαίνει από μέσα του βλέπουν οι συνεργάτες τους και μιλούν για τον συνδυασμό χαρισματικότητας, βασανιστικής ενέργειας και πείσματος που τον χαρακτηρίζει. Ο Τιμπόρης, όπως το έθεσε ένας από αυτούς, είναι «ασταμάτητη δύναμη και ακίνητος βράχος».

Αυτή η ισχυρή ώθηση οδήγησε τον Τιμπόρη προς την επιχειρηματική πλευρά της μουσικής, όπου, παρόλο πως ήταν αρχάριος, τα πήγε εξαιρετικά καλά. Στο τέλος της υπεράσπισης της διδακτορικής του διατριβής ο Professor Leonhard είπε στον Τιμπόρη να φροντίζει τη μουσική και όλα τα άλλα θα ακολουθήσουν. Είναι κάτι που ακούγεται πολύ όμορφο, και το συγκράτησε ο Παναγιώτης που λέει πως βασικά η ζωή του ήταν όλη «για τη μουσική». Αλλά την ίδια στιγμή τα λόγια του Leonhard ακούγονται ως συμβουλή που θα έδινε ένας καταξιωμένος καθηγητής που δεν τον απασχολεί η συγκρουσιακή πραγματικότητα της επιχειρηματικής πλευράς της μουσικής. Ο Παναγιώτης μπόρεσε να χτίσει πάνω στη συμβουλή του Leonhard και παρέμεινε προσηλωμένος στη μουσική και τη ποιότητά της αλλά σιγούρεψε το πως θα μπορούσε να αφιερώσει τη ζωή του στη μουσική δημιουργώντας μία στέρεα οικονομική βάση. Στη πορεία δημιούργησε κάτι καινούργιο, εισερχόμενος σε έναν κόσμο που ήταν πέραν αυτού του πατέρα του και του καθηγητή του. Έπρεπε να χρησιμοποιήσει την εξυπνάδα του και να παίρνει γρήγορες αποφάσεις διότι ούτε η ανατροφή του ούτε η εκπαίδευση του το είχαν εφοδιάσει για το μεγάλο βήμα που πήρε να αποχωριστεί την ασφάλεια που παρείχε η ακαδημαϊκή ζωή και να εισέλθει τον επιχειρηματικό κόσμο της μουσικής στη Νέα Υόρκη.

Ενώ από τη μία πλευρά η φιλοδοξία του τον οδήγησε να πάρει ρίσκα και να καινοτομήσει με κορύφωμα αυτό το πρωτότυπο που εκπροσωπούσε επιχειρηματικά η MidAmerica ο Τιμπόρης μετρίασε τις οικονομικές αβεβαιότητες εφαρμόζοντας τα σχέδια του με μεγάλη προσοχή. Όταν η συγκεκριμένη φόρμουλα έδειξε πως δούλευε, μας εξήγεί, δεν υπήρχε λόγος να αλλάξει. Υιοθέτησε και μία συντηρητική στάση απέναντι στη κλασσική μουσική, όπου οι προτιμήσεις παρέμειναν στο χώρο της κλασσικής και της ρομαντικής περιόδου με μονάχα λίγες στοχευμένες επιλογές πιο συγχρόνων κομματιών.

Στην Οδύσσεια, η μάγισσα Κίρκη περιγράφει τον ήρωα της ιστορίας ως το άνθρωπο που μπορεί να προσαρμοστεί στο οτιδήποτε. Ξεκάθαρα ο Τιμπόρης είχε τη δυνατότητα να προσαρμόζεται στη πορεία. Ο ίδιος αναφέρει τα ονόματα μελών της οικογένειας του, συνεργατών και μεντόρων που τον ενέπνευσαν, το βοήθησαν σε κομβικές στιγμές της καριέρας του, και από τους οποίους με ευχαρίστηση δέχθηκε συμβουλές. Στις περισσότερες περιπτώσεις οι συμβουλές και προτάσεις δεν τον εμπόδισαν να προχωρήσει μπροστά αλλά διαμόρφωσαν το τρόπο που το έκανε. Η MidAmerica Productions και οι επιτυχίες της γεννήθηκαν απο το όραμα του και τα οφέλη για όλους γύρω του ήταν αναρίθμητα. Όπως έχουμε δει, για χιλιάδες μέλη και διευθυντών χορωδιών οι συναυλίες ήταν το αντίστοιχο του να είχαν παρακολουθήσει τις περίφημες συναυλίες για νέους του Μπερνστάιν που είχαν μεταδοθεί από τη τηλεόραση θα μπορούσαμε μάλιστα να πούμε πως ήταν ακόμη πιο σημαντική εμπειρία. Η συνεχιζόμενη επιτυχία και ανάπτυξη της MidAmerica Productions και της MidAm International έχουν φωτιστεί σε αυτό το βιβλίο. Η αξιοσημείωτη έκταση των συναυλιών του Τιμπόρη ανά τον κόσμο αντανακλά ένα ανήσυχο πνεύμα που δεν περιορίζεται από σύνορα και ένα που μπορεί να εγκλιματίζεται σε νέα περιβάλλοντα. Και η δημιουργία του Φεστιβάλ του Αιγαίου και η συνεχιζόμενες επιτυχίες του σε ένα δύσκολο περιβάλλον – που απαιτεί τη προσαρμοστικότητα ενός Οδυσσέα – θα μπορούσε από μόνη της να μετρήσει ως έργο ζωής.

Μπορούμε να δεχθούμε την εκτίμηση του Τιμπόρη πως η ζωή του ήταν «για τη μουσική» μόνο εάν λάβουμε υπόψη την εντυπωσιακή της διαδρομή και τη πλούσια της πολυπλοκότητα. Μία ζωή που τον πήρε από το παίξιμο του εκκλησιαστικού οργάνου στο Sheboygan του Wisconsin κάτω από την ευεργετική καθοδήγηση του πατέρα του μέχρι το Κάρνεγκι Χολ ως αρχιμουσικό και ιδρυτή και γενικό διευθυντή της MidAmerica Productions και στη συνέχεια σε μια σειρά από θέσεις ανά το κόσμο με αποκορύφωση την ίδρυση του Φεστιβάλ του Αιγαίου. Μία καριέρα που επηρέασε τις ζωές χιλιάδων μουσικών και έφερε τη μουσική σε χιλιάδες σε όλο το κόσμο.

Ένα ταξίδι που ενέπνευσαν πολλοί και το οποίο έγινε με ένα μίγμα χαρισματικότητας, πείσματος, καλλιτεχνικής ευαισθησίας και οξύτατης επιχειρηματικής οξυδέρκειας μετριασμένο από μετριοφροσύνη. Ένα ταξίδι αντάξιο του Οδυσσέα, ενός «πολύπλοκου άντρα» εξασκημένου να αντιμετωπίζει διάφορες καταστάσεις με πολλούς τρόπους. Αλλά στη περίπτωση του Τιμπόρη, η Ιθάκη, ο τελικός προορισμός ήταν και συνεχίζει να είναι η δυνατότητα να διευθύνει, να παράγει και να μοιράζεται τη μουσική σε παγκόσμια κλίμακα.

ENDNOTES

1. Interview with James Redcay June 23, 2023.
2. Interview with Tim Sharp June 4, 2022.
3. Alexander Lingas, "John Sakelarides and Greek-American Choral Music for the Divine Liturgy" https://cappellaromana.org/the-divine-liturgy-of-st-john-chrysostom-liner-notes-part-two/
4. "Zante currants are shut out" New York Times April 19, 1896.
5. *Sheboygan Press* January 20, 1908.
6. *Sheboygan Press* August 23, 1916.
7. "Miss Stella Menas is Bride of Dr. Ernst P. Tiboris Here" *The Sheboygan Press* November 16, 1946.
8. *Waukegan News-Sun* November 20, 1916.
9. *The Sheboygan Press* October 12, 1957.
10. *The Sheboygan Press* September 28, 1957.
11. *The Sheboygan Press* January 13, 1961.
12. Clyde Burnett, "New Choral Leader Tells Goals" *The Atlanta Constitution* October 18, 1970.
13. "Roland Johnson Makes Musical History" *The Capital Times* October 19,1970.
14. Robert Labrosca, "5-State Greek Orthodox Choir Conference Here" *The Capital Times* October 10, 1972.
15. "MATC Pop-Rock Concert" *The Capital Times* April 28, 1973.
16. Shirley Jarvis, "Swing Choir Rocks Campus" *Sheboygan Press* March 19, 1974.
17. Roger Rideout, "Travels With Charley" *Journal of Research in Musical Education* April 2006 XXVII: 2 120-131.
18. Kira Zeeman Rugen, "The Evolution of Choral Sound: In Professional Choirs from the 1970s to the Twenty-first Century" Ph.D. Arizona State University, 2013.
19. "New College Singers Whip Up a Wagnerian Storm" *The Capital Times* October 10, 1974.
20. Donald Davies "MATC Will Present Rock Opera in May" *Wisconsin State Journal* April 20, 1975.
21. "Superstar Will Shake Up Audience" *The Capital Times* May 1, 1975.
22. "Peter Tiboris: A Realist Looking for a Way" *The Capital Times* May 8, 1975.
23. Donald K. Davis, "Swing Music Fest Good, But Long" April 5, 1976.
24. Judith Ann Kritzmire, "The Pedagogy of Charles Leonhard: a Documentary Case Study" Ph.D. thesis, University of Illinois at Urbana-Champaign, 1987 1.

25. William C. Child Jr., "Monroe Beardsley's Three Criteria for Aesthetic Value: a Neglected Resource in the Evaluation of Recent Music" *The Journal of Aesthetic Education Summer*, 2000, Vol. 34, No. 2 (Summer, 2000) 49-63.

26. Devan Sipher, "A Reunion that was a Long Time Coming" *New York Times* January 14, 2014.

27. Lisa Sylvester, "Tiboris: Lafayette's Singing Pied Piper" *The Daily Advertiser* October 12, 1980.

28. Tim Page, "Rossini's Sabat Mater at Alice Tully Hall" *New York Times* January 9, 1984.

29. Walt Trott, "Opera Competition a Mix of Drama, Beautiful Music" *The Capitol Times* June 29, 1984.

30. Brook Lea Foster, "Comparing Suburbs: Montclair in New Jersey vs. Dobbs Ferry in New York" *New York Times* February 23, 2018.

31. Allen Hughes, "Concert: Tocco, Tate and Massed Choristers" *New York Times* March 30, 1986.

32. Bernard Holland, "Concert: Youth Choral at Carnegie" May 3 1986.

33. Choral America, "The Chorus Impact Study" (2009).

34. Interview with Lee Kesselman June 3, 2022.

35. Tim Page, "Music: Dinos Constantinides" *New York Times* March 23 1987.

36. Beth Arburn Davis, "Corpus Christi Chorale Gains Conductor's Praise" *The Corpus Christi Caller* March 1, 1987.

37. Whitney Smith, "Conductor to Tune Up Choirs" *The Commercial Appeal* April 21, 1987.

38. Steve Visser, "New York Maestro Demands that Lambuth, Union Choirs Find Perfect Harmony" *The Jackson Sun* April 23, 1987.

39. Associated Press, "Band Defers Bid for Carnegie Hall" *The News Tribune* November 17, 1987.

40. John Rockwell, "Concert: 9 Choruses and an Orchestra" *New York Times* May 7, 1987.

41. John Rockwell, "Classical Music" *New York Times* May 24, 1987.

42. Michael Kimmelman, "Concert: Manhattan Orchestra" *New York Times* June 2, 1987.

43. Riley Drury and Geoffrey Woehlk, "From Grant City to Carnegie Hall" *Times Tribune* September 1, 2023.

44. Burt Wechsler, "From the Heartland, Music Full of Heart" *Daily News* November 29, 1988.

45. Will Crutchfield, "Verdi and Rutter Requiems by 19 Massed Choruses" *New York Times* May 31, 1989.

46. Nadine Brozan, "Chronicle" *New York Times* December 18, 1997.

47. John Rockwell, "Eight Amateur Choruses have Their Day in the Sun" *New York Times* March 25, 1989.

48. Interview with Gene Carr June 5, 2022.

49. Allan Kozinn, "14 Choirs Sing Haydn, Puccini and Liszt" *New York Times* November 23, 1989.

50. Will Crutchfield, "Verdi and Rutter Requiems by 19 Massed Choruses" *New York Times* May 31, 1989.

51. Allan Kozinn, "14 Choirs Sing Haydn, Puccini and Liszt" *New York Times* November 23, 1989.

52. Allan Kozinn, "Venerable Hanoverians Make New York Debut" *New York Times* July 14, 1990.

53. Allan Kozinn, "Manhattan Philharmonic at Allice Tully Hall" *New York Times* April 9, 1991.

54. Jeremy Eichler, "Post Trojan War Turmoil in a Rarely Heard Rossini" *New York Times* June 5, 2003.

55. Interview with John Rutter August 9, 2022; Alex Ross, *The Rest is Noise: Listening to the Twentieth Century* Picador, 2007 562, 575-6.

56. Allan Kozinn, "Lukas Foss, Composer at Home in Many Stylistic Currents, Dies at 86" *New York Times* February 1, 2009.

57. "O Theodorakis Stin NY Gia Tin Opera Electra" [Theodorakis in New York for the Opera Ekectra] *Ethnikos Kyrix* June 7, 2000; "Mikis: Katapliktos apo tin Aplotita tou Archiepiskopou Dimitriou" [Mikis: Amazed by the Down to Earth Archbishop Demetrios] *Ethikos Kyrix* June 9, 2000.

58. AHI Press Release "AHI Honors Greek Composer Mikis Theodorakis at Awards Dinner in New York" June 15, 2000; Steve Brosinski, "Aria Aspirations" *Northwest Herald* June 27, 2000.

59. Allan Kozinn, "Oracular and Talky, an Electra by a Greek" *New York Times* June 13, 2000.

60. Shirley Fleming, "New York: Manhattan Philharmonic: Theodorakis' Electra" *American Record Guide* 63, 6 2000 56-57.

61. Interview with Terre Johnson June 2, 2022.

62. Roy Wood, "A Wild Salome at NYCO" Opera-L Archives October 17, 2002.

63. "By Franz Lehar, directed by Brian Deedrick, Opera Ontario, Hamilton" *Stage Door.com* May 17, 2001.

64. Interview with Eilana Lappalainen, September 8, 2022.

65. William Thomas Walker, "Virginia Opera's Milestone Production of Verdi's Il Trovatore" *Classical Voice of North Carolina,* October 26, 2008.

66. Devan Sipher, "A Reunion That Was a Long Time Coming" *New York Times* January 14, 2014.

67. "How Do You Get to Carnegie Hall? No, Seriously" NPR August 2, 2012. https://www.npr.org/sections/deceptivecadence/2012/07/31/157671080/how-do-you-get-to-carnegie-hall-no-seriously

68. Allan Kozinn, "Murder in Ancient Greece Accompanied by Choirs" *New York Times* June 22, 2004.

69. Bernard Holland, "'Médée': Intrigue and Vengeance Revel in the Sounds of Cherubini" *New York Times* June 5, 2006.

70. Kathryn Mueller, "Taking It on the Road: Touring for Choruses" Chorus America, December 16, 2014 https://chorusamerica.org/management-governance/taking-it-road-touring-choruses

71. https://choralnet.org/archives/532377

72. Katerina Levidou, "Feast in Time of 'Plague' Festivals of Western Art Music in Greece During the Crisis" in Dimitris Tziovas ed. *Greece in Crisis The Cultural Politics of Austerity New York:* I.B. Tauris, 2017 184.

73. Levidou, "Feast in time of Plague..." 192.

74. Giannis N. Dekavallas, *Anamniseis enos Dimarchou* [Memories of a Mayor] Vol. 2 (2003-2014) Ermoupolis 2017 159.

75. Personal communication from Zoe Zeniodi, February 18, 2023.

76. Rory Brennan, "Paros Summer Classical Music Festival: Broadway Comes to Paros" Paroslife.com 13 July 2006.

77. Julia Panayotou, "Third Year Sees Blossoming of Aegean Festival" *Kathimerini* July 9, 2007.

78. Interview with Francis Bardot July 16, 2022.

79. Nick Poulakis, "European Art Music as a Modality of the Greek Crisis: Identities, Practices, and Discourses" IMS-RSMB Series Musicological Balcanica 1.1.2020

80. Constantine P. Carambelas-Sgourdas, "8o Festival Aigaiou (Syros)" [8th Festival of the Aegean (Syros) *Critic's Point*

81. "Epitimos Dimotis Syrou o Piter Tiboris" July 10, 2012 https://www. syrostoday.gr/News/7108-Epitimos-dimotis-Surou-o-Piter-Timporis.aspx
82. Personal communication from Litsa Charalambous July 22, 2022.
83. Dimitris Kiousopoulos, "Monadiki e Butterfly apo tin Syro" [A Unique Butterfly from Syros] *Kathimerini* August 13, 2017.
84. Interview with Giovanni Pacor November 22, 2022.
85. Homer, *The Odyssey* translated by Emily Wilson. New York: Norton, 2018.
86. Προσωπική επικοινωνία με την Ζωή Ζενιώδη, 18 Φεβρουαρίου 2023.
87. Συνέντευξη με τον Francis Bardot στις 16 Ιουλίου, 2022.
88. Nick Poulakis, "European Art Music as a Modality of the Greek Crisis: Identities, Practices, and Discourses" IMS-RSMB Series Musicological Balcanica 1.1.2020
89. Κωνσταντίνος Καράμπελας – Σγούρδας "8ο Φεστιβάλ Αιγαίου (Σύρος)" *Critic's Point*
90. Προσωπική επικοινωνία από την Λίτσα Χαραλάμπους 22 Ιουλίου, 2022.
91. Συνέντευξη με τον Giovanni Pacor 22 Νοεμβρίου, 2022.